STRATEGIC
PLANNING SYSTEMS

STRATEGIC
PLANNING SYSTEMS

PETER LORANGE
Sloan School, M.I.T.
and
RICHARD F. VANCIL
Harvard Business School

PRENTICE-HALL, INC., Englewood Cliffs, New Jersey 07632

Library of Congress Cataloging in Publication Data
Main entry under title:

Strategic planning systems.

Bibliography: p.
1. Corporate planning—Addresses, essays, lectures.
I. Lorange, Peter. II. Vancil, Richard F.
HD38.S744   658.4'01   76-49950
ISBN 0-13-851006-7

Printed in the United States of America

10 9 8 7 6 5 4 3

Prentice-Hall International, Inc., *London*
Prentice-Hall of Australia Pty., Limited, *Sydney*
Prentice-Hall of Canada, Ltd., *Toronto*
Prentice-Hall of India Private Limited, *New Delhi*
Prentice-Hall of Japan, Inc., *Tokyo*
Prentice-Hall of Southeast Asia Pte. Ltd., *Singapore*
Whitehall Books Limited, *Wellington, New Zealand*

CONTENTS

INTRODUCTION

Cases:

1
GOTAAS LARSEN SHIPPING CORPORATION (A)   46

2
NORTON COMPANY (A)   60

3
NORTON COMPANY (C)   87

4
CONTINENTAL OIL COMPANY   112

PART 2
Situational Design   135

Overview Readings:

1
HOW TO DESIGN A STRATEGIC PLANNING SYSTEM   139
Peter Lorange and Richard F. Vancil

2
ROLE OF THE CORPORATE PLANNING EXECUTIVE   151
Robert W. Ackerman

3
BALANCE CREATIVITY AND PRACTICALITY
IN FORMAL PLANNING   159
John K. Shank, Edward G. Niblock, and William T. Sandalls, Jr.

4
DIVISIONAL PLANNING:
SETTING EFFECTIVE DIRECTION   172
Peter Lorange

Cases:

1
THE MASSEY-FERGUSON, LTD. (A)   186

2
THE STATE STREET
BOSTON FINANCIAL CORPORATION   209

3
THE QUAKER OATS COMPANY   229

4
THE GALVOR COMPANY (R-3)   238

PART 3
Developments in Management Technology   259

Overview Readings:

1
A FRAMEWORK FOR THE USE OF COMPUTER-BASED
MODELS IN THE PLANNING PROCESS   262
Peter Lorange and John F. Rockart

2
A FRAMEWORK FOR STRATEGIC PLANNING IN
MULTI-NATIONAL CORPORATIONS   276
Peter Lorange

3
BETTER MANAGEMENT
OF CORPORATE DEVELOPMENT   289
Richard F. Vancil

Cases:

AN INTRODUCTION
AND
AN OVERVIEW OF THIS BOOK

Formal systems for strategic planning are a relatively new phenom-enon in business management. Thus, it is possible, even in a book as short as this one, for the reader to gain an understanding of the historical development of this management tool at the same time that he learns about the existing state-of-the-art and the likely developments in the years ahead. More than possible, it is really mandatory for an executive who wishes to feel comfortable with his command of planning technology to know how that technology has evolved and where it seems to be headed. Three points of view are useful: a retrospective, a current perspective and a prospective for the future. Each of these will be sketched briefly here as a backdrop for the more detailed readings and cases which follow.

RETROSPECTIVE

Planning, of course, is not a new form of mental activity for human beings. What was new in the early 1960s was the attempt by managers in large organizations to formalize this activity and to focus it on affecting the strategic direction of their enterprises. The most vocal and visible advocate of such efforts was Robert S. McNamara, who left the presidency of Ford Motor Company in 1961 to become Secretary of Defense in the Kennedy Administration. At Ford, McNamara had developed a method of multi-year planning which helped him gain perspective on the key strategic decisions in that company. He carried that management technology with him into the Pentagon, applying it to an organization more than ten times the size of Ford with great apparent success. Mr. McNamara's abilities as a manager, and the role of long-range planning as an essential ingredient to his effectiveness, were widely discussed in the popular press. Managers of large organizations all over the country began wondering if they, too, should attempt such an effort.

Managers appear to be just as susceptible to fads as any other groups of people, and it would take ten years for the surge of interest in this new management technique to run its course. There can be little doubt that some companies attempted to formalize their strategic planning during the 1960s simply because it was the thing to do. But there were substantive reasons, as well. The 1960s in the United States was a period of steady economic growth and general prosperity. Corporate executives, realizing that they had many attractive opportunities for growth, also realized that they had to choose. Many businesses during this period chose to diversify, sometimes through acquisition, and to enter international markets. These strategic moves increase the managerial complexity of large corporations in geometric fashion. The problem was particularly intense at the top of such corporations, and new technology was clearly needed to help top management cope with an increasing array of strategic decisions.

Formal long-range planning seemed almost like a godsend to these executives. Its primary virtue was that it focused on the right set of issues. Chief executives knew how easy it was to let current operating problems absorb all their time, and "someday we've got to do some planning around here." Announcing that his organization would undertake a formal program of strategic planning was almost like a public announcement that he was going to quit smoking: It forced the chief executive to attempt to change his own behavior in a way that he knew was desirable. Such an announcement was also warmly received by most second and third level executives because they, too, were concerned about the strategic direction of the corporation to which their careers were attached. The 1960s was also a period of rapid progress in the professionalization of management. These younger executives particularly, many with graduate school training, embraced formal planning as a natural extension of the rational, analytic approach that they applied to operating problems.

To be briefly autobiographical, when our collaboration began in 1968, managerial interest in the design of strategic planning systems was mushrooming. Our research, assisted by many colleagues at Harvard Business School, found a natural and eager clientele. A presidential announcement that the company would begin long-range planning was almost always accompanied by the simultaneous creation of a new executive position: Vice President for Planning. The first incumbents in those positions were lonely people indeed. The new position was obviously important, but they had no precedents to follow in attempting to create an effective planning process where none existed before. Their greatest need was to learn how their counterparts in other companies had approached the task, and they were also willing to share their own experiences. During the five years of 1968-1972, most of the cases in this book were prepared. These planning executives also needed direct contact with each other, and during those same five years, more than a thousand such executives attended short executive workshops sponsored by Harvard Business School.

The development of strategic planning systems matured very rapidly during those years, and for two quite different reasons. First, a great deal *was* learned about the design of such systems. Massive amounts of high-quality talent were devoted to the task by hundreds of executives and scores of academicians. These experiences were pooled in a more or less organized way and some common wisdom began to emerge. The second cause of the sudden maturation of formal strategic planning was quite different: the economic recession of 1970-71. Top corporate managers suddenly realized that good strategic planning did not insure corporate success. The next question was inevitable: Do we need a Planning Department at all? Our informed, but undocumented estimate is that somewhere between a quarter and a third of the Corporate Planning Departments were either decimated or completely eliminated during that recession. It was a sobering experience, even for those who survived. The fad was clearly over, and the survivors knew that they had "arrived"—that the planning activity had been carefully reexamined and found to earn its keep. In those companies where the planning activity failed, the soul-searching was even more intense. Most of those companies would make another attempt to design an effective process, once the wounds had healed, but the effort would be much more cautious and thoughtful.

This history is important, we think, for anyone attempting to learn to design an effective strategic planning system. One reason for its importance is to permit the reader to place the cases in this book into a proper historical context. It is not possible to properly evaluate the planning activities described in these cases without some sense of the state of the art at the time. Even more important, it is possible to learn from history. Each of the cases here provide one or more specific lessons, and there are some general lessons as well. We will state these general lessons, as we perceive them, in terms of our current perspective on the design of strategic planning systems.

PERSPECTIVE

Sorting through our experiences in studying planning activities at dozens of corporations, we have winnowed out five fundamental characteristics of effective strategic planning systems. Stated baldly, as we do below, these characteristics sound obvious—almost vapid. We think it important to state them simply, however, because the successful development of those characteristics in a planning system is not easy; we have seen too many failures as testimony to that fact. These characteristics will appear repeatedly in both the cases and readings in this book, and our hope is that by the time you have finished this book you will have a deeper understanding of both the importance of these characteristics and the subtle ways that they must be nurtured.

General Manager Ownership.   Strategic planning is a line-management function, and the corollary of that is that a strategic planning system must be designed by the general managers who will use it. There is a role for a staff planning officer in both the original design and the continuing maintenance of a planning system, but the wise professional planner has to learn to get his kicks in strange ways. The greatest danger is for him to become identified as the author of the planning system. A better way for him to view his role is as the builder of a planning system according to the architectural specifications laid down by line managers. General managers must feel that they own the system or they will not use it.

The contents of this book reflect that perspective. Almost all of the articles reprinted here were originally published in journals aimed at general managers not staff planners. The cases are also realistic in this regard; the central figures in most of the cases are top line executives. The cases would not be instructive at all if they did not permit insights into the personalities of men like Cushman of the Norton Company, Thornbrough of Massey-Ferguson, and Rockwell of State Street Financial Corporation. The fact that the planners in these cases appear rather colorless *is* a fact—they ought to be, if they are to be effective in their roles.

Decision Orientation.   An effective strategic planning system must help line managers make important decisions. The danger—particularly at the hands of an overzealous staff planning executive—is that the planning system takes on a life of its own, and the production of massive planning documents becomes an end in itself. Line managers are not interested in plans; they like to make decisions. If the planning system helps their decision-making process, they will devote vast amounts of time to it. If the planning system requires filling in a myriad of boxes on innumerable forms, line managers know how to cope with that, too. The greatest strength of most operating managers is that they are effective delegators, once they have routinized an activity to the point where it can be handled by a subordinate. Important decisions by definition, cannot be handled by a subordinate. The clear message for systems designers is to keep the focus on the decisions to be made, not on the routine presentation of information.

Process, Not Structure. An effective planning system is not a system at all; it is an attempt to organize the process by which line managers work together in resolving strategic issues. The title of this book is not intentionally misleading; we do regard an organized planning process as a system, in the sense that it can be consciously designed. The important distinction can best be drawn by contrasting a planning system to other common management systems such as a performance reporting system or a capital budgeting system. In those systems, the major focus is, appropriately, on the design of documents—the content and format of information provided by one manager to another. In our view, the most critical design feature for a strategic planning system is the schedule of planning meetings, not the documents to be presented at those meetings. A well-designed planning calendar specifies when a meeting is to be held, which executives are to be there, what the agenda is to consist of, and how much time is to elapse until the next meeting. Between such meetings, a great deal of work will need to be done, but attempting to structure how that work is to be performed is far less important than assuring that the right cast of characters has been assembled at the right point in time to discuss the right issues.

Situational Design. An effective strategic planning system is unique to the corporate environment in which it resides. One of the primary benefits of studying cases in this book is in the documentation they provide for that obvious fact. Companies are unique in a great many dimensions: the degree of the diversity of their operations, the industries in which they operate, and their strategy in each of those industries. Even more important in many circumstances are the personalities of the people in the organization and the organizational climate or culture in which they work together. The age and history of a company and the extent to which its managers are homogenous in terms of shared values and their orientation toward the world can be very important elements in the design of a planning system. We shall try, particularly in Part II of this book, to provide some more specific guidelines, but the overriding design rule is that there is no general design.

Evolutionary Design. Finally, an effective strategic planning system changes continually. One reason, of course, is that the corporate situation is always changing as a result of changes in the external environment as well as shifts in organizational structure and power. In addition, we believe that a good argument can be made for change for the sake of change. If the system becomes too routinized, those great delegators will devote less and less attention to it. Alternatively, a strategic planning system can serve as a continual challenge to line managers, encouraging them to attempt to look at their business in a different way this year than they did last year. We view strategic planning systems as a major tool for improving the sophistication of managers, and that is a task that can never be completed.

PROSPECTIVE

What does the future hold for the further development of a strategic planning system in large organizations? With the perspective stated just above, the reader ought to be able to anticipate some of our forecasts. One prediction that might be counter intuitive is that we foresee a reduced visibility for strategic planning systems in the future.

What really happened in the 1960s was that many companies realized that they needed to make a rapid improvement in the strategic orientation of their line managers in order to permit those managers to work together more effectively in resolving strategic issues. An explicit, highly visible formal system was one way to meet that objective, even if it also involved a certain amount of bureaucratic documentation and red tape. In many companies, that objective has now been achieved, and some of the trappings of the formal apparatus can be allowed to wither. In those companies, strategic planning has become a natural process for managers with the proper orientation who are focused on the right set of key decisions. For those fortunate companies, this book will be of little value; they already know how to do effective strategic planning in their organization, and need have little concern about how other companies have approached that task. For other companies that aspire to reach that condition, the help that may be provided by this book should be tempered with the realization that the objective is not to build a bigger and better planning system but to build one that is so effective that, eventually, it is almost invisible.

Two other predictions about the future of strategic planning also seem reasonably safe. First, we will continue to see an increasing sophistication in the analytic tools used by managers to evaluate strategic alternatives. Computer-based models went through a fad of their own during the 1960s, producing the inevitable rash of horror stories. That learning curve is also behind us, and as illustrated by the American Airlines case in Part III of this book, a sophisticated and practical computer model is not necessarily a contradiction in terms. Second, managers will continue to develop innovations in both their management systems and in the economic models they use to conceptualize their business. The other two cases in Part III simply illustrate this with the matrix form of organization (A. B. Astra) and the conscious management of development expenses (Texas Instruments). In many cases, innovations such as these will find their implementation facilitated by appropriate modifications in the strategic planning process.

But no one can foretell the future—not the world's greatest strategic planners, nor the academicians who observe them. The future is uncertain, and that's why the world needs its never-adequate supply of intelligent, energetic managers. They are the ones who will bring forth the new developments in strategic planning. By observing them, we will learn from them—and hope that we can reciprocate by facilitating the education of their counterparts in other companies.

Peter Lorange
Richard F. Vancil

STRATEGIC
PLANNING SYSTEMS

PART ONE

Strategy, Structure, and Style

The purpose of the first part of this book is to present an overview of the strategic planning task and to illustrate how planning is affected by such situational characteristics as corporate strategy, organizational structure, and management style. In the course of the discussion, we will outline the major features of a generalized approach to strategic planning.

The first reading, "Strategy Formulation in Complex Organizations," provides a detailed description of how strategy can be formulated to keep pace with changing environments. All too often, managers judge strategy formulation in a complex organization to be a one-time event rather than a dynamic process. In our approach, institutional strategy is treated as a complicated but interconnected set of individual strategies, which are formulated and pursued by the managers who are responsible for making them successful.

In the next reading, "Strategic Planning in Diversified Companies," we propose a conceptual scheme for strategic planning based on two major assertions. First, there is a three-level hierarchy of strategic planning tasks reflecting the division of labor among management. At the corporate level, the concern of the chief executive will be the development and implementation of a corporate strategy and plan for the overall balance of business activities, that is, a corporate or "portfolio" plan. At the division level, the division manager will be responsible for development of a strategy and plan for the specific business that his division is in, that is, business planning. Finally, at the functional level, the department manager will attempt to develop

1

specific action programs to implement the plan of his division, that is, (largely) Interdepartmental programming. This differentiation of major strategic planning tasks will prove extremely useful for putting the necessary focus into planning at the three levels of a corporation while providing a mechanism for overall coordination.

The second major assertion is that the planning process should focus on strategic and often long-term decisions through a process of gradually narrowing down strategic options. Specifically, we propose that gradual organizational commitment can be reached by having the appropriate executives participate in three "cycles" of planning. The first cycle, which might be labeled "objectives setting," involves determining overall portfolio objectives as well as appropriate charters and objectives for each division. The second cycle, which we call the "programming cycle," focuses on the development of specific plans for each organizational unit. Finally, the "budgeting cycle" arrives at detailed and shorter term budget choices consistent with the strategic direction in which the firm wants to move. This "three by three" scheme—a three-level hierarchy and three cycles—gives a useful starting position for the design of a planning system that provides adaptation to environmental opportunities and threats facing all or part of an organization, as well as integration and consistency among the long-term activities of the firm.

Designing a strategic planning system for a company requires matching the system's characteristics to the company's situational setting. Hence, there is no one planning recipe for general use. In the "Five Pillars for Your Planning" reading, however, the claim is made that there nevertheless seem to be a few universally applicable "musts" of strategic planning. One is that the planning system should help to formulate strategic choices and not serve merely as an extrapolative numbers-generating exercise. A second must states that the plans must be understood at all levels in the hierarchy; that is, communication, opinions, interaction, and iterations are to be stressed. Third, the plans must be consistent in formats, methods, deadlines, and such, so that confusion in planning reviews and consolidations can be minimized. A fourth message is that the planning system should be integrated with other management systems, acknowledging that they are elements of the firm's *one* administrative system. Finally, line managers must be centrally involved in planning; otherwise the necessary commitment to carry out the planning decisions will not be achieved. It is useful to acknowledge these five tenets in order not to repeat the errors of others, remembering nevertheless that the planning system must be tailored to a given setting.

The four case studies in Part I of the book all address strategy formulation and design of the basic structure of a planning system. The corporate settings are quite different, but we shall see that the elements of the overall conceptual planning structure are essentially the same.

The first case raises the question of designing a planning system within Gotaas-Larsen Shipping Corporation, a division of I. U. International Corporation. This business is characterized by heavy fixed capital investments and is subject to widely oscillating freight rates and fierce international competition. The number of people employed on the ships is quite substantial, but the strategic decision-making group is exceptionally small. Thus, the case provides a good opportunity for identifying and monitoring key strategic variables and for suggesting what form the strategic planning activities should take. The issue of risk-exposure associated with the strategy is prominent among our considerations.

The second case, Norton Company (A), discusses the process of starting up a formalized strategic planning activity in a quite diversified corporation. The steps taken by Norton, the issues and problems encountered, are quite typical of what we have seen a number of companies face during the initial planning effort stage: what should be the nature of the goal-setting process, in terms of the degree of initiative coming from the corporate level versus the divisions, and the degree of specificity of the goals? What should be the proper role of the corporate planner? How much and in what way should the chief executive be involved? What should be the format of the review meetings and what substantive issues should be reviewed? What planning activities might fruitfully be carried out by the divisions to improve their business strategies? The case illustrates how reasonable people committed to planning go about facing these and other common start-up issues.

The Norton Company (C) case raises several issues regarding the evolution of a strategic planning effort during the years following the start-up. The planning effort becomes complicated by the fact that the company has been running into a harsher competitive climate and, therefore, finds itself in a situation with adversely changing economic conditions. One task then is to explore ways of improving the effectiveness of planning during a profit squeeze. Another factor influencing the evolution of the planning system is turnover of top management. What impact should the style of the chief executive have on the design of the planning process? And what changes in planning are needed as a response to a changing corporate strategy? The case gives an important example of the need to manage the evolution of a planning system, so that it stays in consonance with the changing situational setting. Also, the case illustrates the changing balance between longer time adaptation to new environmental opportunities and shorter time integration with ongoing operations.

The final case in Part I, Continental Oil Company: Coordinating and Planning, presents a company that is heavily engaged in a few narrow businesses, with the major thrust of its activities in one business, oil. Continental Oil is an example of the quite centralized planning that typically takes place in an integrated oil company. In line with its needs for financial coordination, the company has a long tradition of financially dominated long-range planning. The case gives a detailed account of the evolution of planning, especially in terms of achieving a good balance between adaptation to long-term environmental opportunities (and threats) and shorter term coordination. It reevaluates a planning system that has been effective in the past and explores what systems design changes may now be appropriate and feasible.

1

STRATEGY FORMULATION IN COMPLEX ORGANIZATIONS*

The primary source of cohesiveness in an organization is strategy. To be effective, however, strategy must be more than just a ringing statement of purpose or objectives. It must also provide guidance that will assist subordinate managers in deciding how to proceed toward achieving the objectives. Furthermore, strategy should help to weld an organization together by developing among the members of the management team both a shared belief in the efficacy of major action programs and a shared commitment to execute those programs successfully. The purpose of this article is to discuss how strategy can be formulated in such a way that it will be more than simply a statement of purpose but will have an active role in shaping decision making in a complex organization.

SOME DEFINITIONS

Before we proceed we must define three words—*strategy, objectives,* and *goals.* This is necessary because these words will be used in this article to convey a specific meaning which is not always synonymous with their common use in business.

Strategy. The strategy of an organization, *or of a subunit of a larger organization,* is a conceptualization, *expressed or implied by the organization's leader,* of (1) the long-term objectives or purposes of the organization, (2) the broad constraints and policies, *either self-imposed by the leader or accepted by him from his superiors,* that *currently* restrict the scope of the organization's activities, and (3) the *current* set of plans and near-term goals that have been adopted in the expectation of contributing to the achievement of the organization's objectives.

This definition is intended to be read twice. Reading it first and ignoring the italicized words, the definition is not significantly different from the several that already exist in the literature.[1] The second reading, focusing on the italicized words, emphasizes three important additional aspects of this definition of strategy. First, the definition applies not only

---

*(Reprinted from *Sloan Management Review*/winter 1976)
[1]See K. R. Andrews, *The Concept of Corporate Strategy* (Homewood, Ill.: Dow Jones-Irwin, Inc., 1971), p. 18.

to the organization as a whole but to every major component of the organization. The "broad constraints and policies," which is what most businessmen mean by the term "strategy," may be either self-imposed or handed down from above. Strategy in a complex organization is conceived in a hierarchy and there are many levels of strategy in such an organization. Second, the strategy of an organizational component is never really "handed down"; it is conceived by an individual, the leader of the organizational unit, and this definition makes his role explicit. Third, the strategy of an organizational unit is dynamic. At any point in time, it expresses the *current* constraints, policies, and plans, but the likelihood of change in these statements is widely recognized throughout the organization. These three characteristics of strategy, as noted above, have major implications for the development of management systems in the organization.

Objectives and Goals. These two words, often used interchangeably by businessmen, can be differentiated to convey two quite different concepts, as implied in the definition of strategy above. The distinction between these two concepts is important, because a statement of strategy needs them both. The delineation of objectives and goals serves two different management purposes.

An *objective* is an aspiration to be worked toward in the future. A *goal* is an achievement to be attained at some future date. However, these short definitions fail to convey the essence of the difference between these two concepts, that is the distinction between "reach" and "grasp." For example, one of John F. Kennedy's *objectives* in 1960 was to reestablish and maintain this country's position as a leader in the fields of science and technology. One of his *goals* was to land a man on the moon and return him safely before the end of the decade.

The difference between objectives and goals may be drawn in terms of the following four dimensions.

1. *Time Frame.* An objective is timeless, enduring, and unending; a goal is temporal, time-phased, and intended to be superseded by subsequent goals. Kennedy's goal for the '60s was achieved, and it did contribute toward his objective, but new goals for the '70s are needed for the "maintenance of leadership" objective.

2. *Specificity.* Objectives are stated in broad, general terms, dealing with matters of image, style, and self-perception; goals are much more specific, stated in terms of a particular result that will be accomplished by a specified date. It is because of their open-endedness that objectives can never be achieved while goals can. We may believe that landing the first man on the moon did reestablish our scientific leadership, but that perception may not be universally shared. To shift the analogy, we clearly won a battle, but not necessarily the war.

3. *Focus.* Objectives are usually stated in terms of some relevant environment which is external to the organization; goals are more internally focused and carry important implications about how the resources of the organization shall be utilized in the future. Objectives are frequently stated in terms of achieving leadership or recognition in a certain field. A goal implies a resource commitment, challenging the organization to use those resources in order to achieve the desired result.

4. *Measurement.* Both objectives and goals frequently can be stated in terms that are quantifiably measurable, but the character of the measurement is different. Quantified objectives are stated in relative terms. For example, the managers of one growth company have stated that their objective is "to achieve a compound rate of growth in earnings per share sufficient to place its performance in the top 10% of all (relevant) corporations." This objective may be achieved in any one year, but it is timeless and externally focused, providing a continuing challenge for the management of that company. A quantified goal is expressed in absolute terms. Several years ago, the president of a diversifying aerospace corporation stated that the company would "achieve 50% of its sales revenue from nongovernment customers by 1970." The achievement of that goal can be measured irrespective of environmental conditions and competitors' actions.

In order to prepare an effective statement of strategy in a complex organization, the distinction between objectives and goals must be recognized. Objectives are the first element in a statement of strategy; goals are the last. In the time that elapses between the delineation of these two statements, there must be a great deal of interplay between the managers at various levels in the organization's hierarchy. This complex process of starting with a statement of objectives and working toward the development of more specific goals will be discussed at length later in this article. First, however, we will discuss the three major elements of effective strategy.

CHARACTERISTICS OF EFFECTIVE STRATEGY

The effectiveness of a particular strategy can be appraised from two different perspectives. First, of course, is the question of whether or not the strategy is right for the organization in its particular situation. Does it provide a proper match between environmental opportunities and organizational resources? Second is the more subtle question of whether or not the strategy has been constructed in such a way that it facilitates the management processes of the organization. Evaluated from this second point of view, an effective statement of strategy has three characteristics that are not commonly recognized.

Operational Guidance.   The guidance that a statement of strategy provides for subordinate managers is usually cast in the form of what *not* to do rather than in the form of *what* to do. Such guidance, then, is really a set of constraints on appropriate organizational actions. These constraints are usually not stated explicitly both because it would be impractical to do so (the list would be too long) and because constraints have a negative connotation. Thus, an airline, for example, does not say that its strategy is *not* to be in the chemical business or *not* to be in the textile business, but rather that it is "to be a leader in the air transportation industry." The value of such a statement is not what is says explicitly, but the implicit message that a great many other activities which do not fall under the "air transportation industry" umbrella are to be ignored.

The guidance provided by a statement of strategy must be pervasive and operational. The statement must provide guidance to all the managers in the organization in sufficiently explicit terms to allow each manager to proceed with his tasks in the knowledge that his actions are consistent with the objectives of the organization. No single statement of strategy will suffice to provide this kind of guidance in a complex organization. Instead, many layers of strategy are needed, each layer being progressively more detailed to provide strategic guidance for the next level of subordinate managers. As the diversity and complexity of an organization increase, the degree of specificity of strategic guidance provided by corporate-level management appears to decrease. The strategy of a conglomerate corporation cannot be stated nearly as crisply as that of an airline. Nevertheless managers at lower levels of the conglomerate need guidance analogous to that provided to airline managers, and they receive it through a progressive delineation of the strategy of each major operating unit.

Personal Commitment.   Another characteristic of an effective statement of strategy is that it is drafted by the manager who must carry it out. This is obviously true for a corporate president who has no superior officer to tell him what the limits should be on the scope of the corporation's activities. Surprisingly perhaps, it is equally true for several levels of subordinate managers in a well-run corporation.

A personalized strategy is feasible in a complex organization if the statement of strategy is drafted carefully. As discussed earlier, the superior manager devises his strategy and expresses it in the form of constraints on the scope of the activities of his subordinates. However, he should take care to leave them some discretion as to how they operate within those constraints. Each subordinate manager will then accept (or challenge) those constraints, devise "his" strategy within them, and in turn express his strategy to his subordinates in the form of constraints on their activities. The resulting series of progressively detailed statements of strategy are personalized, in the sense that each manager can see his imprint on his part of the series. Furthermore, they are integrated throughout the organization as a whole, because each statement is consistent with the constraints imposed by higher authority.

Two of the several advantages of personalized strategies deserve mention here. First, encouraging each manager to use his imagination to devise the best strategy he can increases the vitality and creativity of the organization. In a complex organization, no one man, not even the president, can identify all the opportunities that exist, and a framework of progressive constraints that elicits personalized strategies multiplies the sources of initiative in the corporation. Second, a personalized strategy engenders a personal commitment. As Andrews says, in discussing the relevance of personal values in the determination of strategy, "Somebody has to have his heart in it."[2]

Expectation of Change. Finally, an effective statement of strategy should recognize explicitly that it is a temporal document. Whereas the objectives of the organization, particularly if carefully drawn, may not change perceptibly over time, the scope of its activities is likely to change in an expansionist fashion and the organization's major plans are almost certain to change as it continues to adapt to its dynamic environment. The inevitability of an evolving strategy does not mean that managers should not take the trouble to make the current strategy explicit or that the task should be done in a casual manner; it does mean that any such explicit statement should be viewed as only currently useful. The implication of this is that provision must be made in the management process for a periodic review and revalidation of all levels of strategy.

TRADEOFFS IN STRATEGY FORMULATION

It is now necessary to look briefly at some of the problems which plague any individual manager in developing his own statement of strategy. Even if we ignore, for the moment, the complexities that arise because his organization is a part of a larger complex, his task is a difficult one. His approach to this task must be both rational and emotional, his analysis of his situation both coolly analytic and unabashedly subjective. As Professor Andrews has described so well, the strategist seeks to reconcile conflicting forces. He must deal simultaneously with four questions: What *might* we do? What *can* we do?, What do we *want* to do?, and What *should* we do? Obviously, the strategy that results from this analysis is based on the manager's personal perception of opportunities, his personal assessment of the strengths and weaknesses of his organization, and his personal aspirations and values.

[2]See Andrews, *The Concept of Corporate Strategy,* p. 117.

In terms of the definition given earlier, strategy consists of three elements: (1) objectives, (2) constraints and policies, and (3) plans and goals. While these three elements are not determined independently in a neat, chronological sequence, it is convenient to discuss them as though they were.

Objectives. The most personal element of an individual manager's strategy is the setting of objectives for his organization. If the task is difficult (and it need not always be), the trouble is frequently caused by a conflict between the manager's personal aspirations and values on the one hand and his professional or positional obligations on the other. Although the nature of the professional obligation varies with the level in the organization, even the highest officer must recognize that the organizational objectives he sets are not the same as his individual objectives. For the chief executive officer, the restraints imposed by his position are primarily external; his objectives for the organization must attempt to relate it to the broader society in which it exists. For a manager at a lower level, personal aspirations must be balanced off against the obligations inherent in his position as the leader of a subunit within a larger organization. For any manager, this tradeoff is essentially subjective; his aim is to frame a set of objectives for his organization which acknowledges his positional responsibilities and which is consistent with his own desires and beliefs.

Constraints and Policies. Determining the scope and balance of an organization's activities is a somewhat more analytical process and is always difficult. In simplistic terms, this task consists of finding the most appropriate match between environmental opportunities and organizational resources; the best set of activities to engage in are those which take best advantage of the organization's strengths, thus permitting the most progress toward achieving the organization's objectives. However, because the time frame involved is so long, this description of the task is insufficient. Stated more realistically, the task is to find a match between opportunities that are still unfolding and resources that are still being acquired. Substantial uncertainty exists on both counts. Opportunities may not develop in the direction or at the rate expected, and the organization may not be able to acquire new resources as effectively as the manager had hoped. Thus, determining the boundaries on an organization's sphere of activities is best conceived of as positioning the organization so that it will be able to capitalize on future opportunities. The choice that this presents for a manager is not simply the result of a neat, economic analysis. It is true that the choice needs to be wrapped in the cloak of rationality, if only to make it more communicable and to engender the commitment of subordinate managers. However, the choice is inevitably influenced, and appropriately so, by the manager's own perceptions and assessments as well as by the aspirations and obligations that he recognized in framing the organization's objectives.

Plans and Goals.   The most specific element of strategy, that is the tangible plans for near-term actions and the results expected from those actions, is the most amenable to rational analysis. Here again the manager's task is to match opportunities and resources, but the choice must be based on the current situation or on what the situation will be in the very near future. The limitations on a purely rational solution occur because of the familiar tradeoff between short-term goals and long-term objectives. A manager's plan of action may be optimal, in the sense that he believes he has achieved the best balance across the time dimension, but that is still a personal belief. He may even attempt to prove the validity of his plan quantitatively, but it is almost inevitable that any such proof will ultimately rely on premises drawn from the broader elements of strategy discussed above.

A statement of strategy, then, is highly situational for two reasons. First, the strategy must reflect the organization as it now exists, its current activities, and its current set of resources. Second, and at least as important, the strategy for an organizational unit is determined by an individual; it bears the mark of his character, perceptivity, and personality. The process of permitting each manager in a complex organization to develop his own unique strategy is the topic to which we now turn.

THREE LEVELS OF STRATEGY

Generalizations about strategy are difficult, not simply because any statement of strategy is situational, but also because strategy in a complex

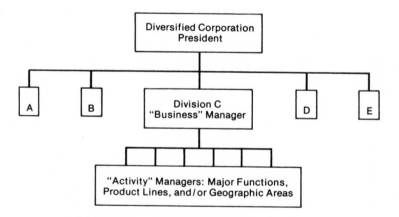

Figure 1   Organizational Chart of Divisional Corporation

organization is so detailed. Most literature on the subject stops short of exploring this detail because it is so messy. We will take the other tack here in order to provide a description that may be useful to practicing managers and more specifically to designers of long-range planning systems.

Even this first attempt at a detailed look at strategy must be simplified to some extent. In this article, we shall deal with a crude stereotype of a diversified corporation. Such a corporation, as shown in Figure 1, is conventionally organized into product divisions each with its own general manager which we will call the business manager. The principal subordinates of the business manager will be called activity managers.

Strategy, even in this simplest of all complex organizations, is an intricate web of personal statements by managers at each of the three levels in the hierarchy. Figure 2 displays the elements of strategy for each of the three types of managers. In order to understand that figure, it must be read both horizontally and vertically. The horizontal reading is the most appropriate to discuss first; it will permit us to examine each statement of strategy from the point of view of the individual manager who enunciates it. Viewed from this perspective, the strategy for this illustrative organization may be conceived of as an amalgam of about three dozen individual strategies: one corporate strategy, five divisional strategies, and perhaps six activity strategies within each division. If properly prepared, these individual statements form an interrelated set. However, it is important to realize that each such statement must be capable of standing alone.

Corporate Managers.   The statement of strategy expressed by the top manager of a diversified corporation can be broken into the three elements shown in Figure 2. Corporate objectives consist of two broad types: financial and nonfinancial. Financial objectives recognize the corporation's obligation to its shareholders and express management's aspirations for fulfilling shareholder expectations. It is increasingly rare, however, for corporate presidents to endorse the simplistic objective of "maximizing earnings over the long run." Instead, by stating the financial objectives in terms relative to what the managers of other corporations are able to achieve, the president recognizes that the performance of his company must be evaluated in the context of the economy as a whole.

In addition to setting financial objectives, many presidents today find it desirable to make explicit the social and ethical obligations of their corporation. Nonfinancial objectives may go beyond mere statements of the corporation's intention to be a good citizen; a corporate "creed" or some similar statement of the personal values shared by individuals in the organization is not uncommon. For example, such statements have been used for decades in large retailing organizations, such as J. C. Penney, Avon Products, and the Jewel Companies. The ability of these objectives

Level in the Hierarchy	Objectives	Constraints and Policies	Plans and Goals
Corporate Managers	Stated in terms for: stockholders other identifiable constituencies society at large. Examples: Financial performance of the corporation Corporate citizenship and "personality" characteristics	Financial policies (debt structure, dividends, diversity of risk, etc.). Specific industries to be in, or characteristics of appropriate industries. Criteria for approving new resource commitments to businesses.	Prospective magnitude of discretionary resources to be utilized by the corporation. Prospective distribution of resources in order to affect the future mix of businesses. Performance expectations for the corporation and for each business over the next 5-10 years.
Business Managers	Stated in terms for: corporate management. Examples: Financial performance of the business Position of the business in the industry	Definition of niche in the industry; relative importance of, and interrelationships between, each activity. Priorities for changing the relative contribution from each activity.	Prospective patterns of resource allocation intended to affect the future contribution from each activity. Performance expectations for the business and for each activity over the next 3-7 years.
Activity Managers	Stated in terms for: business management. Examples: Contribution of the activity to the business Position of the activity in the industry	Delineation of limits on the scope of the entire activity. Criteria for optimizing the use of resources available to the activity.	Prospective sequence of resource utilization intended to affect the future contribution from the activity. Performance expectations for the activity and for each subactivity over the next 1-3 years.

Figure 2 Elements of Strategy in a Hierarchical Organization

to provide a set of ethical guidelines for a large number of employees dealing with an even larger group of customers would suggest that their value need not be restricted to retailing organizations.

The constraints and policies segment of corporate-level strategy consists of two types of statements. One type, statements of financial policy, may not always be critical to the success of the enterprise. Nevertheless, these statements are necessary because there are some elements of financial management, such as dividend policy, which corporate management cannot delegate to subordinates.

The other type of constraints/policies statement deals with the most crucial element of corporate strategy—the diversity of corporate activities. At a minimum, this statement identifies the industries in which the corporation is currently involved and revalidates an intention to restrict corporate activities to those industries over the long term. The top managers of corporations that are continuing to diversify have a somewhat more difficult problem. One useful way of specifying a constraint on the scope of corporate activity in such situations is to identify the major types of business opportunities which seem to capitalize on the resource capabilities of the corporation. Because the opportunities and the resources must be stated in rather general terms, the resulting statement lacks specificity. Still, this sort of statement provides a great deal more guidance for subordinates than a simple statement of the prospective financial performance that is required before a corporation will enter a new business. With the exception of only a few "pure" conglomerates, diversification actions rarely are based solely on financial criteria, and a thoughtful statement of corporate strategy can make the other criteria more explicit.

Finally, a corporate-level statement of strategy must specify the current set of major plans that are to be pursued in the years immediately ahead. In very crude terms, the feasibility of such plans must be related to corporate financial policies. The financial resources necessary to execute the plans need not be in hand, but their availability must be foreseeable. Despite the fact that the prospective distribution of funds across the range of corporate activities is highly tentative, subordinate managers must be given some idea of this distribution so that they may plan in sufficient detail. Similarly, though the prospective effects of such allocations are even more tentative, such goals must be stated in order to provide corporate management with a crude test of the feasibility of all the elements of its strategy.

Business Managers. In terms of the hypothetical organization cited in Figure 1, the manager of a product division is a business manager. He has been delegated the responsibility for formulating and implementing strategy in one of the industries in which a diversified corporation is engaged. Given that set of responsibilities, the statement of strategy which the business manager enunciates contains the same three elements noted above for corporate managers, but the scope and substance of the strategy are different.

Long-term objectives for a business manager in a hierarchical corporation must acknowledge the limitations in scope that are inherent in his position. The range of his activities is usually proscribed within the natural boundaries of an externally definable industry. Accordingly, his objectives for the business may be stated in terms relative to the performance of other companies in the same industry. Objectives need not be limited to financial performance; statements expressing an aim to achieve (or retain) a position as the industry leader in, for example, product development or customer service are also highly desirable. Such statements serve both to express the manager's aspirations to his subordinates and to encapsulate the essence of his strategy.

The cornerstone of business strategy is the concept which Professor Andrews and his colleagues refer to as "niche." Except in the case of a total monopoly, each company in an industry seeks to find a place for itself among its competitors. A niche may be a small nook or cranny in the marketplace where the winds of competition blow with somewhat less force, or it may be the top of the mountain which is occupied by a company with a commanding market share, while the storms of competition range below. But even staying on the mountaintop, or finding a larger and somewhat more comfortable cave higher up the slope, requires a clear understanding of the relationship between a company and its competitors who are seeking to serve the same set of customers.

The constraint/policy element of a statement of business strategy is an attempt to delineate that competitive relationship. Here the manager's task of analyzing and matching opportunities with resources can be somewhat more specific than the task of his corporate counterpart. His major competitors are unlikely to change substantially over the next decade, and the thrust of technological and market development can be foreseen, however, dimly. Some would say that delineating this crucial element of business strategy is more challenging, and more personally rewarding, than the equivalent corporate-level task of determining the strategy of diversification.

Once a business manager has determined the broad constraints that will guide his competitive approach to the marketplace, the remaining element of his strategy is to develop implementation plans and short-term goals for achievement. Figure 2 refers to these plans as *prospective patterns of resource allocation*. This compact phrase is intended to encompass both the expected magnitude of resources that the corporation may be able to make available to the business and the currently intended distribution of those resources among the alternative action programs which the business might pursue. Naturally, such a pattern is highly tentative. Nothing ever happens precisely as forecast, least of all such critical planning factors as the rate of market change and the nature of competitor response. Nevertheless, the performance results must also be forecast in order to permit the business manager to evaluate the cohesiveness and effectiveness of all elements of his strategy.

Activity Managers. The strategy for an activity manager, the third level in the hierarchy shown in Figure 1, is more difficult to generalize about because complex corporations organize their businesses in diverse ways. The principal subordinates of a business manager may be responsible for a major functional area such as manufacturing or sales, a portion of the product line, a geographical area, or some combination of the three. We will use two examples, a product line manager and a functional manager, to illustrate the elements of strategy at the activity manager level.

The first thing to be said about an activity manager of either sort is that his job is where the action is. The scope of his position is, of course, even more proscribed than that of the business manager to whom he reports and the statement of strategy that he drafts as a guide to his activities is accordingly more specific. However, it is the activity manager who must devise and execute the set of actions that will serve to implement the business strategy and, ultimately, the corporate strategy. The need for an activity manager to have a strategy of his own, to develop and maintain his own sense of perspective, is every bit as great as it is for his higher-ranking counterparts.

The objectives of an activity manager must be stated in terms that are appropriate to the nature of his assigned task. A product line manager's objectives might include market share, the rate of growth in sales and profitability, profit margins, and/or the image of the product in the market place. A functional manager's objectives might include costs and productivity, quality and customer service, and/or performance along these dimensions vis-à-vis competitors. For either type of activity manager, the critical characteristics of objectives defined earlier still apply; objectives are externally focused and stated in terms of the relative performance of this activity compared to similar activities performed by others.

For the activity manager the constraints/policies element of strategy is, as it was for the corporate and business managers, the most challenging aspect of strategy formulation. The product line manager's responsibility is to analyze the opportunities and to pick those that are best suited to achieve his objectives. He does this by developing a statement of constraints or priorities concerning the breadth of his product line. In it, he delineates the current and future scope and balance among the various products for which he is responsible.

Similarly, a functional manager also needs to develop a set of self-imposed constraints and policies concerning the scope of his activity. A useful concept here is that of "value added." For a functional manager, the essential question is, "What is the strategically optimal degree of vertical integration within my activity?" A manager in charge of manufacturing must worry about the strategic question of backward integration: can he capture some of the profits of his suppliers efficiently enough to increase the contribution of the manufacturing function to the business? The sales manager's analogous question concerns forward integration: to what extent could the contribution from his activity increase if he attempted to perform some of the functions now performed by others in the distribution chain between him and the ultimate consumer? Careful analysis of opportunities against resources is required to answer these questions and lead to a strategic determination of the limits on the scope of a functional activity.

Finally, the third element of every activity manager's strategy is the set of action programs that he would propose to undertake in order to implement his strategy. The necessary resources are always scarce. Therefore, priorities must be established and, in order to determine a rational sequence of actions, the performance implications of alternative sequences must be examined. Priorities will surely change as events and new opportunities unfold but, for the time at which it is made, the activity manager's strategy expresses both what he is trying to do and how he proposes to do it.

Each of the descriptions above describes the process of strategy formulation by an individual manager as though it were a neatly chronological, three-step sequence. As a practical matter, delineating a strategy is not as pedestrian as outlined, but neither is it cataclysmic in the sense of leaping full-blown from the manager's mind in one great surge of creative insight. However, the elements of a manager's strategy are related to each other, and Figure 3 is an attempt to illustrate that schematically.

As noted above, the most critical element in strategy formulation is that of constraints/policies. Objectives are rarely specified without recognizing their implications on the scope of a manager's activities. Similarly, the availability of an attractive action plan may lead to a modification of strategic constraints in order to legitimatize pursuing that action. Thus, we can see that constructing a cohesive statement embracing all three elements of strategy is a creative, evolutionary process. Plans and goals are expected to change over time; major policies, constraints on scope, and even objectives for the activity will also change, although the rate of evolution should be somewhat slower.

The discussion thus far has emphasized the fact that strategy must be a personalized statement enunciated by an individual manager. The fact that there may be hundreds of such managers in a complex organization

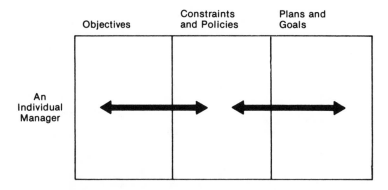

Figure 3   Strategy for an Individual Manager

does not diminish the need for personal analysis and strategic choice within the confines of each manager's positional responsibility. At the same time one would hope that the strategy of a large corporation is something more than a simple melange of independently derived statements by individuals. It is, in fact, the need to coordinate and integrate these individual statements that makes the task of strategy formulation in a complex organization so difficult.

STRATEGIC INTERRELATIONSHIPS

Referring back to Figure 2 and reading it vertically this time, a different picture of strategy in a complex organization emerges. Each manager, working individually, should develop his own statement of strategy, but it is quickly obvious that these statements must still make sense when they are arranged hierarchically. Figure 4 is a schematic attempt to represent the nature of these interrelationships.

The cells depicted in Figure 4 have been numbered for easy reference in correspondence to the sequence of discussion in the preceding section. It is important to point out here that constructing such a strategic grid for a complex organization is not a chronological sequence in involving nine steps. The grid is actually put together like a mosaic and, in order to see how the pieces fit together, we will examine the major elements of strategy within this context.

Objectives.   The citizenship and personality objectives of a corporation in Cell 1 are the only free-standing element of strategy in the entire grid, and yet even corporate management does not have carte blanche. Articulating objectives of this sort will be effective only if they represent a codification of the values shared by most members of the organization.

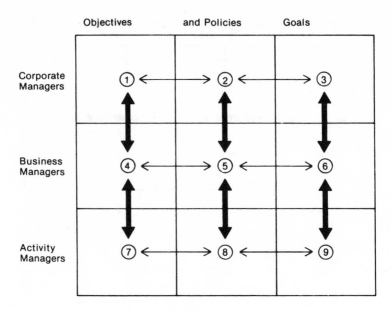

Figure 4   Hierarchical Strategic Relationships

The value of a statement of strategy under these conditions is twofold:

(1) it reinforces and crystallizes the nature and extent to which values are shared in the organization, and

(2) it makes it somewhat easier for a prospective new member of the organization to decide whether he wishes to join it or not.

Generally, as the range of diversity of a corporation's activities increases, the breadth of the values shared by all members of the corporation will decrease. Thus, a highly diverse conglomerate may not state corporate-level objectives of this sort, although such statements might be quite appropriate in some of the businesses in that corporation.

The determination of corporate financial objectives, on the other hand, is clearly not independent of other elements in the strategic grid. The relationship between Cells 1 and 2 has already been noted but, as Figure 4 makes clear, there is also a relationship between Cells 1 and 4. The financial performance objectives for a diversified corporation must relate to the performance objectives for each of the underlying businesses. Perhaps less obvious is the link between Cells 2 and 4, but the importance of that link becomes clear when the problem is viewed from the perspective of one of the business managers in the corporation. He cannot set performance objectives for his business without knowing something about corporate-level constraints and policies regarding diversification. How important is his business in the eyes of corporate managers? How tightly constrained should he expect to be in expanding the scope of his business? He answers these questions by defining the industry and his niche in it (Cell 5), but the delineation of his objectives is directly affected by both of the first two elements of corporate-level strategy.

Similarly, the objectives for any one of the activity managers reporting to a business manager are affected by their hierarchical relationship. The direct link between Cells 4 and 7 is only part of the story; an activity manager's objectives must recognize the constraints and policies that the business manager has specified in Cell 5. An activity manager uses his superior's constraint/policy statement for guidance in drafting an analogous statement of the limits on the scope of his own activity (Cell 8), but that same guidance is also a direct input to the activity manager's thinking as he attempts to enunciate his long-run, externally oriented objectives.

Constraints and Policies. The difficulty of preparing an integrated set of statements of strategy is compounded when we turn to the critical task of delineating a progressive series of constraints on the scope of the organization's activities. At first glance, the integration of this element of strategy in a complex organization might appear to be as simple as following the vertical arrows in the center column of Figure 4. As a practical matter, tying these elements of strategy together is much more involved than that.

The focal point in preparing an integrated strategy is the statement in which each business manager defines his industry and his niche in it. This is the center cell in the strategic grid in Figure 4. It affects, and is affected by, many other elements of strategy. The corporate-level statement of the types of industries that the corporation will participate in (Cell 2) cannot be prepared in a vacuum; corporate managers must understand what opportunities exist in their current businesses before they can decide how to affect the future mix of businesses. Those decisions, set forth tentatively as corporate plans and goals (Cell 3), have an important, and not unintended, side effect. A business manager, trying to delineate his current and future niche in an industry, must have some idea of the magnitude of corporate resources that can be made available to his business over time. Thus, there is a direct link between Cell 5 and Cell 3, which affects the business manager's thinking about the potential scope of his business. The determination of his own plans and goals (Cell 6) also helps him to determine a reasonable set of constraints on his business.

In a similar fashion, the constraints and policies adopted by an activity manager are affected not only by the scope of the business as a whole but also by his superior's tentative plans for the utilization of resources available to the business (Cell 6). Thus, there is a direct relationship between Cell 8 and Cell 6 with regard to the availability of resources for the activity, as well as a relationship between Cells 8 and 9 which concerns how those resources might be used.

Plans and Goals. Finally, the last and most tangible element of strategy, the plans and goals at each level in the hierarchy, must also be integrated. Compared to the complex interrelationships described above, the task of integrating plans is relatively straightforward. The vertical arrows in the last column of Figure 4 point in both directions; the tentative allocation of corporate resources cannot be made without knowing how those resources would be used in each of the businesses, and a business manager cannot plan the use of his resources without knowing what his activity managers expect to accomplish. An activity manager's planning horizon is shorter than that of his superiors. His plans are more action-oriented and definitive, and his performance goals are frequently treated as personal commitments that can and will be achieved. At the business and corporate levels, plans and goals beyond the next year or two are more fluid; tentative plans are needed to express the other elements of strategy in a more tangible form and thus to provide guidance to subordinates. Still, all the managers involved must know that the plans will change over time.

The Strategy Formulation Process. Figure 5 is a graphic representation of the interrelationships discussed above. The heavy, lateral arrows in that chart are intended to emphasize the complex way that the various elements of each manager's strategy are tied together. Even so, the chart understates the extent of the interrelationships. There are several business managers and perhaps several dozen activity managers in a complex organization. Thus, a three-dimensional chart would really be required to express all the interrelationships.

Formulating, revising, or revalidating strategy is more than a task of individual economic analysis and personal soul-searching. In a complex organization, it is also an interactive, iterative process. Dozens, literally hundreds, of two-person agreements must be negotiated, many of them almost simultaneously. The process is never completed because the agreements continue to change and evolve. Each manager, from time to time, may attempt to express his strategy in a written statement, but it is a rare, and very temporary, event for all the managers in a complex organization to develop such statements at the same point in time. On the other hand, organizing the efforts of all the managers in the organization to attempt such an undertaking can be extremely valuable, and this is really the primary purpose of formal planning systems.

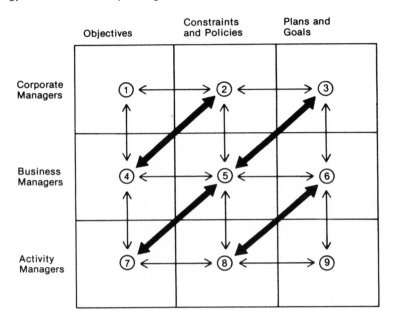

Figure 5   The Strategy Formulation Process

SUMMARY

Strategy is the conceptual glue that binds the diverse activities of a complex organization together. To be effective, strategy must personally affect each manager, constraining the scope of his activities to some extent yet providing him with enough elbow room to devise his own strategy within the broader context. In such organizations it is not very useful to think about *the* strategy. Rather, one should think of the strategy as a collection of strategies, one for each manager, linked together by a progressive series of agreements on objectives, constraints and policies, and plans and goals. Each manager must have *a* strategy in which he believes and which is compatible with the strategies of his superiors, his peers, and his subordinates.

This complex web of strategies is rarely enunciated as explicitly and comprehensively as has been described here. Most of the two-party hierarchical agreements that are required take the form of an implicit understanding between a manager and one of his subordinates. The value of explicit strategies goes beyond the simple fact that a conscious choice among strategic alternatives is likely to be better than an intuitive choice. The process of formulating explicit strategies affects both the quality of the resulting choice and the likelihood that the chosen strategy will be implemented successfully. A good formal planning system is designed to provide orderly processes that permit complex organizations to achieve all three of these benefits.

2

STRATEGIC PLANNING IN DIVERSIFIED COMPANIES*

Step by step through the three-cycle, long-range planning process

RICHARD F. VANCIL AND PETER LORANGE

The widely accepted theory of corporate strategic planning is simple: using a time horizon of several years, top management reassesses its current strategy by looking for opportunities and threats in the environment and by analyzing the company's resources to identify its strengths and weaknesses. Management may draw up several alternative strategic scenarios and appraise them against the long-term objectives of the organization. To begin implementing the selected strategy (or continue a revalidated one), management fleshes it out in terms of the actions to be taken in the near future.

In smaller companies, strategic planning is a less formal, almost continuous process. The president and his handful of managers get together frequently to resolve strategic issues and outline their next steps. They need no elaborate, formalized planning system. Even in relatively large but undiversified corporations, the functional structure permits executives to evaluate strategic alternatives and their action implications on an ad hoc basis. The number of key executives involved in such decisions is usually small, and they are located close enough for frequent, casual get-togethers.

Large, diversified corporations, however, offer a different setting for

*(Reprinted from *Harvard Business Review,* January-February 1975).

planning. Most of them use the product/market division form of organizational structure to permit decentralized decision making involving many responsibility-center managers. Because many managers must be involved in decisions requiring coordinated action, informal planning is almost impossible.

Our focus in this chapter is on formal planning processes in such complex organizations. However, the thought processes in undertaking planning (as described in the opening paragraph) are essentially the same whether the organization is large or small. Therefore, even executives whose corporate situation permits informal planning may find that our delineation of the process helps them clarify their thinking. To this end, formalizing the steps in the process requires an explanation of the purpose of each step.

THREE LEVELS OF STRATEGY

Every corporate executive uses the words *strategy* and *planning* when he talks about the most important parts of his job. The president, obviously, is concerned about strategy; strategic planning is the essence of his job. A division general manager typically thinks of himself as the president of his own enterprise, responsible for its strategy and for the strategic planning needed to keep it vibrant and growing. Even an executive in charge of a functional activity, such as a division marketing manager recognizes that his strategic planning is crucial; after all, the company's marketing strategy (or manufacturing strategy, or research strategy) is a key to its success.

These quite appropriate uses of strategy and planning have caused considerable confusion about long-range planning. This article attempts to dispel that confusion by differentiating among three types of "strategy" and delineating the interrelated steps involved in doing three types of "strategic planning" in large, diversified corporations. (Admittedly, although we think our definitions of strategy and planning are useful, others give different but reasonable meanings to these words.)

The process of strategy formulation can be thought of as taking place at the three organizational levels indicated in *Exhibit 1*: headquarters (corporate strategy), division (business strategy), and department (functional strategy). The planning processes leading to the formulation of these strategies can be labeled in parallel fashion as corporate planning, business planning, and functional planning. We have to define these notations briefly before constructing the framework of the planning process:

Corporate planning and strategy. Corporate objectives are established at the top levels. Corporate planning, leading to the formulation of corpo-

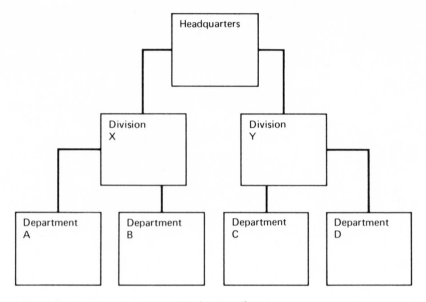

Exhibit 1   Structure of a divisionalized corporation

rate strategy, is the process of (1) deciding on the company's objectives and goals, including the determination of which and how many lines of business to engage in, (2) acquiring the resources needed to attain those objectives, and (3) allocating resources among the different businesses so that the objectives are achieved. (See Footnote 1 later in this article.)

Business planning and strategy.   Business planning, leading to the formulation of business strategy, is the process of determining the scope of a division's activities that will satisfy a broad consumer need, of deciding on the division's objectives in its defined area of operations, and of establishing the policies adopted to attain those objectives. Strategy formulation involves selecting division objectives and goals and establishing the charter of the business, after delineating the scope of its operations vis-à-vis markets, geographical areas, and/or technology.

Thus, while the scope of business planning covers a quite homogeneous set of activities, corporate planning focuses on the portfolio of the divisions' businesses. Corporate planning addresses matters relevant to the range of activities and evaluates proposed changes in one business in terms of its effects on the composition of the entire portfolio.

Functional planning and strategy.   In functional planning, the departments develop a set of feasible action programs to implement division strategy, while the division selects—in the light of its objectives—the subset of programs to be executed and coordinates the action programs of the functional departments. Strategy formulation involves selecting objectives and goals for each functional area (marketing, production, finance, research, and so on) and determining the nature and sequence of actions to be taken by each area to achieve its objectives and goals. Programs are the building blocks of the strategic functional plans.

Obviously, these levels of strategy impinge on each other to some extent—for example, the corporation's choice of business areas overlaps the scope of division charters, and the delineation of the markets by the division can dictate, at the department level, the choice of strategy in the marketing function. But the distinction remains valid and useful.

THREE-CYCLE SYSTEM

An important point to note about the planning process is that it requires formal interaction among the managers at different times. The more formal aspects—business planning, functional planning, and budgeting—are a way of organizing the interaction among managers at different levels in the hierarchy; one way of conceptualizing the planning process is as a series of meetings where executives are trying to arrive at decisions about actions to be taken. In each meeting, obviously, the basic question being addressed is the same: "What should we do?"

A detailed answer to that question is best developed by breaking it into a series of more specific questions dealt with in several meetings. These questions include: What are the objectives and goals of our company? What sort of environment can we expect to operate in? What businesses are we in? What alternative strategies could we pursue in those businesses? What other businesses should we enter? Should we make entry through an acquisition or through our research? What is the best combination of existing and new businesses to achieve corporate goals? What programs should the divisions undertake? What should each division's operating budget be?

The series of agreements among individuals in the corporate hierarchy begin on a very broad level and then are framed in progressively more detailed terms. The options are numerous in the early stages of this ordering process but narrow gradually to the final choice: a set of specific goals (budgets) for each responsibility center in the corporation. Initially, only a small group of corporate executives is involved in the process; later, more and more managers at lower levels become involved. The process eventually engages all the managers who must be committed to making the strategy work.

The reason companies adopt a complex planning process such as that shown in *Exhibit 2* is made clear by the example of a multibillion-dollar, diversified corporation, headquartered in Europe and multi-national,

Formal Planning Cycles	Cycle 1	Cycle 2

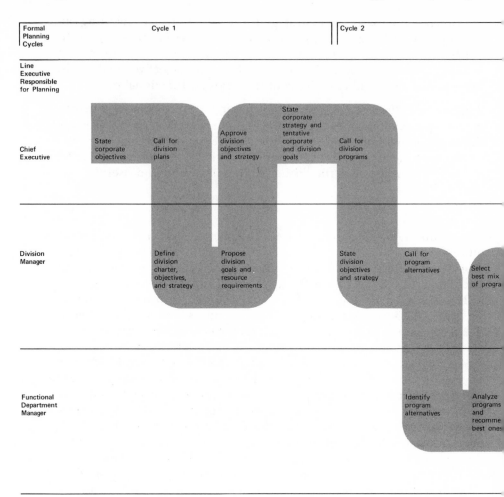

| Line Executive Responsible for Planning | | |

Chief Executive — State corporate objectives · Call for division plans · Approve division objectives and strategy · State corporate strategy and tentative corporate and division goals · Call for division programs

Division Manager — Define division charter, objectives, and strategy · Propose division goals and resource requirements · State division objectives and strategy · Call for program alternatives · Select best mix of progra

Functional Department Manager — Identify program alternatives · Analyze programs and recomme best ones

Exhibit 2´ Steps in the planning process

which had a well-established budgeting process but found "negotiating" the final budget in the closing months of each year to be difficult. The company was divisionalized, but it had decentralized very little initiative for examining strategic options.

Top management, increasingly uneasy over its ability to resolve all the strategic issues implicit in the budget, decided to ask the divisions to prepare formal five-year plans for its approval before drawing up the final corporate budget. The controller's department was to coordinate the preparation of the detailed plans. The company moved from a one-cycle planning system to a two-cycle system, as shown in *Exhibit 3*. The

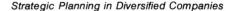

Cycle 3

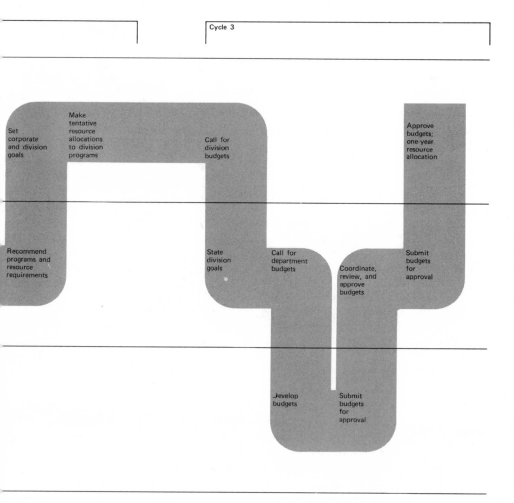

Set corporate and division goals

Make tentative resource allocations to division programs

Call for division budgets

Approve budgets; one-year resource allocation

Recommend programs and resource requirements

State division goals

Call for department budgets

Coordinate, review, and approve budgets

Submit budgets for approval

Develop budgets

Submit budgets for approval

result was a flood of paper work and very little strategic thinking on the division managers' part.

When top management reviewed the first set of five-year plans—a 20-pound packet of neat notebooks—it decided the results were unacceptable. It made suggestions to the divisions and requested a new set. This process was repeated no fewer than five times during the summer and early fall before all sides reached agreement and the budgeting could proceed.

After this experience corporate management agreed that the procedure needed much improvement. So in the following year the company

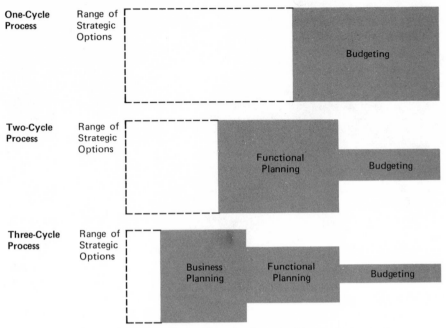

Exhibit 3   Examples of one-, two-, and three-cycle planning processes

installed a three-cycle system. The first step required no comprehensive financial projections; instead, each division manager was asked to identify three or four strategic issues for presentation and discussion at headquarters. Agreement on those issues set the stage for orderly functional planning and budgeting, which had been so cumbersome before.

An important point to note about *Exhibit 2* is its demarcation vertically, by cycles, and also horizontally, by activities at the three managerial levels. The degree of involvement at these levels is different in each planning cycle.

In the first cycle, corporate executives and division managers are primarily involved. A division manager draws his functional subordinates into discussions about the unit's strategy, but the functional managers' role usually remains informal. At this point the division manager regards the strategy as "his"; then, seeking the head office's endorsement, he formalizes it for better communication.

Once the division's strategy is set, the second cycle begins; here functional managers play a much more important part. In both that cycle and the budgeting cycle, they have the primary responsibility for developing detailed programs and budgets. The division manager and his staff are involved more or less actively in these two cycles, while top management limits itself to a review of division proposals.

Exhibit 2, of course, makes no pretense of depicting the planning process as it is universally practiced; it is only illustrative. Nor is the process as neat and orderly as it appears here. For one reason, the process does not start from scratch each year; the previous year's efforts feed into the first cycle. Moreover, while managers plan, the world keeps turning; so during a cycle events may oblige them to hold many meetings involving two levels.

FIRST CYCLE

The first cycle of a formal planning process serves a dual purpose: (1) to develop a tentative set of agreements between corporate management and the division managers about overall strategy and goals, and thereby (2) to provide focus for the more detailed planning in the next cycle. The process of reaching these initial agreements requires three discrete activities: establishing corporate objectives, drawing up division charters, and setting corporate goals. The ensuing discussion centers on these activities in a hypothetical (but representative) corporation whose fiscal year corresponds with the calendar year.

Establishing corporate objectives

In the initial dialogue between corporate and division management —starting in early February—the two groups form a statement of the corporation's purpose and objectives. Naturally, its scope and the degree of detail provided vary greatly from one company to another. Company X prepares a detailed statement, starting this year with the general assertion that it is a "systems-oriented, high-technology, multinational, and socially conscious company."

The principles set out mainly for strategic planning include breakthrough strategies (such as "seek projects, internal or external, waiting for application rather than invention"), resource management (such as "continuous emphasis on market orientation as opposed to product orientation"), financing ("utilization of the borrowing power of subsidiaries to escape the provisions of the debentures and foreign investment regulations"), public relations ("genuine concern for the quality of life, inside and outside the company"), acquisitions, joint ventures, licensing ("export and import technology in the form of licenses or joint ventures, including third countries"), and so on.

The preparation of such a statement gives division managers guidance as they begin strategic planning for their businesses. So as a minimum the statement must include the intended company policies for allocating resources among the divisions. In effect, such policies constitute a statement of strategy for the entire corporation—although many businessmen are uncomfortable using the term "strategy" in such an abstract sense. Therefore, the delineation of an explicit statement of corporate strategy is often deferred until the final step in the first cycle.

Whether corporate strategy should be enunciated early or late in the planning process depends primarily on the degree of diversity in the company's businesses. In general, the more diverse the corporation, the less feasible it is to develop an explicit, cohesive strategy for its businesses and, therefore, the more desirable it is to make the resource allocation policies explicit at an early stage. On the other hand, less diversified companies frequently delay preparing a strategy statement until the division heads have developed strategic proposals for their own businesses. Many large corporations are divisionalized, but not so many are highly diversified. The more common practice is to delay the definition (or redefinition) of corporate strategy until it can be stated in fairly explicit terms.

Drawing up division charters

In mid-March headquarters calls on each division manager to (a) write or review the "charter" of his division, specifying the scope of its activities and his objectives for the business as he defines it, and (b) propose a strategy for the business and a tentative set of goals for the coming year.

Giving the initiative to the division manager at this step challenges him to think strategically about the scope of his activities and then propose a charter broad enough to permit him to contribute significantly to achieving corporate objectives. Formalizing this step in the planning process is an important device by which corporate management widens the horizons of division heads. An explicit charter also serves two secondary purposes: (1) it increases the likelihood of clear agreement between the top executives and the division manager about the scope of his activities, and (2) it reduces the risk of redundant efforts or competition between divisions.

Establishing a division's charter is not a discrete activity; it is inextricably connected to the task of identification and analysis of alternative strategies that exploit the charter selected. Obviously, the decision based on this analysis is crucial because the long-term performance of any division is a function of the strategy it adopts, and the performance of the company as a whole is likewise a function of the strategies of its particular businesses.

Although the initiative for identifying and analyzing strategic options lies with the division manager, guidelines that headquarters gives him for presentation of his proposals affect the way he pursues the task. Increasingly common is a request by corporate management that when he proposes a strategy and specifies goals, at the same time he also present a statement of the alternative strategies which he has evaluated and rejected. The intent is not to permit the head office to second-guess the division manager's thinking, but to ensure that he used strategic thinking in arriving at his recommendations.

In mid-May, four to ten weeks after headquarters presents its request for division proposals, the unit's manager presents his recommendations to the corporate management group. The presentation consists at least of an integrated proposal for the division's charter, its objectives, the strategy to be pursued and tentative goals. The recommendations may also include a general statement of the action programs that would be developed to implement the strategy (developed in more detail in the second cycle) and a crude estimate of the resources that would be required. Detailed financial data are usually not included at this step because such information is not necessary to evaluate the strategy and because the effort of preparing it may go to waste if the recommendations are modified.

In the ensuing discussions, which extend over several meetings in late spring, corporate management and each division chief work toward reaching an agreement about the appropriate division strategy and goals.

Setting corporate goals

By the middle of June top management has prepared an explicit statement of corporate strategy and goals. In some companies this document is, in effect, a set of decisions on how resources are to be allocated among the divisions, as well as a forecast of the results expected from each. In most cases, however, the statement is not intended to constitute a final resource allocation decision; rather, it is designed to provide feedback to the division managers about the corporate implications of the agreed-on business strategies. The presentation and discussion of corporate strategy and goals are also commonly used as a device to initiate the second cycle of the planning process.

The sum of the recommended division goals is likely to be inadequate to achieve the goals envisioned by headquarters for the entire organization. In trying to close this "planning gap," corporate management has only three choices:

1. It can improve division performance by pressing, during the review of division recommendations, for more aggressive strategies and more ambitious goals.

2. It can divert company resources into more promising businesses. This move may give rise to an acquisition program.
3. It can decide that the corporate goals are unrealistic and scale them down.

The fact that the corporation's goals normally are more or less the sum of those division goals sought by top management implies that headquarters is concerned with rather minor adjustments of this portfolio of goals. If so, the first cycle of formal planning has the salutary effect of providing an annual "mid-course correction" to the trajectory of the combined businesses. Momentum is a factor in the continued success of a diversified corporation—as with a rocket headed for the moon—and a wise chief executive does not dissipate it needlessly. Rather, he nudges the bundle of energies represented by his division managers, trying to make minor adjustments early enough to be nondisruptive and at the same time affect the corporation's position several years ahead.

Occasionally—perhaps inevitably—a major corporate shift is necessary, affecting one of its businesses. Care must be taken to isolate the effect on the remaining businesses. In late spring a couple of years ago, for example, top management of a major diversified corporation went through its usual review of division strategic plans. One operation, created to develop a substantial new business for the corporation, presented its usual story: "Buying market share in this high-technology business is very expensive, breakeven is still two or three years away, and additional investment of several hundred million dollars is required. But the eventual profits will be enormous."

The division's management concluded that it was progressing about as expected and that its strategy was sound, and it recommended continued aggressive investment. With minor modifications, top management approved the proposal. Three months later the company abruptly announced that the business would be discontinued and the investment written off.

Poor planning? Obviously, the decision to enter the business was a mistake. But implementation of that decision, and the planning done to minimize the investment exposure without compromising the chances for success, were probably sound. There are two important lessons here about the process of corporate planning:

1. Strategic decisions—like this divestment—are not made in accordance with some precise timetable. They are made whenever top management reaches the conclusion that interference in a unit's affairs is necessary.
2. Formal planning procedures are *not* intended to facilitate strategic decisions such as this—if only because a division manager rarely recommends the disposal of his operation. Rather, formal corporate strategic planning has the more modest, if no less crucial, purpose of seeking to optimize the collective thrust of the continuing businesses.

Approving a division's strategic plan but closing the unit three months later is not hypocrisy or poor planning. The ax is much more merciful than the slow strangulation of providing inadequate resources. In the meantime, until the ax falls, division management must prove the viability of its business. For its part, headquarters must not fail to recognize the difference between a sound plan and a sound business. A sound plan deserves approval, but only top management can decide whether the business is sound enough to continue implementation of that plan.

SECOND CYCLE

The second planning cycle also has two purposes. First, each division head and his functional subordinates should reach tentative agreement on the action programs to be implemented over the next few years. Second, the involvement of functional managers in the long-range planning process should deepen and sharpen the strategic focus of the business and thus provide a better basis for the even more detailed budgeting task to follow.

The division manager in Company X initiates the functional planning process in the middle of June after reaching tentative agreement with top management about his organization's charter, objectives, strategy, and goals.[1] In the first planning meeting with subordinates, he briefly reviews the corporate/division dialogue that has just concluded and describes the approved division objectives and strategy.

At this time he usually does not make explicit the sales or profit goals, even though tentative agreement on targets has been reached. There are two reasons for dealing in generalities at this point. First, being specific might constrain the thinking of the functional managers, who have the chance in this cycle to make a creative contribution toward achieving the division's objectives. Second, division goals will become final only when corporate management has approved the unit's programs and allocated resources to implement them.

Long-range planning by functional managers is conceptually a simple process, being limited by the tentative agreements reached in the first cycle. It is operationally more complex than the planning activity in the first cycle, however, since it requires substantially more detailed plans and involves many more people. The purpose of such "programming"—so-called because the activity focuses on specific programs—is to translate

---

[1] It is worth differentiating between *objectives* and *goals*, since these terms are used separately here. **Objectives** are general statements describing the size, scope, and style of the enterprise in the long term. They embody the values and aspirations of the managers, based on their assessment of the environment and of the capabilities and health of the corporation. For example, the financial objective of a large, diversified, multinational corporation might be to rank in the top 10% worldwide in compound rate of growth in earnings per share. **Goals** are more specific statements of the achievements targeted for certain deadlines. At the corporate level these statements are likely to include such aspects as sales, profits, and EPS targets. Annual budgets constitute goals at all levels in the organization.

the division's externally oriented business strategy into an internally directed, coordinated set of activities designed to implement it. Inasmuch as the resources available for implementation are always limited, programming must help ensure their optimal use.

Obviously, the scope, magnitude, and duration of a program depend on the nature of the goal. In the broadest sense, a product division of a diversified corporation might be conceived of as a "program." The division manager's goal may be stated in simple financial terms and extend over several years, and his discretion may be constrained only by a charter for his product line and the availability of corporate resources. In such a situation, the division program may be international in scope, almost unlimited in breadth of product line, and may involve hundreds of millions of dollars in expenditures. At the other end of the spectrum, the sales manager for a district in the northeast region of that division may have been charged with improving market penetration by 10% over the next 18 months. His actions also fulfill the definition of a program.

Formalized programming

The need to formalize the programming process grows as functional interdependence in the business increases and as more time is required to evaluate the effectiveness of alternative functional plans. Formalization is designed to improve the specification of programs and the matching of programs and goals.

The charter and strategy for the business and the objectives and goals that top management has set for it limit the functional manager's strategic planning. Within those constraints, however, he may still enjoy very broad discretion concerning the best course to take. His challenge is to devise more effective ways to combine the available resources in order to achieve his goals. A useful way to look at the specification of programs is in terms of the chronology for involvement of the functional departments. In a typical manufacturing enterprise there are four types of programs to be developed:

1. *Existing revenue programs*—An example is the development of a set of marketing programs for the existing product lines.
2. *New revenue programs*—Planning the development and introduction of new products is an example.
3. *Manufacturing programs*—Typically, sales forecasts by product line are furnished to the manufacturing function, which develops the programs necessary to meet the revenue goals in the marketing programs.
4. *Support programs*—Managers of other functional support activities, such as administration, may also get involved in the development of programs.

The programming process, even when formalized, is inevitably haphazard because it requires repeated interaction among the departments. The intended result is a plan that is integrated like the two sides of a coin. On one side is the set of action programs and on the other a coordinated statement of the resources needed by each functional manager to execute his part of the program.

A major purpose of the formal programming process is to review the ongoing programs to see whether they can be expected to fulfill the goals for which they were designed. Or, if more effective programs have been devised, the existing ones must be modified or discontinued. At the same time, some "old" programs may be nearing completion, and new ones will need approval if the goals are to be met. Programming also involves coordination of functional activities to ensure that the selected programs can be implemented efficiently. Each functional department must understand the implications of a set of programs for its own activities, and the department manager must accept the tasks assigned him and the resources to be made available to him.

In our mythical Company X, after much analysis and discussion the division manager and his functional subordinates finally agree by the end of August on a set of programs to recommend to headquarters. This time, in contrast to the first, a more elaborate presentation is in order and a large number of managers—corporate and division, line and staff—may attend.

THIRD CYCLE

The third cycle of the formal planning process needs little explanation. Naturally, throughout the planning process top managers and division executives often discuss the allocation of resources among the divisions. But it becomes the focus of attention in the last step of the second cycle, when the divisions have completed their program proposals and sent them to the head office for approval. At this point (mid-September at Company X), decisions on allocation of resources can be made, subject to final approval when the detailed budgets are submitted (in mid-November). These general points are worth making here:

1. Resource allocation is almost always a very informal, unstructured process, heavily dependent on the skill in advocacy and political weight of the executives concerned. Since it is also a continuous process, by the end of the second cycle the risk of serious mismatch between programs and resources is unlikely—if headquarters/division communications have been good.

2. Although programs may have an expected life of several years, resources are usually allocated for only one year at a time. Whether top management

will make a commitment to meet next year's needs will depend on the scale and timing flexibility of the program in the competition for resources.

3. Although resource allocation to projects is based on a perception of the desirability of each, corporate planning attempts to ensure that each also fits into a portfolio of undertakings.

RAISING THE ODDS

The formal long-range planning process in large, diversified corporations is both simple and complex. Conceptually, the process is very simple—a progressive narrowing of strategic choices—although it may involve many steps along that path. Operationally, the process is far more complex than the activities we have described because the formal part of the process is only the tip of the iceberg. Good strategic planning can take place only when qualified managers engage in creative thinking—and creativity, by definition, cannot be produced on a schedule.

Yet there is little doubt that formalizing the planning process is worthwhile; it ensures that managers at all levels will devote some time to strategic thinking, and it guarantees each of them an audience for his ideas. While formal strategic planning cannot guarantee good ideas, it can increase the odds sufficiently to yield a handsome payoff.

3

FIVE PILLARS FOR YOUR PLANNING*

XAVIER GILBERT AND PETER LORANGE

A widely accepted approach regarding the design and implementation of an effective formal system for a company's long-range planning is that the system design should be contingent on the specific situational setting of each particular firm. A given formal planning system should thus be "tailored" to the specific corporate strategy, the organizational structure of the firm, the behavioral styles and preferences of management at hand,

*(Reprinted from *European Business*, Autumn 1974).

and other factors. Because of this, there will be no such thing as a generally applicable implementation of a formal planning system. However, this article will conclude that, in spite of the tailoring approach for systems design, there seem to be at least five general "musts" that do represent necessary, although not sufficient, ingredients in the success of a formal planning process:

1. One of the aims of top management must be that they make use of the formal planning process as a support to formulate strategic choices.
2. The overall purpose of going through a formal planning process must be entirely understood at *all* the levels of the organization that are involved.
3. There must be at least a minimum of common requirements regarding the standardization of contents, formats, deadlines, methods, etc., of the formal planning system.
4. The formal planning system must be integrated with the other management systems of the company, such as, for instance, its management control system or management information system.
5. Line managers must be centrally involved in the formal planning process.

These five rules cannot ensure that the formal planning process will be successful, but at least they will make the task a little easier when they are adhered to. Let us emphasize, however, that the principle of situational planning systems design in no sense will be invalidated by our rules.

Of course, the requirement to tailor the design of the remaining aspects of the planning system to the given situational setting will be just as valid. Nevertheless, there is a significantly smaller chance of success for the planning system when the five design guidelines are not respected, as has been shown by a number of business experiences.

AVOID THE "LAWS"

Strategic choices are those that govern the most basic orientations of the corporation. They deal with the type of industry or industries the company is in, the sort of company it should be, its size and growth, etc. These are some very basic choices that govern all the subsequent ones. However, some confusion frequently exists respecting the process through which they are formulated. They do not exist before and above everything as the Tables of Law. Rather, they are developed through a continuous process in which various coalitions—top management, the unions, the engineers, the stockholders, etc.—try to enforce their own point of view. Top management normally has the final word since it is at the highest level of coordination, but they may nevertheless want to compromise as a consequence of all the pressures that are exercised in and out of the corporation. In this process, what planning may give to the

whole corporation is a sense of direction, namely a commitment to implement a set of future actions, mutually acceptable to all the parties
involved. Top management will be constrained by the plans in two ways
because of the organizational commitment phenomenon, a constraint
surprisingly easy to overlook:

> The key long-range strategic considerations and actions must, at least
> to some extent, be part of the plan, in order to secure that those
> decisions get the full organizational support.
>
> It will be difficult, or may even be impossible, for top management to
> undertake dramatic strategic swings and depart from the planned
> strategy in too dramatic ways. Organizational commitment will not
> easily be obtained for such more-or-less erratic reorientations.

Through the planning process a sort of consensus regarding the overall goals will emerge among the company's many shareholder groups.
Typically, extensive planning revisions, negotiations, reviews and feedbacks will take place before such organizational consensus is reached,
manifested in the finalized plan. We believe that a formal planning
system cannot be implemented unless it is realized that the system should
enhance a sense of direction and organizational commitment, and that,
therefore, strategic decision making to a considerable extent will have to
be part of the planning process.

Some companies may not be aware of this requirement and, as a
consequence, may find themselves at a deadend when it comes to implementing a formal planning process. In a $300 million-sales diversified
company with international operations, top management had decided
that some sort of future planning process ought to be started in order to
better manage the past and future acquisitions. Two joint processes were
supposed to be started. First, the divisions were asked to submit their own
plans which were designed from scratch, without any guidelines or corporate objectives given to them. Second, a group of corporate staff members
were supposed to meet regularly with top management in order to issue
corporate objectives. Consequently, the divisions were left from the beginning with little idea of what was expected from them in terms of future
orientations and results. This would not have been too bad if, concurrently and in conjunction with the way the thinking of the divisions was
developing, top management had been willing to freeze certain options
for the future, made the necessary choices, and brought these to the
knowledge of the divisions. This however did not take place, first, because
the top management committee was working in a vacuum, isolated from
the divisions, and, second, because it consisted only of staff members who
were insufficiently aware of what was really possible for the divisions. In
the year following the start of this formal planning process, a small crisis

affected the company, forcing sales and profits temporarily to decrease sharply. The formal planning process was immediately abandoned in order to save time for more "urgent" matters. In other words, as soon as planning properly done became most required, it got abandoned. The divisions had not developed enough sense of direction before and during their planning process. Consequently, what they had prepared was a series of forecasts that soon turned out to be wrong, rather than a firm commitment and a contribution to the corporate decision-making process. Consequently, the planning efforts could not be of much use, because planning and strategic decision making were entirely separated. Next-to-no organizational commitment to the plans had therefore developed. The only option left to management was to cope with the situation in a firefighter type of reaction.

CONFUSION BETWEEN FORECASTING AND PLANNING

Most companies that undertake long-range planning put considerable emphasis on extrapolating the expected developments of their business activities into the future, so that their top managements may get a clearer notion of where the company is going. Many managers compare this future performance forecast with what might be desirable according to a set of corporate goals, more or less explicitly set. The discrepancy between *desirable goals* and *expected performance according to the forecast* is commonly called the planning gap. For many managers there seems to be a strong perception that the essence of planning is achieved by this. This is what leads us to believe that widespread confusion in fact exists regarding the difference between forecasting and planning, according to our notion of these tasks. *While forecasting involves trying to make educated guesses about the future, planning contains one additional crucial step, namely deciding on specific business actions for the future.* As a consequence, forecasting is only one of the ingredients in planning. A major purpose of planning will thus be to support strategic decision making with the development of alternative actions that will have long-term consequence at the corporate level. It is striking to observe that in several companies that are trying to get formal planning processes started, as well as in some companies with longer traditions in planning, top management often seems to be totally unaware of this major purpose of planning, namely to facilitate the preparation of specific actions for the future. Far too often, this decision orientation of planning seems to get lost.

Another indication of the apparent confusion about the decision-making purpose of long-range planning seems also to be frequently reflected by the interpretation of the term "long-range" or "long-term" planning to mean, say, a five-year planning horizon. Since the major purpose of formal planning is to support strategic decision making for the future, *each such decision calls for the consideration of the appropriate time horizon.* The time horizon is consequently a function of the type of decision to be made, not of the decimal system as would be suggested by the fact that a five-year planning horizon seems to be the most readily acceptable among planners. By choosing a time horizon at random or because everybody does it, rather than accepting that it is a function of the decisions to be made, people are still more inclined to confuse planning with forecasting. This is thus another consequence of the confusion about planning's real purpose that can be observed in a number of companies. One is led to believe that what is required is the preparation of a five-year forecast and nothing more, and, again, the essence of formal planning is lost.

Finally, a *third symptom of the existing misunderstandings about the purpose of formal planning can be found in a number of companies that are trying to implement a formal planning process to an organization structure without proper regard for at what levels in the organization the responsibility for taking long-range strategic decisions in fact should rest.* Companies may be classified all along the spectrum from those in which strategic decisions are all taken centrally to those in which strategic decision making will be highly decentralized. Planning should be undertaken by those levels in an organization which are responsible for the strategic long-term decisions. Thus, in a decentralized company, long-range planning should be undertaken at a number of organizational levels, say, by divisions, groups, and corporate headquarters. Separate forecasting as well as decision identification efforts should be worked out by all these units. Conversely, in a centralized corporation, planning should be undertaken at the corporate level, which, consequently, should prepare its own forecasts and strategic-decision alternatives. Often, unfortunately, one finds that only the forecasting tasks of planning but not the action alternative generation task gets delegated to the divisions in a decentralized company and that the execution of the forecasting task is neglected at the corporate level. The result will be a confusion of the planning task, both at the divisional as well as at the corporate levels. Similarly, in centralized companies, one may find that forecasts are prepared centrally, and that a number of the functional plans containing specific action proposals are prepared further down in the organization without any forecast base at all. Again, the purpose of planning is confused.

THERE MUST BE CONSISTENCY!

The desirability of ensuring a minimum common format and content requirement for the various organizational subunits' plans in a divisionalized corporation does basically arise because, as we have said, formal planning is a decision-making tool that aims at coordinating the efforts of the various operating units. This coordination can be made much easier if the various inputs from the divisions are also consistent among themselves. The degree to which they must be consistent is really a matter of individual cases. The size of the company, the number of autonomous divisions in question, the diversity of business activities, the degree of interdivisionalized interdependence, the geographical spread of the location of the company's activities, and other factors will determine what the minimum format and content requirement must be. The requirement must be, however, that the preparation schedules, contents, and presentation formats must be such as to allow for reasonably effective aggregation of subplans so that corporate planning in fact can take place within the decentralized structure. Planning data must thus be easy to find, comparable and available at the same moment in time.

A necessary requirement, then, for planning in a decentralized company must be that the inputs to the planning process in the various divisions must also be consistent. These inputs include data about the economic environment such as inflation rates, labor cost rates, growth in the economy, etc., as well as data results from corporate constraints and choices such as the cost of capital, the rate of interest for borrowing, etc. All the operating units involved in the planning process obviously have to be given a common set of hypotheses with which to begin. Otherwise, their plans will be impossible to discuss, compare, or coordinate.

In companies that do not take the point of minimum content and format requirement as a "must," it will, of course, be difficult for top management to use the formal plan as a decision-making tool. It frequently turns out that planning deteriorates and becomes less efficient. First, the accuracy of the plans may diminish to less than desirable, because of discrepancies in the underlying definitions for preparing the components of the plans. Second, the time required to complete plans may increase dramatically, because of delays due to incomplete time tables, time needed for clarifying misunderstandings, etc. Finally, quarrels about inconsistencies in plans because of lack of common underlying content and formats may build up hostility among managers and detract energy and attention from improving the decision-support content of planning.

STERILE ARGUMENTS OVER WORDS

Let the following examples illustrate some of the problems that might arise when the various operating units do not use similar methods and languages when they prepare their formal plans. In a large French company, some of the operating units were using different cost concepts under similar names, and no explicit explanation of these differences existed. As a consequence, the review of each divisional formal plan ended up in lengthy and sterile arguments concerning the meaning of the various terms used. In addition to the risk of serious confusions, this also reduced very much the credibility of the whole process. Each time a figure from the plan was under discussion, the immediate answer was: "How can one have confidence in a plan where such a confusion as to the real meaning of 'manufacturing costs' exists?" Obviously, the quantitative part of the formal plan is only a portion of it and not necessarily the essential one. But such arguments are very likely to be used whenever there is already some resistance to the discipline required for going through the formal planning process.

At this point, a note of interpretation may be warranted. *Our plan for minimum common content and format requirements should not lead to the implementation of generalized procedures when "tailored" approaches would be applicable.* For instance, a large multinational conglomerate has developed quite different formats for its major sectors of business involvement, industry, hotels and insurance. Obviously, also, cost concepts, depreciation rules, etc., differ substantially between these sectors. This is the way it should be, reflecting a tailoring of the systems to the given situational purposes. However, differences in definitions, concepts, schedules, etc., are made explicit, so that their effects on planning can be easily recognized and plans aggregated.

Although the formal planning system of a company will be of key importance in terms of the long-term direction setting, there will naturally also be other management systems that support decision making in the company. For instance, the management control system, which typically includes the one-year budget, will help assure that long-term policies and strategic decisions are being effectively implemented. Systems for operational control, such as inventory control systems or production line balancing systems, will assure that specific tasks are carried out effectively. Management information systems will facilitate the process of collecting, manipulating and transmitting information. *Since all these systems, then, in fact will be parts of an overall corporate management system, an overall decision-support system, it becomes essential that the systems be so designed that they will function in an integrated way.* All the different decision-support systems should be tailored to the given situational setting of the company Provided the tailoring of the designs is done properly and carefully, integration between the systems should be a resulting effect. Conversely, lack of integration may be seen as an indication that one or more subsystems have been designed with less than the requisite tailoring care. We may, in fact, say that the requirement that the formal planning system and the other decision-support systems should be integrated may serve as a check of consistency that all the subsystems have been properly designed for a given company setting. This "must"—i.e. that the planning system's design be consistent with the other management systems—is illustrated in Exhibit 1.

LINE MANAGERS MUST BE INVOLVED

The fact is that a number of experts on planning long and vigorously have preached that the line managers must be actively involved in preparing their own plans, because only when those responsible for performance get committed to the plans will the latter stand a chance to get implemented. In spite of this, a number of factors tend to disentangle the line manager from planning:

To attempt to increase the effectiveness of planning, staff planners may get involved and actually do the plans on the line managers' behalf, to relieve the busy line from another burden and to ensure that completion dates are met. Done to a very limited extent this may cause little harm, but the danger is imminent that the line manager will soon get too disentangled to stay committed to the plans.

Planning, and its content, may be seen by some as a tool to obtain power in an organization, which, consequently, may lead to planning being cultivated and "protected" by a small group of executives. We have seen planning as a "political science" happen particularly in a number

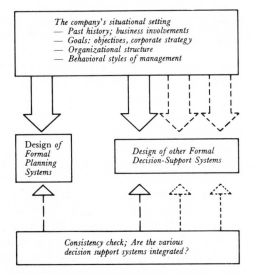

Exhibit 1 Integrating formal planning with other decision systems

of European-based organizations, where there is a long-standing tradition of practicing a more secretive management style. Company executives may easily be led to believe in such settings that the issues dealt with in the formal planning process are so crucial that they should be kept confidential. This will of course be both true and legitimate for some of the issues, but on the other hand, how could one hope to implement a plan when large parts of the organization are unaware of its content? This is even more pertinent these days, as participative management develops from both sides. The confidentiality of certain issues may often be exaggerated, and should never be used as an excuse not to involve line managers.

INFORMATION AS A STATUS SYMBOL

The following example illustrates the source of trouble when information is retained as a status symbol in planning. In a holding company headquartered in France with sales in the vicinity of three billion francs and multinational industrial operations, it turned out that the top managers of the main subsidiaries had never discussed with their own managers the formal plans they were preparing for the headquarters. For them, knowing about the formal plan content was a symbol of their involvement with the strategic issues of the corporation. As a consequence, they did not feel that their immediate subordinate line managers ought to be informed. However, this had the consequence that their plans were mostly wishful thinking and totally lacked the practicality that would have made them implementable. For instance, some of the plants did not have the capacity to produce what the subsidiary top manager had planned for them. Of course, when it came to implementation, the line managers were unwilling to take the formal plan seriously. Had they been involved in the preparation from the beginning, this would have resulted not only in a more realistic formal plan, but also in a stronger cooperation for implementing it.

Let us hasten to stress that we do not, of course, advocate that the entire line necessarily should be kept up to date on all major strategic decisions. For instance, in a major U.S. airline carrier, company planning is highly centralized, and predominantly top down. Key strategic information is shared among a few top executives and the degree of information going to the line further down in the organization is definitely much less than complete. However, given this type of organization, this is all right. The essence is that the line should receive enough information to plan meaningfully in every situation. the amount of information needed will, of course, vary from company to company. In our previous example of the French company, however, the line had definitely not received enough information to get involved in planning in a meaningful manner.

Related to the aforementioned difficulty is *the "empire-building" syndrome*. As an indication of "the bureaucratic phenomenon," the planning organization may have the tendency to grow for its own sake, a process that will blur the real purpose of the planning staff. For instance, in a large U.S.-based industrial company, the first step taken in getting a formal planning process started was to appoint a head of the planning department, who immediately proceeded to appoint assistants to the head of the planning department, and so forth. Subsequently, all these people started designing a system which they thought the company had to follow. However, the way this was perceived by the line people was merely as an additional burden placed on them to satisfy some of the latest fancy information needs of those staff bureaucrats from above. When, after some time, the staff planners, frustrated by the slowness of getting planning to work effectively, offered to undertake parts of the routine tasks of planning on the line people's behalf, the line was more than pleased to let this perceived burden go. Needless to say, this attempt turned into a total failure, which the planning departments for some time desperately tried to ameliorate by adding still more to their empire building. This seems to be a frequent and grave mistake. Those who make the plans should be the line managers, not the members of the planning department. And the plans should be helpful and make sense to the line, not to the members of the planning department. An essential message for the success of a planning process is that planning must become a way of managing for the line people. The best way to convey this is through deeply involving those line people and holding back the growth of the planning staff.

VIOLATING THE FIVE "MUSTS"

The above are five "musts" of formal planning. Some of these principles have been stated before by others, and other principles are simply plain common sense. However, as we have seen, it is surprisingly easy to violate one or more of these "musts" in real life. In designing and monitoring formal planning systems we should thus take the necessary precautions for avoiding such violations.

More importantly, it may be that many of the frequent violations of the basic principles just discussed indicate a basic misunderstanding of planning on the part of those involved, planners and line managers alike. Such symptoms, then, should lead to explanatory actions aimed at straightening out these misperceptions.

Designing and implementing planning systems implies experimenting with one's organization in a real sense, through one's choice of design variables. The expenses of performing the wrong experiments may, of course, become very high when we are dealing with very complex organizations. Our five "musts" may serve as guidelines to prevent the repetition of mistakes done by others before. It should not be necessary to start designing the planning system from scratch, more or less "inventing the wheel."

Again, let us hasten to stress that treating these five points with particular care is not in itself a guarantee of success. They are not cookbook recipes, in the sense that there is no such thing as a general applicable answer to the question of how to implement them. This is pretty much a question of each particular situation. There will never be a universally good way to involve line managers in the planning process, nor a universal set of common content requirements for the formal plans, nor a universal best way to formulate strategic choices before or in relation with the formal planning process, nor a universal approach to integrating planning systems, nor a universal lecture to explain the purpose of formal planning. The "how-to-do-it" procedure depends essentially on each individual situation. Planning is really a way of behaving in the face of situations and, as such, it has to be adapted to each of them.

Case 1

*Gotaas-Larsen Shipping Corporation–A**

By the late 1960s, International Utilities had spent 10 years on a program of acquisition and diversification. To help manage its expanded activities, International Utilities set up a complex formal planning system. In 1970, Mr. Arthur Goldenberg, a member of the planning staff, was transferred to Gotaas-Larsen Shipping Corporation (one of International Utilities' larger subsidiaries), initially as an internal consultant and subsequently as a Vice President of Finance and Administration. Mr. Goldenberg viewed his assignment as being ". . . . to help Gotass-Larsen in setting up a planning system. The output of the planning system was to be compatible with the system established at International Utilities."

---

*This case was written by Steven Alter and Sudeep Anand, Research Assistants, Massachusetts Institute of Technology.

THE PARENT COMPANY

International Utilities (IU), which as the forerunner of I.U. International Corporation, was founded in 1924. During the following 15 years the company grew rapidly into a large public utilities holding company in Canada and the United States. Then, in response to changing regulatory climates, the utility properties outside Canada were sold, the capitalization simplified, and the parent company debt eliminated. From 1944 to 1959 IU grew as the parent of gas and electric utility properties in Alberta, Canada. During the next decade the company embarked upon a program of acquisitions and strategic diversification into businesses whose growth and stability prospects were more compatible with IU's long-term goals. In 1969 the emphasis shifted from acquisition and diversification to consolidation and internal growth. The transition from a utilities holding company to a diversified operating company was symbolized by the change in the company's name from International Utilities to IU International Corporation in 1973.

As of 1973, IU was established in three major industry sectors with eight operating groups:

—Energy Markets: in which the Ocean Shipping (Gotaas-Larsen), Energy Systems and Electric and Gas Services groups operated.
—Transportation and Distribution Markets: in which the Transportation Services and Distribution Services groups competed.
—Environmental Markets: where IU operated through its Waste Management Services, Water Management Services and Land Management and Tourism groups.

Exhibit 1 shows IU's 1973 financial statements. Exhibit 2 shows 10 years of historical data by major market and shows the contribution of each of the eight operating groups to IU's revenues and income.

Today, the breadth of its geographical and market diversification has lead IU to delegate all operating decisions to the management of each operating company. To manage its far flung activities, IU has adopted strong centralized controls in finance and planning, with special emphasis on asset management and long-range strategic planning. Operating management performance is measured against objectives established through IU's planning system. Executive compensation is closely tied to the achievement of approved objectives. It is corporate policy to capitalize each operating group based on its own debt capacity in order that the capital structure of each operating group might reflect the characteristics

Exhibit 1   IU INTERNATIONAL'S FINANCIAL STATEMENT FOR 1973

Statements of Consolidated Income
Years ended December 31, 1973 and 1972
(in thousands, except per share data)

	1973	1972
SALES, REVENUES AND OTHER INCOME	$1,548,559	$1,234,130
COSTS AND EXPENSES:		
Cost of products sold and other operating costs and expenses, excluding depreciation and amortization	1,110,116	876,286
Selling, general and administrative expenses, excluding depreciation and amortization	196,186	166,867
Depreciation and amortization	66,285	59,145
Interest and debt expense	60,942	39,537
Income taxes	32,514	23,586
Minority interests	8,659	8,717
	1,474,702	1,174,138
INCOME BEFORE EXTRAORDINARY ITEM	73,857	59,992
EXTRAORDINARY ITEM	–	684
NET INCOME	73,857	60,676
DIVIDEND REQUIREMENT ON PREFERRED STOCK	1,672	2,231
NET INCOME APPLICABLE TO COMMON AND COMMON EQUIVALENT SHARES	$ 72,185	$ 58,445
EARNINGS PER SHARE		
PER AVERAGE COMMON AND COMMON EQUIVALENT SHARE:		
Income before extraordinary item	$ 2.31	$ 1.88
Extraordinary item	–	.02
Net income	$ 2.31	$ 1.90
ASSUMING FULL DILUTION:		
Income before extraordinary item	$ 2.07	$ 1.65
Extraordinary item	–	.02
Net income	$ 2.07	$ 1.67

Consolidated Balance Sheets
December 31, 1973 and 1972 (in thousands)

	1973	1972*
CURRENT ASSETS:		
Cash	$ 68,878	$ 40,382
Accounts receivable, less allowance, 1973—$4,690; 1972—$4,546	212,753	215,384
Inventories	142,305	116,540
Prepaid expenses and other current assets	27,958	26,174
Total current assets	451,894	398,480
RESTRICTED CASH DEPOSITS (1973—$6,714; 1972—$8,972), NONCURRENT ACCOUNTS AND NOTES RECEIVABLE	39,484	49,514

Exhibit 1 (continued)

LAND HELD FOR SALE OR DEVELOPMENT	22,729	29,170
COOPERATIVES, JOINT VENTURES AND		
SUBSIDIARIES AT EQUITY	76,264	63,206
INVESTMENTS	11,829	25,688
PROPERTY, PLANT AND EQUIPMENT	1,435,346	1,313,722
Less accumulated depreciation and amortization	431,367	386,525
Net property, plant and equipment	1,003,979	927,197
DEFERRED CHARGES, less amortization	18,501	19,707
OPERATING RIGHTS AND OTHER INTANGIBLES, net	40,420	36,093
Total assets	$1,665,100	$1,549,055
LIABILITIES AND SHAREHOLDERS' EQUITY		
CURRENT LIABILITIES:		
Notes payable	$ 91,057	$ 87,912
Accounts payable and accrued liabilities	193,324	177,022
Income taxes	10,288	2,387
Long-term debt—current maturities	50,444	39,066
Total current liabilities	345,053	306,387
LONG-TERM DEBT	583,247	590,656
OTHER LIABILITIES, principally utility construction advances	98,462	87,613
DEFERRED INCOME TAXES	34,628	25,050
MINORITY INTEREST IN SUBSIDIARIES	109,599	97,410
SHAREHOLDERS' EQUITY		
Series preferred stock	28,053	30,868
Series preference stock	41,560	48,107
Common stock	34,676	32,650
Additional paid-in capital	117,486	101,055
Retained earnings	309,280	256,454
	531,055	469,134
Less shares in treasury, at cost	36,944	27,195
Total shareholders equity	494,111	441,939
Total liabilities and shareholders' equity	$1,665,100	$1,549,055

* Certain items have been reclassified to conform to current classification

Source: 1973 Annual Report

of its own industry. Management views cash dividends as a form of corporate discipline, and each subsidiary is expected to pay an annual dividend to the parent company.

GOTAAS-LARSEN SHIPPING CORPORATION

Gotaas-Larsen Shipping Corporation was the successor to a partnership formed in 1946 by the late Mr. Trygve Gotaas and Mr. Harry Irgens Larsen. Initially Gotaas-Larsen managed ships for other owners, but later purchased vessels of its own. Gotaas-Larsen's first purchases were oil

10-Year Financial Comparisons

Adjusted for poolings of interest. (In thousands, except per share data)

SALES AND REVENUES:	1973	1972	1971	1970	1969	1968	1967	1966	1965	1964
Major markets:										
Energy	$ 435,320	$ 356,315	$ 319,183	$ 271,126	$ 219,179	$ 209,841	$ 205,065	$ 187,374	$ 156,189	$ 90,870
Transportation/Distribution	733,967	584,865	521,063	473,734	438,530	407,701	369,260	372,183	313,560	196,234
Environmental	301,422	230,814	200,613	181,761	150,307	41,772	36,199	33,354	30,269	24,723
Total major markets	1,470,709	1,171,994	1,040,859	926,621	808,016	659,314	610,524	592,911	500,018	311,827
Other	77,850	62,136	60,950	59,783	96,949	98,012	75,564	59,843	41,328	20,185
Total sales and revenues	$1,548,559	$1,234,130	$1,101,809	$ 986,404	$ 904,965	$ 757,326	$ 686,088	$ 652,754	$541,346	$332,012
Income from operations (3)	$ 73,857	$ 59,992	$ 51,094	$ 36,641	$ 27,276	$ 27,115	$ 29,233	$ 27,086	$ 22,467	$ 18,571
Earnings per share— operations (1) (3)	$ 2.31	$ 1.88	$ 1.64	$ 1.18	$ .92	$ .97	$ 1.06	$ .97	$ .80	$ .68
Shareholders' equity per share	$ 14.38	$ 13.07	$ 11.93	$ 10.83	$ 10.28	$ 9.01	$ 7.68	$ 6.54	$ 5.61	$ 4.98
Average common and common equivalent shares (1) (2)	31,186	30,646	29,404	28,636	26,313	24,397	23,350	23,766	23,953	21,315
Dividends paid per common share	$ .75	$ .725	$ .70	$ .67	$ .65	$ .60	$ .56	$ .51	$ .46	$ .42
Total assets	$1,665,100	$1,549,055	$1,424,819	$1,337,146	$1,280,914	$1,018,880	$891,268	$794,566	$704,483	$531,610

(1) 1971 and prior years adjusted for subsequent stock split. See note 12 to the financial statements.

(2) 1966 and prior years adjusted for subsequent stock dividends.

(3) Before extraordinary credits of $684, or $.02 per share in 1972, $79, with no per share effect in 1970, $53, with no per share effect in 1965 and before gains on dispositions of properties and investments of $338, or $.01 per share in 1970, $10,891 or $.37 per share in 1969, $12,113 or $.44 per share in 1968, $7,554 or $.28 per share in 1967, $10,188 or $.36 per share in 1966, $2,842 or $.10 per share in 1965, $2,930 or $.11 per share in 1964. Net income after extraordinary credits and after gains on dispositions of properties and investments was $73,857 or $2.31 per share in 1973, $60,676 or $1.90 per share in 1972, $51,094 or $1.64 per share in 1971, $37,058 or $1.19 per share in 1970, $38,167 or $1.29 per share in 1969, $39,228 or $1.41 per share in 1968, $36,787 or $1.34 per share in 1967, $37,274 or $1.33 per share in 1966, $25,362 or $.90 per share in 1965, and $21,501 or $.79 per share in 1964

Exhibit 2   10 Years of Historical Financial Data for I U International

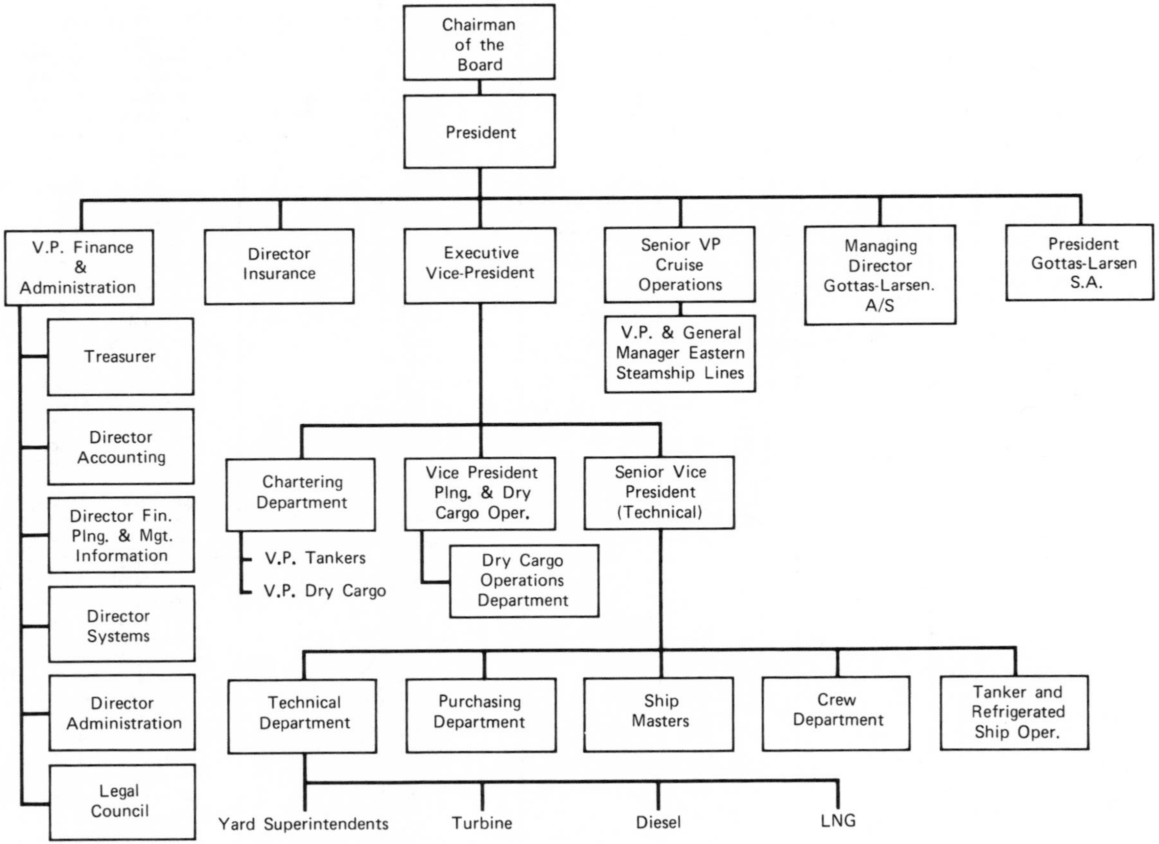

Exhibit 3 Gotaas-Larsen Shipping Corp. Organization Chart

Chairman of the Board

President

Executive Vice-President

Director Insurance

President Gottas-Larsen S.A.

Managing Director Gottas-Larsen A/S

Senior VP Cruise Operations

V.P. & General Manager Eastern Steamship Lines

Senior Vice President (Technical)

Vice President Plng. & Dry Cargo Oper.

Dry Cargo Operations Department

Chartering Department

V.P. Tankers

V.P. Dry Cargo

Technical Department

Purchasing Department

Ship Masters

Crew Department

Tanker and Refrigerated Ship Oper.

Yard Superintendents

Turbine

Diesel

LNG

V.P. Finance & Administration

Treasurer

Director Accounting

Director Fin. Plng. & Mgt. Information

Director Systems

Director Administration

Legal Council

Gotaas-Larsen Fleet March, 1974

Bar indicates duration of charter

TANKERS

Ship	dwt	Ownership	Charter status
Golar Betty	216,629 dwt	100% owned	Time charter expiring 1983
Golar Kanto	215,714 dwt	100% owned	Consecutive voyages expiring 1975
Golar Kansai	215,824 dwt	75% owned	Time charter expiring 1975
Golar Nichu	215,782 dwt	100% owned	Consecutive voyages 6 months to 1974 – Time charter 1974-79
Fernmount	215,529 dwt	40% owned	Consecutive voyages expiring 1975, consecutive voyages winter 1976
Jalta	156,188 dwt	25% owned	Time charter expiring 1976
Jalna	156,188 dwt	25% owned	Time charter expiring 1974
Golar Nikko	111,030 dwt	100% owned	Bareboat expiring 1981
Golar Liz	107,023 dwt	100% owned	Spot
Golar Ron	106,239 dwt	100% owned	Time charter expiring 1975
Golar Toko	86,792 dwt	100% owned	Bareboat expiring 1981
Golar Solveig	60,861 dwt	100% owned	Spot
Golar Siri	55,960 dwt	100% owned	Spot
Golar Martita	42,210 dwt	100% owned	Time charter expiring 1975
Golar Bali	15,540 dwt	65% owned	Time charter expiring 1981
Golar Bintan	15,540 dwt	65% owned	Time charter expiring 1981
Golar Buatan	15,540 dwt	65% owned	Time charter expiring 1981
Golar Surabaya	15,540 dwt	65% owned	Time charter expiring 1981
Golar Bawgan	15,540 dwt	65% owned	Time charter expiring 1981
Golar Sabang	15,540 dwt	65% owned	Time charter expiring 1981
Golar Sigli	15,540 dwt	65% owned	Time charter expiring 1981
Gauchito	1,473 dwt	100% owned	Spot
World Mitsubishi	234,728 dwt	Chartered In	Time charter to 1974 – Consecutive voyages winter 1974-75
Halcyon the Great	226,692 dwt	Chartered In	Time charter expiring outward 1990 – inward 1990
Humboldt	219,087 dwt	Chartered In	Time charter 1974-80 – inward 1980
Golar Robin	215,923 dwt	Chartered In	Consecutive voyages to 1974 – Time charter 1974-79 – inward 1998
Kollbryn	99,347 dwt	Chartered In	Time charter expiring outward 1974 – inward 1974
Sanko Bay	59,200 dwt	Chartered In	Contract of Affreightment expiring outward 1976 – inward 1976
J. T. Higgins	212,010 dwt	Operated As Agent	Bareboat charter expiring 1995
D. L. Bower	212,010 dwt	Operated As Agent	Bareboat charter expiring 1995
Texaco Darien	78,170 dwt	Operated As Agent	Bareboat charter expiring 1987
Chevron Frankfurt	78,872 dwt	Operated As Agent	Bareboat charter expiring 1987

REFRIGERATED SHIPS

Ship	dwt	Ownership	Charter status
Golar Frost	7,400 dwt	100% owned	Time charter expiring 1975
Golar Borg	7,400 dwt	40% owned	Time charter expiring 1975
Golar Freeze	7,130 dwt	100% owned	Time charter expiring 1975
Golar Nel	7,090 dwt	15% owned	Time charter expiring 1975
Golar Fruit	6,090 dwt	100% owned	Time charter expiring 1974
Golar Tryg	6,075 dwt	15% owned	Time charter expiring 1974
Golar Ragni	9,072 dwt	Operated As Agent	Time charter expiring 1977
Golar Girl	9,072 dwt	Operated As Agent	Time charter expiring 1978

Years shown across chart: 1974 1975 1976 1977 1978 (quarters 1 2 3 4)

52

BULK CARRIERS

Golar Sanko	86,795 dwt	100% owned
Gaucho Laguna	30,403 dwt	100% owned
Gaucho Cruz	30,403 dwt	100% owned
Santos Vega	27,021 dwt	100% owned
Golar Arrow	26,139 dwt	51% owned
Golar Bow	26,113 dwt	51% owned
Martin Fierro	15,780 dwt	100% owned
Don Segundo Sombra	15,230 dwt	100% owned
Japan Oak	53,640 dwt	Chartered In
Japan Pine	53,356 dwt	Chartered In
Long Hope	50,900 dwt	Chartered In
Helwig	36,000 dwt	Chartered In
Agia Erini II	31,904 dwt	Chartered In
Gaucho Taura	30,403 dwt	Chartered In
Gaucho Pampa	30,403 dwt	Chartered In

PRODUCT CARRIERS

Bruse Jarl	32,000 dwt	30% owned

DRILLING RIGS

Norskald (Nor-101)	Semi-submersible	39% owned

VESSELS ON ORDER

LNG	125,000 cu.m.	95% owned
LNG	125,000 cu.m.	95% owned
LNG	125,000 cu.m.	95% owned
LNG	125,000 cu.m.	100% owned
LNG	128,600 cu.m.	100% owned
LNG	128,600 cu.m.	100% owned
Tanker	410,000 dwt	100% owned
Tanker	410,000 dwt	100% owned
Tanker	410,000 dwt	100% owned
Product Carrier	32,000 dwt	100% owned
Product Carrier	32,000 dwt	100% owned
Product Carrier	32,000 dwt	100% owned
Drilling Rig	Semi-submersible	49% owned
Drilling Rig	Semi-submersible	65% owned
Drilling Rig	Semi-submersible	65% owned

Year columns: 1974 | 1975 | 1976 | 1977 | 1978 (quarters 1 2 3 4)

Right-hand labels:

- Bareboat expiring 1981
- Contract of affreightment expiring 1976
- Contract of affreightment expiring 1975
- Contract of affreightment expiring 1975
- Time charter expiring 1987
- Time charter expiring 1988
- Contract of affreightment expiring 1975
- Contract of affreightment expiring 1975
- Time charter expiring outward 1978 — inward 1978
- Time charter expiring outward 1977 — inward 1977
- Time charter expiring outward 1978 — inward 1978
- Time charter expiring outward 1974 — inward 1974
- Contract of affreightment expiring outward 1975 — inward 1979
- Contract of affreightment expiring outward 1975 — inward 1981
- Contract of affreightment expiring outward 1975 — inward 1981
- Time charter expiring 1975
- Drilling contract expiring 1976
- Delivery 1975 — Time charter expiring 1996
- Delivery 1976 — Time charter expiring 1996
- Delivery 1977 — Time charter expiring 1997
- Delivery 1977
- Delivery 1977
- Delivery 1977
- Delivery 1976
- Delivery 1977
- Delivery 1978
- Delivery 1974
- Delivery 1975
- Delivery 1976
- Delivery 1974 — Drilling contract expiring 1976
- Delivery 1976
- Delivery 1976

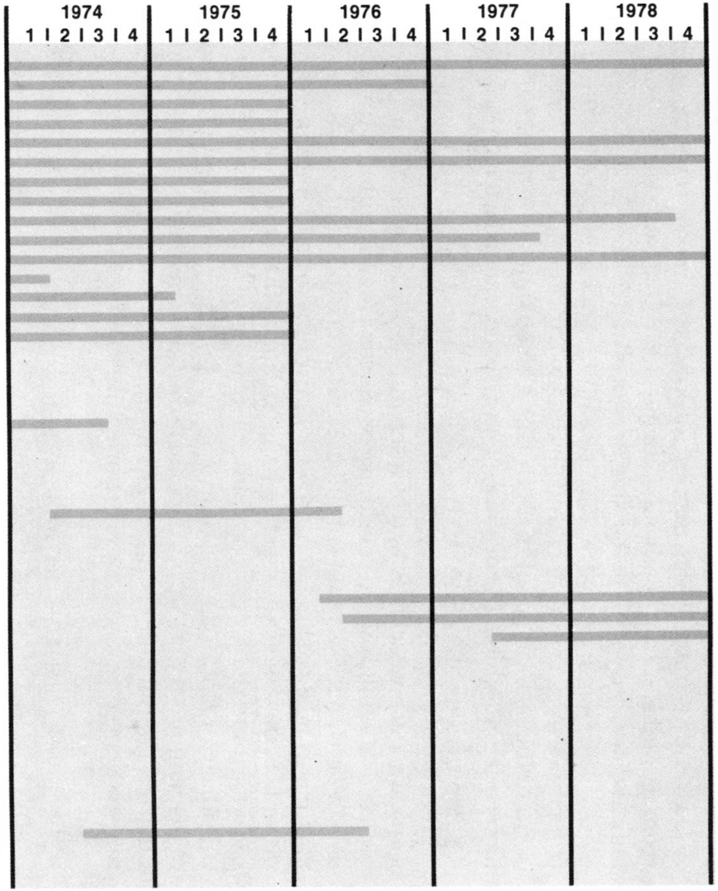

tankers, which were acquired in the early 1950s when it was foreseen that there would be a need for increased U.S. shipping due to the Korean War. Around 1961 the company entered its second major market area, bulk carriers. In August 1963, the company was acquired by IU for $13.2 million in common stock. Gotaas-Larsen's increasing need for capital was a major factor in its becoming part of IU. At the time of the acquisition, Gotaas-Larsen's fleet consisted of 12 ships totalling 350,000 dwts. Over the next 10 years the company grew rapidly. As of 1973, the fleet consisted of 54 cargo ships totalling 4.1 million dwts and 6 passenger cruise ships.

Currently, about 70–80 percent of Gotaas-Larsen's revenues come from its tankers, with the balance being derived about equally from its bulk and cruise operations. Gotaas-Larsen owns (fully or partially) a large part of the fleet it operates. The remaining part is either chartered in from other owners or is operated by Gotaas-Larsen as agents. The breakdown of the major types of trade Gotaas-Larsen ships[1] are involved in can be seen from Exhibit 4 which also shows the current chartering arrangement for Gotaas-Larsen's fleet.

The legal corporate structure of the company is rather complicated. Typically, each vessel is owned by a separate company which is directly or indirectly a wholly owned subsidiary of Gotaas-Larsen Shipping Corporation. For the most part, subsidiaries are incorporated in Liberia or Panama to take advantage of favorable fiscal, tax, and operating conditions. U.S. income taxes must be paid on money that is remitted by these subsidiaries to the parent company. Gotaas-Larsen Inc., a wholly owned subsidiary of Gotaas-Larsen Shipping Corporation, provides centralized management services including chartering arrangements for all the subsidiaries. For purposes of planning and operations, the organization chart may be viewed as one entity, as shown in Exhibit 3.

PEOPLE WHO MANAGE GOTAAS-LARSEN

The style of strategic management at Gotaas-Larsen is largely set by the Chairman, Harry Irgens Larsen, the President, Louis Krall and the Executive Vice President, Finn Grape, while the day-to-day operations of the company are managed by the latter two. All three are provided staff assistance and financial advice by Mr. Goldenberg.

Mr. Larsen (age 66) began his career with a ship brokerage in Norway and later worked for the second World Wartime Norwegian Government Shipping Agency in Montreal and New York. Mr. Larsen cofounded Gotaas-Larsen, Inc. in 1946 with Trygve Gotaas and served as a partner

---

[1] Appendix 1 gives a glossary of common shipping terminology.

until 1956, when he became President and Chief Executive Officer of the Gotaas-Larsen Shipping Companies. In 1963, when Gotaas-Larsen was merged into IU, he became a director and Vice President of IU. Mr. Larsen also continued to be President of Gotaas-Larsen until 1971 when he became Vice-Chairman of IU. Since 1972, he has also been the Board Chairman and CEO of Gotaas-Larsen. Mr. Larsen has been an international figure in the shipping industry for many years.

Mr. Krall (age 54) graduated from New York University with a degree in Business Administration. He joined Gotaas-Larsen in 1948 and became its Treasurer in 1952. He became a Vice President in 1965, the Executive Vice President in 1970, and has been President since 1972. One of Mr. Krall's beliefs is that the way to run a company effectively is to limit the number of people managing it. He also believes that as the company grows, formal planning and control systems have to be instituted to help management make decisions since the management has to become more impersonal. He believes that computers have created profound opportunities for the shipping industry. "They have made possible the building of very large ships, but they have also made possible the planning and control of the companies that own and manage these ships."

Mr. Grape (age 41) joined Gotaas-Larsen as assistant to the President in 1970 after working as a tanker broker with Fearnley and Eger Chartering Co., Ltd., in Norway. In 1972 he became Executive Vice President and assistant to the Chairman.

Mr. Goldenberg (age 42) is a graduate of the Harvard Business School. Before coming to Gotaas-Larsen, he worked in the planning group of IU International. During this time he was intimately involved with the IU planning system. He first came to Gotaas-Larsen as a internal consultant to help upgrade the planning system and make it compatible with that of IU. In 1972 he joined the Gotaas-Larsen management as the Vice President for Finance Administration.

STRATEGIC SEARCH: A KEY COMPONENT OF STRATEGY FORMULATION

Although Gotaas-Larsen makes extensive use of its formal planning system, some key planning activities take place outside the formal system. One such activity is the ongoing search for new business opportunities. This process of environmental scanning is a chief responsibility of Messrs. Larsen, Krall and Grape, all of whom maintain a wide range of contacts throughout the shipping world.

For example, Gotaas-Larsen's acquisition of LNG tankers, VLCC's, semisubmersible drilling rigs, etc, originated from the search activity of the top level management of the company. After years of on-and-off analysis and consideration, when the top managers felt that the time was ripe in terms of the expected development of these markets, the decision was made to proceed with a more formal and thorough evaluation of the acquisition of these new types of ships. At this point, their concepts for developing these new lines of trade began to take operational form through the formal planning process. Thus, many formal planning activities originate from ideas generated by top management through work outside the formal process.

For existing lines of trade, opportunities are often identified in the operating, technical and chartering departments by line managers, who keep close tabs on conditions in the markets where Gotaas-Larsen is already operating. This environmental scanning is fairly easy because the shipping industry is very open, with much information available in shipping journals and through trade associations. Also, the managers maintain close contacts with ship brokers and shippers to keep track of demand for different kinds of ships. To monitor new technology or types of ships, the managers communicate with shipyards, which also contact Gotaas-Larsen occasionally to offer ships for which the orders have been cancelled by another company.

GOTAAS-LARSEN'S STRATEGIC POSTURE AND PHILOSOPHY

Gotaas-Larsen's current strategic philosophy is governed by what top management perceive as its strengths and weaknesses. Since Gotaas-Larsen is a publicly held company, it has audited financial statements. It is felt that this gives Gotaas-Larsen a slight advantage over privately held firms in getting funds from banks and other sources. Also, its management team has a very good operating record which gives Gotaas-Larsen a competitive advantage in arranging new charters. Countering these strong points, are several constraints under which the company operates. Since it is a U.S.-based company, Gotaas-Larsen, when compared to its foreign competitors, is limited in its ability to siphon money through its series of foreign subsidiaries. One reason for this limitation is that U.S. taxes have to be paid when GL repatriates money from its foreign subsidiaries. Since Gotaas-Larsen is relatively thinly manned in terms of members in its management team, it is somewhat limited in its ability to go into businesses which require large amounts of manpower.

Gotaas-Larsen's top management philosophy can be summarized as follows:

Financial.   It hopes to maintain a 60–70% debt to total capitalization ratio. Also, as a constraint set by the parent company, it does not consider any new investments or business areas that will not yield at least a 15% DCF return on equity before tax or a 20% average return on equity after taxes. It must also plan to satisfy IU International's needs for income and dividends.

Trade. Gotaas-Larsen views shipping and other ocean activities and support services as its area of expertise and main line of business. However, due to its lean management organization, it will not enter trades such as containerized shipping or ocean liners, which require major, people-intensive management efforts. Consistent with this Gotaas-Larsen has delegated away the management of its cruise business. Finally, due to risk considerations Gotaas-Larsen shies away from any business or investment which is limited to one country.

Chartering Policies. IU wants to maintain a steady growth path for its reported earnings. Since Gotaas-Larsen contributes nearly 50% of I.U.'s income, it is essential that Gotaas-Larsen also have a stable earnings pattern. To achieve this goal, Gotaas-Larsen follows a policy of sailing a large part of its fleet on medium to long term (2–10 years) charters. Exhibit 4 shows the future commitments of the Gotaas-Larsen fleet of ships. This policy avoids the high risk, volatile spot market. In recent years, however, following a long-term chartering policy has also proved risky (in the absence of cost escalation clauses) due to the unexpectedly high rate of cost inflation in the industry.

Investment. Gotaas-Larsen maintains a fleet of fairly new ships and prides itself on being able to buy "new technology" ships early enough to make good returns. At the same time, however, every ship in the fleet is considered to be for sale at the right price. Of course, each investment must promise at least a 15% DCF return before tax on equity.

QUESTIONS FOR DISCUSSION

Design a planning and control system for Gotaas-Larsen. In doing this it may be helpful to read the overview of management in the shipping industry in Appendix 2. Some of the questions which should be answered in your design include:

What should be the formal cycle of activities?

Who are the people who should be involved and what should they do?

What differences, if any, does it make for the planning system's design that Gotaas-Larsen is a part of the larger IU?

What documents should be produced and who should get them?

What should be the role of models/computers in the process?

APPENDIX 1

Shipping Terminology

Five types of charters are used commonly in shipping:

Time Charter. This is the most common charter arrangement. The vessel is chartered for a specified period of time at a specified rate per deadweight ton of capacity per calendar month. Operating costs for crew, stores, maintenance, insurance, etc. are commonly paid by the owner, while voyage costs such as fuel, port and cargo charges, etc. are paid by the charterer.

Bareboat Charter. This is similar to a time charter, except that the shipper charters the boat "bare," provides his own crew, and pays all operating expenses. This is generally regarded as being analogous to leasing as a financing arrangement.

Consecutive Voyage Charter. Under this arrangement, the ship is chartered for a specified number of consecutive voyages among specified ports over a specified time period. The charterer pays an agreed freight rate per ton of cargo lifted on each voyage. All expenses, including voyage costs, are paid by the owner.

Single Voyage Charter. This is commonly known as a "spot market" charter. The vessel is chartered to lift a cargo from one or more leading ports to one or more discharging ports at a specified freight rate. Single voyage charters are identical to consecutive voyage charters in all respects except their one-time nature.

Contracts of Affreightment. This type of contract provides for the shipment of a specified quantity and type of cargo from and to specified ports over a specified period of time at a certain freight payment per ton. It usually required the owner to use vessels of certain minimum/maximum sizes. As in the case of single voyage charters, the owner pays all transportation costs.

APPENDIX 2

Overview of Management in Shipping[1]

Shipping companies are characterized by a relatively centralized management structure. The management system of most shipping companies is called upon to make three types of decisions. The first type are those

[1] A large part of this appendix is based upon "Portfolio Planning in Bulk Shipping Companies," by P. Lorange and V. Norman in *Shipping Management,* P. Lorange and V. Norman, ed., Institute for Shipping Research, Bergen, 1973.

that chart the business directions of the company and may be termed as "portfolio planning decisions." The second are the actual ship investment decisions and the third are the ship operating decisions. The following are some key aspects of these 3 types of decisions:

Portfolio Planning. The portfolio planning problem has 3 main dimensions. The first is the choice of financial structure of the firm (i.e., the debt/equity ratio). The debt could be of different types, from mortgages on one vessel at one end of the spectrum through a corporate debt issue at the other end. The second important dimension is the allocation of capital to the different types of trades (e.g. tankers, bulk, cruise, etc.). Each trade has different characteristics and different returns to the capital invested. The third important variable is the chartering policy to be followed within each trade chosen (e.g. spot charter, short-term charters, long-term charters, etc.).

Investment Decisions. The investment decisions deal with the buying and selling of tonnage within the portfolio framework. Since the price of new tonnage is very sensitive to conditions in the industry, the timing of placing orders for new tonnage is a crucial determinant of the rate of return on each new ship bought. For new types of ships, ideas take a number of years in moving from the "drawing boards" to common usage. In buying ships involving new technology, timing is especially critical. Also there is a well-developed market for secondhand ships so that the average age of the company's fleet is a controllable variable.

Operating Decisions. These decisions are concerned with the day-to-day activities of running the fleet and are executed within the framework provided by the portfolio planning and the investment decisions. Operating decisions include things like scheduling ships, finding new charters, etc. Normally the ship's captain has control over voyage costs (e.g. the fuel consumed depends on the speed), while the chief engineer is responsible for the maintenance of the equipment. However, many of the operating decisions such as setting up drydocking schedules, finding new cargos, and hiring crews are made centrally.

Of course, these three levels of decision can be broken down much more finely. The planning and control process is designed to ensure that however they are broken down, they are made in a timely and appropriate fashion. The portfolio decisions limit the range within which the more specific goals and objectives of the company can lie. The investment decisions provide the assets which are required to achieve these goals and objectives. The operating decisions are the implementation phase of the strategy.

Case 2

Norton Company–A*

The need for planning occurred only recently. Five years ago we were a one-product company. Abrasives constituted 90 percent of our sales, and we instinctively understood our product's future. We'd been in the business for a lifetime. But now the case is quite different. Abrasives are only about 64 percent of our business.

We started to diversify several years ago. The abrasive industry was not growing very rapidly, and we decided that we weren't properly utilizing our resources for growth. Now we are in new businesses and have many product lines. There is a new demand for capital. We have gone from being a cash-rich to a borrowing company. Now, no man can grasp all the details. Planning helps us understand the alternatives in resource allocation for optimum results. We started our planning none too soon.

These comments were made in the spring of 1967 by Mr. John Jeppson, who was then the Executive Vice President of the Norton Company, Worcester, Massachusetts. He was discussing the development of formal corporate planning at Norton, from its initiation in 1966.

Background of Norton

Starting from the production of grinding wheels (bonded abrasives) in 1885 as a pottery shop sideline, Norton had become the world's largest abrasive manufacturer. In 1966, the company employed over 19,000 persons and operated plants at 45 locations in 17 countries. The financial growth of the Norton Company over the years 1958–1966 is summarized in Exhibit 1.

In the abrasives industry, Norton Company and Carborundum Company accounted for about half of the bonded abrasive market; Norton Company and Minnesota Mining and Manufacturing Company accounted for about half of the coated abrasive market. An estimated 150 smaller companies shared the remainder of both markets.

Norton had expanded its product lines over the years (including 1931

*This case was prepared under the supervision of Associate Professor Francis J. Aguilar based on student reports written by Messrs. Stephen W. Chesebrough, Alfred C. Dix, Carson M. Duncan, Wilfried E. Kaffenberger, and John L. Withers.

Exhibit 1 NORTON COMPANY CONSOLIDATED NINE-YEAR FINANCIAL REVIEW

Operations for the Year	1966	1965	1964	1963	1962	1961	1960	1959	1958
	(thousands of dollars)								
Net Sales	$310,473	$272,668	$250,632	$215,966	$213,409	$189,522	$186,248	$177,919	$151,420
Income Before Income Taxes	37,241	36,269	35,794	28,760	30,431	24,152	24,965	23,541	17,101
Net Income	18,811	18,406	18,213	14,069	14,812	11,613	12,324	11,127	8,507
% of Sales	6.1%	6.8%	7.3%	6.5%	6.9%	6.1%	6.6%	6.3%	5.6%
% Return on Stockholders' Equity	9.5%	10.0%	10.4%	8.4%	8.9%	7.3%	8.1%	7.6%	6.1%
Additions to Property, Plant and Equipment	$ 16,835	$ 17,618	$ 13,846	$ 10,727	$ 11,174	$ 9,568	$ 8,288	$ 7,487	$ 11,134
Depreciation Charges	11,740	10,408	9,532	8,466	8,235	7,625	7,464	7,175	6,487
Long-Term Debt Retired	(11,646)	622	770	483	488	323	760	779	705
At Year End									
Net Property, Plant and Equipment	$103,285	$92,391	$85,829	$78,337	$77,012	$74,310	$72,829	$72,315	$72,116
Long-Term Debt	17,996	6,350	6,972	7,742	8,225	8,713	9,036	9,796	10,575
Stockholders' Equity	197,168	184,518	175,424	166,646	166,348	158,294	152,570	146,105	140,605
Number of Employees	19,210	17,550	16,600	15,160	15,140	14,450	13,990	13,820	12,990
Shares of Common Stock Outstanding	5,669,535	5,579,012	5,611,278	5,649,219	5,652,389	5,655,902	5,651,433	5,654,958	5,665,982
Per Share Statistics									
Net Income	$3.32	$3.30	$3.25	$2.49	$2.62	$2.05	$ 2.18	$ 1.97	$1.50
Dividends Paid	1.50	1.425	1.40	1.35	1.25	1.15	1.10	1.00	1.00
Stockholders' Equity	34.78	33.07	31.26	29.50	29.43	27.99	27.00	25.84	24.82

The 1966 statistics include the operations for U.S. Stoneware, Inc. from August 1, 1966 on and for Chamberlain Engineering Corporation from January 1, 1966 on.
This Financial Review has been restated for the years 1958 through 1962 to include National Research Corporation.

Source: Norton Company 1966 Annual Report

and 1932 mergers with Behr-Manning Company and Pike Company) to include crude abrasives, abrasive grain, machine tools, refractories materials, bonded abrasives,coated abrasives, sharpening stones, pressure-sensitive tapes, and grinding fluids. Recent acquisitions added National Research Corporation (1963: high vacuum equipment, refractory metals, superconductors, and other technological products), Clipper Manufacturing Company and its related companies (1964: specialized construction equipment), and U. S. Stoneware Company (1966: ceramic, metal, and plastic tower packings and internals for chemical processors, plus plastic tubing and other vinyl products).

Norton divisions traditionally enjoyed considerable autonomy. The recent acquisitions had somewhat reduced Norton's dependence on the mature and cyclical abrasive industry, but abrasive products still accounted for 64 percent of the company's sales in 1966.

PLANNING AT THE CORPORATE LEVEL

In 1966 corporate headquarters attempted to inaugurate a corporatewide, recurring planning process for looking beyond one year. On several occasions before, the corporation and some divisions had engaged in limited activities involving planning for more than one year.

In 1955, management showed concern about the future direction of the company by calling for a study to compare Norton's growth rate and profit performance with those of other major companies. Another look at the corporation as a whole was made in 1961, when the assistant to the treasurer tried to assess the future of Norton. His report was presented to the board of directors. (There was little, if any, communication to divisional management on the results of this study.) About the same time another corporate executive was studying acquisition possibilities at the corporate level.

The first corporatewide formal planning effort was one coordinated by Mr. Allan A. Kassay beginning in mid-1962. Mr. Kassay had been head of the Refractory Division's Commercial Development Department, and as such had been deeply involved in the division's efforts beginning early in 1962 to "plan ahead." Mr. Kassay's effort at the corporate level actually began as a search for companies to acquire, since Norton's top management saw the key question to be, "How should we diversify?" Within six months, Mr. Kassay was arguing that the crucial questions to be asked really were: "What are our objectives?" and "What is our potential?"

One result of the dialogue that followed was a request by Mr. Ralph F. Gow, President of Norton, for the divisions to look ten years ahead and to predict sales, profit, cash flow and return on investment. Mr. Kassay composed the actual questions asked of the divisions and coordinated collection of the data. The resulting consolidated growth projection was not ideal in the eyes of top management, but no imminent crisis was seen.

Projections of the economic environment, and lists of strengths and weaknesses pointed out areas needing management's attention. Although the terms "long-range planning" and "planning gap" were not then in use at Norton, and although the 1962–1963 effort had not been intended to start a recurring process, Mr. Kassay claimed as one benefit of that particular effort the realization by Norton's management that much of its time should be spent looking ahead.

Appointment of Mr. Harris

The ten-year look indicated that many of Norton's markets were mature, that its profits were indeed sensitive to cyclical swings, and that a large cash flow could be expected in the coming years. Before the end of 1963, Mr. Richard Harris was appointed Director of Corporate Development, reporting to Mr. Gow. Mr. Harris was to be mainly concerned with growth through acquisition and merger.

Late in 1965, Mr. Harris began reporting to Mr. Jeppson. The two easily agreed that regular formal planning should become part of management's way of life at Norton. They were encouraged to work towards this end when Mr. Milton P. Higgins, Chairman of the Board, suggested that Norton should do some five-year sales forecasting. By the turn of the year, the question receiving more and more attention from corporate executives was, "What should we do to start planning?"

The Corporate Planning Committee

A Corporate Planning Committee was set up in February 1966 by Mr. Jeppson to guide the move toward a regular formal planning process. The planning committee comprised Mr. Robert A. Stauffer, Vice President for Research; Mr. John F. Dingle, Controller; Mr. J. E. Cotter, Corporate Economist; Mr. Jeppson; and Mr. Harris. The latter was named chief coordinator of the committee and was responsible for getting planning activities started. An abridged organization chart of Norton's top management in early 1967, presented in Exhibit 2, indicates the organizational position for each of the planning committee members.

The planning committee met almost weekly for the next few months, and attacked two major questions:

1. By what process should formalized planning be ingrained into life at Norton?
2. What are appropriate corporate goals for Norton Company?

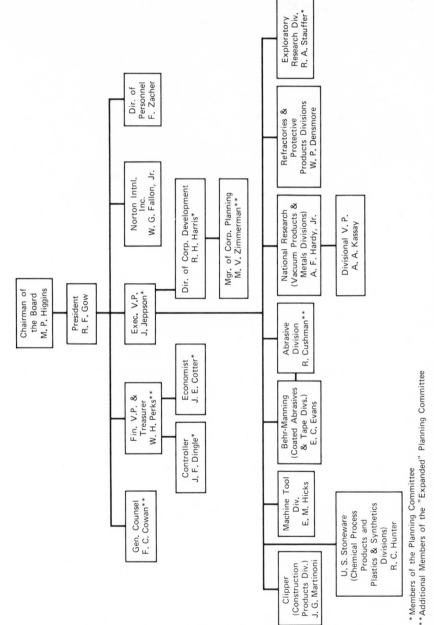

Chairman of the Board
M. P. Higgins

President
R. F. Gow

Exec. V.P.
J. Jeppson*

Gen. Counsel
F. C. Cowan**

Fin. V.P. &
Treasurer
W. H. Perks**

Controller
J. F. Dingle*

Economist
J. E. Cotter*

Dir. of
Personnel
F. Zacher

Norton Intnl.
Inc.
W. G. Fallon, Jr.

Dir. of Corp. Development
R. H. Harris*

Mgr. of Corp. Planning
M. V. Zimmerman**

Machine Tool
Div.
E. M. Hicks

Behr-Manning
(Coated Abrasives
& Tape Divs.)
E. C. Evans

Abrasive
Division
R. Cushman**

National Research
(Vacuum Products &
Metals Divisions)
A. F. Hardy, Jr.

Divisional V. P.
A. A. Kassay

Refractories &
Protective
Products Divisions
W. P. Densmore

Exploratory
Research Div.
R. A. Stauffer*

Clipper
(Construction
Products Div.)
J. G. Martinoni

U. S. Stoneware
(Chemical Process
Products and
Plastics & Synthetics
Divisions)
R. C. Hunter

*Members of the Planning Committee
**Additional Members of the "Expanded" Planning Committee

Exhibit 2 Norton Company Corporate Organization, February 1967 (abridged to highlight people in the case)

A year later, in early 1967, no answer had yet been given to the second question, but decisions were made concerning the first.

A March 21, 1966, memorandum from Mr. Jeppson to division general managers cited a need for regular formal planning and outlined a plan and schedule for starting such an effort. The basic idea was to survey divisional planning history and attitudes and, after discussions, to issue guidelines for the preparation of divisional "provisional plans."

Mr. Zimmerman's Research Report

In late April, a coincidence occurred. Mr. Harris, pressed for time, saw a need for help in starting the planning process. Mr. Marlin Zimmerman, then a second-year student at Harvard Business School, arrived at Norton seeking to do his research report in the area of planning. An arrangement was made whereby Mr. Zimmerman received the cooperation he needed for his research in exchange for helping Mr. Harris evaluate the available alternatives for implementing planning at Norton. Between April 22 and May 12, Mr. Zimmerman surveyed the divisional responses to Mr. Jeppson's March 21 memorandum, investigated planning literature, and wrote a report for the Norton management.

Highlights of the Zimmerman report were a network diagram of a planning process and a recommendation for introducing the process at Norton. The network diagram, with the slight revisions subsequently made, is reproduced as Exhibit 3. The recommendation advised Norton to allow the planning process to evolve from a limited first-year effort, rather than to try to impose at the on-set a complete, ready-made system. Mr. Zimmerman received his M.B.A. degree in June 1966 and took employment in Ohio.

After some discussion of the report, it was decided that the process described in the network diagram appeared useful for Norton, and that in 1966 the divisions should complete the activities contained in the first half of the diagram, up to and including the ". . . TENTATIVE FINANCIAL FORECAST."

Visits by Corporate Groups

The concept of formal planning activities was introduced to the organization through a series of visits to the divisions by corporate groups beginning June 6. The composition of the groups varied somewhat, but always included Mr. Jeppson and Mr. Harris. In these introductory meetings, Mr. Jeppson explained the importance of the planning effort; and Mr. Harris explained the network diagram. One divisional vice president remarked, "It was a good diagram. Dick Harris has found the MAYA (most advanced, yet acceptable) solution. It's a tricky thing to do."

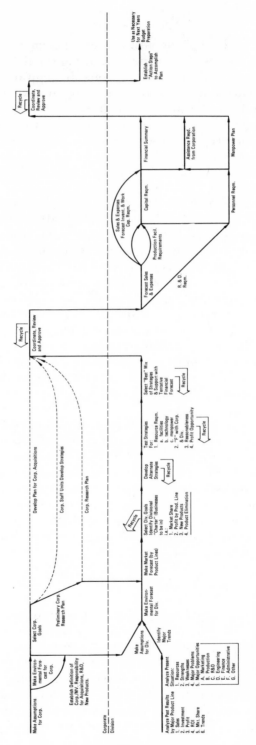

Exhibit 3 Norton Company (A)

Divisions were asked to produce a five-year plan by October 1. It was left to the divisions to decide exactly who would do what in the process and in what format the final plans would be presented.

During interviews in early 1967, several of Norton's executives pointed out the crucial significance of Mr. Jeppson's involvement in designing and implementing the planning process. The fact that he personally endorsed the process during the visit made clear to these executives the intention of top corporate management to make regular formal planning an important part of managing at Norton.

In a memorandum dated July 20, 1966, Mr. Jeppson notified corporate staff groups that they, too, were expected to submit five-year plans by October 1. Attached to this memorandum was a copy of the network diagram and an explanation of the planning effort.

By June 24, Mr. Cotter had issued his annual domestic five-year economic forecast. On July 25 he issued a set of "corporate assumptions" which had been agreed upon by the planning committee. Corporate goals, although continually debated within the planning committee, had not been reduced to writing for the benefit of the divisions. To aid thinking about financial goals, it was decided to undertake a comprehensive financial comparison with other U. S. corporations. The nature of this comparison was defined by Mr. Dingle, Corporate Controller, in a memorandum of June 2, shown in Exhibit 4. As for the up-coming planning effort, divisional executives, by one means or another, had identified criteria which they thought important to corporate management. Chief among these were return on investment and growth rate.

The criteria selected and the general approach to formal planning at the divisional level was undoubtedly influenced by earlier experiences with making up budgets. Budgeting on an annual basis had already been a well established tradition at Norton when formal planning began. The mechanics for compiling the budget (called the financial plan) were the responsibility of the controllership organization. In 1966 a position with the title "Manager of Financial Planning and Control" was created in the controller's department to be responsible for the formulation of capital budgeting procedures. One outcome of this development was a request for a five-year capital requirements forecast from each division. It was anticipated that this information would be prepared in the future as part of the quantitative phase of the planning cycle.

As August ended, Mr. Harris sensed that an exchange of ideas on the planning effort up to that point could benefit divisional planners. Hence, on September 8 representatives from all divisions met to hear how the others were going about planning.

On September 19, Mr. Zimmerman was hired by Norton and appointed Manager of Corporate Planning under Mr. Harris.

Exhibit 4 NORTON COMPANY –A   A Memorandum from
the Corporate Controller on Setting Corporate Goals
or Long-Range Planning

June 2, 1966

MEMORANDUM - CONTROLLER

This is a skeleton outline for the development of corporate goals. Please comment.

Qualitative Areas
1.   Degree of technological, product, distribution, and
     market diversification. Service industries vs. mfg.
2.   Penetration of international markets.
3.   Government business. How much and what kind?
4.   Acquisitions vs. development balance.
5.   Quantity of new stock which management and/or stock-
     holders will approve.
6.   Management & stockholder attitudes/desires.
     (a) Size, growth, EPA, ROI, dividends.
     (b) Relocation of plants and other operations.
     (c) Financing - Leverage, classes of equity, etc.

Quantitative Areas
     Problems:
          Determine objective P/E ratio.
          Full use of internally generated funds.
          Dividend policy.
          Position in U.S. industrial "pot."
          Optimum use of leverage.
          Optimum ROI.
     Determine objectives in following areas in order to
achieve best balance of above and qualitative goals.
          Sales growth
          Profit $ growth
          EPS growth
          ROI
          Dividend policy

Exhibit 4 (continued)

<u>Specific Studies</u>
These would be carried out·in order to provide information for decisions on quantitative and qualitative goals.
1. Internal
   (a) P/V relationship and B/E point for each division and/or major product group, and over-all.
   (b) ROI factors:
       Sales/(Assets - Current Liabilities)
       Op. Profit/Sales
2. External
   (a) Corporate profits vs. GNP. - Trends and correlation.
   (b) Durable goods profit vs. FRB. - Trends and correlation.
   (c) Norton vs. corporate and durable goods profits.
   (d) Study of 1st 250 "Fortune" companies
       Sales: Growth and trend vs. GNP and durables.
       Profits: Growth and trend vs. corporate and durables.
   (e) Study selected public companies similar to Norton
       1) Those with P/E above 15:1
       2) Sales, profit, and EPA growth
       3) ROI analysis
       4) Dividend policy
       5) Use of leverage
       6) P/V characteristics
   (f) Study of principal competitor(s)

<u>Decision Steps</u>
1. Based on quantitative studies, project growth rates for:
   GNP
   Sales and Earnings:
     All corporate
     Durables
     "1st 250" Fortune companies
     Selected public companies
     Principal competitor(s)
2. Based on policy that Norton must be = or + some of the above, select growth criteria.

Exhibit 4 (continued)

3. Based on study of selected public companies (2(e) under
    specific studies), determine objective for ROI, dividend
    policy, leverage, growth in sales, profit and EPS.
4. Test 2 + 3 vs. qualitative goals and preliminary con-
    solidated plan (sum of divisions) for fit.
5. Reappraisal of goals in light of 2, 3, & 4.

(initialed)

J. F. Dingle
280
JJ
JEC
RHH
RAS

Planning Review Meetings

Meetings to review divisional plans were held in November and December. As was expected, the format of the divisional plans and presentations varied widely. Attendance at the planning reviews varied also. The planning committee always attended, as did Mr. Zimmerman and the head of the division being reviewed. In addition, members of the Executive Committee: Messrs. Higgins, Gow, Perks, Cowan, and Cushman attended on occasion. The three executives named last became regular attendees and, with the original planning committee and Mr. Zimmerman, made up what came to be called, informally, the Expanded Planning Committee. Divisions were free to bring whomever they wished to their planning review. Representatives of divisions other than the one being reviewed on a given day were not invited to attend.

At the planning review, questions were asked concerning the divisional plans. One member of the Expanded Planning Committee noted that the quality and sophistication of the questioning rose noticeably between the first planning review meeting and the last.

Planning Response Meetings

A second series of meetings was started December 28, 1966. In these meetings, the Expanded Planning Committee commented on the divisional presentation to the division general managers. The divisions had been expecting some reaction by corporate management ever since the planning reviews, and these planning responses were designed to meet this expectation. Typical of these meetings was that of the Abrasive Division, whose General Manager, Mr. Cushman, was also a member of the Expanded Planning Committee. The Abrasive Division discussion lasted three hours, with Mr. Cushman and the rest of the committee openly evaluating the Abrasive Division's plans and its planning review.

Mr. Jeppson sent a memorandum to the general manager of each division after its planning response meeting. Each memorandum summarized the major points agreed upon in the meeting, thanked the participants for their effort in 1966, and expressed the desire for continued progress in making planning a way of life for the Norton manager.

PLANNING AT THE DIVISIONAL LEVEL

Some planning had been done by the divisions for themselves prior to the 1966 corporate effort. Mr. Cotter, the corporate economist, stated that Behr-Manning had been doing five-year forecasting and some planning since the early 1950s.

Another example could be found in the Abrasive Division, which under the leadership of Mr. Jeppson had begun annual five-year forecasting of sales by aggregate product groups in 1957. Two committees, one for forecasting grain sales, the other for forecasting wheel sales, had thus been in existence for several years previous to 1966. These committees turned out to be a useful starting point for the more thorough 1966 effort.

In 1961, the Refractories Division (later the Refractories and Protective Products Division) had organized a combined planning and reevaluation effort headed by Mr. Kassay. By 1964, the re-evaluation of market needs and divisional resources was complete. It led to an extensive redeployment of resources and considerable reorganization.

In March 1966, Mr. Jeppson sent out a memorandum to the divisions asking them to list their present planning practices. The responses, mostly received by April 4, included descriptions of the planning of those divisions mentioned above, as well as the others. National Research, Clipper, and the Machine Tool Divisions all stated in their letters that they had no formal, long-range planning activities at that time.

The 1966 Divisional Effort: National Research Corporation

On July 1, 1966, Mr. Kassay was appointed an N. R. C. vice president in charge of three of N. R. C.'s five internal divisions.[1] Because of Mr. Kassay's background, Mr. Hardy, N. R. C.'s president, had designated him as divisional planning coordinator.

N. R. C.'s "Management Committee," consisting of Messrs. Hardy and Kassay and the divisional and staff managers that reported to them, became a planning group. The purpose of this committee was seen as twofold:

1. To discuss and coordinate the various divisional plans as they were put together.
2. To thrash out the charters for the N. R. C. divisions.

However, as Mr. Kassay explained, the main burden of the planning effort had deliberately been placed on the divisional managers. "The responsibility was made clear."

Mr. Kassay indicated some dissatisfaction with the impact of the 1966 effort at N. R. C. Each divisional manager had tended to restrict the involvement to the departmental managers reporting directly to him. "This wasn't far enough," said Mr. Kassay. "More managers further down the line should have been involved. However, we were under the pressure

---

[1] N. R. C., a division of Norton, also had its own divisions.

of time and a new concept, so perhaps our results were the best obtainable under these conditions." He indicated an intention to make sure that the impact would go further in 1967 to get the benefits of wider participation. He also noted that the divisional managers had not properly appreciated the scope of a continuing planning effort.

Mr. Kassay described the 1966 planning as a "housecleaning effort" for N. R. C. He acknowledged that a great many previously recognized problems had been, this time, formally recognized and recorded. It was expected that in ensuing years the N. R. C. plans would deal less with cleaning up old problems and more with evaluating the environment and planning future strategies.

Drawing some notebooks out of his desk, Mr. Kassay explained how he had combed through the divisional plans to list specific problems. He had then asked the division managers to draw up specific action programs involving expected corrective actions, priorities, due dates for solutions, and follow-up dates. He indicated that this program was already in effect.

"In 1967," stated Mr. Kassay, "we will definitely be giving more attention to charters and strategies. We expect more involvement, and more sophisticated and probing questions. We want more understanding of the use of planning by the line managers."

The 1966 Divisional Effort: Abrasive Division

"Planning must become a way of life," said Mr. Cushman. "When we got the planning assignment, our first move was to try and excite people. This was done by both group and individual discussion on what benefits to expect, and how to go about planning.

"One person should be accountable for all this," he added, explaining the appointment of Mr. Harold White (Director of Process Development) as coordinator for planning within the Abrasive Division. "I was too busy in 1966," said Mr. Cushman, "but in 1967 I will have to be more involved. I couldn't have done it as well as Mr. White did, considering all the other things I had to do." Several sources commented that the Abrasive Division had done one of the best jobs in planning.

On the subject of goals, Mr. Cushman indicated that this was still an unresolved area. "The corporate management wanted to see what would come from the bottom up." Mr. Cushman also indicated that during the period of charter formation there had been much lively debate and that he had ultimately felt obliged to settle the debate by fiat in order to meet the deadline.

"Management by results" was a recent undertaking by Mr. Cushman, and he felt that planning made an excellent fit with this. Indicating a notebook, he explained that his subordinates had submitted written plans of action, with check-up and completion dates, for correcting the divisional problems noted in the five-year plan.

Mr. Cushman had appointed Mr. White and three other staff men to serve for 1966 as a four-man, divisional planning committee. According to Mr. White, the planning committee decided that the line should do the planning; and this intention was communicated to the line managers in a meeting convened for that purpose.

"We had some trouble keeping everyone on schedule," said Mr. White, "but by September 15 we had the data in and began to consolidate it. The paperwork on something like this is tremendous." By the end of September, the consolidation was ready for Mr. Cushman's approval. Mr. Cushman had a weekend to review the plans. "On the next Monday," said Mr. White, "we hand-carried the finished document over to Mr. Harris, on time, with great satisfaction." The plan formed a notebook about three-quarters of an inch thick.

According to Mr. White, time pressures had prevented any extensive discussion of departmental problems, and he admitted that "some grey areas went into the plan grey." He added, however, that these problems subsequently formed the basis of a list of areas for immediate action with target solution dates.

Mr. Robbins, a member of the planning committee and Assistant to the Divisional Vice-President of Sales, further described the process. He explained that each line manager had turned in a report on what specific action he would take over the next year. He mentioned that the 1962–1963 effort (which he considered mostly a forecast, as distinguished from planning) had produced a list of divisional strengths and weaknesses, and that the planning committee had had the line managers update the list for inclusion in the five-year plan.

Mr. Robbins was of the opinion that the "numbers game" had been played a little bit, in order to meet deadlines. He expressed some concern over the tendency of managers to worry more about deadlines than plans. He hoped aloud that 1967 would see more emphasis on strategies. Also, Mr. Robbins admitted that he did not fully understand the network diagram, "But," he said, "that's not important. What is important is that we are planning at last."

Mr. Robbins also believed that the "tentative financial forecast" requested by Mr. Jeppson for inclusion with the five-year plan was not sufficiently detailed. "To assess the impact of a strategy properly, you have to work it out in considerable detail." Exhibit 5 contains a memorandum from Mr. Dingle, Corporate Controller, to the divisions setting forth guidelines for the financial forecast.

Mr. William Howard, Sales Manager for Grinding Wheels, explained his part in planning. "My group had to develop marketing strategies," he

Exhibit 5 NORTON COMPANY –A A Memorandum from
the Corporate Controller
on Financial Planning for 1966

Mr. R. Cushman   July 19, 1966
Mr. W. P. Densmore
Mr. E. C. Evans
Mr. W. G. Fallon, Jr.
Mr. A. F. Hardy, Jr.
Mr. E. M. Hicks
Mr. J. G. Martinoni

Tentative Five-Year Financial Planning

The planning meetings held thus far have mentioned the
need for rough financial data as part of the initial phase of
the five-year planning program. The following is meant to
be only a guide for your consideration in developing the
provisional financial plan for five years. Each division
will wish to tailor its data to suit its own particular needs
and characteristics; however, we wish to stress the need
for thinking through the projection of a five-year plan so
that some perspective will be available as indicated below:

Sales - Please state past and future sales at 1966 prices
and also in actual $, in total, by major product group, and
by market group (e.g., domestic customers, export customers, inter-company).

Profit before Taxes - Analyze projected $ profit in
terms of variance from projected 1966 $ profit. The four
significant areas of variance should be:

Price Realization - The change in profit due to
prices being higher or lower than 1966.

Volume and Product Mix - The change in profit contribution due to changes in physical volume and
product mix. This is calculated by applying
1966 contribution ratios to the change in physical volume, by product line.

Exhibit 5 (continued)

Cost Variances - Changes in unit variable costs or aggregate fixed costs should be stated. These aggregate changes should be separated into price (wage & material rates) variances and efficiency (all other) variances.

A simplified variance summary would then appear as follows:

			Variance			
					Costs	
				Vol.	Wage +	
		196_		Price and	Mat'l	
P&L Category	1966	Forecast	Total	Real. Mix	Prices	Other
Sales						
Cost of Sales						
S&A Costs						
Operating Profit						

Profit after taxes - Translate pretax to after-tax profit dollars for future years at the 1966 tax rate. Show income taxes and investment credit separately.

Cash Flow - The following should be shown by years in total and by product line where a determination can be made. Full product line data is not required, but some indication of cash flow, say inventories and capital expenditures, by product line will be helpful.

Profit after taxes
Depreciation
Accounts receivable
Inventories
*Capital expenditures
Other working capital items:
    Cash (working balance only)
    Prepaid expense
    Accounts Payable and Accruals
    etc.
All other
    Total Cash Flow

Exhibit 5 (continued)

<u>Do</u> <u>not</u> <u>project</u> <u>overdraft</u> <u>or</u> <u>debt</u> <u>of</u>
<u>any</u> <u>kind</u>.

*Detail by projects over $100,000, <u>if</u>
<u>possible</u> at this stage.

Excluding profit after taxes, the above projection can
be used to project the change in divisional net assets. This
can be used, in turn, to project % return on net assets.

NORTON COMPANY
/s/
J. F. Dingle   Controller
280
JAB PIW
FSH JEC
JPL RHH
BHM JJ
RSM RAS
JIO

said. "We had to figure out how to get where we claimed we were going to be." Mr. Howard was of the opinion that the discipline imposed by the planning process had been very beneficial. He further stated that concrete actions, regarding manpower and pricing strategy, had already been motivated by the planning effort. "Otherwise, we wouldn't have made those decisions at this time."

Mr. H. W. Davis, Superintendent of Abrasive Crushing Mills and Supplies, stated dissatisfaction with the various forecasts. As evidence, he pointed out that several individual products had already had their forecasts altered. In his opinion, Norton's internal data was generally inadequate to meet his needs. He conceded, however, that the people making the forecasts had to deal with a great many uncertainties. Mr. Davis also explained in some detail the extent to which he and his engineers had labored in developing plans for the various types of equipment needed to meet the sales forecasts. "I'm the guy who has to get the men and materials in and out of here," he said. "When those forecasts are off, it hurts." He hoped that the 1967 effort would be easier than the first go-around.

On several occasions in the Abrasive Division, comments were made to the effect that the five-year plan had, in fact, resulted in actions being taken that would not otherwise have been taken. In addition, Mr. Jeppson indicated that in one of Norton's other divisions a significant materials position had been taken as a result of planning intelligence.

The Abrasive Division was the first Norton division to present its plan to corporate management (i.e., the first of the planning review meetings). The presentation, using copies of the five-year plan and charts projected on a screen, took more than two hours. Mr. White, who helped Mr. Cushman and the Abrasive Division's department managers prepare their presentation for the Expanded (corporate) Planning Committee, commented on the reception by the Expanded Planning Committee. "Since we were the first division, we were sort of like guinea pigs," he said. "But we found the response disappointing. We were ready with a lot of information and expected difficult and probing questions. Perhaps we expected too much of the corporate group. But I heard from Dick Harris that later meetings with other divisions were much better."

DEVELOPMENTS IN EARLY 1967

The results of the first planning cycle were judged as mixed by Messrs. Harris and Zimmerman and by members of top management. It was generally felt that the divisions had made a good beginning, but that they had only begun to dent the planning task. Divisional plans were seen generally to be optimistic extrapolations of past operating trends. Some members of management criticized the effort as having been a "numbers game." Others countered that these results were a necessary first step. Most agreed that the plans had been helpful in providing information that would aid top management in understanding better the various business activities of the corporation.

Organizational Changes

1967 witnessed a number of organizational changes that were to affect planning in major ways. Chief among these was the elevation of Mr. Jeppson to president in April. The corporate planning function moved up with Mr. Jeppson, continuing to report directly to him.

Several other important organizational changes followed shortly after. Two corporate staff functions were created. Mr. D. R. Melville, was hired from outside the company to become Vice President of Marketing, and the Exploratory Research Division was elevated from an operations level. While the number of staff functions reporting to the president was increased, operating responsibility was further delegated. The International Division was to report to the new Executive Vice President, Mr. R. Cushman, the former General Manager of the Abrasive Division. The Abrasive Division was divided along product lines to become the Grinding Wheel and the Abrasive Materials Divisions. As a result, the total number of operating divisions at Norton had grown to nine.

To handle the increasing number of divisions two new executive line functions were created. Mr. A. F. Hardy, Jr. and Mr. H. G. Brustlin were named Group Vice Presidents, each responsible for three divisions, with the remaining three reporting directly to Mr. Cushman. Previously, Mr. Hardy had managed the National Research Corporation, and Mr. Brustlin had been the Marketing Vice President of the Abrasive Division. Meanwhile, Mr. Kassay became General Manager of National Research. An organization chart showing these changes is presented in Exhibit 6.

Objectives for the 1967 Planning Activities

As a result of the "numbers" orientation of the 1966 planning efforts, Mr. Harris recommended an increased emphasis on strategic concepts in 1967. After some discussion, the planning committee decided to separate the formal planning cycle into three phases. The first phase, to be held in the spring, covered the first third of the network diagram and was termed the "Strategy Development" phase. The second or "Quantitative" phase would summarize, during the fall, the financial and manpower implications of the strategies selected in the first phase. The final or "Action" phase would aim to translate the results of planning into specific programs for action. Mr. Zimmerman revised the network diagram to em-

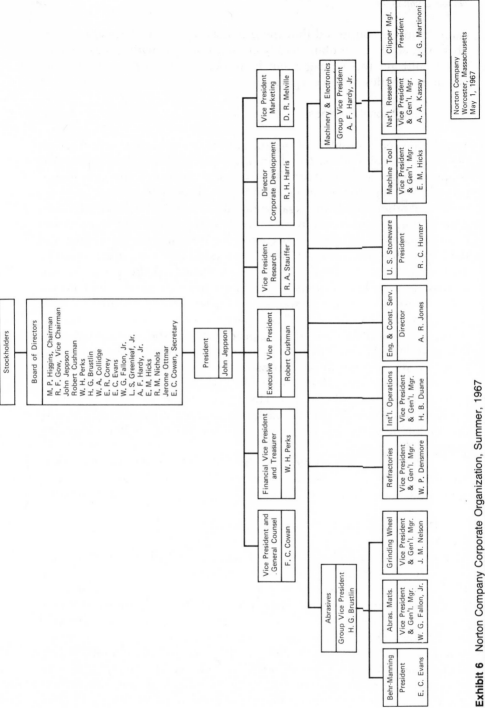

Exhibit 6 Norton Company Corporate Organization, Summer, 1967

Stockholders

Board of Directors

M. P. Higgins, Chairman
R. F. Gow, Vice Chairman
John Jeppson
Robert Cushman
W. H. Perks
H. G. Brustlin
W. A. Collidge
E. R. Corey
E. C. Evans
W. G. Fallon, Jr.
L. S. Greenleaf, Jr.
A. F. Hardy, Jr.
E. M. Hicks
R. M. Nichols
Jerome Ottmar
E. C. Cowan, Secretary

President

John Jeppson

Vice President and General Counsel

F. C. Cowan

Financial Vice President and Treasurer

W. H. Perks

Executive Vice President

Robert Cushman

Vice President Research

R. A. Stauffer

Director Corporate Development

R. H. Harris

Vice President Marketing

D. R. Melville

Abrasives Group Vice President

H. G. Brustlin

Behr-Manning President

E. C. Evans

Abras. Matls. Vice President & Gen'l. Mgr.

W. G. Fallon, Jr.

Grinding Wheel Vice President & Gen'l. Mgr.

J. M. Nelson

Refractories Vice President & Gen'l. Mgr.

W. P. Densmore

Int'l. Operations Vice President & Gen'l. Mgr.

H. B. Duane

Eng. & Const. Serv. Director

A. R. Jones

U. S. Stoneware President

R. C. Hunter

Machinery & Electronics Group Vice President

A. F. Hardy, Jr.

Machine Tool Vice President & Gen'l. Mgr.

E. M. Hicks

Nat'l. Research Vice President & Gen'l. Mgr.

A. A. Kassay

Clipper Mfg. President

J. G. Martinoni

Norton Company
Worcester, Massachusetts
May 1, 1967

80

phasize the distinction between the three phases. He also deleted the caption "Tentative Financial Forecast" from the last step in the "Strategy Development" phase to further reduce the temptation for divisions to get caught up in pushing numbers.

In mid-March, Mr. Jeppson sent a letter to each division manager outlining the planning cycle for 1967 and the objectives for the planning efforts that had been agreed to by the planning committee. This letter, contained in Exhibit 7, pointed out that while members of the planning committee would participate in the review meetings, actual approval of divisional plans was strictly to be a line function.

In April, Mr. Cotter issued his annual five-year economic forecast which included environmental assumptions and projections of economic growth rates for the industries which constituted Norton's markets. Later that month Mr. Zimmerman issued a forecast of the social environment to 1975 which he had compiled from Stanford Research Institute sources. The purpose of this report was to familiarize division planners with anticipated long-term developments in the general environment and in the marketplace. Also, around that time, a Corporate Goals Committee comprising Messrs. Jeppson, Cushman, Perks, Cowan, and Harris was attempting to develop a statement of corporate goals. Each of these activities contributed to the formal planning process that was evolving at Norton Company.

ISSUES AND QUESTIONS

In developing a program for Norton's 1967 planning effort, Mr. Zimmerman had identified a number of specific issues warranting attention. Three of these issues are discussed in more detail below.

The Role of the Corporate Planning Staff Group

The corporate planning staff had a "philosophy" of developing the planning process through nondirective means. From the beginning, however, the divisions had been welcome to seek planning advice from the staff. For example, early in 1967, Mr. William P. Densmore, Vice President and General Manager of the Refractories and Protective Products Divisions, requested assistance in divisional charter-writing. Mr. Zimmerman provided the assistance.

In many other corporations, planning staffs issued standard forms to the divisions. This possibility was also being considered by Mr. Zimmerman. Arguments which were presented against standard forms in 1967 included the following: some divisions have yet to go through a planning cycle and should not have forms forced upon them; imposed forms run

Exhibit 7 NORTON COMPANY –A
The President's Letter Concerning
Formal Long-Range Planning for 1967

March 15, 1967

Division General Managers

1967 Planning Cycle

The 1966 formal planning cycle produced some
excellent thinking and communication on major issues of
concern to Norton Company. As a result of the planning,
we are better informed on the problems and opportunities
facing us, and we also see considerable action resulting
from the plans.

During 1967, our major objectives are to complete
the corporate steps required for planning, to improve
attention to the strategy development phase, and to extend
planning to all parts of Norton. Exhibit A gives details of
our 1967 objectives.

The program planned for this year is described in
Exhibit B (not included in this case.) Major milestones in
the program are as follows:

1. Strategy Review Meetings. These will be
   scheduled from May 15 to June 15 (approximately.) They will focus only on the
   strategy phase.

2. Plans Review Meetings. These will be
   scheduled from September 15 to November 15 (approximately.) They will focus
   on the numerical results of the planning
   process.

3. Interaction Meeting. December or later.
   We hope to have a meeting with all division managers in attendance where each
   division can briefly present the key elements of its plan. The idea is to provide
   communication and encourage interaction
   among divisions.

Exhibit 7 (continued)

Division General Managers

I should like to make a comment about the review meetings planned in order to help clarify the roles of line and staff. I have chosen to include members of the Planning Committee to participate in the review of divisional plans because they have specialized skills which should be represented in an in-depth review. I want to make it clear, however, that the approval of divisional plans is a strictly line function and, therefore, is not done by the Planning Committee.

I should be pleased to hear from you concerning your reactions to our program and/or your ability to mesh your planning with the corporate schedule this year. I am hopeful that we can build upon the good beginning we made last year in planning and make significant progress this year in improving this valuable management tool to serve better both divisional and corporate ends.

NORTON COMPANY

/s/   John Jeppson

J. Jeppson   Executive Vice President
gmo

RC
WPD
ECE
WGF, Jr.
AFH, Jr.
EMH
RCH
JGM

Exhibit 7 (continued) Objective for 1967 Planning Exhibit A

General Objective

    To improve the utility, efficiency, and acceptance of planning.

Specific Objectives

  I. Improve attention to strategy development phase

      A. Separate "strategy development" and "Quantitative summary"
      B. Encourage explicit statements of strategy for each division and/or product line/ markets

        1. Our present strategy and proposed strategy
        2. Strategy of each major competitor

      C. Encourage competitive analysis - resources, strengths, and weaknesses

  II. Extend coverage to whole company

      A. U.S. Stoneware
      B. Clipper Manufacturing Company
      C. Norton International Inc.
      D. Staff Departments

  III. Complete corporate steps

      A. Goals
      B. Assumptions
      C. Environment
      D. Strategy
      E. Identify "Gap"

  IV. Improve planning techniques

Exhibit 7 (continued)

  A. Extend historical information back 10–15
       years (to include business cycle)
  B. Provide more planning aids
  C. Planning committee assistance

  V. Promote divisional interaction

  VI. Emphasize role of action steps (programs)

  VII. Establish progress reviews

  VIII. Think about management climate for change

  IX. Evolve structure appropriate to new strategies

contrary to the tradition that divisions in Norton are quite autonomous; the staff does not yet have the wherewithal necessary to design good forms. The big advantage to be gained in using standard forms was that of facilitating the coordination, consolidation, and review of plans.

The Goal Setting Process

In 1966, the divisions were asked to set their own goals and charters, with no explicit guidance from corporate management. Meanwhile, the Expanded Planning Committee discussed corporate goals.

Armed with divisional ideas about their goals, the Corporate Goals Committee in 1967 was wondering if and when corporate goals should be announced. Mr. Jeppson, for one, believed that divisions should receive guidelines in the form of corporate goals. The Corporate Goals Committee, however, had not yet decided what these goals should be. One possibility that had been suggested was to issue "provisional corporate objectives" for the 1967 cycle.

The Use of Planning as a Management Tool

All of the executives interviewed at Norton agreed that planning was useful. Exactly how planning should be used was, however, an important issue which had not yet been settled. One question was the extent to which the planners should be held responsible for executing their plans. Messrs. Kassay and Cushman had already begun to expect realization of 1966 plans according to certain schedules. Managers in the Abrasive Division said they were committed to their plans and realized that they would be evaluated in light of them. As Mr. William C. Howard, Jr., Sales Manager, Grinding Wheels, said, "When you write a plan, you realize that there will be a day of reckoning." Mr. Zimmerman had reservations about the use of planning as a control tool, particularly in the early years. His fear was based on the following consideration: "When you let a man know his plan is for control purposes rather than to help him, you aren't going to get the same product." Both Mr. Jeppson and Mr. Zimmerman stated that, "We have to do more thinking in this area."

QUESTIONS FOR DISCUSSION

1. As Mr. Zimmerman, prepare recommendations for Norton's planning committee regarding the three issues discussed above.
2. What other issues should Mr. Zimmerman be concerned with as he plans for Norton's future planning efforts?
3. Predict what will take place at Norton in 1967 with respect to the progress and development of formal planning at Norton.

Case 3

Norton Company–C*

Synopsis of Norton Company (B) In mid-1967, following a round of strategic planning at the divisional level, the Planning Committee of the Norton Company decided to discontinue the remaining steps in the annual planning cycle because of severe pressures on management's time. These pressures resulted from a combination of major organizational changes, a recent acquisition, and depressed market conditions that ultimately caused sales to lower by 1.6% and profits by 38.5% as compared to 1966 results. Despite the abbreviation of the planning cycle in 1967, John Jeppson, newly appointed president of Norton, reaffirmed his intention to emphasize planning at Norton in his statement for the 1967 annual report: "Long-range planning will become a way of life at Norton Company. By this medium we will set specific goals, allocate resources of talent and money, and measure our progress. There will be increased emphasis on the delegation of responsibility and in the measurement of performance against predetermined goals."

The Norton Company recovered financially in 1968 with a 6.2% improvement in net sales and a 58-cent gain in earnings per share, as shown in Exhibit 1. The year also witnessed recovery from many of the organizational pressures: the newly assembled top management team had become increasingly seasoned in its task; the fission of the Abrasive Division into a Grinding Wheel Division and an Abrasive Materials Division had strengthened those operations; and the problems of assimilating the recently acquired U.S. Stoneware were generally under control. In his review of the year 1968, Mr. Jeppson renewed his commitment to planning: "We are continuing to emphasize long-range planning by constantly refining and updating our objectives and strategies for the future."

Despite the apparent return to earlier conditions, the whole approach to formal planning had changed from its original conception. Following a brief historical review of planning developments at Norton, this case describes planning activities during the latter half of 1967, the initial plan for formal planning in 1968, certain fundamental changes in the company that led to major alterations in the planning process, and the newly emerging pattern of planning.

*This case was prepared under the supervision of Associate Professor Francis J. Aguilar based on student reports written by Miss Irene N. Leary and Mr. Wouter Goedkoop. Copyright © 1970 by the President and Fellows of Harvard College.

Exhibit 1 NORTON COMPANY CONSOLIDATED FINANCIAL REVIEW

	1968	1967	1966
Operations for the Year		*(thousands of dollars)*	
Net Sales	$324,020	$305,039	$310,473
Income Before Income Taxes	*31,174	24,912	37,241
Operating Income (Income before			
Extraordinary Item)	*15,247	12,107	18,811
% of Sales	4.7%	4.0%	6.1%
% Return on Stockholders' Equity	7.4%	6.0%	9.5%
Additions to Property, Plant and Equipment	$ 12,334	$ 15,417	$ 16,835
Depreciation Charges	12,948	12,748	11,740
Increase (Decrease) in Long-Term Debt	3,278	12,728	11,646
At Year End			
Current Assets	$174,586	$159,696	$164,297
Current Liabilities	38,810	36,910	56,360
Current Ratio	4.5	4.3	2.9
Net Property, Plant and Equipment	101,829	104,312	103,285
Long-Term Debt	34,003	30,725	17,996
Stockholders' Equity	207,083	200,792	197,168
Number of Employees	18,380	18,200	19,210
Shares of Common Stock Outstanding	5,610,838	5,670,433	5,669,535
Per Share Statistics			
Operating Income	*$2.72	$2.14	$3.32
Cash Flow (Operating Income and			
Depreciation)	*5.02	4.38	5.39
Dividends Paid	1.50	1.50	1.50
Stockholders' Equity	36.91	35.41	34.78

* Excluding non-recurring gain on the sale of mining properties of $1,789,214, equal to $.32 per share.

The 1966 statistics include the operations for U.S. Stoneware, Inc. from August 1, 1966 on and for Chamberlain Engineering Corporation from January 1, 1966 on.

Source: Norton Company 1968 Annual Report.

Norton Company

The Norton Company was the world's largest abrasive manufacturer, operating plants at 45 locations in 17 countries and employing over 19,000 people in 1967. Norton had expanded its product lines over the years (including 1931 and 1932 mergers with Behr-Manning Company and Pike Company) to include crude abrasives, abrasive grain, machine tools, refractories materials, bonded abrasives, coated abrasives, sharpening stones, pressure-sensitive tapes, and grinding fluids. Recent acquisitions added National Research Corporation (1963; high vacuum equipment, refractory metals, super-conductors, and other technological products), Clipper Manufacturing Company and its related companies

(1964; specialized construction equipment), and U.S. Stoneware Company (1966; ceramic, metal and plastic tower packings, and internals for chemical processors, plus plastic tubing and other vinyl products).

Norton divisions traditionally enjoyed considerable autonomy. The recent acquisitions had somewhat reduced Norton's dependence on the mature and cyclical abrasive industry, but abrasive products still accounted for over 60% of the 1968 company sales.

FORMAL PLANNING UP TO 1968

Formal planning began at Norton in 1966 with what might be characterized as a "bottoms-up" approach. The major planning efforts —instigated and coordinated at the corporate level by Mr. Richard Harris, Director of Corporate Development—were to take place in the operating divisions. The divisions were asked to prepare accounts of opportunities, threats, strengths, weaknesses and alternative strategies. Mr. Harris favored a nondirective approach for the initial effort, and thus each division was given wide latitude as to the content and format of its plans. The resulting reports were reviewed by top management and then served as a basis for preparation of a tentative financial forecast. The 1966 effort was purposely limited to covering the first half of the planning cycle, as described in a widely distributed chart known as "the network diagram."

These first efforts were criticized by some executives as having resulted largely in sterile numerical projections without sufficient strategic thinking. To offset this tendency, the planning cycle for 1967 was divided into three distinct phases: a strategic phase to be completed in the spring; a quantitative phase to be completed in the fall; and an action program phase to be completed in the winter. The modified network diagram is shown in Exhibit 2. (The original network diagram is contained in the Norton Company (A) case.)

In general, planning had become more structured and formal in 1967 when compared to 1966. Several members of management were of the opinion that much of the undue optimism that characterized planning in 1966 was again evident in the strategies submitted in 1967. Despite these shortcomings, the consensus of top management was that the divisions had gained a great deal from the difficult and thought-provoking task of developing strategies. The aim of completing the network planning cycle beyond phase one, however, was frustrated for the reasons given in the opening paragraph of this case.

While the formal planning cycle had been curtailed in 1967, several other related activities continued with more or less impetus. Among these organized efforts were those concerning corporate goals, product line evaluation, and management by objectives.

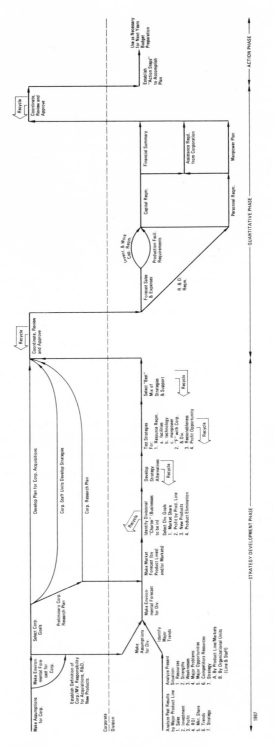

Exhibit 2 Norton Company (C) Modified Planning Network Diagram

Corporate Goals

The Corporate Goals Committee, made up of Messrs. Jeppson, Cushman, Perks, Cowan, and Harris,[1] was in Mr. Harris' words, "organized to do the spade-work necessary to formulate corporate goals." Several informal dinner meetings were held during the first half of 1967 to discuss a framework developed by Mr. Harris for arriving at corporate goals. Although a definite statement of corporate goals was not drawn up, the members generally felt that much progress had been made and that it had been a useful and educational experience for all who had participated. The committee as originally constituted was inactive in late 1967 and early 1968, but Mr. Harris continued to work independently with Mr. Jeppson on the task. Mr. Harris pointed out, "Goal setting at Norton started out as a bottoms-up process with the planning performed during 1966 and 1967. Through the development of corporate goals, we are now starting to give it the balance that it needs." In line with these activities, Mr. Jeppson was quoted in the business press as stating corporate expectations to include a minimum annual profit growth of 10% and a return on equity of 12.5%.[2]

Product Line Evaluation

One result of the 1967 planning review meetings held in May and June of 1967 was the conclusion that Norton had numerous unpromising product lines. Accordingly, a committee chaired by Robert Cushman, Executive Vice President, was established to prepare "position papers" on each of the approximately 75 product lines.[3] The Product Line Study Committee (PLSC) planned to report its findings to the Executive Committee in the spring of 1968.

As Mr. Cushman later explained, "We tried to see if the product fit our picture of Norton five years out. If it did not, we made a decision on how and when it should be phased out. We examined the possibility of regrouping the product lines to take advantage of any synergistic benefits and also were concerned with identifying weaknesses in our present lines which could be rectified through acquisition."

Decisions reached by the PLSC were forwarded to the divisions, and

---

[1] President, Executive Vice President, Financial Vice President and Treasurer, Vice President and General Counsel, and Director of Corporate Development respectively. See Exhibit 6 of Norton Company (A) for the relevant organizational chart; Exhibit 5 of this case portrays their positions in a subsequent organizational structure.

[2] *Forbes*, December 1, 1967.

[3] Other members included: H.G. Brustlin, Abrasives Group Vice President; A. F. Hardy, Jr., Machinery Equipment and Engineering Group Vice President; D. R. Melville, Advance Materials Vice President; R. A. Stauffer, Vice President, Research; and J. F. Dingle, Corporate Controller.

each general manager had the opportunity to challenge the committee's opinions if he did not agree. According to Mr. Cushman, the PLSC did not make any in-depth market studies; therefore, subsequent discussions with some of the general managers brought out new information which resulted in changes to the report.

In advance of this study, each division was requested by the controller's office to furnish product line data for 1966 and 1972 including sales, profits after taxes, net assets, market share, principal market, and a qualitative statement of the risks involved. Mr. Crocker of the controller's office saw this effort as a one-shot study and not part of the formal planning cycle. He noted that many divisions were unable to come up with all the numbers, and in some cases could only report net sales.

Members of the PLSC felt that the final report and subsequent action on it by the Executive Committee would take much of the strategic uncertainty out of divisional planning. "They will know where we want them to go in the future."

Management by Objectives

Mr. Cushman also instituted during 1967 a program of management by objectives. Each line manager had to prepare a list of objectives which he could achieve by a given point in time. The manager then discussed the objectives with his superior until agreement was reached.

In early 1968, many managers were still unsure of how planning was to be used in evaluating managerial performance. Evaluation had been based customarily on the annual financial plan (budget). Mr. Cushman distinguished between the budget and management by objectives in the following way, "The financial plan is what you feel will actually happen during the year, and you are fully committed to accomplishing it. This is your job and does not warrant an incentive. However, an incentive bonus is earned if you reach your objectives, which employ difficult but attainable goals."

Mr. Cushman took a great deal of time to explain to the various management groups in Norton the aims and procedures of the management by objectives program. As he remarked, "I want it to be a way of life at Norton, all the way down to the first line supervisors; and I take advantage of every chance I get at operating meetings to make sure that the program is understood. Planning isn't much use unless something is done to follow up on the strategies and action programs that have been developed." Exhibit 3 contains excerpts from several charts used in explaining the differences between forecasts and goals.

Exhibit 3

NORTON COMPANY –C

Excerpts from a Memorandum on Planning Definitions

Forecasts vs. Goals

This year we have had a great deal of trouble distinguishing between forecasts and goals. There seems to be a need for some uniformity in our definitions so that when we look at figures, we know at what we actually are looking.

. . . a forecast starts at the bottom of the organization . . . and works itself up in the form of a prediction. However, a goal starts at the top of the organization with the chief executive officer stating what his targets or objectives are beyond the forecast. The difference between the two equals the amount of improvement he expects.

To reach a goal there must be an organized effort with everybody assigned and held responsible for meeting certain objectives. This is where the theory of management by objectives is put into practice. Although the setting of the goal must start at the top and work down the organization to any given level, it is appropriate for an individual to first approach his supervisor with what he hopes to accomplish during the year. The final objectives set at any level must be in agreement between the man and his supervisor.

* * * * *

CHART 1

A FORECAST IS THE MOST REALISTIC PREDICTION
OF WHAT IS MOST LIKELY TO HAPPEN

1.   A FORECAST IS NOT COMPLETELY INSURED.
IT IS NOT A SURE BET.

Exhibit 3 (continued)

2.   THE ATTAINMENT OF A PROFIT FORECAST,
     FOR EXAMPLE, WILL REQUIRE THE SUCCESS-
     FUL COMPLETION OF MANY PLANNED PRO-
     JECTS SUCH AS COST REDUCTION PROGRAMS
     AND THE REALIZATION OF SALES PROJECT-
     IONS OF NEW PRODUCTS PERHAPS NOT
     FULLY TESTED.

3.   A FORECAST WILL INCLUDE THE RESULTS OF
     WHAT WOULD BE CONSIDERED NORMAL
     GROWTH IN A PRODUCT LINE OR IN THE
     INDUSTRY.

4.   THE REALIZATION OR REACHING OF A FORE-
     CAST IS EXPECTED. IT DOES NOT REPRE-
     SENT OUTSTANDING OR DISTINGUISHED PER-
     FORMANCE.

5.   BECAUSE MAJOR INFLUENCES BEYOND OUR
     CONTROL MAY MAKE THE ATTAINMENT OF
     A FORECAST EASIER OR HARDER, A FINAL
     FORECAST SHOULD INCLUDE A SECOND
     FIGURE.

* * * * *

CHART 2

A GOAL IS AN OBJECTIVE WANTED ABOVE
THE FORECAST AND FOR WHICH
AN EXTRA EFFORT IS MADE

1.   A GOAL REPRESENTS EXECUTIVE JUDGE-
     MENT ON WHAT REASONABLY MIGHT BE
     EXPECTED IF THE ORGANIZATION AND ITS
     INDIVIDUALS WERE MOTIVATED TO A HIGH
     DEGREE.

2.   ONCE SET, A GOAL IS TRANSLATED INTO
     CURRENT PROGRAMS FROM THE TOP DOWN
     THROUGH THE LINE ORGANIZATION.

Exhibit 3 (continued)

3. INDIVIDUAL GOALS MUST BE MUTUALLY
    AGREED UPON BETWEEN AN EMPLOYEE AND
    HIS SUPERVISOR. THEY MUST BE CLEARLY
    STATED IN WRITTEN FORM WITH MEASUR-
    ABLE MILEPOSTS ALONG THE WAY.

4. WHEN CIRCUMSTANCES BEYOND CONTROL
    ARE LIABLE TO BE MAJOR FACTORS, AL-
    TERNATE GOALS SHOULD ALSO BE AGREED
    UPON.

5. THE DEGREE OF SUCCESS IN THE ACHIEVE-
    MENT OF A BASIC GOAL BECOMES THE MOST
    IMPORTANT MEASUREMENT OF INDIVIDUAL,
    DIVISIONAL OR DEPARTMENTAL PERFOR-
    MANCE.

6. UNLESS A PROGRESS READING IS TAKEN ON
    AT LEAST A QUARTERLY BASIS, THE CHANCES
    OF REACHING A GIVEN GOAL ARE SUBSTAN-
    TIALLY REDUCED.

7. IF THE SUCCESSFUL ATTAINMENT OF THE
    GOAL IS NOT REWARDED OR RECOGNIZED,
    FUTURE GOALS WILL BE UNSUCCESSFUL
    EXERCISES.

THE PLAN FOR FORMAL PLANNING IN 1968

After two years of formal planning, the company had still to complete the entire cycle shown on the network diagram. Among its aims for 1968, the planning committee intended to accomplish this act. It also called for completion of an explicit statement of corporate goals and objectives. These planning objectives were listed among others in a memorandum entitled "Objectives for 1968 Planning," contained in Exhibit 4.

These plans for planning at the Norton Company were not to be followed. Certain developments occurred in the company which were to change the whole approach to formal planning.

MAJOR DEVELOPMENTS AT NORTON IN 1968

Among the many developments that occurred at Norton during 1968, probably most important to planning activities were the changes in organizational attitude and the related change in corporate strategy promoted by Robert Cushman, the Executive Vice President. Mr. Cushman, who had moved up from head of the Abrasive Division when Mr. Jeppson assumed the presidency of Norton, enjoyed the reputation among his colleagues as a hard-driving, no-nonsense line manager who had little patience for elaborate staff support. He felt strongly that planning should be an integral part of line management's regular duties and that the existing format and structure tended somehow to separate planning from a line manager's central concern.

A shift in corporate strategy was also taking place. Mr. Jeppson, in reviewing the company's position in the early sixties noted that Norton's products were generally in areas of slow growth, concluding, "We, therefore, felt the necessity for diversifying into products and markets with sharper growth rate possibilities. In addition, we wanted more strings to our bow in the event of technological and product obsolescence."[4] By 1968, however, top management had already begun to question the extent to which the company had come to spread its attentions, and eventually came to favor having the company "pull in its horns" somewhat. The new approach would have Norton concentrate on six or seven major product areas where the company had a distinct competence.

Since management would now be much more closely familiar with the business areas to be managed than was true under the earlier strategy, Mr. Cushman felt that planning could and should be totally integrated in line decision making. The shift from staff involvement in planning was thus seen in terms of line management no longer requiring "outside" expertise

[4] *The Wall Street Transcript*, June 17, 1968.

Exhibit 4 NORTON COMPANY –C

Memorandum by the Planning Committee

OBJECTIVES FOR 1968 PLANNING

General Objectives

TO IMPROVE THE UTILITY, EFFICIENCY, AND
ACCEPTANCE OF PLANNING

Specific Objectives

1. Update and refine "Strategy Development Phase" as
   necessary and complete "Quantitative Phase" of
   planning.

   a. Include rough manpower plan and capital require-
      ments.

2. Translate plans into specific programs for action
   ("Action Phase").

   a. Include timetable

3. Complete major corporate steps.

   a. Goals and objectives
   b. Strategy
   c. Review the impact with each division general
      manager by fall, 1968.

4. Achieve complete participation by all divisions.

5. Introduce specific techniques into planning.

   a. Format for financial summary

6. Consolidate quantitative phase results.

   a. Identify "planning gap"
   b. Prepare information needed for staff planning
      (Worcester & corporate)

Exhibit 4 (continued)

7. Establish progress reviews by line management.

8. Promote divisional interaction.

9. Introduce additional training of people deeply involved in planning at divisional and corporate level.

10. Make formal planning a part of the day-to-day management and begin integration with the use of annual control budgets.

in the areas to be planned and the related need to elicit strong commitment from the operating managers.

Several organizational developments accompanied these changes in leadership and strategy with further impact on formal long-range planning. In 1968 the NRC and the Grinding Wheel Divisions each created the post of divisional planner. This staff member was to perform many of the functions that had formerly been done by the corporate staff planner. On January 18, 1969, two group vice presidents were appointed to improve communications between the divisions in the major product lines. Exhibit 5 contains a chart of the executive organization in Norton as of early 1969.

Formal Planning in 1968

In 1968, the planning process at Norton, in large part, came to be influenced and administered by Mr. Cushman. The major thrust of change in Norton's planning activities was to cut down on details and to make planning a part of regular line activities.

In Mr. Cushman's opinion, division managers had been planning in previous years largely to satisfy the requirements set by the planning staff and had failed to become committed to the plans. He saw voluminous documentation required in 1967 to present a divisional strategy and financial plan as one reason for this failure to identify with the planning output. Thus, in 1968, division managers were asked to present each product group strategy in a statement of two pages or less and the related financial five-year plan on only one page.

The divisional strategy statements were to cover information on such items as industry trends, market size, competition, and major opportunities or threats as well as a description of the proposed strategic response. For the financial plan, divisions were required to submit figures for only the first, second and fifth years of the five-year plan. The purpose of this abbreviation was to reduce the time spent on the numbers, thereby allowing divisional management more time for strategic considerations. Exhibit 6 contains a memorandum to divisional managers in which Mr. Cushman lays out the new approach to planning in 1968.

The management review process was also altered. Divisional presentations before the Expanded Planning Committee[5] were replaced by two other meetings. The first of these was a one-hour "premeeting" attended by Mr. Jeppson, Mr. Cushman, the division general manager, and the responsible group vice president. In this premeeting Jeppson and

---

[5] The Expanded Planning Committee had comprised J. Jeppson, President; R. Cushman, Executive Vice President; R. Stauffer, Vice President for Research; J. Dingle, Controller; J. Cotter, Corporate Economist; R. Harris, Director of Corporate Development; W. Perks, Financial Vice President and Treasurer; F. Cowan, Vice President and General Counsel; and M. Zimmerman, Manager of Corporate Planning.

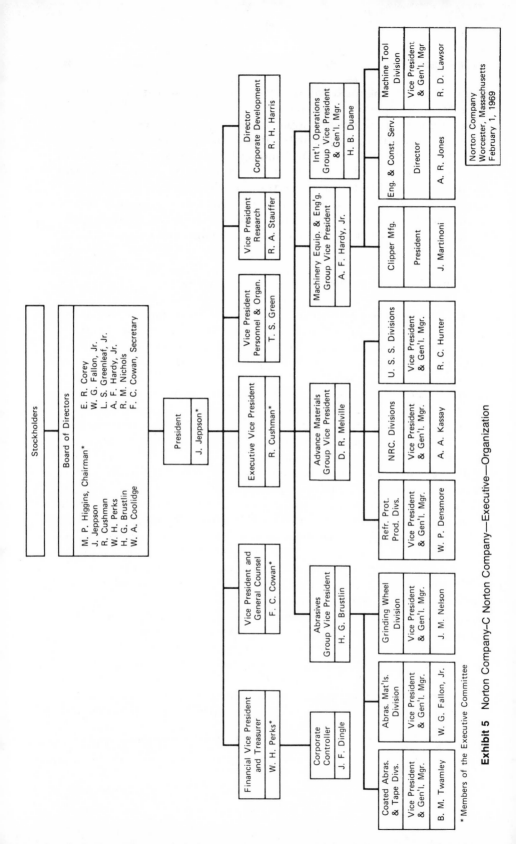

Exhibit 5 Norton Company–C Norton Company—Executive—Organization

Stockholders

Board of Directors

M. P. Higgins, Chairman*
J. Jeppson
R. Cushman
W. H. Perks
H. G. Brustlin
W. A. Coolidge

E. R. Corey
W. G. Fallon, Jr.
L. S. Greenleaf, Jr.
A. F. Hardy, Jr.
R. M. Nichols
F. C. Cowan, Secretary

President

J. Jeppson*

Financial Vice President and Treasurer

W. H. Perks*

Vice President and General Counsel

F. C. Cowan*

Executive Vice President

R. Cushman*

Director Corporate Development

R. H. Harris

Vice President Research

R. A. Stauffer

Vice President Personnel & Organ.

T. S. Green

Corporate Controller

J. F. Dingle

Abrasives Group Vice President

H. G. Brustlin

Advance Materials Group Vice President

D. R. Melville

Machinery Equip. & Eng'g. Group Vice President

A. F. Hardy, Jr.

Int'l. Operations Group Vice President & Gen'l. Mgr.

H. B. Duane

Coated Abras. & Tape Divs.

Vice President & Gen'l. Mgr.

B. M. Twamley

Abras. Mat'ls. Division

Vice President & Gen'l. Mgr.

W. G. Fallon, Jr.

Grinding Wheel Division

Vice President & Gen'l. Mgr.

J. M. Nelson

Refr. Prot. Prod. Divs.

Vice President & Gen'l. Mgr.

W. P. Densmore

NRC. Divisions

Vice President & Gen'l. Mgr.

A. A. Kassay

U. S. S. Divisions

Vice President & Gen'l. Mgr.

R. C. Hunter

Clipper Mfg.

President

J. Martinoni

Eng. & Const. Serv.

Director

A. R. Jones

Machine Tool Division

Vice President & Gen'l. Mgr.

R. D. Lawsor

Norton Company
Worcester, Massachusetts
February 1, 1969

*Members of the Executive Committee

Exhibit 6

NORTON COMPANY –C

MEMORANDUM - EXECUTIVE VICE PRESIDENT

March 6, 1968

Long-Range Planning 1968

The 1967 formal planning cycle effectively focused on the strategy development phase of planning and resulted in better communication concerning major issues facing Norton Company. Although the work on the quantitative phase was postponed last fall, we assume you and your division management have continued to develop and refine your projections of the future.

Considerable thought has been given to how our planning program should be structured and implemented during this year. In outlining our plans, it may be helpful to think of the planning program as serving two purposes. First, there is certain basic divisional information which is required at headquarters in order to establish and monitor a corporate program. Secondly, there is that planning which must be done by and for the divisions in order to insure proper management and adequate growth.

Focus on Opportunities

We are aware that a well-delineated picture of what we want the company to look like in the future has not been made available to you. Your strategy presentations during 1967 were helpful in the formation of such a picture. The recent Product Line Study which has, or will shortly be described to you, has been completed. The next steps now in process include an evaluation of our current major R & D programs followed by a careful definition of those major areas of opportunity which Norton will pursue.

Examples of major opportunity areas might be:

1. Electronic materials, devices, and instrumentation

Exhibit 6 (continued)

2. Chemical Process products
3. Coated products, etc.

In addition to those major areas on a well defined but broad front which might approximate five or six in number including abrasives, there are important opportunities which are related to presently established products and which logically should be pursued by the individual divisions. An example might be chemical specialties used in the metal-working industries.

A major area might be one where we could develop or acquire up to one hundred million dollars in sales in five years. In addition to those "nitch filling" product extensions, a related opportunity area probably should be targeted at a minimum of twenty million dollars in five years.

Corporate management will attempt to define carefully the major opportunities. We would expect to work closely with you in planning those opportunity areas which are related to or extensions of your present product and market positions. We would expect growth in both areas to include internal growth activities as well as acquisitions.

With this background, we outline the 1968 planning program. We will expect all nine divisions to cooperate and carry out each step as requested.

I. The Quantitative Phase

The quantitative phase for figures required in Worcester is described on the sample report attached. It constitutes a minimum number of figures. You already have developed them for 1968. We believe that in a four hour meeting with your key managers, you could make the adjustments necessary to arrive at a pretty accurate forecast or financial plan for 1969.

When it comes to 1972, we would expect you to plug in the effect of major shifts in direction or performance but to extrapolate and use historical ratios to arrive at the

Exhibit 6 (continued)

1972 figures. Done thoughtfully, it will provide us with what we need and preclude your building up in every product line all the detail calculations that you performed in making your 1968 forecast.

II. The Strategic Development Phase

The qualitative phase of this request includes your submitting a statement on each major product line grouping. This statement should include your current strategies. We would expect you would want to include comments on such items as industry trends, market size, market share, competition, research effort, capacity, major problems or opportunities you see, and any unusual requests for capital that are predicted.

We ask that you also submit a description of those related opportunities that you are pursuing or might wish to pursue and which you believe will be compatible with our corporate objectives as you now understand them.

It is important that the statements on the strategy development phase be kept to a minimum necessary for effective communication to corporate management. While we recognize that more detail normally would be useful within the divisions for product line planning, please keep the material submitted succinct. A statement on each major product line grouping of two pages or less should be adequate.

Please feel free to consult with any members of our corporate staff whom you think may be helpful in providing format suggestions. Rigid uniformity in preparing these statements is not a criterion. However, your planned strategies should be clearly understandable and believable to be helpful for our purposes.

We hope the information requested in I and II can be in our hands no later than May 1, but please submit when ready and sooner than that date if possible.

Exhibit 6 (continued)

III.   Between May 15 and June 30, each division manager
will be asked to come to Worcester to review his plans.
This will be an informal meeting. You may come alone or
bring any members of your staff. It will enable us to ask
questions and evaluate progress. Such a series of meetings
would take place at this time each year.

IV.   The meetings we have held in early January each
year with the Executive Committee to present the year's
financial plan will be pushed ahead and held in December
starting in 1968.

At that time, you will be asked to cover the coming
year and then forecast a second year and fifth year in
exactly the same manner as described in section I and the
attached supplement.

To this same meeting, you would be asked to
bring the same summary statements described under the
qualitative phase in paragraph II. This would give management a second time during the year to evaluate progress.

/s/ Robert Cushman
cp
Exec. Committee
Group Vice Presidents
Division Managers
Planning Committee

Please forward both the financial
projections and the strategy statements to
this office.

Exhibit 6 (continued)

Q-1

Quantitative Phase
Summary Data

NORTON COMPANY
5 YEAR PLAN 1968 – 1972
$ Millions
(Nearest $0.1 Million)

Division	1968	1969	1972
	___	___	___
1. Net Sales			
2. Net Income			
3. Net Assets:			
Receivables			
Inventories			
P.P.&E. – Net			
All Other			
TOTAL	___	___	___
4. Turnover: Sales/Net Assets			
5. Profit Margin: Profit/Sales			
6. Return on Net Assets:			
Profit/Net Assets			
7. Net Funds Generated/(Consumed)			
8. Capital Expenditures			
9. Depreciation			
10. Inter-Division Net Sales			
11. After-Tax Interest Expense/(Income)			

Exhibit 6 (continued)

Instructions to be Followed in Preparing Form Q-1 Quantitative Phase

Summary Data

Although the captions contained on form Q-1 largely are self explanatory, the following comments should clarify any questions which might arise concerning the interpretation of the data required.

1. Net Sales - The figure shown for sales should be net of returns, cash discounts, and allowances. In addition, all intra-division sales should be eliminated in arriving at the net sales figure for your Division.

2. Net Income - The figure shown for net income should be the adjusted net income used in measuring your Division's return on net assets. This means that such items as goodwill amortized and the after tax cost of interest expense should be added back to the book income. Adjustments of this type only will be necessary for those divisions which currently are subsidiaries of the parent company and have debt in their capital structures.

3. Net Assets - This is the investment base for your Division. It consists of total assets less current liabilities. Intercompany items, debt, overdraft, and surplus cash should be excluded from the investment base. The net assets to be shown on form Q-1 should be stated as of January 1 of each year. Specifically, the net assets to be shown under the year 1968 should be the net assets of your Division as of 1/1/68 etc.

Exhibit 6 (continued)

4. Turnover – Self explanatory.

5. Profit Margin – Self explanatory.

6. Return on Net Assets – Self-explanatory.

7. Net Funds Generated/(Consumed) – This figure is derived by determining the change in the net assets of your Division during the year and deducting the profit. If the profits of your Division exceed the increase in your net assets, then your Division would be a net generator of funds. If the increase in net assets exceeds the profits, then your Division would be a net user of funds. Two examples are shown below to clarify exactly how the calculation is made.

	($000) Division "X"	($000) Division "Y"
Net Assets as of 1/1/68	$47,000	$11,000
Net Assets as of 1/1/69 *	48,000	17,000
(Inc.)/Dec. in Net Assets	(1,000)	(6,000)
Net Income	5,000	500
Net Funds Generated/(Consumed)	4,000	(5,500)

8. Capital Expenditures – The planned capital expenditures for your Division should be stated on a gross basis. Expensed costs associated with planned capital projects should not be reported under this caption.

107

Exhibit 6 (continued)

If the capital expenditures for your Division are expected to be considerably above or below the historical norm during the years 1970 and 1971, please indicate the level of capital expenditures during each of these two years as a postscript at the bottom of the form.

9. Depreciation – Self explanatory.

10. Interdivision Net Sales – The figure to be shown should be the sales made by your Division to other divisions and subsidiaries of Norton Company. Do not report intradivision sales under this caption.

11. After-tax Interest Expense/(Income) – The figure to be shown should be the after-tax cost of any interest expense or income which is added to or deducted from your book income in arriving at the net income reported on line No. 2 of the form. This information, along with the intercompany sales detail, is required in order to determine the consolidation adjustments.

Any technical questions regarding the information to be supplied on this form should be addressed to the Corporate Controller.

Cushman explained Norton's strategy and acquisition policy, and reviewed the findings and conclusions of the Product Line Study. During the remainder of the hour, the division manager had to explain and to defend the division's strategy for the coming year. At the end of the one-hour meeting the president gave his decision on the division's plans. This review was immediately followed by a three-hour meeting in which the division manager and his staff presented their plans for the first time to the remaining members of the Executive Committee and to selected members of the corporate staff. Exhibit 7 contains the memorandum announcing these arrangements.

SOME OPINIONS OF THE 1968 PLANNING EFFORT

Recent developments and changes in formal planning at Norton were followed with considerable interest by key managers throughout the organization. It was generally conceded that the corporate staff planners had provided valuable impetus and guidance to the organization during the initial period of planning. The International Division, where planning was recently inaugurated, continued to follow the network diagram closely. Other divisional managers deplored continued use of a uniform, detailed approach arguing that the increased emphasis on strategic planning necessarily led to more diversity among divisional plans. Divisional staff planners were appointed to devise and implement planning efforts appropriate to the division's needs.

The change in corporate planning at the Norton Company was thus viewed by some as a natural evolution, rather than as an abrupt reversal or as a redress of earlier efforts. As one possible future development, Mr. Melville, Group Vice President, suggested that some of the divisional planners might move up to the group level after helping divisional line executives get on top of their immediate planning problems.

The Corporate Staff Planner Speaks Out

Mr. Harris, Director of Corporate Development, had become visibly disturbed by the recent turn of events in planning. He felt himself increasingly limited to corporate merger and acquisition studies. His subordinate, Marlin Zimmerman, Manager of Corporate Planning, was left in an entirely ambiguous position in terms of duties to perform.

Mr. Harris was fearful that the company would revert to a short-term orientation if it continued along the present path. In voicing these objections to Mr. Jeppson, he realized that the formal planning system that he and Mr. Zimmerman had worked so hard to develop was at stake. As a result of these discussions, he felt that he still had the full confidence and

Exhibit 7

NORTON COMPANY –C

May 3, 1968

To Executive Committee
   Group Vice Presidents
   Division Managers

Agenda for Mid-1968
Planning Meetings

Dates for these meetings are being finalized. It
might be helpful for you to know now what kind of an
agenda we are planning. During the first hour of the half
day session, you will meet with JJ, RC, and your Group
Vice President. At this time, we will summarize for you
our corporate strategy and programs. We will review the
key decisions resulting from the Product Line Study and
discuss our acquisition policy. This should take about a
half hour.

During the remainder of the hour, we will ask you
to brief us on your key plans for growth within your division.

Following this meeting, we will be joined by other
members of the Executive Committee plus those members
of our corporate staffs who, we believe, it is important to
be kept informed on divisional plans and progress. Each
of these participants will have received and read your
May 1 report.

1.   We will ask you to give us a brief report on 1968
     commenting on any variances from your original
     forecast or plan.

2.   Briefly cover the highlights of changes anticipated
     in 1969 as outlined in your Summary Data (Q-1).

3.   Discuss the Strategic Development Phase or your
     general plans for growth in the division referring
     to the 1972 data submitted.

Exhibit 7 (continued)

As stated in our memorandum of March 6 on this subject, we will keep the meeting informal. You may bring others on your staff if you feel it important. However, frank discussions regarding people during the first hour could be helpful and informative.

NORTON COMPANY

Robert Cushman   Executive Vice President

cp
JEC   WCW   MUZ
JFD   DRM   RHH
RAS

support of the chief executive. At the same time, Jeppson publicly acknowledged the benefits of getting increased line involvement in planning.

QUESTIONS FOR DISCUSSION

1. Appraise the new approach to planning at Norton:
   In what ways does it improve on the earlier approach?
   What possible problems does the new approach introduce?
2. What purposes does formal planning serve at Norton in 1968?
   How do these differ from the purposes of formal planning in 1966?
3. As a divisional general manager, which approach to planning would you prefer?
4. If you were Mr. Harris, what would you try to do at this point?
   What if anything, should Mr. Harris have done differently in the past with respect to planning at Norton?
5. If you were Mr. Cushman, what would you do next to improve planning at Norton?
6. Predict what formal planning will be like at Norton in 1975.

Case 4

Continental Oil Company*

Coordinating & Planning

In 1971, Mr. Samuel Schwartz, Vice President, Coordinating & Planning of Continental Oil Company (CONOCO), spoke of his planning responsibilities as follows:

> It is really quite a challenge to plan and coordinate an organization which sells close to $3 billion worth of products . . . expands at the rate of $400 million per year in new facilities . . . returns a net income of $160 million . . . is responsible to 75,000 stockholders . . . has operations in 34 countries and has an employee force of 35,700 people.[1]

---

*This case was made possible by the cooperation of Continental Oil Company. It was written by Ronald M. Hall, Research Assistant, under the direction of Assistant Professor John S. Hammond III, based partly on a research report submitted by Messrs. Keval K. Bhasin, Diep La Vu, H. R. Seshagiri Rao, and Claude Sorel.

[1] Additional financial information for 1961-1970 is contained in Exhibit 1.

With assets averaging $75,000 per employee, CONOCO's people must know their businesses to efficiently handle the high volume of cash flow and production while simultaneously keeping CONOCO growing at a rate exceeding most other major U.S. oil companies.

To make it even more interesting, there's plenty of drama in today's business. The recent surfacing of a major fuel shortage in North America . . . political instability and rising nationalism in foreign oil producing countries . . . the continuing uncertainty of discoveries of energy sources such as the Alaskan North Slope . . . these factors and countless others point to the necessity for skillful, comprehensive planning.

CONOCO has evolved a complex and largely effective planning system which matches to a considerable extent the unique qualities of the company. In maintaining and improving the system I have adopted the approach of thinking about two separate topics: What planning should include (content) and how it should be done (organization and form).

CONOCO, AN ENERGY COMPANY

The planning system of CONOCO reflected the company's growth, organizational evolution and the styles of its chief executive. The company, which was organized in 1875 to peddle coal oil from wagons in Utah and Wyoming, referred to itself in 1971 as an "energy company" whose relevant sphere of operations lay in the finding, producing, and marketing of natural resources as fuels, chemicals, and plant foods. For most of CONOCO's life, the company's activities had been largely confined to petroleum operations in the western United States and Canada. But, during the period 1950-1971, CONOCO had expanded both its product line and market coverage enormously. New petroleum marketing areas throughout the United States and Western Europe had been successfully penetrated. Exploration, production, and refining activities had been expanded to match the growing market demand. The largest producer of coal in the U.S. had been acquired. New energy sources such as nuclear fuel were being developed.

Management Structure. The growth of the company also appreciably altered the tasks of top management. In particular, during the fifties and sixties the upper levels of management found themselves increasingly involved in issues concerning the coordination of CONOCO's far-flung operations. They were concerned that their effectiveness in controlling the corporation might be jeopardized. Intermediate layers of management were created to accommodate the company's growth. CONOCO entered new business areas such as coal, plastics, plant foods, and minerals. Because of these factors, top executives noted an ever-widening distance between themselves and subordinates with substantial operating authority.

Exhibit 1 CONTINENTAL OIL COMPANY TEN-YEAR FINANCIAL REVIEW, 1961–1970

(millions of dollars, except per share amounts)

	1970	1969	1968	1967	1966	1965	1964	1963	1962	1961
Source and Application of Funds										
Funds from operations	352.8	316.8	330.7	314.3	266.3	232.7	229.5	214.9	185.3	170.9
Addition to long-term debt	88.4	264.3	62.8	90.4	98.5	54.3	48.2	66.9	2.2	101.7
Issuance of equity securities	—	5.3	—	173.4	78.1	—	—	—	—	—
Property sales and other	55.0	71.1	72.2	31.8	75.2	18.8	31.3	36.6	71.4	15.0
Total sources of funds	496.2	657.5	465.7	609.9	518.1	305.8	309.0	318.4	258.9	287.6
Capital outlays	377.8	352.8	409.6	393.7	295.0	212.8	233.6	268.6	203.2	172.3
Dividends paid	85.5	85.7	81.0	71.6	61.0	59.0	52.0	45.2	41.7	41.2
Reduction of long-term debt	69.7	52.8	33.2	38.1	94.2	19.5	16.2	14.5	9.4	42.6
Other applications (net)	—	37.8	7.7	22.8	—	1.5	—	—	—	—
Total applications of funds	533.0	529.1	531.5	526.2	450.2	292.8	301.8	328.3	254.3	256.1
Increase (decrease) in working capital	(36.8)	128.4	(65.8)	83.7	67.9	13.0	7.2	(9.9)	4.6	31.5
Revenues										
Sales by product—Refined petroleum	1,175.4	1,014.3	970.9	909.5	782.5	671.0	627.3	583.1	523.7	477.5
—Excise taxes collected	200.5	179.5	168.7	150.2	145.4	140.5	134.8	126.2	115.6	109.4
—Crude oil	678.4	621.9	542.0	486.4	463.6	414.5	354.8	322.6	250.4	249.0
—Natural gas	78.4	70.1	64.5	61.0	58.1	51.2	48.2	42.8	36.0	26.6
—Coal	312.3	244.7	221.1	209.6	61.7					
—Chemicals and plastics	206.8	198.3	195.1	174.7	168.0	132.3	86.9	64.8	51.9	50.5
—Plant foods	121.9	122.2	137.8	155.3	158.2	142.6	118.5	102.0	83.6	83.2
Other sales and operating revenues	154.6	128.1	124.4	91.2	62.0	42.9	36.7	44.0	33.9	19.7
Nonoperating revenues	35.5	27.8	18.7	16.9	15.1	14.6	13.6	15.8	10.8	9.1
Total revenues	2,963.8	2,606.9	2,443.2	2,254.8	1,914.6	1,609.6	1,420.8	1,301.3	1,105.9	1,025.0
Costs, Expenses and Taxes										
Purchases of crude oil	645.5	570.4	520.2	449.5	443.5	406.2	357.7	314.9	267.5	270.4
Other purchases, costs, operating and general expenses	1,268.6	1,169.9	1,101.1	1,067.0	827.6	658.1	578.6	542.2	456.7	410.7
Depreciation, depletion and amortization	158.5	130.1	133.0	120.5	106.7	105.4	98.3	96.1	89.8	84.1
Dry hole costs	20.6	18.8	17.1	19.6	18.4	19.4	17.9	20.1	19.1	15.9

										1969
Interest and debt expense	10.7	12.3	14.4	15.0	17.1	18.6	23.4	29.0	39.8	**51.3**
Minority interest in subsidiaries' net income	3.2	4.1	5.2	5.5	6.4	7.7	8.5	11.3	11.6	**9.6**
Income taxes	8.8	7.2	12.3	11.9	45.9	89.0	92.4	91.4	91.8	**140.6**
All other taxes	152.9	175.4	208.7	235.8	254.9	287.5	337.8	390.1	428.1	**508.6**
Total costs, expenses and taxes	956.7	1,032.1	1,213.9	1,320.7	1,513.4	1,799.0	2,118.7	2,293.2	2,460.5	**2,803.3**

Earnings and Dividends

Earnings before extraordinary gains	68.3	73.8	87.4	100.1	96.2	115.6	136.1	150.0	146.4	**160.5**
Dividends on Preferred Stock[1]	4.1	4.1	4.1	4.1	4.1	4.1	4.0	3.4	1.7	**1.7**
Earnings applicable to Common Stock	64.2	69.7	83.3	96.0	92.1	111.5	132.1	146.6	144.7	**158.8**
Dividends on Common Stock	36.2	37.4	40.7	45.4	52.0	53.8	63.6	72.6	78.3	**78.1**
Extraordinary gains	—	—	—	—	—	41.3	12.9	—	10.7	**—**

Per Share Data Applicable to Common Stock

Earnings before extraordinary gains[2][3]	1.50	1.63	1.94	2.22	2.13	2.54	2.75	2.88	2.77	**3.06**
Dividends[3]	.85	.875	.95	1.05	1.20	1.225	1.325	1.425	1.50	**1.50**
Extraordinary gains[2][3]	—	—	—	—	—	.94	.27	—	.21	**—**
Book value[3][4]	14.82	15.53	16.65	17.91	18.85	21.93	24.26	26.09	27.22	**29.65**

Balance Sheet Data[4]

Net working capital	194.7	194.6	184.7	191.9	204.9	272.8	356.4	290.6	419.0	**382.2**
Ratio of current assets to current liabilities	2.50	2.22	1.96	1.95	1.80	1.64	1.93	1.66	1.83	**1.67**
Long-term debt	247.2	240.1	292.5	324.4	359.3	363.6	415.9	445.5	657.0	**675.6**
Minority interest in subsidiaries	34.0	34.2	41.9	38.9	42.3	50.0	82.1	91.8	94.2	**110.4**
Stockholders' equity	756.6	787.1	836.3	898.1	939.3	1,117.2	1,346.0	1,416.5	1,496.6	**1,525.1**
Total assets	1,270.9	1,319.8	1,462.8	1,554.4	1,679.5	2,069.8	2,354.5	2,537.4	2,896.6	**3,023.4**

1. Pro forma prior to October 21, 1963.
2. Based on weighted-average number of shares outstanding during the year.
3. Adjusted for share-for-share distribution declared February 1969.
4. At December 31.

Source: Continental Oil Company Annual Report; 1970.

The organizational evolution of CONOCO reflected the senior executives' attempts to maintain effective control over the direction of the company. In 1947, CONOCO was a small, closely knit, functionally organized oil company. However, throughout the fifties operations were expanded internally and by acquisition. The other regional oil companies that were acquired usually encompassed a new geographic market and were allowed to operate semiautonomously. Over a period of years the proliferation of regional general managers and the increasing technological complexity of basic operations demanded closer contact between regional operations and corporate staff. Regional general authority for domestic petroleum operations was diminished and the various regional functional departments were absorbed by their corporate counterparts. International petroleum operations, and the coal, petrochemicals and minerals businesses were acquired and/or organized as semiautonomous profit centers. The company maintained this organizational mixture of functional corporate petroleum departments and diversified profit centers until the late 1960s.

In August 1969, CONOCO underwent a structural reorganization accompanied by a management change. Overall operating responsibility shifted from Mr. Andrew W. Tarkington to Mr. John G. McLean. Mr. Tarkington was elevated from president to the twin posts of vice chairman of the board and chairman of the finance committee. Mr. McLean became the new president. Simultaneously, the company's operations were organized into four business areas, encompassing six operating divisions. Exhibit 3, on page 133, indicates the revised organization structure of CONOCO. The four business areas, Western Hemisphere Petroleum, Eastern Hemisphere Petroleum, Consolidation Coal Company, and CONOCO Chemicals, were each envisioned as major profit centers. The heads of these areas were each given the title of division president.

Mr. McLean, a former teacher of industrial organization, stated that the move from a largely functional to a "moderately decentralized organization" was intended "to strengthen the organization at the top." Mr. McLean expected a friendly rivalry to develop between the two petroleum divisions, which he said would "proceed somewhat independently." The president of each division was given general responsibility for his business area as well as a role in parent company management through membership in the Policy and Planning Committee.

Following are sketches of the four business areas:

The Western Hemisphere Petroleum Division was engaged in the full spectrum of the petroleum products industry from exploration through marketing to final consumers. This division, headquartered in Houston, Texas, held sole responsibility for petroleum operations in North and South America. The WHPD, as the division was termed, generated approximately one-half of the corporation's total revenues and two-thirds of its earnings. This operation ranked as the 14th largest producer of petroleum liquids in the U.S. The WHPD's operational emphasis was in 1971 being directed towards the location and development of additional oil and gas reserves, largely offshore.

The Eastern Hemisphere Petroleum Division ranked as the fifth largest U.S. producer of petroleum liquids abroad, providing over half CONOCO's total petroleum supply. The EHPD, as this division was termed, contributed approximately one fifth of CONOCO's revenues and earnings through integrated operations outside the Americas. Expansion had recently been rapid in the EHPD. Net undeveloped reserves were doubled in 1969 while crude oil production increased 16% and sales of refined products rose 28%. In 1970 EHPD's first wholly owned refinery commenced operations, completing the establishment of EHPD in all phases of petroleum operations. This division expected to continue its drive to become an important factor in the West European petroleum market based upon its substantial reserve position in North Africa and the Middle East.

The Consolidation Coal Company (CONSOL) was, in 1971, the world's largest producer of steam and metallurgical coal. Since its acquisition in 1966, CONOCO had approximately tripled the rate of capital investment in this division. Expansion had proceeded on several fronts. In research, CONSOL originated and developed the transport of coal by pipeline and had pilot programs in various stages of development designed to produce gasoline and high BTU gas from coal. Through new mine development, CONSOL expected to increase coal production by about one-third over the next few years.

The CONOCO Chemicals Division, engaged in converting crude oil, natural gas, and minerals into petrochemicals, plant foods, and plastics, contributed approximately 6% and 4% to CONOCO's revenues and earnings, respectively. This division, while small by CONOCO standards, ranked domestically as the largest manufacturer of organic detergent intermediates and among the ten largest manufacturers of vinyl plastic resins. Petrochemicals, plastics, and carbon black were produced in 31 locations throughout the world.

In addition, CONOCO conducted uranium exploration through drilling and planned the construction of an uranium mine-and-mill complex. Commercial production of nuclear fuel was expected in the early 1970s. CONOCO also participated in a joint venture researching the use of nuclear energy in mining, construction and the stimulation of oil and gas fields.

FORMAL PLANNING, TO 1968

Early Years. The first formal effort to institute long-range planning at CONOCO was initiated in 1953, by Mr. Leonard F. McCollum, the president at that time. Five-year financial plans, highlighting future sources and applications of funds, were requested from operating and staff managers.

This request keynoted a significant change in CONOCO's operating and financial policies. Mr. McCollum expressed the intention of breaking the company away from its historical role as a regional oil and gas company. He expected this expansion to require more funds than would be available under CONOCO's traditional, debt-free, financial policy. Mr. McCollum intended, therefore, to seek funds from outside sources. He anticipated that the company would have to strengthen its financial planning ability to satisfy the investment criteria of those sources and to insure that the funds secured would not threaten the financial flexibility of the company.

In the years after 1953, under the leadership of Mr. McCollum and his successors, the company continued to develop increasingly sophisticated financial planning tools and apply them to operating decisions. The five-year, essentially financially oriented, plan continued to serve as the nucleus of CONOCO's planning effort for the next 15 years.

Genesis of C&P.   Mr. Schwartz, who left Harvard Business School's doctoral program in 1957 to join CONOCO's Coordinating & Planning Department, spoke of the period prior to his arrival:

> From the information I have been able to piece together about the two or three years before I came to C&P, it appears that top management was still dissatisfied with the kind and level of control they had over operations.
> This became particularly apparent in the resource allocation process. Those corporate managers responsible for capital expenditure approvals began to suspect that lower level weeding-out processes were preventing them from even seeing projects which might be extremely beneficial for the company as a whole though not particularly beneficial for any single operating unit.
> Those same managers also felt that they were not getting enough background information on current operations, plans, and environmental factors to really contribute to the allocations process. The five-year plans were thought to be too narrowly financial in perspective and thus did not render explicit the actions and events which were expected to determine the stated financial results.
> To remedy the situation, Mr. McCollum strengthened the Coordinating & Planning Department in 1956 to (1) study the company's planning needs; (2) organize an effective approach to filling those needs; and (3) provide analytical support for Mr. McCollum in the development of his growth program.
> Mr. McLean was selected to organize and head C&P. Under his leadership the department became heavily involved in studies designed to improve the methods by which managerial decisions were made and to improve managers' understanding of their businesses.
> One of the former studies, undertaken in cooperation with the controller's

office, resulted in a wider and more uniform application of discounted cash
flow analysis in resource allocation decisions.

Some of the latter studies, undertaken jointly with operating departments, involved investigations of:

The breakeven price for purchased versus found crude oil reserves,
with indications of the relative profitability of onshore versus offshore
operations.
The attractiveness of CONOCO going abroad in its petroleum operations.

Mr. McLean headed C&P for about three years. During that time the
basic thrust of CONOCO's planning system for the next decade was
established. The five-year financial plan continued to serve as the basic
formal mechanism for long-range planning. Accountability for the
formulation and implementation of plans rested with the operating managers. The Coordinating & Planning Department supervised the collection and consolidation of operation units' plans, provided methodological advice as requested, and established itself as a source of economic,
environmental, and corporate policy information through its participation in studies of corporate policy and investment issues. C&P also
identified the corporate issues or possible uncertainities involved in the
proposed investments and plans for consideration by Executive Management.

Planning Process, Late Fifties to 1968. The annual planning cycle remained more or less unchanged from the late 1950's to 1968: 1) the C&P
Department performed preliminary, ten-year, economic forecasts and
established five-year, "bench mark," operational forecasts for dissemination as inputs to divisional plans; 2) corporate opportunities and strategies
were explored by Continental executives at a single meeting during the
spring of each year; 3) strategic issues arising out of the executives'
discussions were assigned for analysis to staff task forces consisting of
representatives of the concerned divisions and C&P; 4) drawing on the
experience and information derived from the above activities, individual
divisions prepared five-year plans during the summer; 5) the C&P Department presided over the uniform transmittal of division plans and
consolidated them for corporate review; 6) in the early fall the consolidated plans were reviewed by a standing committee of the company's top
managers and then presented to the board of directors for final approval.

Mr. Schwartz noted that the content of the plans submitted by the
operating units changed very little from 1956 to 1966. The plans contained "a statement of policies, programs, and expected results in a
somewhat abbreviated, narrative form with supporting quantitative data

contained in exhibits." The supporting material was often insufficient to appraise the merit of the plan.

Management Changeover.   Shortly before he relinquished his position as chief executive officer in 1966, Mr. McCollum created the Policy & Planning Committee (PPC) reporting to the board of directors. PPC gradually supplanted the Management Executive Committee which had functioned since the mid-fifties as the company's chief advisory body.

The membership of the two committees was nearly identical; both were comprised of the company's top executives. The Management Executive Committee had acted as an advisory committee to the president on operating matters. The purpose of PPC, however, was directed more towards guiding the company's future growth. This committee was intended to provide a high-level body for the generation and assessment of expansion opportunities, the evaluation of long-range plans, and the identification and investigation of issues of importance to corporate management. By contrast, the Management Coordinating Committee, identified in Exhibit 3, sprang up to provide a forum for the weekly exchange of operating information. This committee met very informally and had no decision-making authority or responsibility.

When Mr. Tarkington succeeded Mr. McCollum in the presidency of CONOCO the corporate goals changed little, although emphases were differently placed. Mr. Tarkington assumed operational responsibility at a time when there was considerable stringency in the nation's financial system. Also at that time, CONOCO's long-term debt to total capital ratio was approaching 30%. Mr. Tarkington modified CONOCO's investment and capitalization policies. The rapid growth in capital outlays was stopped, the maturities of long-term debt repayments were harmonized and CONOCO issued equity in 1967. (In retrospect, CONOCO's management felt that the sagacity of these policies was proven as the company maintained a position of financial strength and flexibility through the economic fluctuations of the late sixties and early seventies.)

Mr. Schwartz expressed the opinion that the years 1966-1968 probably witnessed "the very apex of CONOCO's formal planning system." Mr. Howard W. Blauvelt, the head of C&P in 1966, was charged by Mr. Tarkington with the responsibility of "expanding the planning activities and making planning a more vital and continuing part of the company's overall activities." Mr. Blauvelt greatly expanded the narrative section of the five-year plans and requested more substantial documentation of each of the projections contained therein. Then C&P began to perform a more detailed critique of each operating unit's plans, indicating areas of additional information needs, inconsistencies and potential coordination problems. Once the critique had been completed, C&P reorganized the plans into a standardized format, condensed, and rewrote the operating units' plans for corporate management's review.

FORMAL PLANNING 1968-1971

As CONOCO approached the 1968 planning cycle Mr. Tarkington decided that the heavier demands for quantitative information which had characterized the two previous years' planning had produced mixed results. On the one hand, the corporate staff had been able to build a bank of standardized, detailed data covering all of CONOCO's operations which provided helpful insight into performance of operating units. The availability of this information facilitated the kinds of strategic studies which C&P had been performing for the president and top level management committees since the mid-fifties. On the other hand, the formal requirements for more detailed plans had revealed that the projections and programs relating to years four and five in the five-year plans were little more than gross extrapolations of the first several years' plans. CONOCO's managers apparently felt reasonably comfortable and committed to thinking in concrete terms for two or three years, but considered effort expended on fourth and fifth year projections largely wasted. Mr. Schwartz and several line managers expressed the opinion that five years was neither long enough to accurately present most investment proposals nor short enough to allow an intensive consideration of operating programs.

To ensure that the planning system more adequately reflected the thinking, goals, and strategies of operating management and to promote critical thinking beyond the three-year horizon, the following changes were introduced in 1968's planning practices:

1. Projections and programs for years four and five were no longer required. The three-year plan which remained was termed the Action Plan.

2. Actions planned for the next three years were to be accompanied by several alternative programs together with the reasons for their selection or elimination.

3. Increased attention was to be allocated by operating units to studies of their environment and future beyond the three-year horizon of the Action Plans. Operating managers were particularly urged to consider more speculative growth projects.

A diagram of the planning process, as it occurred in 1970-71, is shown in Exhibit 4, on page 134.

Mr. Tarkington expressed the hope that the explicit delineation of short-term (3 years) and longer-term (4 to 20 years or more) planning horizons would encourage a more productive and effective effort on each. He stated:

> The thrust of the changes in our planning program will be to provide greater flexibility and responsibility to each business area to undertake

probing studies and develop appropriate courses of action. We expect that the benefits of these changes will be a greater degree of creativity in, and commitment to, our plans.

The Action Plan. The core of Continental's 1968-1970 planning activities was the Action Plan, prepared at the divisional level. Conceptually, action planning was expected to facilitate the achievement of corporate objectives by performing three functions:

1. motivating operating management to think ahead, identify key opportunities and challenges, define major goals, and to develop steps to attain the goals;
2. facilitating communication and coordination of operating activities and policies at, and through, all levels of management;
3. providing an explicit review of management plans and an information base for subsequent postauditing and control.

In essence, the Action Plans were alternative programs which covered all aspects of divisional operations. They provided a basis to evaluate rank and finally select from the proposals submitted. Upon final approval of the plans by corporate management, the first year of the Action Plans was hardened and became the basis for a more detailed, annual operating (termed by CONOCO the Profit Objective) and capital budget.

Annual action planning commenced in January when the president of CONOCO issued oral guidelines at meetings with key operating people (most notably the Policy & Planning Committee members). Mr. Schwartz commented:

> The thrust of the guidelines is the tentative allocation of resources among the diversified operations of the company. This is accompanied by a review of CONOCO's general earnings outlook, financial position, etc., so that the operating people share the same perspective (and problems) of the chief executive officer.
>
> The guidelines sessions are usually quite lively. There is a give and take of questions and comments which is eventually reported to the board of directors, enabling them to update their expectations and recognize the issues that confront operating management.

The president's guidelines and instructions were interpreted by the division presidents and transmitted to their functional departments and subsidiaries. The divisional instructions were generally detailed, precisely denoting the content and format of departmental plans and specifying deadlines for the submission of these plans to divisional management. Also as guidance, the divisions had their proposed Action Plan from the previous cycle with the Coordinating and Planning Department's commentary on it, as well as the final plan, approved by the board. Frequently, the chief executive officer would have traveled to the company's main operating centers to explain the thinking back of the approved plan.

Functional departments and subsidiaries then developed Action Plans during February and March. Operating management analyzed changes which had occurred since the previous year and formulated financial projections and supporting programs for the action planning period. Sufficient financial detail was required to ultimately permit the corporate controller to compile corporate pro-forma income statements and funds flows. The operating data provided had to enable division and corporate management to monitor changes and progress in selected variables affecting the company's operations. These variables included physical volumes, unit prices, revenues and costs, assets employed, etc.

Department managers and subsidiary heads were also asked to supplement their proposed plans by submitting statements containing the following information:

1. The department's major goals and objectives and the means by which they were expected to be achieved over the next few years.

2. Environmental conditions and assumptions underlying the financial projections; the effect of change in each key variable was to be quantified.

3. Brief descriptions of the major projects not yet approved but which had been incorporated into the financial projection.

4. Brief descriptions of more speculative projects not included in the financial projections but which might be initiated during the next five years, and their impacts on earnings.

5. A manpower requirements forecast complementing the proposed action programs.

6. A strategic study progress report providing brief information on the studies in progress and those desired studies which would not be initiated due to staff or financial limitations. The information expected to be included involved: a) the purpose of the study; b) the departments involved; c) progress to date; and d) the estimated completion date.

The departmental Action Plans were submitted to the respective division's Control and Planning & Economics Departments for review and consolidation. Following this staff review the Action Plans were presented to the Management Advisory Committee, comprised by the division president and department heads, for review and modification or tentative approval. The consolidated divisional Action Plans were then submitted to the corporate C&P and Controller's Departments.

The C&P and Controller's Departments critically reviewed with the division managements their respective Action Plans. The thrust of the controller's review, directed primarily at an examination of the accounting policies used and comparisons of financial projections with historical performance, was to affirm the integrity of the figures given in the plans. C&P's review was aimed at identifying any inconsistencies between plans, corporate guidelines, policies or operating and environmental information available to C&P through its review of other divisions' plans and strategic studies.

C&P's task was facilitated by the assignment of senior department personnel as advisors and observers to each division during the planning period. The presence of these people, Mr. Schartz had found, prevented many problems from developing and lessened the friction which sometimes occurred between divisions and C&P during review.

After the controller's and C&P's reviews, the Action Plans were consolidated and both the consolidated and division plans were examined by the Policy & Planning Committee. At that time division managers had the opportunity to present their reasons for any deviations from the president's guidelines. The committee discussed the divisions' plans and the corporate implications of these plans. Once the president had given his approval, the consolidated plans were presented to the board of directors in June. Upon final approval by the board, the Action Plan became the basis for the fall Capital Commitment Budget and the Profit Objective for the next year.

The Capital Commitment Budget.　　The annual capital budgeting process took place in the fall of each year. In September and October each year the divisions began to prepare their capital budget for the following year. These budgets included all the projects which the division wished to have approved in the following year. A member of the Coordinating and Planning group advised divisional management on his department's view of individual projects, but his advice was in no way binding on the operating managers. In November these budgets were reviewed by the Coordinating and Planning and the Controller's departments prior to an executive management review in December. At this review in December two processes took place:

1.　Establishment of the size of the budget for the next year.
2.　Determining the allocation of capital to each division by deciding which projects to leave out.

The size of the budget was determined by several considerations, the expected cash flow for the next year, the dividend payment required and the availability of external capital from debt sources given the debt level which had previously been determined. An additional problem in the oil industry was that exploration expenditures, which were reviewed with the capital expenditures budget, were largely expensed in the year occurred and had an impact on reported earnings. Therefore, the size of the exploration budget was dependent to some extent on the level of earnings desired.

The projects to be included in the budget were reviewed by the Management Executive Committee, which included all the chief operating managers of the divisions.

After the capital budget had been determined by the Management Executive Committee it was further reviewed by the Finance Committee and then finally by the board. Once approved, the division had authority to proceed on the capital expenditure appraisals that were included in the approved budget.

The Strategic Studies. Undertaken on a noncyclical basis, strategic studies were intensive and extensive analyses performed by staff personnel for executive and operating management. By this means, complex issues bearing upon the division's (and company's) future were given greater attention than individual managers could afford in terms of their other duties. Normally the responsibility for the initiation, progress, and presentation of strategic studies was assumed by the line manager responsible for the area to be studied. However, in instances in which studies required the extensive cooperation of two or more divisions, primary responsibility for conducting the studies was assigned to the Coordinating & Planning Department. For example, C&P coordinated the efforts of about 30 professional research, engineering, operating and economic people in analyzing the relative attractiveness of alternative processes to manufacture synthetic hydrocarbons.

Usually, major policy or investment issues were considered by formal task forces termed Strategic Study Committees, rather than by individuals. Committee members were selected on the basis of their expertise, availability, and ability to represent effectively the operating units' interests in the study of critical issues. The strategic study committees were often formally organized in three parts: 1) the committee chairman retained responsibility for the overall coordination and execution of the study; 2) the working committeemen were assigned responsibility for specific portions of the total task; and 3) an advisory group, composed of representatives drawn from corporate staff departments (Controller and C&P) and other interested operating divisions, functioned separately from the main body of the committee to provide objective opinions and recommendations regarding the committee's work.

The strategic study committees' activities typically involved the development and evaluation of various alternatives for allocating resources, taking into consideration Continental's position, industry trends, and competitors' actions. The recommendations often involved specific strategic actions to be performed during the planning period (usually 10-20 years) in the interest of enhancing Continental's long-term profitability growth. After the committee reported its findings and recommendations to the sponsoring management, it usually disbanded.

"There is no means," Mr. Schwartz said, "of assuring compatibility between studies' findings and division's Action Plans. The divisions are at liberty to submit plans and budgets at variance with prior corporate decisions or recommendations, but are then requested to provide written reasons for the variances. C&P, in its commentary during the review process will certainly point out any failure to do so!"

The United States Marketing & Supply Study (USMSS) was perhaps the best-known strategic study group in WHPD. Unlike most study groups, this committee had been in continuous existence for over five years. In 1971, USMSS was well-established as a fixture in WHPD's strategic planning and continued to develop "optimum long-range programs" for the division's refining, transportation and marketing operations.

The study had been initiated in the mid-sixties in an effort to coordinate and optimize market and transport activities east of the Rocky Mountains. It was soon realized that regional marketing and supply strategies could not be made independently. Concurrently, domestic petroleum operations were restructured, with regional authority subordinated to corporate functional authority. Responsibility for the study was picked up by the domestic Supply & Transportation Department which further broadened the perspective of the study to include nearly all of the other corporate functional departments. Following the 1969 decentralization of domestic petroleum operations, the functioning of USMSS became the responsibility of WHPD. The composition of the committee was as follows:

Department	Number of Representatives
Production	1
Refining	3
Computer	1
Marketing	2
Products Supply	1
Crude Transportation	1
Pipeline	1
Planning & Economics	1 (chairman)

The scope of the study had evolved to the point where one of its regular responsibilities was to provide annual guidelines for the formulation of the Action Plan and the Capital Budget. Consequently, the annual results of the study had to be available in July in order to influence capital expenditures. The USMSS also helped to assess how current decisions and future strategies could be expected to affect sales and earnings of the division in 10 to 20 years.

The analytical techniques used by the USMSS included several computer models for marketing, product supply and distribution, refinery design, scheduling, and the critical path method for the coordination and scheduling of information gathering and task performance.

The committee worked on major analyses, each of which involved a package of decisions that formed action programs consistent with selected strategies. Starting with environmental assumptions, the committee ran alternative action program simulations on computers to help determine the best strategy. The committee's principal problem lay in sound environmental appraisals and in internal data gathering, because for such projections inputs had to be provided by all the departments involved.

Mr. Schwartz considered USMSS one of CONOCO's most effective strategic studies. He stated that he could cite many instances in which the work of this committee had had a profound effect on management's thinking. For example, he noted that the acquisition of the Sequoia refinery in Ponca City, Oklahoma would probably never have been considered by division management without this committee's campaign for such a move. Division management had a strong "bias" for coastal refineries, because of long-term outlook for growing crude oil imports. However, USMSS "proved" that the Sequoia refinery's operations, coordinated closely with existing CONOCO facilities in Ponca City, could (1) be adequately supplied and (2) remain as competitive as a new coastal refinery.

THE ROLE OF THE COORDINATING & PLANNING DEPARTMENT

Mr. Schwartz estimated that his department's personnel (numbering 22) were, "about half new MBA's and half professional economists or experienced people from our operating departments." He went on to say, "We seek to get people who are analytically sharp and intellectually curious."

Many of CONOCO's top executives had at some time moved through or headed the department and had valued the experience through the breadth of exposure it afforded them. For example, besides Mr. Schwartz, the 1971 members of the Policy & Planning Committee included Messrs. McLean, Blauvelt and Morrow . . . all of whom had been members of C&P at an earlier time.

In addition to its role in the formal planning system, as previously outlined, the department undertook independent projects to guide executive management in long-range planning and investment decisions including: (1) individual and team work to analyze basic economic and political information and evaluate and forecast for the company's worldwide growth; (2) studies evaluating the results flowing from the corporation's major investment and operating decisions, including competitors' performance and ways to improve management control; and (3) evaluating new projects both for expansion and new businesses.

Mr. Schwartz indicated that within the past few years department studies on the desirability and the means of CONOCO entry into new business areas had been completed. Currently underway was more rigorous and definitive work on basic price projections for important products and the criteria used in considering capital budgets (e.g., right alternatives considered? fit with long-range plans? methods of enhancing profitability and/or diminishing risks? etc.).

Interface With the Rest of CONOCO.   Mr. Schwartz stated:

Historically, the company has had a number of strong, aggressive, entrepreneurially minded young line managers who are very good at smoking out opportunities for investment. This has been a considerable asset to the company and accounts for its rapid growth. However, the rate of expansion in the company's capital spending program is moderating. The C&P reviews, which are necessary to discriminate among proposals so only the highest quality ones can be selected, no doubt seem at times an impediment to bold, fast action.

Historically, there have been differences in analytical perspective between C&P and the operating departments. One key issue has been the matter of incremental analysis. In our opinion adding to the present operations as a base tends to favor existing areas of business (both from a product and geographic viewpoint) and to favor near-term over long-term considerations. Other groups did not see this as a disadvantage. In fact, C&P's frequent suggestion of departures from existing areas of business was considered by many operating managers to be ivory tower intellectualism. Over the decade of the sixties some, though not total, resolution of this difference in perspective had been achieved.

We have not always adopted the right approach in our dealings with the operating people. In part, we have had some learning to do ourselves. I fear that we tended in the earlier years to accuse our upstream brethren (in exploration and development operations) of a lack of planning. It might just as fairly be said we failed to come up with specific techniques to take economic considerations into account in the technical planning program. That is to say, we should have directed greater effort toward finding an explicit way of dealing with the uncertainties they faced in translating geological and technical information into economic terms which would facilitate the evaluation of alternative programs.

These difficulties aside, I think C&P has played an important role in influencing major company moves, and I believe that this view is shared by most line managers. Some line managers come to us for considerable informal counselling—they want to have a dry run on their forward thinking. Others tend to minimize contact to the essentials of the budget and action planning. They evidently feel that our contribution is in succinct reporting rather than new insights. Indirectly, C&P attempts to be involved in most major studies, particularly at the beginning (definition of scope and methodology) and at the end (interpretation of findings and the recommendations).

I believe operating management eventually places considerable weight on the findings of our in-depth studies. Reactions are not instantaneous, of course, and this is a frustration to any staff man. Our former chief executive officer, Mr. McCollum, once told me that a large corporation is like a ship—it turns a few degrees at a time. Any attempt to make a very sharp turn might capsize it. On another occasion, he told a meeting, assembled to discuss recommendations of a task force which were not endorsed by the line management, that he had to support the line managers—at least until such time as he became convinced that the staff people had better over-all grasp of the situation. At that time he would promote the staff people to the line jobs!

Mr. Schwartz went on to say:

In fact, there are some significant differences between C&P-controlled studies and operator-controlled studies. We (C&P) are more inclined to gloss over the intricacies of the existing situation (because we understand it less perfectly) and to strive for a broader-gauged study (a study which considers a wider range of alternatives). Extreme alternatives, like "sell the entire operation," is the ultimate difference between an "objective" C&P study and a "vested" departmental study!

In the more important middle ground of alternatives, C&P is a little less likely to be influenced by current developments and instead to rely on long-term trends. Sometimes this causes us to miss a turning point which the operators have spotted. We (C&P and operators) increasingly spend time in dialogue in these areas in the hope that this will improve both the operators' imaginativeness in options considered and our perceptiveness with regard to the input data. Specific people in C&P are assigned for this purpose.

Mr. Schwartz concluded his remarks saying:

My definition of our (C&P's) purpose reflects my bias towards the needs of our executive management—the resource allocation process. Planning seeks to rationalize the allocation of scarce resources to alternative uses. A formal planning system's purpose is to assure that these decisions are made in a timely fashion on the basis of a complete and objective assessment of all relevant knowledge, projections and conjecture. I am sure that our operating people would say that the system, if it works well, serves to upgrade their efforts—they can develop projects, etc., with a surer knowledge of what our top management expects from them and itself.

I might note, parenthetically, that C&P is involved in setting the ground rules and running the system. I like to think of C&P as a high fidelity record player in which I'm the needle. The divisions press the records (plans) and play them awhile to see if they like what they hear. When the records are played to corporate management, I want both the recorders and the listeners to be sure that they are getting a complete and accurate rendition.

Exhibit 2 CONTINENTAL OIL COMPANY   PROFILE, MR. McLEAN*

PERSONALITY

Conoco President Encourages Innovation

By WILLIAM D. SMITH

The credentials of John G. McLean are impeccably establishment.

He is a trustee of the Presbyterian Church, lives in Darien, Conn., golfs and sails, was a professor at the Harvard Business School, and is now the president and chief executive officer of one of the nation's major corporations, the Continental Oil Company.

Yet the chief tenet of his management philosophy could be paraphrased "power to the people."

"To remain successful, a big company must encourage the development of individual centers of initiative and interest. I mean groups of six, eight, or 10 people under a strong leader, who are interested, imaginative and enthusiastic about what they are doing."

"We must encourage such groups to use initiative and place a minimum of restraints upon them. Better they should be alive and active, even though we may not always like what they do, than they be tightly controlled and unresponsive."

Mr. McLean grinned as he added, "I've seen some pretty odd suggestions and plans cross my desk, but you have to give people a chance to run —otherwise they stand around marking time."

The small, gray-haired executive's second management tenet would also be close to the heart of impatient, anti-establishment types. "I try to make decisions as quickly as possible and encourage other Conoco executives to do the same. A major curse of large corporations is the time it takes to get decisions made."

Mr. McLean is direct but soft-spoken. He smiles easily but always seems to be completely aware of every word he says.

John McLean was born in Oregon but grew up in Santa Barbara, Calif., where his father was a Presbyterian minister. His grandfather and great grandfather, who had come over from the Isle of Mull in Scotland, were also Presbyterian ministers.

Mr. McLean followed his older brother to the California Institute of Technology, where he studied physics. "Actually I spent most of my time in extra-curricular activities. I was president of the student body and of the

*Reprinted from the New York Times, Sunday June 28, 1970

senior class and played varsity football and track." He added wryly, "Cal Tech is probably the losingest school in the history of intercollegiate athletics."

Physicist, athlete, class leader next went to the Harvard Business School, "which opened up a whole new world to me."

"I became totally involved, and I devoted all my time to work." After graduating in 1940, he was asked to stay on as a research assistant.

Mr. McLean stayed a while, 15 years to be exact, during which time he received his doctorate and rose to the rank of full professor. "It was a fine life."

He also found time to act as a consultant to oil companies and wrote a book called "The Growth of Integrated Oil Companies."

In 1954 he took a leave of absence to work as an assistant to the president of Continental Oil. Two years later he had to decide whether to return to Harvard or remain in industry. He chose industry, and was named vice president of Continental in charge of coordination and planning.

When Mr. McLean joined the company in 1954, Continental had earnings of $41.6-million on revenues of $500-million. In 1969 Conoco earned $146.4-million from operations on revenues of $2.6-billion.

In 1954 Continental was a provincial domestic oil company, some of whose officers vowed, "We will never put bricks and mortar overseas." Despite these views the company began to make moves overseas, and Mr. McLean began to become more and more involved. In 1958 Continental as part of a consortium with Marathon and Amerada discovered big oil in Libya.

Mr. McLean was named financial vice president in 1959 and became deeply involved in the complicated negotiations to sell the Libyan oil in Europe. From that point he became more and more an expert in the company's foreign operations and plans. "It was partly fascinating and partly self-serving. I realized that this was a growth area and one in which I could get in on the ground floor since we were just starting to become an international oil company."

In 1963 he was named chairman and managing director of the Continental Oil Company, Ltd., in London with responsibility of spearheading the company's drive into European markets. A year later he was brought back to New York to become vice president in charge of European international operations. "My wife and I hated to leave. In a year we had found a real home in London."

In 1968 he was named executive vice president in charge of international affairs with responsibility for Continental's activities in more than 30 countries. When Mr. McLean joined the company, it had had interests in Egypt, British Somaliland and Italian Somaliland.

Mr. McLean was named president and chief executive officer of Continental in September, 1969.

He defined his goals for Continental last week quietly but confidently with a faintly professional air. "My chief objective is to build a steady growth in our share earnings.

"We can make money doing anything, but the way to score big is to find natural resources. We have gone out and gotten exploratory acreage. Continental now controls more than 400 million gross acres.

"This is more than any other company in the world. We think we have the finest set of exploratory acreage in existence. Our exposure-to-discovery is outstanding."

Mr. McLean ticked off the locations—"North Sea, Libya, Dubai, Iran, and we have vast acreage in the South China Sea."

Despite the present accent on discovery, Mr. McLean is a firm believer in an integrated oil operation. "We believe we will hit it big in the South China Sea, and we already have many laying the groundwork for the integrated company that will follow the oil, if we find it."

Mr. McLean is hopeful about the future of the international oil business. "The companies should press forward when they are right, but must be flexible. Oil companies can't fight rear-guard actions with foreign governments. Oilmen must take forward-looking positions, not keep trying to reclaim the past."

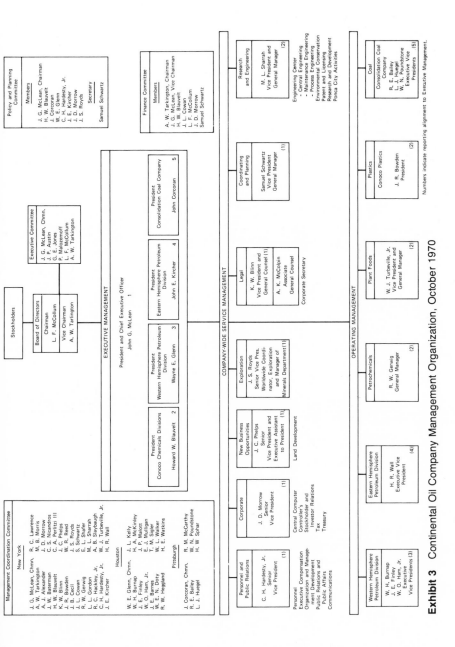

Exhibit 3 Continental Oil Company Management Organization, October 1970

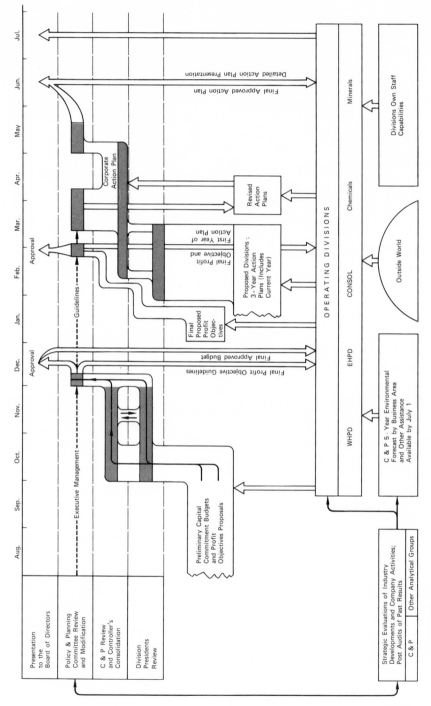

Exhibit 4

PART TWO

Situational Design

The second part of the book explores in detail the most critical factors in the design of formal planning systems. The central idea is that planning systems must be tailored to an individual company's circumstances in terms of its goals-setting process, the planner's role, linkage of planning and budgeting, and management control processes. In Part I we presented the conceptual foundation for our approach to strategic planning and provided a framework consisting of three levels of strategy and three cycles of planning. We stated that the task of designing a planning system would be one of tailoring the system to a given unique corporate setting, but deferred the discussion of how such contingent design of planning systems might take place. Instead, we offered several generally applicable musts for planning. In this part we will return to and specifically address the question of situational design.

The first reading, "How to Design a Strategic Planning System," distinguishes between the task of designing a planning system for a larger, typically divisionalized and diversified corporation versus a smaller corporation, typically functionalized and with less product diversity. Another important situational factor under discussion is whether the planning system is relatively new or more mature and well established. There are other important situational factors in addition to the two contingencies, size/diversity and age of system. However, as we introduce more contingencies, it becomes impossible to draw valid generalizations about the choice of systems design factors. We have, therefore, elected to delimit the choices, allowing for further individual tailoring of each case.

Six strategic planning systems design issues are identified. These are the degree of explicitness in the communication of corporate goals; the "top-down/bottom-up" flavor of the goals-setting process; the strategic versus statistical nature of the corporate environmental scanning effort; the strategic versus financial nature of the subordinate managers' planning focus; the role of the corporate planner; and the degree of linkage between planning and budgeting. Each of these design issues should be solved differently according to the situational setting. A second important aspect of contingency design is also stressed, namely the need to keep redesigning the planning system in response to the changes that take place both in and outside the company. Thus, the task is not completed even when a system has been successfully tailored to a given corporate setting; a continuing updating of the system will also be required.

The second reading, "Role of the Corporate Planning Executive," deals with the planner's role. Potentially, there are several alternatives for the corporate planner, and what will be the appropriate role depends on the specific corporate setting. For the corporate planner to be effective, a working relationship must be maintained with three classes of executives, the chief executive, the line management, and other staff, particularly the controller's office. Four classes of situational contingency factors are identified as important for dictating what would be an effective role for the planner. First, the state of the planning system itself might be important—new or old; internally developed, or "prepackaged, off-the-shelf." Second, the type of industry might be important—old and static versus technological and dynamic, for example. Third, the company itself, in terms of corporate atmosphere, may be important. Finally, the style of the key executives involved, particularly the chief executive, may be significant. Depending on the particular set of contingencies, three different roles for the corporate planner are identified. He can be a "broker" who will be solely concerned with maintaining the planning system and will not play any role in deciding on the substantive issues of the plans. Alternatively, he might be an "advisor" who will offer his own opinions on the plans, in addition to maintaining the system. Finally, he might be an "evaluator" and have an even greater substantive influence. There will be no universally best role, however; this will depend on the situational setting.

The third reading, "Balance Creativity and Practicality in Formal Planning," is concerned with how to link the longer range planning activity with more near-term budgeting. A loose linkage might foster a more creative, innovative approach to the planning activities; a tight linkage might lead to more realism and action orientation. How much linkage will be appropriate will vary with the situational setting. An inappropriate balance might result from too much linkage, that is, too little creative adaptation to new environmental opportunities. Alternatively, and just as bad, too little linkage might lead to unrealistic and irrelevant planning.

Three major types of linkage between planning and budgeting are then discussed. Content linkage addresses the question of how directly the content of the budget and the first year of the long-range plan match each other, in terms of degree of specificity, reconciliation of differences, and explanation of differences from what was said last year. Organization linkage is concerned with the degree of overlap in responsibility among executives for administering the planning and control processes. If the controller is directly involved with both systems, then there is tight linkage; if the corporate planner and the controller report to different corporate executives, then we have an example of loose organizational linkage. Finally, we have timing linkage, referring to the sequencing of the planning and budgeting activities; if there are large gaps in the time schedule between the two activities, or if all activities are "packed in" during a short time period, then we have examples of loose timing linkage.

The question of what will be an appropriate degree of linkage is, of course, entirely dependent on the situational setting. Further, as this setting commonly might change, there is a need to manage the evolution of the degree of linkage. For instance, a division that goes through a life cycle set of stages for its product thrust—from early growth with consumption of more funds than it generates, through balancing the funds inflows and outflows, through a period of "milking" the division, that is, generating more funds than consumed—might have a plan-budget linkage that starts out loose but is gradually tightened.

The final chapter of Part II, "Divisional Planning: Setting Effective Direction," examines the question of what might be good practices for the business planning activities of the divisions and how to ameliorate some potential pitfalls. Useful divisional planning practices include an analysis of a product's position along a business attractiveness dimension, such as the market's growth rate, as well as along a dimension capturing the strength of one's own position, such as one's market share. The effects of a planned program can then be judged according to how it will reposition the product and what the funds flow implications will be. Other useful tools include a practice of first planning strategic programs across the functions of the division, each function manager preparing his own budget. This ensures both strategic direction and proper coordination and control. Thirdly, appropriate procedures for the "staging" of a project in its development from one function to another must be developed.

In addition to these practices, the divisions will commonly have to strengthen their planning efforts to cope with two additional problems. First, it is often unrecognized that the division might tend to be overly risk-aware in its selection of projects. As a result, the corporation often misses out on potential high profit projects, which would be viewed as less threatening in light of the overall risk-distribution of the corporate portfolio. The second problem area is that a strategic project analysis which only considers a product along the business attractiveness and competitive strength dimensions might be too simplistic. A third dimension will be needed that addresses how well the project fits into the overall divisional and corporate picture in terms of both cash flows and synergy effects.

Each of the four cases in Part II raises aspects of the issue of how to tailor the strategic planning system, or parts of it, to a given corporate setting. Many of the same systems design considerations will emerge in all cases, but we will see that the choice of design configuration often will be different, reflecting distinctive situational settings.

In the Massey-Ferguson case, we are faced with a worldwide corporation pursuing a set of business activities that are highly interdependent and require careful integration. The planning system has evolved over a long time and is heavily formalized. The goals-setting process is heavily top-down-oriented, Massey-Ferguson's planning system being an archetype of this approach. We shall soon have an opportunity to see how this contrasts with the bottom-up approach in the Quaker Oats case. A second major issue is the question of linkage between the plan and the budget. Given Massey-Ferguson's objectives, chief among which is the efficient development of its existing businesses rather than further diversification, a planning system with heavy emphasis on integration is described.

The second case, State Street Boston Financial Corporation, discusses planning in a company that is in a rather traditional industry, namely banking, but which has undergone a large influx of nontraditional banking executives, including a chief executive and a corporate planner who are new on the job. The bank's willingness to go new ways has resulted in development of such management systems computer-based MIS, MBO, and performance measurements. The strategic planning activity faces several challenges, such as how to get executives involved who are operating in a traditional business climate and often with an industry-specific background. The objective of the planning activity is to strengthen the environmental adaptation capabilities of the bank; this is, to identify and implement new venture opportunities and respond quicker to changes. A long list of issues is raised regarding the role of the corporate planner.

The Quaker Oats Company case too often offers a unique situational corporate setting: a business diversification drive has led to a recent reorganization into business divisions, and as a consequence the previous planning system is obsolete and a new system is being introduced. This system is relying heavily on a bottom-up, goals-setting process. The case raises in particular the design issue of planning-budgeting linkage: what is an appropriate degree of linkage in this contingency setting, given Quaker's present objectives for appropriate adaptation-integration balance in its system? All three classes of linkage issues, contact, organization, and timing, are apparent in this case.

The final case in the situational design section of the book, Galvor Company, describes an integrated, elaborate planning, and control system as it has been developed within a major multinational, highly diversified corporation. The case focuses on the business planning task within a division and the corporate-divisional planning interface. The planning system features an interactive top-down/ bottom-up balance and a three-cycle narrowing down of strategic options. Thus, many of the features of the conceptual planning model described in Part I of this book are apparent, as they are in the top-down approach at Massey-Ferguson and the bottom-up approach at Quaker Oats. The case also spells out in detail which variables go into the business plan. It is worthwhile to compare this with our discussion of divisional planning in Part I, and ask what would be an appropriate choice of variables for business planning—again a situational planning systems design issue. Another situational design issue not raised before is what would be an appropriate sequence of feedbacks from plans, requirements for plan revisions, and for follow-up corrective actions. A final prominent situational design issue deals with whether it is appropriate to implement standardized, elaborate, highly formalized planning systems in all divisions, irrespective of size and/or nature of business differences.

1

HOW TO DESIGN A STRATEGIC PLANNING SYSTEM*

PETER LORANGE AND RICHARD F. VANCIL

Every business corporation does strategic planning, although the formality of that process varies greatly from one company to the next. Conceptually, the process is simple: managers at every level of the corporate hierarchy must ultimately agree on a detailed, integrated plan of action for the coming year, and they arrive at that agreement through a series of steps starting with the delineation of corporate objectives and concluding with the preparation of a one or two-year profit plan.[1] As a practical matter, however, the design of that process—deciding who does what, when—can be fairly complex. And our experience shows that the design of a strategic planning process can be crucial to the success of the planning effort.

A strategic planning *system* is nothing more than a structured—that is, designed—*process* that organizes and coordinates the activities of the managers who do the planning. There is no universal, off-the-shelf planning system for the simple reason that companies are different in terms of their size, the diversity of their operations, the way they are organized, and the style and philosophy of their managers. An effective planning system requires "situational design"—it must take into account the specifics of a particular company's situation, especially along the dimensions of size and diversity.

In this chapter, we shall attempt to provide some guidelines for the design of strategic planning systems, hoping that the reader recognizes that, for the reasons just stated, such generalizations can be treacherous. We do not aspire to prescribe the specifics of a planning system for your company; you must do the final tailoring. But some useful generalizations are possible, particularly in distinguishing between large companies vs. small ones and between highly diverse companies vs. less diverse ones. As a general statement, size and diversity of operations go hand-in-hand, although there are many exceptions to that rule. Several of the billion dollar airlines, for example, are essentially in one business, and there are

---

* (Reprinted from Harvard Business Review, Sept.-Oct. 1976).
[1] These steps are described in detail in Part 1, Reading 2.

also a number of miniconglomerates with sales of less than one hundred million that have divisions in disparate industries. For convenience in this discussion, we shall talk about companies as "large" or "small," defining those labels in terms of a set of typical characteristics shown in Exhibit 1.

Exhibit 1 TYPICAL CHARACTERISTICS OF "LARGE" AND "SMALL" COMPANIES

	"Large" Companies	*"Small" Companies*
Annual sales revenue	More than $100 million	Less than $100 million
Diversity of operations	Two or more different industries	Single industry
Organization structure	Product divisions	Functional departments
Industrial expertise of corporate management	Less than that of divisional subordinates	Greater than that of functional subordinates

While your company may not match up neatly along either set of characteristics, understanding why an effective strategic planning system is different in these two types of companies may enable you to design a system that fits your situation. It should also be noted that the characteristics of "small" companies also describe a "typical" division in a large, diversified firm. Thus, division managers in such firms can follow the discussion below at two levels simultaneously:

(1) their role as a part of the corporate planning process, and

(2) their role in the strategic planning for their own "small" business.

We have identified six issues on which an explicit choice must be made in the design of a strategic planning system. For each of these issues the proper choice for large companies, in most cases, will be different than for small companies. The issues are:

1. Communication of goals for corporate performance.
2. The goal-setting process.
3. Environmental scanning.
4. Subordinate managers' focus.
5. Role of the corporate planner.
6. Linkage of planning and budgeting.

Each of these design issues is described in turn below, along with a brief discussion of why the design choice is different in the two corporate settings.

COMMUNICATION OF GOALS FOR
CORPORATE PERFORMANCE

A common problem in the design of a formal planning system occurs when second-level managers request corporate guidelines in order to focus the preparation of their strategic plans. Such managers, faced with the uncertainty of how to tackle the planning assignment, may ask, implicitly or explicitly, "Tell us where you want us to go and what you expect from us by way of performance, and we'll present a plan of how to achieve it." These questions are not unreasonable, but acceding to them may violate the very purpose for which strategic planning is being undertaken. To determine how goals should be communicated and how specific they should be is an important design issue for the planning system, and the "right" answer will differ from company to company.

Small companies

When the president of a small company (or the general manager of a division of a diversified firm) initiates a strategic planning process, he shares with his functional subordinates his thoughts about the objectives and strategy of the business. In most situations, however, he does not make explicit his performance goals for the business. Instead, he asks his functional managers to devise a set of *action programs* that will implement the strategy of the business in a manner consistent with its objectives. All the managers involved know that one result of the "programming" process will be a mutually agreed-upon set of performance goals for the business, but they also realize that there is no need to anticipate the results of their planning efforts by trying to establish goals before the programs have been created and evaluated. This would be unnecessarily time-consuming and burdensome, and might create false expectations among the functional managers.

The programming process is oriented much more toward the analysis of alternative actions than toward the establishment of corporate goals. The primary reason for this is that the functional managers involved in programming tend to have (properly) a parochial point of view. They have a somewhat shorter time horizon than the president and focus their attention on one special function of the business. The president is the only executive who puts all the functional pieces together. He is the one who decides which subset of alternative action programs should be selected in order to achieve the goals that he has set for the business. Functional managers do not need to know what the president's performance goals are, only that he wants them to recommend the best possible set of action programs.

Because of its action orientation, the programming process tends to have relatively little continuity from one year to the next. The objectives and strategy of the business may not change, but each year it is necessary to reexamine all existing programs and try to devise new ones. Thus, even though the programming activity commonly uses a time horizon of three to five years, relatively little attention is paid to the tentative goals established in the preceding year. The focus, instead, is on the current situation, on the best set of action programs now, and on the development of an achievable goal for the forthcoming year.

Large companies

The diversity of the portfolio of businesses facing corporate management in large companies is often so great that their capacity for in-depth perception and familiarity with each business diminishes. Consequently, corporate management has to rely on the relatively unconstrained inputs from the divisions.

Division managers do heed corporate guidance in the form of broad objectives, but it is usually desirable for top management to delay the development of an explicit statement of performance goals for the corporation. This forces the division manager to think through his business with a long-term, external focus; the fewer constraints placed on his thinking, the better. Another reason for delaying the specification and communication of corporate goals to division managers is that corporate management is also changing the approach it takes to an old task. In the absence of a formal strategic planning process, corporate management may have developed explicit goals for itself, but it cannot be sure that the goals will seem appropriate when viewed in the context of a set of independently-arrived-at divisional goals. Divisional recommendations permit corporate management to do a better job of corporate goal setting.

THE GOAL-SETTING PROCESS

A major issue in the design of a planning system is the goal-setting process itself. From the point of view of the division manager, are the division's goals to be established by corporate management or by the division manager himself? This issue is sometimes cast as a dichotomy, the choice being between "top-down" goal setting or "bottom-up" goal setting. As a practical matter, of course, both corporate and divisional management must agree upon divisional goals. An important issue, however, concerns which level in the hierarchy initiates or first suggests what the divisional goals should be. The same issue arises between the general manager and functional managers of a homogeneous firm. The design of the planning system can have a strong influence on how this issue is resolved.

Small companies

The goals for a small company that emerge from the programming process are tied to an approved set of action programs. Until the president has decided which programs should be approved, it is impossible for each of the functional managers to set goals for his sphere of activity. Once a set of action programs is selected, therefore, the performance goals for each functional department are more or less automatically determined. In this sense, functional goal setting is a top-down process. The functional managers propose action programs, but it is the president with a businesswide perspective who decides which programs to undertake and what the goals for his functional subordinates should be.

Large companies

When it comes to tailoring the corporate-divisional goal-setting process in a large company with a relatively diversified set of businesses, "capacity limitations" at the corporate level will dictate a relatively bottom-up approach. A major share of the goal-setting initiative should probably come from the divisions, since intimate knowledge of the industry-specific set of business conditions will be necessary.

Initiating an effective corporate-divisional goal-setting climate in a large company can be tricky. For the first year or two of a formal planning effort, the best approach in most situations is to allow the initiative for recommending divisional goals to rest on the division manager. This approach serves to enhance his sense of running his own business and encourages broad strategic thinking at the divisional level. Subsequently, after the corporate and divisional managers have had some experience in hammering out a mutually agreeable set of divisional goals, the division manager's annual proposal for divisional goals will not be as unconstrained as in the early years. It should be stressed that divisional goal setting is really a negotiation and, although it is formalized as an annual event in the planning process, the cumulative experience of previous negotiations tends to improve the effectiveness of the goal-setting process. Top corporate management can help to nurture this development by creating a system that maintains a proper top-down/bottom-up balance, given the particular situational constraints. In part, this may be accomplished by withholding an explicit statement of corporate goals for the first year or two, while requiring the division manager to recommend goals for his division.

ENVIRONMENTAL SCANNING

A strategic planning system has two major functions: to develop an integrated, coordinated, and consistent long-term plan of action, and to facilitate *adaptation* of the long-term efforts of the corporation to changes in the environment. When introducing and developing a formalized system for strategic planning, a common tendency is to concentrate on the *integrative* aspects of the system. Designing the system to focus explicit effort on the task of environmental scanning will help to assure that the planning effort also fulfills its adaptive mission.

Corporate management of both large and small companies will usually wish to provide all subordinates with a more or less detailed set of forecasts and assumptions about the future business environment. Since each manager, initially at least, will be doing the strategic planning for his sphere of responsibility more or less independently of his counterparts, corporate management will be aided in its task of reviewing plans and proposals if all managers have used the same set of economic and other environmental forecasts.

Small companies

Corporate environmental scanning in small companies is a strategically oriented analytic task that can go far beyond the mere gathering of data about markets, competitors, and technological changes. For example, a company that has a large share of the market for a consumer product used primarily by middle and upper-income teen-agers and young adults might devote considerable effort to analyzing demographic trends and changes in per capita income. A fairly accurate forecast of the size of the total market five years hence is possible, and would be useful in appraising the potential for corporate growth. Similarly, companies involving products with rapidly changing technology may devote more attention to forecasting future technological advances, and those operating internationally will appraise political trends in foreign countries.

Large companies

In large companies, this task of monitoring detailed environmental changes is too immense to be performed by top corporate management alone. Division management, therefore, will be expected to study the external environment that may be relevant to their particular business. Typically, in these circumstances corporate managers will provide only a minimal number of environmental assumptions, primarily statistical economic forecasts, in order to reinforce the importance of division thinking about future environmental conditions.

Corporate environmental scanning may play an additional important role in large companies that are interested in further diversification through acquisitions. Division managers can do little to assist in this important strategic task, so an important determinant for the success of an acquisition program will be the quality of the corporate scanning effort. Needless to say, adequate attention to this scanning effort will be particularly crucial for the aggressive, highly diversified corporation.

SUBORDINATE MANAGERS' FOCUS

What should be the focus of the second-level managers involved in a corporate strategic planning effort? What roles will the division manager, the functional manager, and top management play? We shall consider these questions in terms of whether plans should be relatively more quantitative or qualitative; more concerned with financial detail or with broad strategic analysis.

Small companies

Preparing a functionally coordinated set of action programs for a small company may require a great deal of cross-functional communication. Much of this interchange is most efficiently expressed in dollar or other quantitative terms, such as numbers of employees, units of product, square feet of plant space. Focusing on financial or quantitative data in devising or reviewing a set of action programs is appropriate for two reasons. First, it helps to insure that each functional manager understands the specific dimensions of a proposed program and has thought through the implications of executing it. Second, dealing with the financial implications of alternative programs in some detail permits the president to select more confidently the subset of programs to be implemented. In practice, the financial and quantitative aspects of functional planning become progressively detailed as the programming process continues, culminating in very specific plans that constitute the operating budget.

Large companies

In a diversified larger corporation the aim of corporate management is to insure that a timely strategic outlook is taken by each division, and the focus of division management is primarily on achieving that outlook. Division managers should be permitted to develop as much financial detail to support their proposals as they think is desirable, particularly during the early years of planning. This permissiveness may result in the creation of more financial detail than is really necessary for strategic business planning. After a year or two, therefore, the corporate requirements for financial detail to support division proposals should be made explicit—and should be explicitly minimal. Division managers should be asked to shift the focus of their efforts to the identification and analysis of strategic alternatives, using their expertise to estimate quickly the financial implications of these alternatives. This new focus is the one that was intended from the beginning, of course, but it is difficult to achieve at the outset of formal planning. Failing to shift the focus is an even greater danger; the planning activity will become a "numbers game" and will never achieve its purpose.

Considering that, prior to the initiation of a formal planning activity, the division manager may never have seen or prepared long-range financial projections for his business, preparing them should be a useful activity in itself. Such projections help him to lengthen the time horizon of his thinking; he is being asked to make his intuitive economic model of the business more explicit to be able to forecast changes in the financial performance of the business. The result is that, the first time through a formal planning process, a division manager's efforts tend to be financially oriented and, in many respects, analogous to long-range budgeting. Corporate management, which is aware of the new pressures that formal planning poses for a division manager, should design the formal requirements of the system to mitigate these pressures.

One important caveat for the chief executive of a large company: he should never allow himself to get so involved in the development of business plans that he is trying to do the planning job on behalf of the division managers. Such interference might inhibit the division from coming up with a realistic business plan to which it will commit itself.

ROLE OF THE CORPORATE PLANNER

A major issue in the design of the planning system is the role to be played by the corporate planner himself. It must be emphasized that strategic planning is a line-management function. A sure route to disaster is to have plans produced by staff planners and then issued to line managers. Strategic planning is essentially a people-interactive process, and the planner is one of the cast of characters involved. He needs to have a clear understanding of what his proper role is if the process is to function effectively. It is important to distinguish between the corporate planner's function in large and small companies because their roles are quite different.

Small companies

The planner's role in a small company (or a product division of a large company) is effectively that of staff planning assistant to the president (or the general manager) of a business. He must coordinate the planning activities of the functional managers, but he is even more concerned with the problem that his general manager faces in selecting the best subset of alternative action programs. Only the general manager—and his staff planning assistant—have a businesswide perspective of the alternatives, and it is the assistant who must do the bulk of the analysis. Cast in this analytical role, the planner may become a very influential member of the general manager's executive team. If he uses his power sensitively, his effectiveness with his peers running the functional departments need not be diminished. They can appreciate the need for a cross-functional analysis of program alternatives. The entire team is searching for the "right answer," in the substantive sense of the right package of action programs. Managing the planning process is an almost incidental role for the general manager's planning assistant in that he merely formalizes the analysis that leads to a coordinated set of action programs.

Large companies

The corporate planner's organizational status in a large company can have significant symbolic value in conveying to division managers both the importance of formal strategic planning and the difference between it and conventional budgeting. The corporate planner's role is best conceived of, initially, as that of a catalyst, trying to encourage all line managers to adopt a strategic orientation. He is trying to help corporate management do a better job of resource allocation among the divisions, and one way to do that is to assist the division managers in strategic planning for their businesses.

The planning system may be seen as setting the "rules of the game" for planning. Managing and implementing the system should be an explicitly stated management task and assigned to the corporate planner. Since systems maintenance and coordination is the primary function of his job as the planning effort matures, he should have a thorough understanding of the working of a planning system to be able to monitor its evolution and maintain consistency.

LINKAGE OF PLANNING AND BUDGETING

The chronological steps in a typical planning system represent an orderly and gradual process of commitment to certain strategic alternatives. Each step in the process is, theoretically at least, linked to the steps that preceded it. In financial terms, this linkage may be quite explicit; a division's profit forecast prepared in the first planning cycle may subsequently become the profit commitment for next year's operating budget. Although few companies expect to achieve this financial linkage in narrowing down the alternatives, all the parties involved in the process should understand the intended relationship between the cycles. How fast or slow this narrowing down should be is a situational design question, depending on the particular corporate setting. A tight linkage between planning and budgeting indicates that relatively more strategic commitments have been made at an earlier stage. A loose linkage, on the other hand, implies that the narrowing down process is slower and will occur mainly during the latter part of the process, in the budgeting stage. Exhibit 2 shows examples of rapid versus slow narrowing down profiles. Notice that a company which does little narrowing down at the early stages will face the task of considering a larger number of strategic issues during the budgeting stage. This implies that either the company must be equipped with an adequate organization to process an immense and peaky budgeting workload, or that some alternatives will be neglected or disregarded altogether, with the result that the quality of the company's allocation decisions is likely to suffer.

Small companies

A company that has relatively little diversity in its operations may wish to undertake an early or rapid narrowing down, since the functional and

Exhibit 2 Examples of Slow vs. Rapid Narrowing Down Profiles, Implying Loose vs. Tight Linkage Respectively between the Cycles of the Planning Process

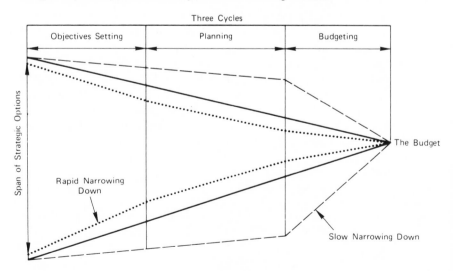

corporate executives involved will be thoroughly familiar with the few businesses in question. The basic strategy in most small companies is thoroughly understood by the top managers, and they can proceed directly to the task of developing action programs to continue their implementation of that strategy. Quantitative financial linkage between the selected programs and the resulting budgets is feasible, and "tight" linkage of this type is common practice.

Large companies

Linkage will probably be looser and the narrowing down process slower in a large company when it initiates a formal strategic planning system. During the start-up phase relatively more emphasis should be put on allowing division managers to come up with "inventories" of creative ideas for their businesses and encouraging their strategic thinking, differentiating that activity from long-range budgeting with its related requirement of divisional performance fulfillment. As the system matures, however, a gradual increase of narrowing down can occur without jeopardizing the creative aspect of planning. A natural result of this progress is that the linkage between the planning cycle and the budgeting cycle will become increasingly explicit.

SUMMARY

We have discussed six issues that must be addressed by corporate management as it seeks to design an effective process for formal strategic planning. The issues, and our attempt to delineate what is current good practice in large and small companies, are summarized in Exhibit 3.

Our major finding is that there are significant differences between the planning procedures used in the two broad types of companies that we have examined. "Small" companies—those that are not very diversified and are functionally organized—rely heavily on corporate management for the real strategic thinking about the future of the business. In such companies, a formal process to help organize that thinking is frequently not necessary, given the handful of managers involved. Instead, "strategic planning" as a formal activity is focused on the development and review of innovative action programs to implement the strategy. The planning system reflects that focus: goal setting is top-down, linkage to the budget is tight, and the staff planning officer plays a major role as cross-functional program analyst and environmental scanner. These comments also apply to strategic planning within product divisions of diversified corporations.

Corporate planning in "large" companies—those that are operating in several industrial sectors and are organized into product divisions—is

Systems Design Issues	Situational Settings		
	"Small" Companies	"Large" Companies	
		New Planning Systems	Mature Planning System
1. Communication of Corporate Goals	Not Explicit	Not Explicit	Explicit
2. Goal-Setting Process	Top-Down	Bottom-Up	"Negotiated"
3. Corporate Environmental Scanning	Strategic	Statistical	Statistical
4. Subordinate Managers' Focus	Financial	Financial	Strategic
5. Role of the Corporate Planner	Analyst	Catalyst	Coordinator
6. Linkage of Planning and Budgeting	Tight	Loose	Tight

Exhibit 3   Design Issues for Strategic Planning Systems

quite different. Initiating a formal strategic planning process in such companies is a major task in itself. The first year or two of such an effort must be viewed as an investment in developing a strategic planning competence among division managers; the explicit payoffs, in the form of better strategic decisions at the corporate level, will not be realized until the system matures. To be effective, the planning system must evolve rapidly along several dimensions if it is to survive as anything more than an exercise in pushing numbers into the blank spaces on neatly designed forms. A mature system, however, can be invaluable, helping both corporate and divisional executives to make better, and better coordinated, strategic decisions.

Concluding Note

In conclusion, we wish to reiterate three important general considerations about the design of strategic planning systems. First, the choice of systems design depends on the nature of the company at hand; thus, careful analysis of a company's specific situation is a necessary preliminary step before choosing among the design alternatives described above. Issues to be considered might include assessment of past and present strategy, organizational structure, style(s) of the key-line managers, and the need to integrate the planning activity with the existing management systems in the company.

Second, the design issues discussed in this article and listed in Exhibit 3 should be seen as tools at management's disposal, and the importance of the choices must be recognized by the president. If he overlooks any of the issues, he may jeopardize the functioning of the entire system.

Third, any company should be viewed as a dynamically evolving entity whose situational setting is subject to change. The result is that the design of the planning system must constantly evolve if it is to continue to be effective. Thus, implementation of a planning process is a continuous task requiring vigilance and insight on the part of management.

2
ROLE OF THE CORPORATE PLANNING EXECUTIVE*

ROBERT W. ACKERMAN

The literature on long-range planning, and the seminars and workshops devoted to this topic, tend to be directed toward the design and installation of systems of various sorts to execute planning. Among the more specific issues considered, for instance, are the linkages between long-range plans and budgets, the use of models in planning, environmental scanning, technological forecasting and so forth. This emphasis on the substance and technique of planning is, of course, necessary and desirable. It is also understandable. The system, after all, is the part of planning that is most visible and tangible; there are timetables, procedures, and the contents of the plans themselves to consider. Moreover, there are experts in the field who consider systems to be portable—with appropriate tailoring, one system can be introduced in many situations—and hence generalizable.

Designing and installing the planning system, however, is only one part of the planning task. Of critical importance is the relationship of planning to the process through which strategy in the corporation is formulated and resources are allocated toward its attainment. In most instances when there is a planning system, there is also a planning executive responsible in a broad sense for *managing* the planning *process.* To secure influence for the output of his planning system, the planner must relate his function effectively to the organization that forms the context in which strategic decisions are made. He must be a manager able to negotiate the halls of power in the corporation as well as a professional in the field of planning. He needs to develop an explicit strategy for himself and his office that can be consciously implemented.

The purpose of this paper is to lay out some of the major alternative roles available to the corporate planner and, because his situation may vary from company to company, to examine some of the contingent factors that may influence the choice of roles.

PROBLEMS FOR THE CORPORATE PLANNING EXECUTIVE

The corporate planning job, particularly in a large corporation, is not an easy one. In the first place, the planner has a number of complex and often difficult relationships to manage. He must have the respect and trust of the chief executive. If there is one basic truth in the lore of planning, it is that the exercise is futile unless it has the continuing, visible support of the CEO. Without his dedication to the proposition that planning is useful and, more importantly, without his willingness to make commitments to his line managers on the basis of their planning activities, the function loses its effectiveness. On an interpersonal level, the perceived relationship between the CEO and the planning executive will, of course, have a major bearing on how the latter is viewed by the rest of the organization.

The planning executive must also manage his relationship with line managers. It is naive for him to think that they will happily grasp the benefits of corporate planning. Their concerns are broad and sensitive, having to do with the course of their careers as well as the chart they have plotted for their division or department. They are continually monitoring the opportunities for securing resources and are sensitive to the nuances of performance evaluation. The planner and his system represent elements at least partially beyond the line manager's control and to that extent constitute a disruption and possibly a threat to previously existing decision processes.

Finally, the planning executive must relate to other staff functions, especially those responsible for financial controls. Unless he is to build a sizeable analytical and clerical staff, the planner may have to depend on the controller's office for assistance. Without it, his efforts may be either hopelessly mired in detail or so far removed from the detail that his advice is not grounded in fact. There is, of course, a tension between planning and budgeting; to give precedence to one tends to lessen the influence of the other. It is not unusual that the planner and the controller find themselves in competition for the attention of both the CEO and line managers. Given the importance frequently accorded the budget in the evaluation of executive performance and the greater bulk of the controller's task and organization, it is not surprising that the planning executive finds the odds untenable in the event of battle.

In the context of these relationships, none of them easy to manage, the corporate planner has a difficult task. He is generally expected to secure information from managers down the line regarding the nature of their activities and future plans. This information is to be forthright and truthful. More importantly, it is to be useful in guiding the future activities of the corporation. He is also expected to help the corporation develop objectives and goals and strategies for attaining them. One planner commented, "My job is to be the manager in charge of tomorrow." For him to be successful in measuring up to that responsibility, he will have to secure influence in the process through which strategic decisions are made. Unhappily for him, his office is rarely endowed with the power of position. His portfolio at the outset is thin and his mandate often superficial. In a head-to-head confrontation with line management, he will normally lose. With good reason, a strong CEO will most likely sacrifice his staff advisors rather than disrupt reporting relationships with those responsible for operations.

HOW SITUATIONAL IS THE PLANNER'S ROLE?

Let me be clear about the nature of the conclusions that can be expected from this discussion piece. It is doubtful that there is an appropriate universal role for the corporate planner. In fact, there may be several broad role types to be described later that, consistently adhered to, constitute useful models. My suspicion, however, is that a careful diagnosis of the context in which the planner is to operate and the individuals involved will point toward one of them as preferable to the others *in his situation*. How then is the planner's role bounded?

The Planning System. The most obvious, although perhaps the least useful, way of describing the planner's role is in terms of the tasks demanded of him by the system he manages. Executing the procedures required by the system defines the need for certain communications, relationships, and activities, which cannot be ignored.

To those who take a professional's view of planning, these aspects of the job are of commanding importance. This view hinges on the assumption, however, that a well-designed system, professionally administered, will result in effective planning. Such, unfortunately, is not always the case. The system itself cannot dictate either the contents of the plans or the level of organizational commitment to using them as a basis for setting corporate strategy. Securing relevance for planning in the decision-making process may relate more to the planner's interpersonal competence than to his skills as a planner.

On the other hand, the corporate planner should be aware of the implications of the system for his job, especially when he is given the responsibility for initiating planning. In the start-up situation he frequently has the choice between installing a prepackaged system, such as that offered by the Stanford Research Institute, or developing one of his own. Ironically, interpersonal skills may be considerably more demanding in the former situation than in the latter. With the basic design questions decided beforehand (and without wide participation), the prepackaged system can be activated more rapidly. Relationships, which might otherwise evolve over time, must be managed under the strained conditions of a new but fully elaborated system.

The Industry.   A second source of contingent propositions is the planning requirements imposed on the corporation by the nature of the industry(ies) in which it operates. Putting aside for the moment the case of a corporation represented in widely diverse fields, is the planner's role bounded by the competitive environment of the firm? Should the corporate planning executive in a high technology business, all other factors being equal, define a role for his office significantly different from his counterpart in a one-bank holding company? It is conceivable that the same individual, because of background and level of technical understanding, may be able to perform nicely in one situation but not the other. However, that is not necessarily the same as maintaining that industry characteristics serve as a constraint on the choices of role available to the planning executive.

While comparative research has not, as yet, been undertaken to help answer these questions, one study on the role of the planner in the commercial banking industry has been completed.[1] The findings are revealing because commercial banking involves operating functions and environmental factors that are considerably different from those in manufacturing firms where planning has been more widely established. The

[1] Patricia Rapoport and Robert Schultz, *The Role of the Planner in Commercial Banks* (Boston: Harvard Business School, 1972).

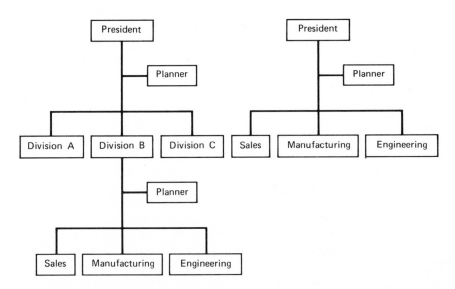

dimensions of the planner's task, as line and staff executives in five major banks described it, appear remarkably similar to those traditionally associated with industrial enterprises.

The Company. There are two characteristics of the firm that may have an important bearing on the role of the corporate planner. The first, relating to organization structure, has been suggested by Lorange and Vancil.[2] He notes that the corporate planning task is sharply different in corporations organized by product divisions vs. those organized by function. Whereas in the latter case the corporate planning executive can have a vital hand in coordinating the integration of interrelated functions and the articulation of a business plan, in the former these jobs are performed by managers in the divisions. Consequently, in the divisionalized firm, the corporate planner is more likely to be left with the job of overseeing the system, evaluating plans, and worrying about the allocation of resources among businesses and between internal uses and acquisitions. Vancil[3] suggests that a more passive, neutral posture in this situation is desirable to retain the support of division managers and to insure that the planner does not interfere with the vital relationships between the chief executive and line management.

There have been a number of extensive descriptive studies in the past decade, starting with Chandler,[4] on differences between divisionalized and functionally organized enterprises, which support the Vancil posi-

[2] Reading 2, Part 1.
[3] Reading 1, Part 2.
[4] Alfred D. Chandler, *Strategy and Structure* (Cambridge: M.I.T. Press, 1963).

tion. In describing the allocation of duties between corporate and operating levels, these studies also point to a changed, and generally diminished, role for the corporate staff as the divisionalized structure came to dominate the population of large corporations in the United States and more recently in Europe.

Despite the clarity and intuitive appeal of this distinction, does it necessarily hold true? There are a number of situations involving divisionalized firms in which the corporate planning executive might consider a neutral role inappropriate. In general, this may occur whenever the flow of resources is to be diverted from normal channels. For instance, in times of financial crisis (or a national crisis for that matter) corporate executives frequently seek to reassert their authority over the affairs of operating units. If divisions are to be liquidated or divested, the chief executive may find it foolhardy to expect those involved to adopt corporatewide views. Similarly, planning for entry into a major new field and implementing that decision by accumulating the necessary resources from existing businesses may also be a task that cannot be delegated to second-tier line managers. In short, stated rather grandly, a neutral role for the corporate planner may rest on the assumption that the firm is functioning satisfactorily relative to its potential and that the chief executive does not see the need for intervention in the *initiation* of business plans and resource allocation proposals.

Individuals. A final source of particularity in defining a strategy for the corporate planner is the personal characteristics of those most critical to the planning process and the nature of their interpersonal relationships. To some degree, perhaps to a very large degree, the corporate planner must look beyond the planning system and the organization structure to the human dimensions of his task.

Frequently, the planner's principal client is the chief executive and it may be worthwhile to consider him first. The diagnosis includes at least two types of inquiry. The first relates to the personal needs of the chief executive and the pressures placed on his job. The new president brought into a crisis situation clearly has different concerns than his long-tenured counterpart in a successful company. The former may view planning as a mechanism for sorting out what is to be kept from what is to be liquidated, while the latter may hold planning to be one means of developing managers and insuring against unforeseen long-term consequences of environmental change. Their time horizons, mandates for change, and power in the organization may be radically different. Moreover, the nature of the relationships *they* must manage may vary, and this should be of great importance to their advisors. Most presidents have personal needs and goals that help to define what they expect from the planning function.

The second inquiry relates to the chief executive's management style and in particular the means he adopts to solve problems. For example, what is his tolerance for detail and how deeply does he tend to intervene in the decision-making process? Some chief executives place great reliance on delegated responsibilities and indirect methods of guiding decisions through performance appraisal and rewards; others are willing to share responsibility in exchange for the chance to influence the outcome directly. The emphasis has a great deal to do with how much the chief executive needs or wants to know about operating matters and where he looks for guidance.

The needs and ambitions of other managers involved in planning constitute a second source of differences among preferred roles for the corporate planner provoked by human concerns. The power and attitudes of, for instance, the controller, the manager of the most profitable division, the executive who was passed over for the presidency, the executives who are vying for the top spot next, are all relevant concerns. The corporate planner must be aware of likely allies and likely enemies and the intensity and significance of their feelings. He is, after all, dealing with a process that affects the careers of the managers involved; it is natural that they calibrate its usefulness in personal terms.

Finally, the planning executive should take into account his own objectives and capabilities. The options available to the planner are, of course, constrained to some extent by the place his position has had in the career paths of his predecessors if there have been any. Nevertheless, the strategy he adopts will certainly have a bearing on his future opportunities in the firm.

THE ROLE OF THE CORPORATE PLANNER

The central point of view in this discussion is that the corporate planner, despite the constraints and difficulties associated with his task, has a measure of freedom in the role he chooses to play in the organization. That is not to say that one alternative is as good as another or that a role, once chosen, can be easily altered. Such is seldom the case. In fact, a careful diagnosis should suggest a preferred role from which to fashion a personal and departmental strategy. In broad terms, I believe there are three: a planning broker, a presidential advisor, and a strategic evaluator. While there may be some overlap, the roles are, by and large, distinct.

Planning Broker. In this role, the corporate planner struggles to maintain neutrality and impartiality in his relationships with other managers. He manages the long-run planning system, insures that the plans are comprehensive, and promotes the ideas and techniques of planning. However, he avoids taking positions whenever possible on the strategic issues confronting the corporation or its components. In a sense, he acts as a weather bureau by reflecting the chief executive's concerns to managers down the line and as a broker by giving advance exposure for their plans in corporate circles. He tends to view his career as a planner in professional terms and avoids getting caught in the crossfire between line managers on the same or different levels in the organization. He limits his exposure to criticism, keeping, as the current saying goes, a "low profile."

Presidential Advisor.   Alternatively, the corporate planner may see the president as his client and the president's needs as his concerns. Rather than attempting to maintain neutrality, the planner may take and make use of "the president's ear" to further his client's purposes. He ties his success and influence to the strength and resolve of the chief executive. While this position may seem extreme and dangerous for the planner, it is not necessarily so. It depends heavily on the relationships between the chief executive and his line managers. If the chief executive is a respected leader, the planner benefits from his close association. Moreover, the organization understands his point of view, knows how to approach him, and may in fact deal with him as the chief executive's stand-in.

Strategic Evaluator.   Finally, the planner may attempt to define a role that permits him to have his own position on strategic issues. In this case, he seeks independence rather than neutrality or subjugation to the chief executive. His client is the corporation and his efforts are directed toward defining strategy that will be to its long-run advantage. In fulfilling this role, the planner must have freedom to evaluate plans and the influence to have his assessments taken seriously. To assess, however, is to judge the competence of the managers submitting plans and to influence is to exert some control over the allocation of resources. In effect, the corporate planner adopts a position akin to that of a line manager. While clearly the most active role, it is also the most exposed. The stakes are higher and the planner must decide whether the opportunities justify the risks.

A serious consideration of alternative roles forces the planning executive to diagnose his position in the organization. He should think very carefully through such questions as:

(1) "Who is my client?"
(2) "What distance should I maintain in my relationships with various other executives?"
(3) "What degree of independence do I want or need for my views on the substantive issues confronting the enterprise?"

With an identification of his role or the role he would like to have, the planning executive can then begin to develop a strategy that will serve as a guide for future action. If planning is useful in managing the corporation, the planner has the responsibility for insuring that his office is managed in a fashion that insures that the benefit is obtained.

3
BALANCE 'CREATIVITY' AND 'PRACTICALITY' IN FORMAL PLANNING*

Study of six companies shows how different combinations of system-design features can be used to achieve workable equilibrium

JOHN K. SHANK, EDWARD G. NIBLOCK, AND
WILLIAM T. SANDALLS, JR.

Every company engaged in long-range planning would like its efforts to attain two fundamental but often conflicting goals. On the one hand, management wants the planning function to reflect pragmatic judgments based on what is possible. On the other hand, it wants planning to reflect forward-looking, assertive, and creative thinking.

The primary way of enhancing "realism" is to give the planning function a clear action orientation. Generally, this is done by relating long-range planning closely with short-term budgetary control. And this is where the difficulty lies. While close linkage between planning and budgeting puts the stress on the desired action, it also promotes a focus that can be disastrous to mind-stretching "reach."

We are making the assumption, of course, that for the formal planning system to operate effectively it must achieve a balanced compromise between realism and reach. In this article, we shall argue that these dual objectives need not be mutually exclusive. In fact, our purpose is to illustrate that the long-range planning system can be structured to achieve

* (Reprinted from *Harvard Business Review*, January-February 1973).

both an action orientation and a focus on mind stretching. Our discussion will proceed in two steps.

In the first stage, it is important for long-range planners to begin thinking about the realism-reach trade-off as a problem they can do something about. That "something" involves varying those aspects of the long-range planning system which relate to its interface with the short-range budgeting process. In this regard, we shall summarize the general features of the planning system which relate to plan-budget linkage, illustrating both the "tight" and "loose" form of each "linkage device."

Then, in the second step, we shall illustrate some of the most interesting devices actually being used. These reflect the experiences of six companies which we selected because they

(1) are successful in terms of compound earnings growth and
(2) have long-range planning systems with both action-oriented and mind-stretching characteristics.

In short, we believe that management can control the focus a planning system will exhibit with respect to the realism versus reach problem. It may not always be possible to achieve a totally satisfactory trade-off, but we shall describe the mechanisms being used by a sample of successful companies to achieve what for each of them is a satisfactory compromise.

PLAN-BUDGET DESIGN

On close examination, it quickly becomes apparent that the different aspects of plans and budgets can be linked in three distinct ways:

1. *Content linkage* relates to the correspondence between the data presented in the plan document and that presented in the budget.
2. *Organizational linkage* focuses on the relationship between the units responsible for planning and budgeting.
3. *Timing linkage* concerns the sequencing of the annual planning and budgeting cycles.

Within each of these categories, there are several specific features of the planning system that can be manipulated to influence the extent of plan-budget linkage. Let us take a closer look at each of these linkage devices.

Financial features

One important feature of content linkage is the amount of detail in the financial statements included in the plan document. The tightest linkage would be to include statements with the same level of detail as in the monthly reporting package which compares budgeted with actual results. The loosest linkage would be not to include financial statements at all.

Another design feature related to the financial content is the level of rounding in the plan document. Although it may not seem particularly significant at first blush, there is evidence that rounding to a much higher level in the plan than in the budget (e.g., millions of dollars in the plan versus thousands in the budget) can foster a kind of mental distinction between plan and budget numbers which reduces the tendency to view the plan as solely a long-range budget. This can in turn facilitate a much more creative planning effort by making it clear that the managers do not have to commit themselves (in a budgetary sense) to delivering the planned financial results.

Still another important content feature is the conformity between plan and budget numbers for those years which are common to both documents. If the numbers differ, planning may face a credibility gap. Many companies, however, feel that allowing such differences is critical to maintaining the aggressive forward thrust of the planning effort.

For example, one conglomerate includes in the first year of its five-year plan the earnings from acquisitions that are projected to be closed during the next twelve months but which are not yet finalized. The company does not include these earnings in the budgeted results for the next year which line managers are asked to commit themselves to deliver.

Several other companies show differences between planned and budgeted profit for the next year because the two documents are prepared at different times. The one prepared later in the year would reflect the latest thinking and this might differ from projections made earlier in the year.

Situations like these may or may not be desirable, but they certainly reflect loose content linkage. If numerical differences are permitted, one way of moving back toward tightness is to require that some kind of formal reconciliation of them be included in the plan. Many companies which permit differences require such reconciliation.

Related to plan-budget conformity for years common to both documents is the issue of the uniformity of the numbers for any given year as they appear in succeeding annual plan documents. If the planned figures for any one future period change significantly each time a plan is put together, the perceived realism of the planning effort can suffer.

Our evidence suggests, however, that rarely do companies require the numbers for a given year to be "cast in concrete" the very first time that year appears in a plan document. This degree of linkage is probably unrealistically tight.

As we shall illustrate later, a few companies do require formal explanations in the plan for any changes in the projections related to a given future year. This clearly reflects a tighter linkage form of this planning-system variable than would otherwise be reflected by complete freedom to change future years' projections at each iteration of the planning cycle. At least a few companies feel that some tightness at this point is desirable.

A final important design feature is the structure of the content of the plan. In most companies, the budget is structured in terms of the organizational units which will be responsible for carrying it out. Such an approach is a fundamental part of what is often referred to as "responsibility accounting."

Given this situation, it is possible to restructure the plan to focus on programs rather than on the organizational units. The total expenditures for a given year are the same in either case, but there is nevertheless a distinctly looser impact on the way in which the plan document is interpreted.

Organizational relationships

The major design feature in this category is the relationship between the organizational units responsible for the budgetary-control processes. The loosest form is to lodge planning and long-range planning and those responsible for the budgeting in separate organizational channels reporting to different top-level executives. The tightest form is to have the two functions combined in one department.

Even in those situations in which planning and budgeting are separated in terms of formal organizational relationships, there is wide latitude in the extent to which the controller is formally involved in the long-range planning effort. Naturally, the loosest linkage situation is to have scant involvement on the part of the controller. However, because of his expertise in analyzing and communicating financially oriented data, it is probably neither possible nor desirable to exclude him completely from the formal planning effort.

Between this extreme of separate planning and budgeting channels and the complete integration of these functions lies a very broad middle ground which can be probed to achieve an appropriate level of involvement for any given company. Among the relevant questions to ask in this regard are the following:

1. Does the controller provide staff support for the preparation of the financial data in the plan document?
2. Does the controller review the plan document before it is finalized?
3. Does the controller have any direct or indirect responsibility for approving the plan?
4. Does the controller have any direct or indirect responsibility for monitoring planned financial results against actual results?

The more questions of this kind that can be answered *yes,* the tighter the plan-budget linkage, even though the functions may officially be separate.

Timing considerations

The most important design feature here is concerned with the sequencing of the annual planning and budgeting cycles. If the two cycles are carried out sequentially, which one is done first? How much time elapses between the completion of the first cycle and the beginning of the one which follows it? If the two cycles are undertaken concurrently, what is the relationship between initiation dates, completion dates, and approval dates?

The loosest timing linkage is to have the planning cycle done before the budgeting cycle and to have several months elapse between the two. One major food products manufacturer, for example, completes the annual planning cycle in February and does not begin the budgeting phase until November. Situations like this are least inhibiting to the achievement of "reach" in the planning effort.

The tightest form of the design feature related to sequencing would be to complete the budgeting cycle first and to have the planning cycle follow it with minimal elapsed time in between. Since the budgeting cycle almost always concludes in the last quarter of the fiscal year, it is rare to find a company in which the planning cycle comes last. There are, however, many companies that undertake the two cycles concurrently.

In general, the more the budget process precedes the plan preparation—in terms of initiation, completion, and approval dates—the tighter the linkage, since the budgeting focus will tend to dominate the joint planning-budgeting effort.

One final timing-related design feature is the time horizon for the long-range planning effort. Usually, the shorter this span, the closer the relationship between the budget and the planning process and thus the tighter the plan-budget linkage. Conversely, the longer the time frame, the easier it becomes to clearly distinguish the process from budgeting and thus the looser the plan-budget linkage.

Nowhere in the whole range of system-design features is the trade-off between realism and reach more clearly defined than in the choice of a planning horizon. The longer the time frame, the wider the range of factors which can be varied and thus the broader the range of strategies which can be considered in moving the company toward its long-range objectives.

At the same time, a longer time span increases the uncertainty regarding environmental assumptions, corporate strengths, and the financial parameters which shape the strategy formulation and evaluation process. At some point, uncertainty overcomes the gain in flexibility.

What constitutes an appropriate time horizon certainly varies from industry to industry. It is probably easier, for example, for most public utilities to do fifteen-year planning than it is for defense-aerospace companies to do five-year planning. Within the reasonable range for any given industry, however, the longer the time considerations, the looser the plan-budget linkage. Furthermore, in our opinion, a planning horizon of three or four years reflects a heavy emphasis on realism at the expense of reach, regardless of the industry.

LINKAGE EXAMPLES

In the preceding section of this article, we concentrated on a general framework for considering the plan-budget problem. Now, we shall turn our attention to some of the interesting devices actually being used by the six manufacturing companies that we selected as a small but representative sample of those which have

(1) participated in formal planning studies,
(2) earned the reputation for having both action-oriented and creative planning systems, and
(3) been highly successful in terms of compound EPS growth.

Since we believe it unlikely that their records of sustained performance could have been achieved without the help of good planning, it should be revealing to examine in some detail how these companies cope with the linkage problem.

The six companies we observed were Cincinnati Milacron, General Mills, Quaker Oats, Raytheon, Toro, and Warnaco. In them, we encountered such a large number of different linkage devices that we concluded the variety of specific links is limited only by the imagination of the personnel. We shall use the same categories as in the preceding section in reviewing the most interesting linkage practices in these sample companies.

But, first, a note of caution. It is not our intent to propose *the* right answer to the linkage problem, but only to identify some of the more important factors to be considered in determining *a* right answer for a given company at a specific point in time.

Content-related approaches

One of the most innovative attempts to use structure as a mechanism to overcome the creativity-practicality problem is the distinct separation between group and division planning at Warnaco. Each division manager prepares a three-year plan, while each group vice president plans five years out.

Warnaco's objective here is to encourage the group vice presidents to think in more general and longer range terms. They then carry this framework with them to meetings with their division managers. This encourages them to do more creative planning.

It is important to note that the formats of these two plans are much different, with the divisional plans being done in much greater detail than the group plans. This serves to focus the group manager's attention on the strategy of the group itself rather than on the specific details of the divisions' operating programs.

A mechanism we mentioned earlier to overcome the problem of loose linkage is the comparison of a plan with its predecessor from a year earlier. Consider, for example, this situation taken from the planning records of a large paper manufacturer. Here are this company's profit projections for 1971 as shown in

Five-year plan done in 1966 ....$60 million
Five-year plan done in 1967 ....$50 million
Five-year plan done in 1969 ....$36 million
1971 budget prepared in 1970 ....$16 million

At the very least, a plan-to-plan comparison would have called the company's attention to the increasing lack of realism the further the projections extended into the future. The threat of having to formally justify this ever-receding bonanza might have served as a sobering influence to the planners.

It is also possible to use plan-to-plan comparisons to overcome the problems of overly conservative forecasting. Thus, if the paper company's profit projections had demonstrated an ascending pattern, the happy surprise of realizing more profits than expected might also have been accompanied by the undesirable development of capacity shortages and missed market opportunities. In such a case, a plan-to-plan comparison could serve as an impetus for more expansive projections.

Of the six companies we visited, only General Mills requires the reporting and justification of significant changes from the preceding year's plan. At General Mills, management feels that this checking device is sufficiently useful in preventing blue-sky fantasizing to justify its risk in terms of discouraging open-ended mind stretching.

A third-content-related mechanism worth noting is the relationship between the plan and budget formats. As we noted earlier, if the two documents differ in form and style, it is more difficult to directly transpose the plan to the budget. Both Toro and Raytheon approach a program format for planning and a functional format for budgeting, but they also retain the program and project breakout in the budget as well as the functional allocation. In the other companies we sampled, this split is less distinct since the divisions are largely organized by program area or product line. We view this loosening device as a very significant one that has potential applicability in many companies.

Finally, all six of the sample companies vary the level of detail between the plan and the budget. It is interesting to note, however, that the absolute level of detail in the plan also varies significantly among the six companies. Cincinnati Milacron shows only very highly aggregated summary data, whereas Raytheon's plans approach the same level of detail as its budgets. The other four companies fall in between these extreme approaches.

Organizational coordination

At the corporate level, it is important to understand who is coordinating the planning and who is coordinating the budgeting. The basic question here is whether the company wants to split the two processes. The splitting of this coordination function has the effect of loosening the linkage between planning and budgeting. Both Toro and Cincinnati Milacron provide excellent examples of this.

At Toro, planning is coordinated by the Corporate Planner and budgeting by the Controller. No formal attempt is made to ensure that these two functions proceed in a similar fashion. Cincinnati Milacron handles this in much the same way that Toro does.

At General Mills, the end result is the same but the mechanisms are much more complex, with coordination being handled by groups instead of individuals.

Different handling at the division level can also affect the linking process. The basic split here is between strategy formulation and the quantified explication of that strategy. While in almost all instances both are coordinated by the division manager, the degree of delegation of the quantification phase can vary significantly.

It is noteworthy that there is very little divergence in the way quantification of plan results is handled by the six companies. All of them largely delegate this phase to the divisional controller. This has a loosening effect by focusing the division manager's attention on policy rather than on detailed profit and loss information.

Although it is not a "device" in the usual sense, a company's informal communication process can function in a way that tightens the linkage between planning and budgeting. A great deal of informal information transfer across the corporate/divisional interface increases top-management's cognizance of what is in the plan and how it relates to the budget. The presence of informal channels of communication may make top management appear to have an omniscient awareness of these issues even if this is actually not the case.

At Cincinnati Milacron, where the planning and budgeting systems are very closely linked, one division manager stated that he really felt strongly committed to delivering the performance projected in his five-year plan. At Quaker Oats and Toro, where there are loose linkage systems, two division managers reported similar feelings of commitment. It is difficult for us to assess what precise influence the informal communication processes in the foregoing companies had in forging the personal commitments of these three division managers to delivering the planned results. However, the counter-intuitive coincidence of loose systems and strong commitments at least offers circumstantial evidence that this influence does exist and should not be overlooked.

Time horizons

A separation in time between the end of the planning cycle and the beginning of the budgeting cycle, as we noted earlier, has the effect of loosening the linkage between the two processes. When the time to worry about next year's performance commitment is still several months away, it is easier to be expansive about the future. In addition, since forecast conditions are always changing, the more time that elapses subsequent to submission of the plan, the easier it is to justify a revision in the budget.

Of the six sample companies, only Raytheon pursues its planning and budgeting cycles concurrently. Cincinnati Milacron has a six-month separation between the end of planning and the beginning of budgeting. General Mills, Quaker Oats, Toro, and Warnaco all have at least a two-to three-month separation.

In general, as the number of years in the budget is extended, or the number of years in the plan contracted, the similarity between the plan and the budget increases. Different time horizons for the two processes tend to emphasize the different purposes of each. Five of the six companies we sampled have either a four- or five-year planning range and a one- or two-year budget span. The exception is Warnaco, which we noted previously.

APPROPRIATE EQUILIBRIUM

Individual linkage devices impact on the planning system by facilitating an overall planning effort which is either more creative or action oriented. As is evident from the preceding discussion, some devices serve to promote a stronger action orientation in planning while others encourage more creativity.

Since a single planning system will utilize several devices which may have opposing effects on the plan-budget balance, an "algebraic" sum of the devices is needed to determine where the planning system is located on the linkage continuum. This plays a pivotal role in achieving an appropriate equilibrium between divergent requirements for both creative and action-oriented planning.

Whether or not a particular planning balance is appropriate for a given company hinges on the corporate setting. Thus, if the underlying essence of planning is to improve a company's ability to cope with changes, it follows that, as the changes are realized, the need for specific forms of planning will also change. In other words, a dynamic corporate setting may call for heavy emphasis on creativity at one point in time and heavy emphasis on practicality at another. The implication is that, as a company's needs change, devices must be added or subtracted in order to adjust the balance between these planning objectives.

The concept of a dynamic corporate setting seems particularly relevant to the four of the six sample companies which are now diversifying extensively beyond the boundaries of their traditional industries. Consider:

1. The Toro Company is changing from a manufacturer of lawn mowers and snow blowers to a broad-based participant in the environmental beautification market.

2. General Mills's Fashion Division, which was established only three years ago, already contributes significantly to the company's sales and earnings and competes in markets dramatically different from those served by Cheerios and other ready-to-eat cereals.

3. Quaker Oats, in its most recent fiscal year, derived 25% of its sales from nongrocery product sources, including 12% from Fisher-Price Toys. The company has since further diversified in nongrocery areas through acquisition of Louis Marx & Co. Toys and the Needlecraft Corporation of America.

4. Cincinnati Milacron, the largest manufacturer of machine tools in the world, is seeking points of entry into the minicomputer and semiconductor markets.

A dynamic corporate setting, however, is not necessarily dependent on the diversification activity of a company. For example:

1. Cincinnati Milacron, with 80% of its sales in the machine tool industry, contends with market cycles which brought machine tool sales volume in 1970 down 50% to 60% below the peak reached two years earlier.

2. The Raytheon Equipment Division, a defense contractor, faces rapid turnover in electronics technology—a contract bidding process that sometimes makes a ticket in the Irish Sweepstakes look like a sure bet—and concomitant uncertainties and headaches in dealing with mercurial government customers.

3. Warnaco, competing with 30,000 other companies in the apparel industry, finds that although total sales volume is relatively stable, individual markets are highly volatile as fashions come and go in quick succession.

Whether the result of extensive diversification programs or corporate response to the challenges of traditional markets, all six companies are in a state of perpetual change.

Given this state of flux, it is significant to note that the planning systems in five of the companies have recently been changed, are in the process of being changed, or will be changed in the near future (the exception is Raytheon Equipment). To illustrate:

1. At Toro, David M. Lilly, Chairman and Chief Executive Officer, recently projected the development of looser linkage between the planning and budgeting systems.

2. At General Mills, the 1971 planning instructions announced a procedure to highlight where the 1971 plan deviated from the 1970 plan; the same instructions reemphasized a year-old procedure which required "new" businesses to be differentiated from "present" businesses.

3. At Quaker Oats, the corporate planner foresees the emergence of tighter linkage as the company becomes acclimated to its new divisionalized structure.

4. At Cincinnati Milacron, a new planning system is in its first year of operation; this system is very loosely linked to budgeting and shifts the burden of planning from the division managers to the group managers.

5. At Warnaco, as we noted earlier, a systems modification has been implemented; this requires group vice presidents to plan five years into the future and their subordinate division managers three years ahead.

In seeking a comprehensive explanation of the planning system changes just described, we find particularly pertinent the observation that management control systems must be consistent with top management's objectives in order to be truly effective. If the same can be said of formal planning systems, then it follows that a change in an effective planning system is usually triggered by a change in top management's objectives.

The implication here is that whether or not a given change improves a planning system may be beside the point. To paraphrase Marshall McLuhan, the planning system and the changes made in it may be "the medium that is the message"—i.e., the message from top management.

Criterion of consistency

In this section of the article, we shall examine more closely two of the planning system changes previously mentioned to see what inferences about top management's objectives we can draw from them.

Since 1971, Cincinnati Milacron has been pulling out of a severe recession that afflicted the entire machine tool industry. Operating management's ordeal during the past two years has been something akin to a day-to-day struggle. As the company has begun to emerge from this traumatic experience, top management has installed a new planning system to allow maximum opportunity for broad-level mind stretching. Furthermore, the burden of planning has been shifted upward to a level of management where there exists the opportunity and authority to implement a diversification program.

The message of Cincinnati Milacron's two planning-system changes appears to be rather straightforward: top management wants aggressive diversification planning.

In his memorandum covering General Mills's 1971 planning instructions, James P. MacFarland, Chairman and Chief Executive Officer, indicated the need for a more aggressive capital investment program in the years ahead to achieve the company's sales and earnings objectives. He also referred to progress in the control of capital use and to a change in the planning procedures which would allow top management to focus easily on the changes made subsequent to the previous planning cycle. His general instructions described this procedural change in more detail and reiterated a year-old procedure which separated the planning for new businesses from that for current businesses.

In our judgment, it is a fair guess that it will be a tougher task to revise estimates upward in order to justify additional capital for a current business than to submit new estimates in order to justify seed capital for a new business. The message of the announcement of both a new procedure and reemphasis on an old one appears to be that the encouragement of heavier investments is intended for new and not for current businesses.

(This message, incidentally, is clearly reflected in the chairman's and president's letter to General Mills's stockholders and employees in the 1971 Annual Report.)

The procedure at General Mills of separating current and new businesses is particularly noteworthy in that it creates an opportunity to differentiate the planning perspectives, and to apply different standards of expectation to each type of business. In this manner, top management can encourage a division manager to be creative in planning for his new businesses and action oriented in planning for his current businesses.

Future-oriented businesses will be best suited for loosely linked planning/budgeting systems. As the potential of a business begins to be realized, tighter linkage will be desirable in order to transform promises into results. At that point, a balance between creative planning and action-oriented planning would be especially appropriate. Later, as the business exhausts its growth potential and evolves into a "cash generator," even tighter linkage will be desirable to accommodate the corporation's capital needs for the next generation of new businesses.

In short, recognition of divergent corporate objectives for both the mature and the future-oriented business is manifested in different degrees of linkage in their respective planning/budgeting systems. As evident at Quaker Oats, for example, a divisionalized company can find itself at several points—up and down—on the linkage continuum at the same time. In evaluating whether or not any point on the continuum is "right" or "wrong," the sole criterion must be its consistency with corporate objectives.

CONCLUSION

To be effective, every formal long-range planning system must achieve a workable compromise between creativity and practicality—twin goals that are often in conflict. This problem of maintaining a satisfactory balance between "reach" and "realism" can be directly addressed by varying those design features of planning which relate to its interface with budgeting. However, in order to put in perspective the importance of loosening the plan/budget linkage, it is important to consider the role of informal communications and the personalities of management.

At the corporate/division interface, companies that have a great deal of informal communication transfer are likely to be constantly aware of what was written in the plan and how that relates to the budget. This has the effect of very tightly linking the plan and the budget, even in structurally loose systems, unless management makes a conscious effort to demonstrate that this is not wanted. Even if this intent is demonstrated at the corporate level, there still may be tight linkage built in at the division level because of the division manager's personality.

Generally speaking, the divisional planning and budgeting are either both done by the division manager himself or at least coordinated by him. As he coordinates the preparation of the budget, he often feels —either consciously or subconsciously—an obligation to justify the value of the plan by reflecting much of it in the budget which represents his short-term game plan for the division.

Briefly, loosening devices have much broader applications than to just those companies which have structurally tight linkage systems. In fact, some of them may be needed in any action-oriented planning system.

We believe that managers should consider these devices as variables they can and should manipulate in the interest of more effective planning. Viewed in this context, the linkage continuum can be considered as a powerful interpreter of the top-management objectives implicit in the planning system.

Although at first this may seem to be counter-intuitive, we believe that it is not the planning system which generates corporate objectives but rather the corporate objectives which dictate the appropriate planning system. We are neither proposing that there is a "correct" form for any of these design features, nor that it is always possible to structure a planning system so that "realistic creativity" is ensured.

We do believe, however, that "realistic reach" in planning is not just an illusory phenomenon which exists independent of management's actions. Rather, it is well within management's control to influence the focus of the efforts by changing the structure of the planning system. That, we feel, is all any manager can ask.

4

DIVISIONAL PLANNING: SETTING EFFECTIVE DIRECTION*

PETER LORANGE

INTRODUCTION

The state-of-the-art of long-range planning displays a number of strengths; not the least of these is the progress which has been made in developing effective planning systems for divisions within divisionalized corporations. Much is now known about the development of sound business plans by divisions and about the blending of these plans into one overall corporate "portfolio" plan.[1] In fact, within many corporations, one finds that the strongest planning is being done within the divisions.

---

* (Reprinted from Sloan Management Review, Fall 1975)

[1] See Reading 2, Part 1. In this reading we shall follow Vancil and Lorange's terminology: at the corporate level—corporate or portfolio strategy and planning; at the divisional level—business strategy and planning; and at the functional level—project strategy and programming.

Planning at the divisional level will generally be built around strategic projects such as new product introduction, R&D projects and marketing campaigns. The common approach to planning for these strategic expenditures is fairly well understood. Despite the progress made in the areas of strategic development planning and divisional planning in general, however, we find that present divisional planning practices may have shortcomings. First, we find that there is often a tendency towards planning too conservatively within each division when seen in the light of the total capacity and potentials of a large corporation. Second, divisions frequently encounter difficulties in developing a business strategy for setting priorities among business lines and among strategic projects.

This article discusses these potential problem areas of effective direction-setting in divisional planning. We believe such a discussion is merited, not only because we have observed these problems in a number of divisional planning settings but also because they represent a "stumbling block" to further progress in divisional planning. Furthermore, these pitfalls often go unrecognized or unacknowledged within actual divisions. In order to put these planning problems in perspective, we shall begin with a brief review of the major aspects of divisional long-range planning and then focus on each of the problem areas more specifically.

COMMON PRACTICES OF DIVISIONAL PLANNING

In order for a division to ensure that strategic projects will be consistent with the overall strategy of the division and of the firm, and to maintain congruence between the desired and actual impact of strategic projects, three planning measures are commonly undertaken. These are (1) identifying a business project's fit as part of a business strategy, (2) programming across functions while budgeting for each function, and (3) planning the stages of new business projects in accordance with several specific characteristics of the strategic business project management task.

Identifying a Business Project's Fit as Part of a Business Strategy

It is of primary importance that the selection of strategic business projects be closely aligned to the long-range planning process. Because a division will be largely responsible for its long-term success within its business area, a significant portion of the responsibility for strategic business project development should also rest on each division. Through research, development and market analysis, a division should provide the new products and maintain the existing business lines necessary to hold or expand its position within the business. Clearly, strategic business project development plays a vital role in the implementation of the overall strategy of a division.

Since strategic business project selection will be determined primarily by a division's objectives and strategies, it becomes particularly important that these objectives and strategies be stated in sufficiently operational terms to provide meaningful guidance. The common method of defining business line strategy in operational terms is to specify it in a two-dimensional classification; each division's major product segments are located according to the general attractiveness of its business (i.e., market growth) and its competitive strength in that business (i.e., market share).[2] This two-dimensional classification results in a matrix of possible product typologies, each with distinctly different prospects for profitability, capacity for funds generation or requirements for funds consumption. Figure 1 gives an example of such a two-dimensional matrix for strategic positioning of a business line.

Product A is an example of a product which would require a "build" strategy, that is an attempt to improve competitive strength. This strategy will generally require a net outflow of funds. Product B is in a "hold" strategy position. Here the objective would be to protect the position "as is"; consequently, inflows of funds to the line should be in approximate balance with outflows. Product C is an example of a product which would require a "harvest" strategy; such a strategy involves intentionally allowing one's competitive strength to gradually diminish with the likely result of a net funds inflow contribution from the product.

This type of analysis, which is now universally practiced, helps to determine what might be an appropriate strategy to follow for a new or existing product line. In summary, a division's business plans should emphasize specifically the types of product lines that will be most desirable. Such specification should include a delineation of product line strategies and individual strategic projects.

Programming Across Functions While Budgeting for Each Function

The second measure which is commonly taken to maintain control of the strategic program process is a response to the danger that separate planning for each function might fragment the overall business project selection. This measure requires that the functional departments first construct plans for the project in cooperation *across* organizational lines and then develop budgets *for each* organizational unit across business project segments. As indicated in Figure 2, step one is programming to ensure the

---

[2] See B. D. Henderson, "Perspectives on Experience," *The Boston Consulting Group*, 1968, and "The Experience Curve Reviewed," *The Boston Consulting Group*, 1970; S. Schoeffler, R. D. Buzzell, and D. F. Heany, "Impact of Strategic Planning on Profit Performance," *Harvard Business Review*, March-April 1974; and R. D. Buzzell, B. T. Gale, and R. G. M. Sultan, "Market Share—A Key to Profitability," *Harvard Business Review*, January-February 1975. For an article concerning reservations about going uncritically after market share, W. E. Fruhan, Jr., "Pyrrhic Victories in Fight for Market Share," *Harvard Business Review*, September-October 1972.

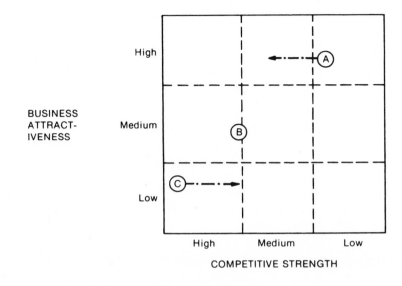

Figure 1   Business Line Strategic Posture Matrix

strategic direction; step two is budgeting to ensure that each department's resources are adequate to carry out its share of the program activities.[3]

Planning the Strategic Business Project Stages

The task of managing business projects involves certain elements which merit specialized planning procedures. First, management must acknowledge the fact that specialized functional skills will be needed to carry out each of the tasks associated with the development of a new project. Examples of such functional skills are research development and marketing activities. Second, because these functional departments are more or less limited in their ability to adjust their capacity for processing work, at least in the short run, it is necessary that the work loads of each functional department be carefully balanced. An important related divisional planning task will be to plan the capacity of the functional departments in such a way that the "capacity profile" remains relatively even. Figure 3 gives examples of two strategic project organizations which are not in balance. It would be the task of the management of these two organizations to "flatten" their capacity profiles over time.

A third characteristic of the strategic project process which must be considered by divisional planners is the issue of whether and when to transfer a given project from one functional stage to the next. This

[3] See Reading 3, Part 3. Figure 4 of that reading is altered slightly and reproduced here as Figure 2.

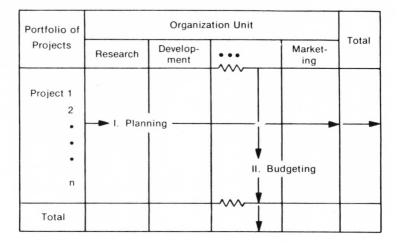

Portfolio of Projects	Organization Unit				Total
	Research	Develop-ment	•••	Market-ing	
Project 1 2 • • • n	→ I. Planning —————————→ → II. Budgeting				
Total					

Figure 2   The Planning/Budgeting Sequence of Functional Departments

decision-making procedure should be based to a large extent on management's best subjective estimate of the probability of final success for the project in the marketplace, and should not merely consider whether the project is physically ready to be moved from one stage to another.

As we stated earlier, many corporations have divisional business planning systems which incorporate variations of the three classes of procedures discussed in this section. The particular design considerations should be to a large degree a function of the situational setting of the

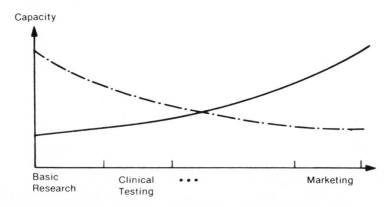

Figure 3   Profiles of the Capacity of the Strategic Project Organization of Divisions with Scarce Capacity in Basic Research (Solid Line) and in Marketing (Dashed Line)

organization in question. Thus, there will be no single right way of incorporating the planning procedures, given that all corporations are more or less unique. It should be emphasized that all three aspects must be taken into account in order for a division to plan properly. If any one issue is neglected, the overall effectiveness of the division's planning will be substantially diminished even if the other aspects of the planning are very well executed. Still divisions which do a reasonably balanced job of planning may yet face two additional problems; there may still exist a lack of proper divisional risk-handling and/or inappropriate strategic business attractiveness/strength analysis. In discussing these two classes of problems, we shall suggest that they might be highly interrelated and that they might be avoided by more properly structured divisional planning systems.

PROBLEMS OF RISK-HANDLING

We have observed that the long-term success of a company's businesses depends to a large extent on the ability of the divisions to generate sufficient strategic business projects. It should be noted that new strategic business project developments are by nature uncertain and that the more uncertain projects typically have higher potential rewards associated with them. Now, consider a corporation with two divisions, each one in the process of finalizing its business plans regarding which strategic business projects to emphasize. The first division is faced with setting priorities among ten projects and the second division has fifteen projects to consider. Each division will weigh the probability of success of each project and its resulting payoff against the probability of failure and its cost and set its priorities accordingly. In the end, each division will probably give priority to some "safe" and some "risky but promising" projects among their ten and fifteen projects respectively. If on the other hand, we hypothetically assume that the two divisions have been merged into one, the task would be to set priorities among twenty-five projects. In this case, there is a greater likelihood that high risk projects would be chosen, since they would be "averaged out" against a larger number of safe projects. Thus, in this situation we might well include a project that both divisions independently would have deemed too risky because of their smaller number of options.

For the company as a whole, the overall riskiness of its business project portfolio, given that the portfolio is of some size, will not increase significantly with the undertaking of a very risky but potentially promising new project, because the risk will "average out" over the entire portfolio. A division with its smaller portfolio has fewer projects among which to average out a risky project. Consequently, a division manager will be more reluctant to take on risky but potentially promising projects[4] because his/her division normally will be held accountable for performance and incentive compensation is based on this.

Where the divisions construct their strategic project portfolios in total independence of one another, the corporate project portfolio, with its implicit risk characteristics, can be found by adding together the division portfolios. We can assume that this corporate strategic project portfolio will have more conservative risk characteristics than if the corporate portfolio had been chosen directly by top management. Thus, by delegating the responsibility for choosing the divisional portfolios, the company as a whole may move in a more conservative direction.[5]

The traditional scheme for business planning, then, would seem to promote plans that tend to view the company as a collection of independent companies. In terms of risk-taking, the advantages of being big are not realized. There still remains the question of what can be done to modify business planning so that ". . . the large organization . . . can do things the small organization cannot do. It can commit resources for a much longer time, for instance, to long-term research projects that are beyond the staying power of the small business."[6]

We shall offer a suggestion for at least partially overcoming this. The corporate level may play a more active role by attempting to assess overall corporate risk-taking and, if necessary, "upgrading" some of the divisional business project portfolios toward greater "riskiness." This implies that the division will have to undertake its business strategy analysis in a different way than is now being done so that the corporate/divisional interaction on risk-taking can be an orderly part of the planning review procedures.

BUSINESS STRATEGY ANALYSIS

We have suggested that the issues involved in arriving at more appropriate corporate risk-taking may be a function of better business strategy analysis. This may be done in part by incorporating proper business

---

[4] Several research studies have documented a tendency toward risk aversion in research project selection in large divisionalized firms. For further details, see D. Hamberg, "Invention in the Industrial Laboratory," *Journal of Political Economy*, April 1963.

[5] In the above, we have assumed, of course, that the attitudes towards risk-taking will be determined as a consequence of portfolio size variations. Nevertheless, we might encounter a very conservative corporate management which is more cautious than its young, aggressive division managers. In such a situation, a conservative attitude might more than counterbalance the risk-taking advantages due to project size. We shall, however, not discuss this situation here.

[6] See P. F. Drucker, *Management: Tasks, Responsibilities, Practices* (New York: Harper & Row, 1974).

strategy analysis into a formal planning system. Another issue, however, focuses on what might be the most appropriate measures for "business attractiveness" and "business strength" in various situations. An emerging consideration deals with a division's evaluation of business lines together and with corporate evaluation of a portfolio of divisional plans.

Measurement of the Strategic Dimensions

Business Attractiveness. The factors governing attractiveness of the business should be seen as given and beyond the control of the company, at least in the short run. This does not imply, however, that a division will have no power to bring a product out of a relatively unattractive business and into a more attractive business. For instance, it might attempt to resegment a product so that it ends up in a higher growth segment. Several measures of business attractiveness are listed below.

1. Market growth rate. Traditionally, this has been the most frequently used measure of business attractiveness, and was originally suggested by the Boston Consulting Group who have pioneered business strategy analysis.[7]
2. Frequently vs. infrequently purchased products. Data collected by the Marketing Science Institute through their PIMS project indicated that businesses with infrequently purchased products seem to enjoy a slightly higher return on investment than businesses with frequently purchased products when normalized for market share.[8] As a result, businesses with infrequently purchased products seem more attractive.
3. Concentrated vs. fragmented customers. The PIMS study found the same effect to hold for businesses facing fragmented customers as contrasted with businesses facing a concentrated set of customers.[9] Thus, businesses with fragmented customers seem more attractive.
4. Barriers to new competition. Another factor which often affects the attractiveness of the business is how easy or difficult it will be for competitors to enter the business. This is determined by such considerations as the investment intensity required, patent protection, and know-how advantages.[10]
5. Size of market. The absolute size of a market will be a major influence on the long-term economic potential for a business line.
6. Structure of competition. The final factor to be mentioned relates to the nature of the competition. Are there many competitors? What is the

---

[7] See Henderson, "Perspectives" and "Experience Curve."

[8] PIMS is an abbreviation for "Profit Impact of Market Share." See Schoeffler, Buzzell and Heany, "Impact," and Buzzell, Gale and Sultan, "Market Share."

[9] See Buzzell, Gale and Sultan, "Market Share."

[10] See J. S. Bain, *Barriers to New Competition.* Cambridge, Mass.: Harvard University Press, 1956).

degree of concentration? These factors will affect the degree of freedom one will have regarding pricing. The more freedom one has in pricing, the more attractive the business.[11]

Each of the above factors is likely to play an important role in judging the attractiveness of a business. It would, however, be utopian to assume that there exists one universal ranking of these factors as to their relative effect on business attractiveness. The choice of relevant factors for measuring the attractiveness of competing business lines should therefore be situational, and each division must develop its own ranking system. It will thus be an important task in planning systems design to come up with the list of ranked factors that is most relevant for a given division. It follows that the factors might differ from one division to another within the same company as well as among divisions of different corporations. An attempt should be made to hold the variables list, including its implied ranking, relatively constant over time in order to minimize potential "gaming" in planning as well as to facilitate communication and review.

Relative Competitive Strength. Unlike business attractiveness, competitive strength can be influenced by the organization. Policy choices on the divisional and corporate levels significantly affect this dimension. The following is a list of factors commonly used to measure competitive strength.

1. Market share. This is the most common measure of competitive strength—the higher the market share the stronger the competitive strength. The PIMS study has found clear positive correlation between market share and returns on investment.[12]

   One should distinguish between absolute and relative measures for market share. Normally market share will have to be measured relative to one or more competitors. This implies that there will often be the difficult task of measuring competitors' market share. After having obtained a market share picture, however, one might merely want to compare one's own absolute sales against past sales, a considerably simpler procedure. It should also be noted that considerable emphasis should be put on what might be a reasonable definition of what constitutes the market. How broadly the market should be defined will probably differ from case to case.

2. Strategic expenditure level. Another indication of competitive strength might be the level of strategic discretionary expenditures, such as R&D expenditures and marketing expenditures. This measure assumes that each of the dollar expenditures to be compared is spent with approxi-

---

[11] Economic theories of the firm have been very preoccupied with this issue. For a survey, see W. D. Maxwell, *Price Theory and Applications in Business Administration.* (Pasadena, Calif.: Goodyear Publishing, 1970).

[12] See Buzzell, Gale and Sultan, "Market Share."

mately equal effectiveness. Unwise strategic expenditures, of course, will add little, if any, to competitive strength.

3. Product quality. High product quality may significantly enhance competitive strength.
4. Capacity utilization. High capacity utilization may also contribute to competitive strength since it means wider absorption of fixed investment costs. This factor is more important for capital intensive industries.

It should be reiterated that these are not necessarily the only factors which may affect a given division's competitive strength. Furthermore, as was the case with business attractiveness, the relative importance of each factor may vary from division to division and thus we do not offer a general ranking. The key question for determining the balance between factors will be "which factor is the one which the division wants to influence through its policy?" Or to phrase the question slightly differently, "which factor does a particular division want to build, hold or harvest?" It should be emphasized that the situational choices of business strength variables should be seen as part of the planning system design task, and should not be left to each business manager to choose according to his preference (and possible advantage).

Let us conclude our discussion of the measurement of the strategic dimensions of business line strategy analysis by suggesting the importance of two issues which often are overlooked. First, the actual choice of variables with regard to both business strength and business attractiveness is a vital aspect of the *design* of a division's planning system and second, it should be remembered that these design choices ought to be done on a contingency basis.

Consolidation of Product Line Strategy Analyses

Product line strategy is an important building block in the business plans of both the division and the corporation as a whole. After the product line strategy has been completed, a number of analytical tasks still must be performed. One will concern the consolidation of the business project or line strategies into an overall business strategy for the divisions. A second task will be to evaluate these business strategies at the corporate level in order to arrive at a sound corporate strategy. In the discussion which follows, we shall see that a third dimension of analysis is required to effectuate these two consolidations properly.

Consolidation into a Division Strategy. Viewed in isolation a business line or project is valued according to its position with regard to business attractiveness and competitive strength. Within this limited framework, a strategy which emphasizes high market share/market growth potential (assuming appropriate measures of these dimensions have been stressed) is likely to imply a set of cash flows which, when discounted to net present value, will have a higher net worth than cash flows generated by strategic projects which rank less advantageously on these dimensions. Thus, a business project "cost/benefit" analysis is undertaken, and the projects are ranked according to this. When considering strategic line analysis in its context as part of a formal corporate long-range planning system, however, it turns out that this ranking based on a two-dimensional approach is inadequate. A third dimension should come into play when more than one business strategy is being put together into a broader planning portfolio, namely, a measure of how well the total "package" of business projects or line strategies fit together. We shall call this third dimension the *consolidation attractiveness dimension*. As we shall explain below, this dimension should focus primarily on cash flow and synergy-potentials considerations. Figure 4 summarizes the business line strategy matrix in its revised version.

The following factors might be used to measure the consolidation dimension.

1. Shape of cash flow. For the division as a whole it is not sufficient to set priorities among business lines according to net present value of expected cash flows. The timing of these cash flows must be considered as well. The balance of cash flows should be positive over time if the division wishes to avoid the need for additional outside liquidity.

2. Size of cash flow. It may be important that a balance be maintained among expected cash flows from all projects. Division management will often prefer an evenly distributed set of cash flows from projects rather than the more exposed position which may arise when cash flows are largely dependent on one business line.

3. Risk of cash flow. Another important consideration for division management is the riskiness of the expected cash flows from the product lines. High risk/high potential payoff projects must be traded off against safer but less glamorous ones. Thus it is the job of division management to plan its business lines in such a way that the riskiness of the division's overall expected cash flow does not become too large.

4. Covariance of cash flows. Division management must also consider the extent to which business cash flows will be expected to fluctuate along the same or different patterns. The less the covariance among the business line cash flows, the better.

5. Production synergy effects. There may be instances where several products originate from the same production process thereby enabling division management to take advantage of economies of scale. An example of this is the silicones industrial chemistry where highly integrated production leads to a wide variety of product options.

6. Marketing synergy effects. Often existing marketing capabilities, such as a sales force, can be utilized to promote an additional product. New projects should relate to existing products in such a way that they may be promoted through existing marketing facilities.

7. R&D synergy effects. Large R&D expenditure savings may be possible if general research capabilities and know-how can be applied to new projects.

8. Substitution opportunity. Last but not least, comes an often overlooked factor that relates to whether it will be easy or difficult, risky or not risky to deemphasize one existing business line in favor of a new one. Because it is easier to give up competitive advantage than to develop it, we need a measure which indicates the consequences of shifts in emphasis in a business project portfolio.

We see that the strategic planning task of the division will be to systematically evaluate the business line or project strategies and to construct a comprehensive business plan from these "building blocks." It should be stressed that the divisional business strategy should not be based on a business attractiveness/business strength analysis for the division as a whole, but should result from an aggregation of separate attractiveness/strength analyses for each of the division's product lines. It will be a primary task of the formal planning system to facilitate the derivation of the divisional business plans through a proper aggregation procedure. Again it will largely be a situational question to determine which factors to put primary emphasis on along the consolidation dimension. At one extreme, a division that operates within a single business line will have no consolidation problem. At the other extreme, a division which operates in a large number of business lines will probably consider all the consolidation factors relevant.

Consolidation into a Corporate Strategy. It is outside the scope of this article to review the entire divisional-corporate planning interface through which the divisional plans become consolidated into an overall corporate portfolio plan.[13] We shall, however, discuss the effects such a consolidation may have on product-line strategies. Two sets of considerations will be relevant in this respect.

1. Assessment of overall corporate risk-taking exposure. As we discussed in the section on risk-handling, there is a tendency toward an overly conservative risk-taking profile when business line priorities are set by the divisions entirely on their own. A proper evaluation of the implicit risk exposure of the proposed divisional plans can only be accomplished

---

[13] See Reading 2, Part 1.

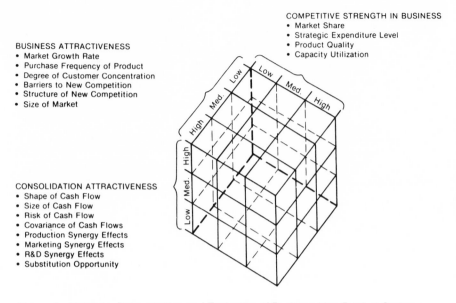

BUSINESS ATTRACTIVENESS
• Market Growth Rate
• Purchase Frequency of Product
• Degree of Customer Concentration
• Barriers to New Competition
• Structure of New Competition
• Size of Market

CONSOLIDATION ATTRACTIVENESS
• Shape of Cash Flow
• Size of Cash Flow
• Risk of Cash Flow
• Covariance of Cash Flows
• Production Synergy Effects
• Marketing Synergy Effects
• R&D Synergy Effects
• Substitution Opportunity

COMPETITIVE STRENGTH IN BUSINESS
• Market Share
• Strategic Expenditure Level
• Product Quality
• Capacity Utilization

Figure 4   Matrix for Determination and Evaluation of Business Line Product Strategy

through a divisional-corporate interface. Consequently, information on risk dimensions must be readily available from the divisional proposals themselves. The planning system should ensure such communication in order to facilitate adjustment of divisional plans to take advantage of the risk-absorption capacity of the corporation as a whole.

2. Proper assessment of divisions' proposals. Once the potentials of divisional business lines have been assessed, corporate performance targets should be set at levels consistent with the divisional business strategies. While this may seem elementary, it is actually quite difficult unless the planning system is carefully designed to provide sufficient information about business line strategies which can be used in target setting. The consequences of failure to collect and utilize such information are illustrated in the following recent example.

A large U.S.-based multinational corporation embarked on a major diversification effort in the 1950s and 1960s. The company was well-known for its rigorous management systems, centered around a detailed planning and control system which was implemented across the company. Typical of the way the system worked was a tight linkage between planning and control and heavy pressure on subsidiary managements to fulfill ambitious, centrally-set performance targets as exemplified by the agreed upon budgets. Plans and budgets were determined at negotiations meetings where subsidiary managements met with corporate and European area managements over extended periods of time and where the atmosphere was one of "no-nonsense pressure" on the subsidiaries. Each subsidiary was held to specific targets in five key areas: sales, net income, total assets, total employees and capital expenditures. No attempt was made at evaluating the divisions' business strategies directly by addressing the nature of the underlying business line or project strategies. As a result, divisions were virtually forced to let their market shares erode in order to satisfy corporate performance requirements in the short run. The long-term profitability prospects were seriously jeopardized because of these market share sacrifices. This has become painfully evident in the ensuing years.

An important adjunct to this discussion is the acknowledgment of the fact that incentive compensation for division managers should recognize that the criteria for division success are more complex than profits alone. Overly simplistic incentive compensation measures should be avoided but instead long-term track records should be developed for the division managers over the broader set of relevant dimensions. There should be an audit procedure for business project failure to identify what dimensions of the project have been fulfilled and what portions have failed. In total, the incentive compensation system should be consistent with the relevant set of variables as indicated by Figure 4. If it is not, it will probably become dysfunctional for desired risk-taking.[14]

CONCLUSIONS

Long-range planning at the divisional level, is, in many respects, the "backbone" of the overall long-range planning activities of the firm. Luckily, much is now known about sound divisional planning practices and a set of useful business planning tools has evolved. In this article, we have briefly reviewed the more commonly used tools, and have identified two interrelated deficiencies which frequently appear when examining long-range planning activities within divisions. First, we pointed out that while the divisionalized structure offers important advantages, implicit in its makeup is the threat that divisions will encounter risk considerations as if they were independent companies. Such individual planning by divisions forfeits certain benefits which may be accrued if the corporation as a whole interjects its larger perspective. The second problem we identified dealt with the way in which strategic business analysis is performed. We pointed out that not only will many divisions define business strength and business attractiveness inappropriately for their given situations but also that divisions have a tendency to overlook a third dimension of overall corporate fit when constructing their business plans. The absence of this

---

[14] See W. H. Newman, *Constructive Control* (Englewood Cliffs, N.J.: Prentice-Hall, 1975).

third dimension, which we called the consolidation attractiveness dimension, makes it exceedingly difficult for corporate management to interact with the divisions. It is this dimension which enables corporate management to evaluate business plans in terms of risk and to judge the degree of fit among divisional plans.

It will be the responsibility of the planning system to facilitate effective incorporation of risk-handling through a proper identification of the dimensions of the business plans. A planning system which is designed with these problems in mind should be able to keep the difficulties we have pointed out to a minimum.

Case 1

Massey-Ferguson, Ltd.-A*

INTEGRATED PLANNING AND CONTROL

In November 1970, Mr. Peter Breyfogle, the Comptroller of Massey-Ferguson, Ltd., was considering several problems which had plagued corporate management in recent years. Poor sales forecasting was not at all uncommon in the farm machinery industry, but at Massey-Ferguson (MF) this problem had been compounded by slow operational response times and what he suspected to be a conscious delay by optimistic field managers in reporting adverse operating conditions to the corporation.

The recent economic downturn in North America had made it especially important that a solution to these problems be found. Economic and monetary conditions were likely to temporarily dampen MF's growth rate and the primary source of new earnings was likely to become improved operating efficiency. But satisfactory improvements in operating efficiency depended to a considerable extent on the quality of the information reported by the operating units to corporate headquarters where major resource allocation and product strategy decisions were made.

Mr. Breyfogle held administrative authority and accountability for not

---

* This case was prepared with the cooperation of Massey-Ferguson, Ltd. It was written by Ronald M. Hall, Research Assistant, under the direction of Professor Richard F. Vancil, based partly upon a research report submitted by Messrs. Dick Travers and Carlos Williams. Copyright © 1971 by the President and Fellows of Harvard College.

only regular control reporting, but also for the planning function through MF's Integrated Planning and Control (IPC) system. In the latter capacity he worked under the general guidance of the Senior Vice President—Corporate Administration. He suspected that some of the company's problems could be traced to the way in which goals were set for the operating units. However, Mr. Breyfogle knew that he would have to have a very strong case if he wished to effect a change in management's goal setting philosophy.

CORPORATE PROFILE

In 1970 Massey-Ferguson, Ltd, was the world's largest manufacturer of farm tractors, combines, backhoes and loaders, and diesel engines. In addition, the company produced a wide line of other farm machinery, office furniture, and recreation equipment. Tractors comprised 35% of 1969's sales; other farm machinery accounted for an additional 28%. The remainder of Massey-Ferguson's Canadian $1,043,000,000 volume was divided approximately equally among industrial and construction equipment, engines, and replacement parts. Exhibit 1 presents a ten-year statistical summary of the company's operations.

Massey-Ferguson had customers in more than 180 countries and 57 plants either manufacturing or assembling MF products in 22 countries spread throughout the world. Several other factors besides the geographic dispersion of MF operations helped to create what one corporate executive termed "a bloody complex operating situation." While worldwide sales of farm machinery were expected to grow at an average rate of 3%-5% per year in the foreseeable future, sales growth rates had fluctuated between 0.5% and 13.0%, with little discernible pattern, over the last 10 years. Nearly one-third of annual sales were concentrated in a three-month period coinciding with annual farm crop harvests. Mr. John G. Staiger, Senior Vice President-Corporate Administration, commented upon the farm equipment industry as follows:

> This is such a terrifyingly cyclical industry. It is affected by environmental forces which are so much more difficult to control than is the case in other industries which can appreciably influence their environments by inputs of advertising, promotion or personal contact. When there is a drought and crops fail, you just aren't going to sell anything. You can't cure a drought, or a hailstorm, or a fungus epidemic—it's a natural disaster. The farmer won't buy unless he needs the machine—if he needs it, he wants it today—and his need did not develop until yesterday. This situation demands that your harvesting equipment be manufactured and sitting in the showroom and warehouses at the same time the market breaks.
>
> When you consider also all the other things that can, and do happen to you

Exhibit 1 MASSEY-FERGUSON, LTD. STATISTICAL SUMMARY

		1969	1968	1967	1966	1965	1964	1963	1962	1961	1960
Net Sales	($)	1043.4	916.8	913.3	932.1	808.5	772.0	685.7	596.1	519.3	490.4
Asset Turnover	(%)	94.9	97.5	98.6	110.2	109.0	124.2	122.3	111.7	102.2	107.1
Gross Margin	(%)	22.7	23.1	21.7	22.5	22.0	23.6	22.6	21.4	20.8	20.4
Net Income	($)	33.1	28.4	26.6	45.2	40.1	45.0	24.1	18.1	15.2	13.2
Return on Equity	(%)	7.1	6.3	6.1	10.6	12.4	15.5	9.5	8.1	7.2	6.6
Net Current Assets	($)	355.6	358.4	353.7	365.0	274.8	265.1	250.4	189.7	179.4	175.6
Current Ratio		1.8	2.1	2.1	2.4	2.0	2.4	2.6	1.9	1.9	2.1
Depreciation and Amortization	($)	33.0	34.0	32.5	30.2	26.0	23.0	20.4	20.2	19.1	18.8
Total Capital Additions	($)	41.3	33.2	53.2	50.8	47.0	40.7	29.3	21.6	25.7	16.9
Capital Structure											
Current Liabilities	(%)	42.7	34.6	34.0	30.8	36.7	29.6	28.8	38.2	37.7	33.8
Other Liabilities	(%)	15.2	17.8	18.8	18.5	19.7	23.7	26.0	20.0	20.8	22.3
Shareholder's Equity	(%)	42.1	47.6	47.2	50.7	43.6	46.7	45.2	41.8	41.5	43.9
Per Common Share											
Sales	($)	57.34	50.56	50.37	51.42	53.69	52.09	50.81	48.59	42.56	40.54
Net Income	($)	1.82	1.57	1.47	2.50	2.66	3.04	1.68	1.36	1.13	0.97
Dividends	($)	1.00	1.00	1.00	1.00	0.90	0.57	0.50	0.40	0.40	0.40
Equity	($)	25.46	24.68	24.11	23.64	21.48	19.60	16.81	15.97	15.03	14.34
Price—High	($)	25[4]	24[6]	27[2]	37	36[1]	31[4]	17	14[1]	14[5]	12[1]
—Low	($)	16[3]	14	15[2]	20	27[2]	16[7]	12[2]	10	10[2]	8[2]

Note: Per Common share figures based on weighted average of shares outstanding during year. Share figures in United States dollars. All other figures represent millions of Canadian dollars.

Source: MASSEY-FERGUSON, LIMITED, *ANNUAL REPORT 1969*; Pitfield, "The Farm Machinery Industry," MacKay and Co.; *The Wall Street Transcript*, January 12, 1970.

in this industry, such as fluctuations in the availability of financing, competitive innovation, inflation, currency adjustments, strikes, and local government economic regulations, the asset management implications are enormous. There is always a great deal of capital tied up relative to current income and the return on this investment is exceedingly vulnerable. The normal techniques for assuring growth are a little more difficult to apply. However, we, meaning the senior management of the company, have decided that there is sufficient untapped potential in our existing businesses. And, we are not at this time interested in entering new industries but rather in improving our position in the ones we are now in.

The largest concentration of ownership of Massey-Ferguson had for many years been the interests of the Argus Corporation, Ltd. The operations of Argus had been characterized by one prominent investment service as follows:

> This investment company places a major portion of funds in a limited number of enterprises which show probability of future growth and expansion. It makes an investment sufficiently large to have representation in formulating policy.

The approach that top management had selected for assuring Massey-Ferguson's growth was a "delicate balance between centralized and decentralized management." Since Mr. Albert A. Thornbrough took over the leadership of the company during a mid-1950s crisis, MF had moved generally in the direction of increased organizational and procedural uniformity. Mr. Thornbrough and others of his senior management considered an explicit and consistent definition of individual management tasks, responsibilities and accountability a prerequisite to the effective functioning of a management system which coupled the market sensitivity of a decentralized structure with the economic and competitive advantages of a centralized structure.

Massey-Ferguson engaged in two major corporate reorganizations as management sought to achieve a satisfactory balance between centralization and decentralization. The first, in 1959, organized the company into profit centers called operations units. These, through 1970, comprised the building blocks of MF's structure. Each operations unit was headed by a General Manager who, until 1966, formally reported solely to the President, Mr. Thornbrough. Operations units activities were marketing in defined geographic areas and often also manufacturing for one or several markets. General Managers were responsible for all MF functions within their assigned area except decisions relating to product line strategy and design, the locations of facilities, the allocation of capital for investments and expenditures, and interunit transfer pricing and volumes. However, in each of these areas the General Managers played an important part in initiating and reviewing proposed actions.

Essentially, the General Managers were charged with the responsibility for decisions that capitalized on local opportunities to increase sales volume, reduce manufacturing costs, and raise operating efficiency. Corporate level executives felt that even though there was substantial interunit trade based upon economic sourcing patterns, the profitability of individual operation units due to local management actions was accurately identifiable. And, the General Managers were held fully accountable for the profits of their operations units.

In practice, the General Managers' relationship with the President took precedence over their relationships with the Vice Presidents of Farm Machinery and Industrial & Construction Machinery. While the latter were in the process of building Group operating authority, their relationships with the operations units could in 1970 be characterized as advisory. The Engines Group maintained a strong group Vice President function largely due to the fact that this group had existed as an autonomous unit prior to its 1959 acquisition by Massey-Ferguson. Exhibit 2 depicts MF's 1970 management structure.

THE DEVELOPMENT OF INTEGRATED PLANNING AND CONTROL

Following the 1959 reorganization, management said, "Okay, we are going to plan and control from now on. We now have the uniformity, the organization and structure established, so that we can get a uniform approach to planning and get uniform results out." However, MF management then discovered an additional problem, which was the identification of the information inputs and sources required to effectively monitor and control the operating units at the corporate level without building a large staff. To help identify and resolve these information needs, the services of a management consulting firm were employed. Subsequently the scope of the project was widened and the joint effort of the McKinsey & Co. consultants and Massey-Ferguson's people produced a management system which was entitled "Integrated Planning and Control" (IPC). One of MF's top executives recalled that the selection of this appellation was a deliberate attempt to emphasize that the ultimate objective was to develop a worldwide consolidated plan that *committed* management to growth. The adjective "integrated" was also to serve as a continual reminder of the coordination and cooperation, both horizontal and vertical, which was deemed necessary to achieve this objective.

IPC Theory. The logical core of the IPC system which evolved over the ten-year period, 1960–1970, was the supposition that "The most effective approach to corporate planning and control is the one that maximizes the proportion of the company's financial results that is attributable directly

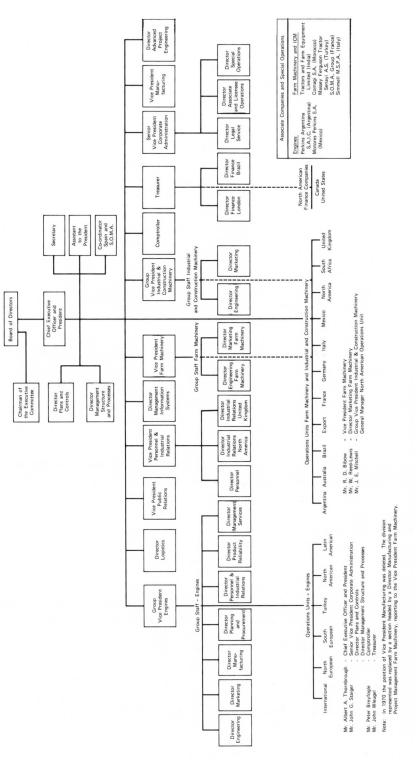

Board of Directors

Chief Executive Officer and President

Chairman of the Executive Committee

Secretary

Assistant to the President

Co-ordinator Spain and S.O.M.A.

Director Plans and Controls

Director Management Structure and Processes

Group Staff - Engines

Director Engineering
Director Marketing
Director Manufacturing
Director Planning and Procurement
Director Personnel & Industrial Relations
Group Vice President Engines

Operations Units - Engines

International | North European | South European | Turkey | North American | Latin American

Director Logistics

Vice President Public Relations

Vice President Personnel & Industrial Relations

Director Management Services
Director Product Reliability
Director Personnel
Director Industrial Relations North America
Director Industrial Relations United Kingdom

Director Management Information Systems

Vice President Farm Machinery

Group Staff Farm Machinery

Director Engineering Farm Machinery
Director Marketing Farm Machinery

Operations Units Farm Machinery and Industrial and Construction Machinery

Argentina | Australia | Brazil | Export | France | Germany | Italy | Mexico | North America | South Africa | United Kingdom

Group Vice President Industrial and Construction Machinery

Group Staff Industrial and Construction Machinery

Director Engineering
Director Marketing

Comptroller

Treasurer

Director Finance London
Director Finance Brazil

North American Finance Companies
Canada
United States

Senior Vice President Corporate Administration

Director Legal Service

Director Associate and Licensee Operations

Vice President Manufacturing

Director Special Operations

Director Advanced Project Engineering

Associate Companies and Special Operations

Engines	Farm Machinery and ICM
Perkins Argentina S.A.I.C. (Argentina)	Tractors and Farm Equipment Limited (India)
Motores Perkins S.A. (Mexico)	Comagi S.A. (Morocco)
	Massey Ferguson Tractor Senayi A.S. (Turkey)
	S.O.M.A. Group (France)
	Simmell M.S.P.A. (Italy)

Mr. Albert A. Thornbrough – Chief Executive Officer and President
Mr. John G. Staiger – Senior Vice President Corporate Administration
 – Director Plans and Controls
 – Director Management: Structure and Processes
Mr. Peter Brevfogle – Comptroller
Mr. John Wleugel – Treasurer

Mr. R. D. Bibow – Vice President Farm Machinery
Mr. W. Reed-Lewis – Director Marketing Farm Machinery
Mr. J. E. Mitchell – Group Vice President Industrial & Construction Machinery
 – General Manager North American Operations Unit

Note: In 1970 the position of Vice President Manufacturing was deleted. The division represented was replaced by a section headed by a Director Manufacturing and Project Management Farm Machinery, reporting to the Vice President Farm Machinery.

Exhibit 2 Massey-Ferguson Limited World-Wide Management Organization

to change and improvement initiated by managers."[1] From this fundamental statement the entire structure of the IPC system was derived. The
purpose of IPC was to maximize the impact of change and improvement.
The corporate profit and sales objectives were to be achieved by action
initiated by individual managers. Progress in the achievement of objectives was to be measured in terms of two variables: 1) The financial impact
of changes occurring independently of management action, and, 2) the
financial impact of changes resulting from management initiative.

The dynamics of the IPC theory consisted of three phases: 1) directing
management effort toward the attainment of acceptable financial goals;
2) obtaining firm personal commitment to achieve agreed-upon goals;
and 3) encouraging flexibility in the implementation of plans by the
development of new or revised courses of action when required by
changed circumstances.

Messrs. S. R. Wilson and John O. Tomb, the authors of *Improving
Profits Through Integrated Planning and Control,* were involved in the development of IPC at Massey-Ferguson. They identified in their book
several management activities necessary to complete each of the three
phases noted above. Directing effort effectively towards goal achievement
involved developing management understanding of the business and the
way it reacts to change, determining the expected financial results if
management does not introduce significant change during a planning
period, and establishing an over-all financial goal that reflects the
achievement of demanding (but realistic) new management tasks. Obtaining firm personal commitments to achieve goals involved developing the
detailed management action programs required to achieve the financial
goal and evaluating these programs in terms of their overall potential to
satisfy the financial performance requirements. Encouraging flexibility
of management action involved adhering to agree-upon goals as the
standard of satisfactory performance, identifying in advance probable
deviations from the financial goal, and responding quickly to changed
circumstances in a manner which would ensure achievement of the
planned results.

IPC Evolution.   The first application of IPC theory to operations management was conducted in 1960 in the United Kingdom unit. The project
was supervised by a team of MF managers and outside consultants. Their
initial objectives were to construct ambitious plans, well supported by
realistic action programs for 1961, and to establish a working model of a
planning and control system which could be extended to the whole
company. Anticipating procedural start-up difficulties, the project team
deliberately limited the planning horizon of this initial effort to one year.

[1] S. R. Wilson and John O. Tomb, *Improving Profits Through Integrated Planning and Control* (Englewood
Cliffs, N.J.: Prentice-Hall, Inc., 1968), p. 4.

The advisability of this policy was later borne out when it was found necessary to devote substantial time to what later became known as a "responsibility audit" before actual planning activities could be undertaken. The responsibility audit involved an investigation of functions and tasks performed within the operating unit which were essential to the effective management of operations. The audit first uncovered large areas of duplication and ambiguity, and later aided the operations unit's management to resolve these shortcomings with clearer lines of communication, explicitly identified individual responsibilities and closer interfunctional coordination. The responsibility audit proved so beneficial that the practice was repeated later by other operations units as they were brought into the IPC system.

Exhibit 3 presents the simple cycle through which the operations unit moved in 1960. In June of that year, Mr. Thornbrough, the President, issued a profit goal for the operations unit. At that time this profit goal produced considerable consternation among the operations unit management as it called for substantial immediate profit improvement. The simple statement of a profit goal was not accompanied by any explanation, justification, or direction, and management entertained severe doubts about their ability to produce the profits demanded. (It later developed that the profit goal was exceeded by 10%.) The detailed planning by managers commenced in late June when the project team disseminated the Planning Guide. This set of instructions, designed to provide a more or less uniform approach to the preparation of plans, suggested charts or tabular formats for describing 1961's expected operating environment, contained samples of each form with the identification of probable information sources, suggested methods of preparation and analysis, included a summary of points that should be covered in supporting data for plans, and provided an outline of the approach that managers should use in formulating action programs.

While the initial attempt at Integrated Planning and Control involved what management felt to be an excessive cost in terms of manhours and paper work, management also felt that 1960s experience had demonstrated the utility of the IPC system. There was a marked, favorable contrast between the detailed action programs which appeared to provide realistic support for an ambitious profit goal for the United Kingdom operating unit, and the simple budgets, based upon historical experience and market trends, which the remaining operations units produced in 1960.

On the basis of lessons learned, in 1961 the IPC system was extended to cover three additional operations units. In order to satisfy the general managers' requests for a greater understanding of the rationale underlying the President's goal setting, the General Managers were given an opportunity to submit to the President a preliminary assessment of their

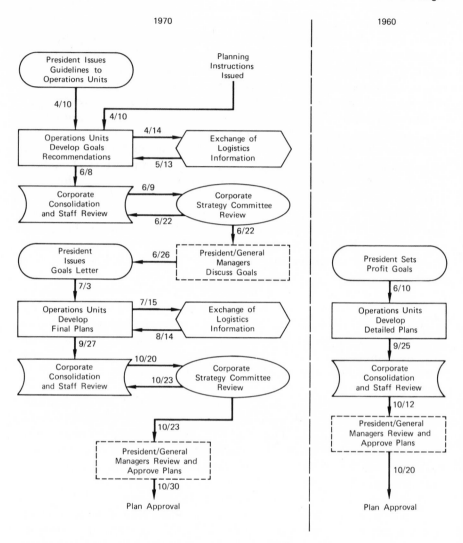

Exhibit 3   Massey-Ferguson, Ltd. Planning Cycles—1960 and 1970

units' prospects for the coming year. These assessments or goals recommendations were found by corporate management to be lacking in that they did not appropriately reflect the overall corporate needs. Corporate management decided that, in subsequent years, it would be necessary to provide an additional input of presidential guidance to establish the order of magnitude of corporate goals prior to asking the General Managers for their profit goal recommendations. Also in 1961 a technique was devised and implemented to resolve difficulties experienced in 1960 in comparing plans with the budget. The technique basically consisted of adjusting the current year's profit, sales and assets forecasts to reflect the profit, sales and asset impacts expected to be realized from (1) previous years' projects, (2) nonrecurring events and environmental changes, and (3) new management actions. Exhibit 4, MF's Impact Summary Format, demonstrates this technique as it was practiced in 1970s planning.

During the planning efforts of 1962 and 1963 the remaining Massey-Ferguson operating units were brought into the IPC system. Although the operating units' General Managers continued to be dissatisfied with their lack of understanding of the rationale in goal setting, an increasing proficiency in developing plans to achieve the President's goals was observed by corporate management. In 1963 the time spent by individual operating units in going through the entire planning cycle was less than that taken by the U.K. in the detailed planning portion alone in 1960.

In 1965 two changes in the planning system were made. The emphasis in control reporting was changed from a comparison of actual to planned performance-to-date, to a comparison of actual with planned performance on an entire year basis (as represented by forecasts updated monthly). The explanation given for this change, which continued in effect through 1970, was the statement that the purpose of variance analysis and control was to serve as a guide for future action rather than to merely review past performance. Various members of MF's planning and control staff at both the corporate and divisional level concurred in the opinion that the necessity of updating forecasts for the year on a monthly basis forced managers to focus on current remedial or opportunistic alternatives.

A major change in the IPC system's format initiated in 1965 resulted from Mr. Thornbrough's desire to gain a commitment from each General Manager for not only short-term sales and profit growth but also the effective, long-term utilization of all resources placed at his disposal. In 1965 the General Managers were required to submit two-year plans. To aid them in this undertaking special corporate study teams visited each operating unit in 1965, assessing operating conditions, reviewing their findings with the General Managers involved and reporting their findings to the President. In 1965 and 1966 (when this activity was repeated), the discussions of the study teams with the General Managers supplanted the initial round of goal-setting recommendations and review which had occurred from 1961 through 1964.

Great changes occurred in Massey-Ferguson's mode of operations in 1966. Continuing the course of closely examining MF's future in greater detail, during 1966 the planning horizon was extended to three years. To aid the operations units in formulating the three-year plans, the corporate staff developed a set of preliminary over-all assumptions to serve as the foundation for the plans. Basically these assumptions consisted of

Currency CUMULATIVE CDN. $ MM	1971-1975 Area Operating Profit Impact Summary			Location	
	1971	1972	1973	1974	1975
1970 Latest Forecast	100	124	142	163	190
1970 Carryover and Non-recurring					
Events					
Major Project Carryover	+9	+4	+5	+6	+8
Environment					
Competition	−2	−3	−2	−1	0
Industry Volume	+3	+4	+4	+5	+5
Industry Mix	+2	+1	+1	+2	+2
Economics - Material	−1	−1	−1	−1	−1
- Wages	−1	−2	−2	−2	−2
- Salaries	−1	−1	0	0	0
Export Sales	+4	+4	+4	+5	+5
Intercompany Sales	+2	+2	+2	+3	+4
Others	+1	+1	+1	+1	+2
Planning Base	116	133	154	181	213
Management Action					
Major Projects	0	+2	+3	+3	+4
Price	+2	+1	0	+3	+2
Merchandising Programs	+2	+2	+2	0	+3
Product Cost Changes	+1	0	+1	+1	+1
Structural Cost Actions	0	+3	+2	+1	+1
Volume Decision Costs	+2	+1	+1	+1	+1
Other Actions	+1	0	0	0	0
1971 - 1975 GOALS	124	142	163	190	225
Range of Certainty					
Plus	+12	+15	+17	+20	+25
Minus	−8	−13	−16	−19	−25

Exhibit 4   Massey-Ferguson, Ltd. Impact Summary Formats

information statements concerning important future events and conditions which would be beyond the control of the operations unit managers. For example, the introduction of new products and the establishment of new intercompany price and volume levels were noted for the years covered by the plans. Arising out of top management's continuing concern for providing long-range direction for the company, and based upon management's discussions and the special corporate study team's analysis

CURRENCY CUMMULATIVE CDN. $ MM	NET SALES IMPACT SUMMARY	LOCATION 1. Consolidated O.U. 2. ICM				
Factor and Commentary		1971	1972	1973	1974	1975
1970 Sales						
Major Project Carryover						
Non-recurring Events						
Environment						

Competition
  Industry Volume
  Industry Mix
  Intercompany (All factors)
  Export						

Management Action Carryover						
ICM Net Environmental Impacts						
PLANNING BASE						
New Actions						
Price Merchandising Programs Major Projects						
Other Factors						
ICM Actions						
Total Actions and Projects						
Current Year Sales						
Range of Certainty	PLUS MINUS					

Exhibit 4 (Continued)

of the company's operations in 1965 and 1966, Massey-Ferguson's management organization was partially restructured in 1966.

PLANNING IN 1970

Exhibit 2 indicates a Director of Plans and Controls reporting directly to Mr. Thornbrough in 1970. Mr. Staiger held this title in addition to his other titles listed in Exhibit 2. However, he had delegated primary responsibility for the administration of the IPC system to Mr. Breyfogle who, in turn, also consulted with Mr. Wleugel, the Treasurer.

During the years immediately preceding Mr. Breyfogle's appointment as Corporate Comptroller in 1969, the planning and control system suffered from a lack of consistent leadership. Since the 1966 corporate reorganization, responsibility for the administration of the IPC system had passed from an internal plans and controls coordinator reporting directly to Mr. Thornbrough, to a succession of corporate comptrollers. Each of the latter attempted to fill the increasing demands for information from the system by simply appending his own ideas without exorcising the old ideas. By 1970 the planning process was, in Mr. Breyfogle's

CURRENCY CDN. $ MM

LOCATION Consolidated ICM

1971 PROFIT IMPACT SUMMARY

ACCOUNT	1970 Forecast	Non-recurring & Carry-over	Major Project Carry-over	Competition	Ind. Vol. & Mix (Incl. Export Interco.)	Economics	Others	PLANNING BASE	Price	Project	Programs	Struct. Organization	Others	1971 Plan	Range of Certainty Plus	Range of Certainty Minus
Gross Sales																
(Sales Discounts)																
Net Sales																
- Home market																
- Export																
- Other																
- Intercompany																
TOTAL NET SALES																
Direct Variable Cost																
Direct Variable Profit																
Engineering																
Manufacturing																
Physical Distribution																
Marketing																
Group Administration																
Group Operating Profit																
Allocated Area																
ABSORBED GROUP OPERATING PROFIT																
Area																
Administration																
Interest																
Miscellaneous Income																
Miscellaneous Expense																
Management Information Ser.																
Allocated Area																
AREA OPERATING PROFIT																
Non-operating Items																
Taxes																
NET INCOME																

Exhibit 4 (Continued)

CURRENCY CDN. $ MM   LOCATION _____   Consolidated ICM Engines

1971 ASSET IMPACT SUMMARY

ACCOUNT	1970 Forecast	PLANNING BASE												1971 Plan	Range of Certainty	
		Non-recurring & Carry-over	Major Project Carry-over	Competition	Ind. Vol. & Mix (Incl. Export Interco.)	Economics	Others	Price	Projects	Merchand. Programs	Asset Controls	Others		Plus	Minus
Receivables - Home market - Export - Other															
TOTAL RECEIVABLES															
Inventories Raw Material & Work in Process Finished Goods Parts In Transit															
TOTAL INVENTORIES															
Prepaid Expenses															
TOTAL CURRENT ASSETS															
Accounts Payable Other Operating Liabilities															
TOTAL NET CURR. OP. ASSETS															
Fixed Assets, Gross (Accum. Depr. and Amort.)															
TOTAL NET FIXED ASSETS															
Investments Other Assets															
TOTAL NET OPERATING ASSETS															
Decision Cost in Inventory															
TOTAL NET ASSETS															

Exhibit 4 (Continued)

words, "a complete mixture of everybody's ideas." The content of the plans and reports had suffered from one comptroller's attempt to move away from pure IPC theory by taking the income statement and using it as the foundation for extensive analytical work. The next comptroller perhaps over-reacted by going back to the impact summary and attempting to make it the complete analytical and accounting tool. In Mr. Breyfogle's opinion two of the most serious consequences of this vacillation in direction were (1) that operations units had responded by individually selecting planning and control practices without due regard for the necessity of maintaining a degree of corporate uniformity, and (2) that the demands for information placed on the operations units had become so great that the involvement/commitment of the General Managers was threatened and the corporate and group staffs had more information than they could use.

As he had directed the company through the 1970 planning cycle Mr. Breyfogle had taken actions which he felt had partially resolved the above difficulties. The Comptroller had conducted a critical review of corporate/group information needs which had allowed him to prune the system's demands upon the operations units to what he felt was an acceptable level. And, Mr. Breyfogle felt that he had achieved a workable coordination between reporting for control purposes and accounting for external reporting. However, Mr. Breyfogle had not been able to devote as much time to maintaining and evolving the system as he would have wished. In 1970 a general economic downturn in North America had forcefully altered MF's perspective from one of continued sales and profit growth to greater emphasis on effective asset utilization and control of overhead expenses. This altered perspective had placed heavy demands for analysis on the Comptroller's office and had made it difficult for him to devote more attention to the problems with the IPC system.

The Planning Cycle. Planning in 1970 formally commenced with the issuance of the Planning Guidelines by the President to each General Manager of an operations unit. Exhibit 3 indicates the chronology of the cycle which followed. The content of the guidelines received by each manager was similar; the Guidelines included discussions of:

1. Some of the problems in the prior years' planning cycles. Sample problems noted were:
    a. Operations units' managements were given insufficient strategic planning framework for the development of goals.
    b. Major projects, the core of management action, tended to become mixed in with on-going operations.
    c. The impact analyses looked only at changes and tended to overlook the basic performance trends that indicate the health of the business.

d. There was no differentiation in degree of precision requested between short-term (one year) planning and medium-term planning. The three-year time span was not long enough to show major project effects but was too long to review operational detail.

2. A summary of the proposed changes for the current year's planning, including the establishment of strategic guidelines at the outset of the planning process. The basic aim of the changes was to improve the quality of communication between the General Managers and the President and the Group Vice Presidents. The changes included, but were not restricted to, the following:

   a. Strategic guidelines for the corporation and for the relevant unit were presented in this letter.

   b. Goals recommendation submissions were requested to stress strategic thinking via the development of specific and measurable objectives within the context of the planning guidelines, the definition of management tasks (i.e., action steps required to reach each objective), and the determination if tasks could be accomplished within financial guideline limitations.

   c. Goals recommendations were expected to be assessed on the basis of the clarity of communication and the completeness with which significant environmental factors and management actions were identified and evaluated, rather than the precision of their calculation.

   d. The changes in planning methods and format were explained as being intended to permit goals recommendations to be prepared directly by the General Manager and his senior managers.

   e. Review and discussions with General Managers regarding goals would be focused on the actions taken to achieve results rather than on the results per se.

3. The basic strategic guidelines within which the total company would develop. This section accorded top priority to improving profitability from existing resources in the next year but called for more strategic projects in the years thereafter. The amount of gross capital expenditures intended in the planning year was noted, along with the amount expected to be available for new projects. A qualitative assessment of capital availability for four additional years was also included. In line with these constraints and policies the criteria for planned investments were stated.

4. The specific strategic goals guidelines for the relevant operations unit, developed by application of the basic corporate strategy to the unit's operating environment. This section stated preliminary goals recommendations in terms of improvements in direct variable profit (DVP) margins, decision costs (overhead and operating expenses), and current asset utilization, etc. Suggestions for programs to achieve these improvements were included.

Following the receipt of the Planning Guidelines, the operations unit Comptrollers received from Mr. Felker, the Forecast Evaluation Manager, a letter containing goals planning instructions and the goals submission package. This package, which chronologically preceded the final plan submission package, was with minor exceptions identical to the latter. Mr. Felker cited this duplication as a deliberate attempt to forcefully demonstrate the linkage between goal setting and action planning. Mr. Felker's letter contained a schedule of planning events and deadlines, reviewed the Presidential guidelines, communicated the decision to extend the planning horizon to five years to reflect average project lifespans, suggested the use of percentage ranges of uncertainty in describing goals, and suggested that goals recommendations be done primarily by the general managers and senior executives. In addition Mr. Felker's letter stated that the intent of the June 8th goals recommendation was to be a statement from each General Manager that, based on the events and actions outlined in the package, his assessment of profits and assets for his unit for 1971–1975 were those indicated, subject, however, to a range of uncertainty which was also indicated. Furthermore it was intended that these figures form a basis for back and forth communication regarding their acceptability and/or capability of improvement. Since they were to be a starting point for a future commitment, emphasis should be placed on actions to achieve results rather than results themselves. To develop such action, goal setting within the operations unit should be from "top down" involving the General Manager to develop the basic logic of the goals and directing the strategies to be used in the planning period. Relative to final plan submission, Mr. Felker stated that the plan should cover 1971 in detail adequate for performance control and that the following years should be covered in detail adequate for control of planning. The goals instruction letter also stated that, "Forecast sales should be based entirely on anticipated demand, considering dealer and company inventory levels (pipeline) for our major products during the planning period, as determined by market requirements and without consideration of known or assumed capacity restraints." A procedure for identifying imbalances between supply and demand through the Logistics Exchange was noted. After the exchange of information between the Logistics Department and the operations unit, the latter was assumed to have adequate information regarding new and old product availability and specifications to finalize goals and plans. Mr. Felker's letter concluded with a listing of intercompany price assumptions for the five-year planning period.

During the period from April 10 to June 8, 1970, the General Managers prepared their goals recommendations. In North American Operations (NAO) the goal setting procedure was described by members of that unit as follows:

The General Manager, Mr. Mitchell, who is incidentally also Group Vice President of Industrial & Construction Machinery, sits down with Mr. Brown, the NAO comptroller, and goes over the President's Guidelines and Mr. Felker's letter. Based on the corporate instructions, Mr. Mitchell and Mr. Brown formulate *pro forma* balance sheets, income statements and spending schedules. They then break down the *pro forma* financial statements further to approximate the operations of each functional department and subsidiary within NAO. Several rounds of discussion follow in which each department and subsidiary director is asked to develop objectives, spending schedules, and impact summaries to enable his subunit to achieve its portion of NAO's goals.

The goals recommendation section of the planning cycle involves all the managers in NAO in a nearly complete formulation of plans. You just don't know how realistic your goals are without developing the plans to support them. In going into such a high degree of detail we are running contrary to Corporate instructions as well as creating a significant additional workload for ourselves. We are continuously exploring new approaches to resolve this situation, but so far have been unsuccessful. Our problem in the past has been that the goals always seemed to be just a little bit too ambitious. We would present arguments, supported by plans, why we could make some goals or not make others and then we would be instructed to crank up our plans another notch to make some of those goals we didn't think that we could make.

This year we took a different approach and got a realistic set of financial goals. This year we have two sets of goals and plans. One set, called the financial goals and plans, describes our commitment to the corporation and reflects say a small stretch factor. This commitment to the corporation is one which I feel we can achieve. We in this unit need to achieve a set of goals and I think that we can do it this year, though it won't be easy. Our other set, the operating goals and plans, reflects a very demanding stretch factor. These represent the target that we expect NAO managers to shoot for. We recognize that these are really ambitious plans but they do not commit NAO to gearing up capital investment and other expenditures ahead of time. The thrust of the operating plans is to squeeze greater efficiency out of the resources allocated in the financial plan. Our operating plan shows how we intend to do it but does not tie us to a commitment to the corporation which would jeopardize the corporation's resources if we failed.

Following submission of the financial goals recommendations to corporate headquarters, they were reviewed and consolidated by the corporate staff and comments were prepared regarding the recommendations' logical consistency with guidelines and their financial implications. These comments were passed on to the President and the remainder of the Corporate Strategy Committee by the Comptroller and the Treasurer. The Corporate Strategy Committee was comprised of the President, the Senior Vice President—Corporate Administration and the Group Vice

Presidents. This committee, which convened periodically throughout the year, advised Mr. Thornbrough on matters relating to corporate strategy and policy. Other corporate executives, such as the Comptroller and the Treasurer were invited to attend these meetings when their opinions were required. After the discussions of the consolidated goals recommendations among top management, the President met with individual General Managers and discussed with each the fit of his goals with the needs of the corporation and the President's expectations of performance.

Following the President's discussions of the goals recommendations with the staff and General Managers, Mr. Thornbrough issued final 1971 goals to the General Managers on July 3rd, 1970. The President's goals letters compared the individual goals of the operations unit to the Planning Guidelines, stressed and explained the need for improvement in critical areas such as asset turnover, liquidity, direct variable profit margins, decision costs, and return on investment. A goal for improvement in each of these areas was stated. Suggestions of strategies that might be considered in achieving the stated goals were included.

With the receipt of the Goals Letter, the General Managers commenced assembling their final plans. Much the same procedure was utilized as had been evident in the goal setting process. Mr. Charles Kalb, NAO's General Financial Planning & Analysis Manager, described the application of IPC's impact concept to the goal setting and final planning stages as follows:

> In practice the profit impact is a logical sequence of events in planning, on one sheet of paper.[2] It provides a compact yet comprehensive way for managers to focus on their entire operation. In setting goals and assessing plans it provides a convenient way of relating and summarizing individual programs. Major programs such as pricing policy changes are indicated individually. However, the impacts of all management actions and decisions cannot be isolated. Therefore there is not a great deal of difference between the impact approach to planning and run-of-the-mill planning and forecasting. The essential advantage to the impact approach is that all managers are reminded of the influence upon current and future performance of previous years' actions, the environment, competition and such, and current project decisions.

Mr. Kalb said that the real usage of impact summaries stopped at the directors' level. He noted that at the NAO senior management level, which included the directors, the impact summaries were supported by the itemization of accounts which, of necessity, created supporting staff involvement. These accounts indicated totals for particular types of costs and were not quantitatively identified as being due to any particular event or decisions.

---

[2] See Exhibit 4.

The NAO directors' final plans were collected and consolidated by Mr. Kalb and his staff of three analysts. For both the goal setting submission and the final plan submission the General Manager of NAO, and the other General Managers, utilized additional qualitative and quantitative descriptions of their detailed plans. The length of individual operations units final plans in 1970 varied between forty and one hundred and twenty pages; the total planning package, including goals and plans submissions, comprised up to two hundred pages per operating unit. The timeliness and relevancy of the plans was facilitated by the issuance of updated forecasts of year-end performance in every month with more detailed analysis in May and August, and the update of corporate product, price and volume assumptions based upon trends and decisions prior to final plan formulation. During October the corporate staff consolidated and reviewed the operations units' planning output and passed their comments on to the Corporate Strategy Committee. The latter, including the President, reviewed the plans and noted any modifications necessary. During the President's meeting with the individual General Managers, the plans were discussed, modified if necessary, and approved by the President by October 30, the end of Massey-Ferguson's fiscal year.

IPC Control. In 1970 the basic instrument of corporate control was the monthly General Managers' Letter. The purpose of this report was to identify major changes in operations, and their causes, and to note any other factors of importance affecting the operations units. The General Managers' Letter included a profit and an asset impact summary which compared planned results to forecast results on a total year basis. These summaries noted the impact of various events and actions upon sales, direct variable profits, decision costs, area operating profits, liquidity, inventory and fixed assets. The summaries were supported by management's comments and a more detailed quantitative variance analysis on both a year-to-date and entire year basis.

One member of the Comptroller's staff observed that the General Managers' Letters and consolidated monthly reports were widely distributed among the officers and staff at corporate headquarters. Based on the information contained in the reports, the control staff identified apparent operational trends, noted their planned or unplanned impacts upon operations and passed this information both back to the appropriate General Managers and to the appropriate corporate staff officers. The data base over which the control staff presided was not limited to financial data since the Comptroller's office held responsibility for collecting regularly required information for all the corporate staff functions. The data available to the control staff on a monthly basis included sales units by product group and assessments of MF market shares and industry volume.

The monthly control report circulated within the NAO was a more detailed, yet pocketsize, edition of the monthly General Manager's Letter, though without the qualitative assessment section sent to corporate headquarters. This control report showed performance against both the financial plan and the operating plan on both a year-to-date and an entire year forecast basis. The forecasted performance which provided the basis of control evaluation was essentially the first year's plan. After final plan approval, NAO managers spread the first year's planned costs and revenues over the full year on a quarterly basis.

MANAGEMENT ASSESSMENT

Mr. Breyfogle commented:

I think that the good features of this system far outweigh the bad, and I have no intention of dropping the IPC approach. We are running a billion dollar company employing nearly fifty thousand people from here in Toronto with a headquarters of only 120 people including all staff and clerical workers.

However, in recent years a situation has developed which is blocking the smooth functioning of IPC. Our sales forecasts have been off, and this created problems, complicated by slow response times, with inventory control, facilities planning, etc. The operations units have begun to slip away from a reasonably uniform planning and control system, and if this trend is not stopped we may find that we are managing badly or ineffectively here at headquarters. I think that these problems may actually be symptoms for deeper problems with the application of IPC. It is towards identifying and attacking this deeper problem that I intend to direct my effort.

Several of Massey-Ferguson's top executives, both line and staff, agreed that the overly optimistic forecasting of sales and profit levels in recent years was at least partially due to the corporate emphasis upon growth. Mr. Thornbrough believed in setting "very, very demanding goals" for the operations units. Mr. Staiger, who had had a long and close relationship with Mr. Thornbrough and acted in his behalf when he was absent, said that the President based his evaluations of the General Managers' performance not on whether or not they achieved these sometimes arbitrarily demanding tasks, but on how close they came to achieving them. "Both he and I," continued Mr. Staiger, "look somewhat quizzically and critically at managers who year after year can hit their plans right on the nose. We know that we should have made it hard enough so that he couldn't possibly have hit it once in awhile just on the basis of the underlying economic variables." One high level executive termed the managers who hit their sales and profit objectives year after year "cynics." This executive stated that, "The 'cynics' think that they are putting something over on corporate management, but sooner or later they will fall flat on their faces—and we'll still be around."

Various executives cited additional reasons, besides compliance with Mr. Thornbrough's demands for sales and profit growth, why the general managers were prone to over-forecast. Mr. Staiger noted that in recent years for one reason or another, there had been a shortage in the supply of equipment from the factories. The general managers had reacted to these shortages by raising their forecasts of sales by 10% or higher simply to be certain of receiving 80% of what they thought they could sell. Mr. Staiger cited the continued shortage as preventing corporate management from really cracking down on the general managers for failure to achieve their goals. Mr. Breyfogle was of the opinion that the IPC system might contain a natural bias toward optimism because the impact summary so clearly identified planned results. He felt that there was a tendency on the part of all management to believe that no plan was acceptable unless it showed worthwhile improvement in market shares, for instance. However, he noted that there were times when you just couldn't get an improvement in market share and you were doing well just to maintain your position. Mr. R. D. Bibow, who was recently appointed to the position of Vice President Farm Machinery, admitted that a poor job of sales forecasting had been done in recent years. He stated that the blame could not be totally laid on the operations units because they had had little technical support from the group staff. It was one of his missions to activate the support function to help achieve good quality forecasts.

Mr. William Reed-Lewis currently filled the position of Director of Marketing—Farm Machinery which was vacated by Mr. Bibow on his promotion to Vice President. Mr. Reed-Lewis agreed with several other executives that the corporate desire for substantial growth contributed to the general manager's tendency to over-forecast. He stated that in his experience, general managers hesitated to present goals or plans which did not appear to support the corporation's desires for good growth. Mr. Reed-Lewis stated that as the year progressed and it became evident to the General Managers that the planned objectives would not be reached, there was a reluctance on the part of the General Managers to spell this out in a control report to the corporation. The General Managers feared that this would be interpreted as a lack of commitment, both by corporate management and by their subordinates who also received copies of the monthly General Manager's Letter. Mr. Reed-Lewis noted that in 1970, corporate recognition that the planned objectives would not be reached did not come about until the seventh or eighth month of the fiscal year. The General Managers had simply spread the unachieved sales and profits from the first quarters over the forecasts for the last quarters.

Mr. Reed-Lewis outlined a program designed to sharpen the operations units' ability to forecast accurately. This program was based on a retail sales reporting system that had been tried with some success in the ICM group and the North American Operations Unit of the Farm Machinery Group. Mr. Reed-Lewis hoped to create a computer based system which would enable the FM group marketing staff to maintain a more current awareness of all the operations units' market performance. He intended to build a data base which would ultimately allow the application of sophisticated computer forecast techniques to farm machinery operations. At the moment, however, Mr. Reed-Lewis indicated that sales for farm equipment products exhibited a range of variances of 26–41% of forecast.

Mr. Felker, the Forecast Evaluation Manager, noted that the problems arising from the poor quality of sales forecasts were widely recognized among all levels of management. These errors led to eroded returns on assets through premature capital expansions, excessive purchasing commitments and inventories, and unnecessary capital charges. Mr. Felker thought that prompt remedial actions could mitigate much of the damage to the return on assets, but in the past the responses had been too slow in forming and taking effect. Mr. Felker observed that remedial actions often had to be initiated prior to the third quarter of the fiscal year if one expected to receive the benefits of such action for even as much as the last quarter.

In a move to reinforce the General Managers' commitment to achieving their planned objectives, Mr. Breyfogle had suggested to them that they build into their goals and plans a bit more flexibility. Though Mr. Breyfogle insisted that a goals commitment, once agreed-upon, was absolute, he was of the opinion that the goals set should fully reflect the uncertainties involved. Mr. Breyfogle cited the use of probabilities applied to expected profit impacts as one means to inject flexibility.

Case 2

The State Street Boston Financial Corporation*

The long-range planning program of the bank is a companywide undertaking aimed at determining how to achieve top management's objectives through a program of planned growth. In particular, the planning program should facilitate the development of strategies to meet these objectives in view of the need to allocate the bank's available resources between existing traditional bank business and its response to its customers' demands for new products.

The need for sound planning practices will continue to intensify in view of the rapidly changing environment in which the bank will be seeking to consistently improve its growth and profitability. Furthermore, the expanding size and complexity of the organization, coupled with increasing competition from both within and outside the banking industry, will accelerate the frequent necessity for making major decisions which will significantly commit the bank's resources for long periods in the future.

The above excerpt from the statement of "Purpose and Objectives" of the Corporate Long-Range Planning Manual of the State Street Boston Financial Corporation reflected the management philosophy of George B. Rockwell, who in April 1971 became Chief Executive Officer of the one-bank holding company which owned the State Street Bank and Trust Company. It also provided an indication of the mission Richard Gallant, Vice President, was asked to assume as Corporate Planning Officer in January 1972.

Mr. Gallant was concerned during his first few weeks in this new job about how he should define his position, how he should apply his knowledge of the bank's various operations, and how he should capitalize on his reputation and talents for getting new management systems installed and operating in a short period of time.

STATE STREET BANK AND TRUST COMPANY

The State Street Bank and Trust Company, since its inception in 1792, had been an important factor in Boston financial circles. Historically, the

---

* This case was prepared by Ms. Patricia Rapoport and Mr. Robert Schultz under the direction of Assistant Professor Robert W. Ackerman.
Copyright © 1972 by the President and Fellows of Harvard College

bank had stressed loans to other financial institutions and to commerce and industry and as a result had been "interest sensitive"—a change in the prime interest rate had a dramatic impact on earnings. Beginning in 1924, State Street also developed strong ties to the mutual fund industry becoming in time the world's largest mutual fund service agent which meant, in essence, performing the bookkeeping function and acting as custodian for the funds. In addition to fees and commissions, the bank also obtained substantial demand deposits in this way. Trust, investment and agency services for individuals, corporations and institutions provided a third major source of income. State Street, on the other hand, had been limited by law to Suffolk County in retail banking and this type of business had not been an important factor for the bank.

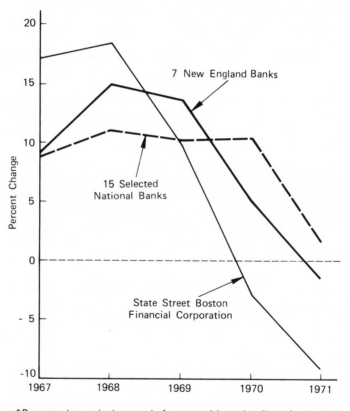

*Percent change in income before securities gains (losses) per share against each previous year.

Exhibit 1   The State Street Boston Financial Corporation Annual Earnings Performance of Comparative Banks*

In 1961, the Rockland-Atlas National Bank, a smaller but more rapidly growing bank with seven offices in Suffolk County, was merged into State Street. Under the strong leadership of H. Frederick Hagemann, formerly President of Rockland-Atlas and subsequently President and Chairman of the Board of the combined organization, the bank began to enlarge the scope of its business. Diversification into certain banking functions, particularly savings accounts and mortgage loans, had been inhibited by the fact that historically a high proportion of the bank's shares were owned by savings banks. Although declining over time, these interests continued to own about 40% of the shares in 1972. In addition, several directors were also officers of savings banks.

A massive conversion to computers was completed in 1964 enabling the bank to become a pioneer in extending data processing services to financial institutions, mutual funds, trust accounts, and others. It was hoped that this capability would forestall the trend, especially among mutual funds, to take their business to computer service bureaus. A wholly owned subsidiary, State Street Bank Boston International, was established the following year to meet customers' expanding international financial needs. In 1966, the bank joined a nationwide credit card system by launching the State Street BankAmericard. In 1969, the Automated Customer Services Division was created to provide computer services to commercial accounts.

Then in June 1970, a one-bank holding company was established to hold the stock of the bank and three new operating subsidiaries, the State Street Boston Securities Services Corporation (to sell securities collection and clearing services to the financial community); the State Street Boston Credit Company, Inc. (to raise funds for bank lending through the sales of commercial paper); and SSB Investments, Inc. (to invest equity funds in venture capital markets). In addition, a bank was opened in Munich, Germany to conduct international commercial banking as well as to service the mutual funds industry in Europe.

Despite the enthusiasm with which new ventures were undertaken, not all of them were as successful as originally envisioned. Lower earnings in 1970 and 1971 were attributed in part to unsettled economic conditions which depressed loan activity in New England. However, internal problems played a part as well. In particular, the BankAmericard Department incurred losses due to operating problems and larger than anticipated fraud and credit losses. The Munich office, which had been staffed in anticipation of increasing volume, fell prey to a 95% decline in offshore mutual fund sales due to the well-publicized failings of certain funds, and the stock market decline. As a result the staff was halved.

Nevertheless, management remained committed to growth and increased diversity of services through "the maximization of ideas for the purpose of generating opportunities." A goal of performing in the top quartile of 22 leading banks had been publicly stated. Although State Street's performance had fallen below the average of this reference group in 1970–71 as shown in Exhibit 1, management was confident that relative performance would indicate a substantial improvement in 1972. Financial performance for recent years is reflected in Exhibit 2.

GEORGE B. ROCKWELL

During this period of realignment and expansion of the bank's services, Mr. Hagemann also moved to strengthen the organization and introduce new management systems into operations. In 1963, George Rockwell was hired from IBM as Vice President of the Computer Services Division. Under his direction in that capacity and later as senior and then executive vice president, a number of management techniques were introduced which had been extensively used in manufacturing industries, but had seen little application in banking. Mr. Hagemann, however,

Exhibit 2 The State Street Boston Financial Corporation

Ten-Year Financial History

Year End Totals	1971	1970	1969	1968
Deposits	$966,471,686	$1,017,467,782	$939,097,550	$985,407,506
Cash and U.S. Govt. securities	350,473,340	424,895,506	378,487,508	396,787,724
Loans	613,558,186	592,007,865	579,911,768	546,710,838
Total capital accounts	05,772,154	104,796,351	100,269,665	75,886,892
Daily Averages				
Deposits	942,850,000	820,460,000	861,049,000	878,857,000
Loans	609,375,000	581,387,000	564,370,000	502,739,000
Yearly Results				
Total Operating income	92,507,418	94,992,384	82,263,310	64,426,863
Income before securities gains (losses)	8,395,465	9,300,856	9,596,198	8,767,651
Securities gains (losses) less related tax effect	235,606	353,678	406,664	(210,531)
Significant Ratios				
Income before securities gains (losses) to total operating income	9.1%	9.8%	11.7%	13.6%
Income before securities gains (losses) to equity capital (average)	9.8%	11.3%	12.3%	11.8%
Loans to deposits (average)	64.6%	70.9%	65.5%	57.2%
Total capital to deposits (average)	11.2%	12.5%	11.0%	8.4%
Per Share Data				
Income before securities gains (losses), on average outstanding common shares	$4.20	$4.63	$4.78	$4.37
Regular dividends declared	2.40	2.40	2.40	2.40
Equity capital at year end	43.73	42.23	39.97	37.79

continued to exert a commanding influence in important operating and policy decisions.

In March 1970, Mr. Rockwell became President and the following year, at the age of 45, chief executive officer of the bank. His selection to head the second largest Boston bank caused a stir in the financial press:

> The important story behind Rockwell's promotion is its implication for the banking industry generally and State Street in particular. He is the first "computer man" to become a top banking administrator. But that is really only the tip of the iceberg and Rockwell is quick to say that the computer is nothing more than a tool. . . .
> The real point is that Rockwell is a manager, in the modern sense of the term. He is an organization man rather than being exclusively a financial man, as very often has happened in banking. . . .
> Rockwell sees the establishment of management by objectives not only for the entire organization but for the individual as well as the way to encourage and utilize the young managers who are now moving into the business. There's enough growth ("we've got a thousand more employees this year than we had last") and pay ("if Fidelity Management can pay 50 grand for a good man, I don't see why we can't") so that the young may stay interested a long time. . . .

1967	1966	1965	1964	1963	1962
$876,802,678	$696,544,517	$682,042,048	$615,999,459	$579,522,682	$529,396,346
344,154,376	282,787,868	296,920,921	264,086,222	259,365,294	242,913,172
463,725,169	420,681,268	384,427,982	341,010,864	320,505,635	305,581,782
69,575,803	68,423,510	63,320,761	63,320,761	61,202,098	59,323,932
743,252,000	654,856,000	598,703,000	534,237,000	503,380,000	487,413,000
426,560,000	409,373,000	369,088,000	318,867,000	308,495,000	270,523,000
50,957,964	44,801,806	36,141,925	31,900,018	29,091,108	28,593,239
7,406,051	6,335,554	6,783,654	5,914,768	5,228,973	5,027,307
3,980	(288,622)	(332,700)	(65,019)	154,527	110,289
14.5%	14.1%	18.8%	18.5%	18.0%	17.6%
10.4%	9.1%	10.1%	9.5%	8.7%	8.6%
57.4%	62.5%	61.6%	59.7%	61.3%	55.5%
9.6%	10.6%	11.2%	11.7%	12.0%	12.0%
$3.69	$3.15	$3.38	$2.95	$2.60	$2.50
1.90	1.80	1.64	1.55	1.45	1.43
35.97	34.65	34.07	31.53	30.48	29.54

Exhibit 3

THE STATE STREET BOSTON FINANCIAL CORPORATION

Incentive Compensation System

The incentive compensation system developed in 1969 at State Street has three components:

a. The bank's performance relative to those 22 banks against which it was compared.

b. The organization unit's performance relative to its budget.

c. The individual's performance relative to the objectives he had set for himself.

The weight given to each and the proportion of incentive relative to salary varied by position and individual. In general, however, managers fell into one of four categories:

Perform- ance of	Corporate Officers	Line Division Managers	Operating Officers	Corporate Staff
Bank	100%	40%	40%	40%
Unit	---	40	30	20
Individual	---	20	30	40

The compensation system was managed by the Salary Committee composed of the President, Chairman and five outside directors with the following staff officers in attendance.

First Vice President and Corporate Staff Coordinator

Vice President and Corporate Planning Officer

Vice President and Comptroller

Assistant Comptroller (Corp. Budget Administrator)

"Those banks that can mobilize funds are the ones that will move ahead successfully," he said. He thinks State Street can use its services to customers as ways of generating cash flow through the bank and even sees such functions as the finding of venture capital and setting up of computer programs as sources of fees.[1]

At the time of Mr. Rockwell's elevation to chief executive officer, Mr. Hagemann, 65, retired as Chairman to be replaced by John Nichols, 58, formerly vice-chairman, who also continued to supervise the mutual fund and money management divisions. Membership on the Executive Committee of the Board, which met weekly, and the Trust Committee, which met biweekly, remained essentially unchanged.

Although discouraged by the Board from making major organizational changes during his first year as President, Mr. Rockwell took several other actions to insure that his managerial approach became an integral part of the bank's operations. For instance, increased attention was given to the recruitment of MBA's, and a new incentive compensation system, under development since 1969, was given increased impetus.[2] Then in 1971, two division manager positions (Credit and Loan and Mutual Funds) were filled, a new vice president was appointed to head the BankAmericard Department and the Mutual Funds Division was reorganized. Finally, the corporate planning office was created and staffed by Mr. Gallant and one assistant. Organization charts for the holding company and the bank are shown in Exhibits 4 and 5. A description of the activities of each division is provided in Exhibit 6.

The following comments provide an indication of the context in which these organization changes took place:

> Mr. Rockwell places exceptionally heavy reliance upon extensive, detailed, mathematical data to measure performance in every aspect of the bank's operations, to set objectives for the future and to fix with precision the degree of progress toward those goals.
>
> An integral part of this process is the competitive determination of executive compensation. Mr. Rockwell contends that by achieving the right mix of planning and quantitative analysis of the performance of its top officers, State Street will advance through a healthy internal interaction of teamwork and competition.

Some of the bank's older officers find Mr. Rockwell's methods cold and overly mechanistic, but it seems that this problem is no greater at State Street than at any other institution where a young man is put in charge. "Rockwell's tactics have been hard on some people who have been in the bank for a long time, because they aren't used to being measured so objectively," says one young executive.

---

[1] *The Boston Globe,* March 24, 1970.
[2] See Exhibit 3 for description of the incentive compensation system.

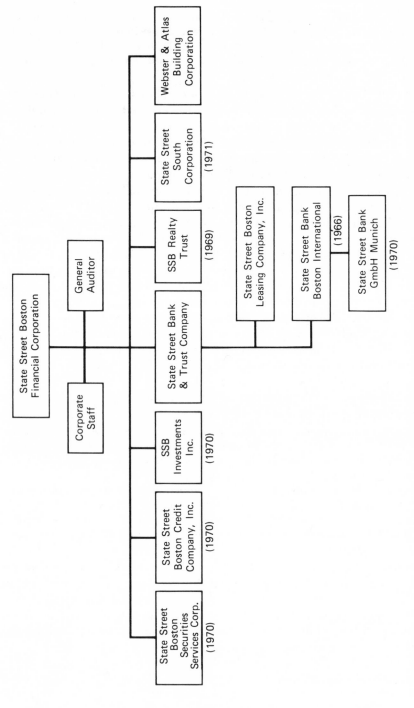

Exhibit 4 The State Street Boston Financial Corporation. One Bank Holding Company Organization—April 1972. Formed June 15, 1970

State Street Boston Financial Corporation

General Auditor

Corporate Staff

State Street Boston Securities Services Corp. (1970)

State Street Boston Credit Company, Inc. (1970)

SSB Investments Inc. (1970)

State Street Bank & Trust Company

SSB Realty Trust (1969)

State Street South Corporation (1971)

Webster & Atlas Building Corporation

State Street Boston Leasing Company, Inc.

State Street Bank Boston International (1966)

State Street Bank GmbH Munich (1970)

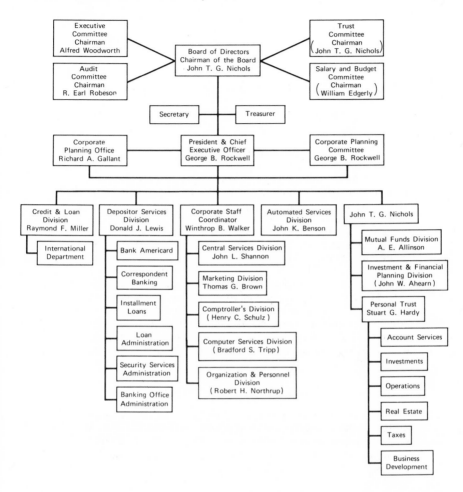

Exhibit 5 The State Street Boston Financial Corporation Organization Chart—April 1972

Most of the officers interviewed—and even some personnel below officer rank—are enthusiastic about Mr. Rockwell's stewardship. "The reason I stay at State Street is because it's run like a corporation and not like a bank, and I prefer to be judged objectively," comments one young man.

The enthusiasm, however, does not seem to be accidental nor solely because State Street employees enjoy being judged "objectively." Probably more important is that Mr. Rockwell works hard at maintaining good rapport with his staff. In fact, he estimates that about 70% of his time is devoted to dealing with questions concerning personnel, either encouraging employees or recruiting talent. He sees no conflict between his precise

Exhibit 6

THE STATE STREET BOSTON FINANCIAL CORPORATION

Activities of State Street Bank Divisions

Credit and Loan Division

The division has primary responsibility for corporate banking relationships within the United States. Its officers specialize in making business loans to companies of all sizes and in all industries. Its services include lines of credit, accounts receivable loans, term loans, real estate construction loans, merger and acquisition assistance, and tax collection.

The International Department of the division has primary responsibility for corporate and correspondent banking relationships outside of the United States. It also serves the international requirements of domestic commercial customers. Its officers specialize in making business loans to companies and banks in various areas of the world.

Depositor's Service Division

The division is responsible for retail banking and satisfies the many deposit and loan requirements of individual customers and businesses. This includes checking, savings, and time deposits, as well as complete loaning services - installment, commercial and real estate mortgage loans.

Automated Customer Services Division

The division offers a wide range of computer time-saving services to banks, credit unions, manufacturing and commercial enterprises, government and community agencies. It operates one of the largest IBM banking computer installations in New England and processes payroll, demand deposit, on-line savings and mortgages and other related data processing services.

Exhibit 6 (continued)

Mutual Funds Division

The division is the world's largest service agent for the mutual funds industry and serves as custodian or agent for investment companies with assets amounting to over 20% of the entire industry. The division also acts as corporate agent in various capacities.

Mutual fund agency services include acting as transfer agent, dividend disbursing agent and redemption agent. Custodian services include safekeeping of fund portfolio securities and cash, control, and daily net asset value computation. Corporate agency services include the Corporate Trustee Department for bond indentures and the Industrial Department which maintains corporate stock records.

Investment and Financial Planning Division

The division provides advice on money markets and on investments in securities which are issued by all levels of government. These services are an outgrowth of the management of the bank's investment portfolio. Customers are provided advice with regard to economic trends and technical factors in the marketplace.

Personal Trust Division

The division provides complete trust, investment and agency services to individuals, partnerships, corporations, and institutions. It acts as executor of estates, as trustee for various types of trust, and as investment advisor to individuals, corporations, institutions and others. Investment services are tailored to fulfill the specific objectives of each account. Pension and profit-sharing services are offered to many industrial and financial companies.

Source: Company documents.

mathematical style of management and his aspirations for high employee morale and productivity.

Although he has been working on it for eight years, Mr. Rockwell finds that his programs constantly need fine-tuning. Asked whether his views toward bank management have changed since he joined State Street, Mr. Rockwell replied: "The major change in my own thinking is that things are changing so rapidly you have to be more nimble than ever. I used to think that with planning, everything would be all right in six months. Now I see it's more difficult. We need greater adaptability for short-term changes. We need facilities to quickly introduce changes or modify ideas to get things corrected." And the way to do that, he believes, is through good personnel well directed and well motivated.[3]

THE EVOLUTION OF LONG-RANGE PLANNING

Although five-year planning had been initiated as a pilot program in the Computer Services Division in 1964 and five-year financial forecasts had been in existence for some years, the design of a formal bank-wide business plan was not attempted until 1969. As a first step, Mr. Rockwell selected Richard Gallant, (41), then Deputy Comptroller and Director of Long-Range Financial Planning, and another member of the comptroller's staff to work with him in the preparation of a manual to delineate the planning procedures.

Mr. Gallant joined the bank in 1962 from Arthur Andersen & Co., with an initial assignment of devising and installing a responsibility accounting system. During the next seven years, he gained the reputation of being an aggressive manager who was able to get financial controls implemented. He had first collaborated with Mr. Rockwell earlier in 1969 in the design of the incentive compensation system which he then had responsibility for coordinating during its first year of operation.

In general terms, planning was viewed by Mr. Rockwell as a means of determining how the bank's objectives might be achieved through a program of planned growth. Its most important function, as the Planning Manual stated, was, however, more specific:

> The most important reason for implementing a long-range planning program is not compulsion, but opportunity—the opportunity to derive a profit from new programs of action or new ways of carrying on traditional bank business more efficiently and effectively. A system of planning serves best when it is broad enough to include not only plans for the solution to problems, but plans for the discovery and exploitation of opportunities as well. As a system, long-range planning is concerned with the management

---

[3] *American Banker*, Wednesday, November 10, 1971.

of ideas; it provides top management with a definite vehicle for gathering, analyzing and interpreting ideas; and *fusing them into solid, profit-making courses of action.*

As a consequence, a focal point for planning at the division level was the generation of Major New Ventures, defined by the Planning Manual as:

A proposed undertaking unrelated to existing activities or which represents a significant extension or supplement to an existing activity and is considered to be of such importance that it should hold priority over all other programs and projects for your division. The undertaking may be either revenue producing, operational, cross selling of services between divisions or other matters of significance.

Each division was required to submit one Major New Venture as well as other programs of lower priority as part of its plan. A separate "project priority reporting system" was developed for projects drawing on working capital to the extent of $25,000 or more to provide corporate management with the means of evaluating them and setting priorities for subsequent implementation.

The Planning Manual specified the following framework for division plans:

1. Mission
2. Objectives
3. Goals
4. Guidelines (policies)
5. Environmental assumptions
6. Position audit
7. Major new venture
8. Other programs and projects
9. Problems and challenges
10. Definition of needs
11. Alternative strategies

The plans were to be formulated in the context of previously articulated corporate objectives, goals, guidelines and environmental assumptions. Provision was also made for reconciling the first year of the detailed financial summary accompanying the plan with the budget for the next year.

Although a trial run was made in 1969, the first full-blown planning cycle occurred in the spring of 1970. Each division manager was asked by Mr. Rockwell to prepare a plan to be presented at a three-day Planned Growth Conference in June attended by all senior bank officers. Although sparingly requested, help was available in interpreting the planning manual from Messrs. Rockwell and Gallant.

The results of the 1970 planning efforts were disappointing. While the formal process was presumably followed, the plans contained little more than financial extrapolations of the short-term budget outlook. One participant of the Planned Growth Conference remarked, "it was a real show—pictures, music, the works." More specifically, the Major New Ventures tended to be of minor significance. Further investigation disclosed that, with few exceptions, the division managers or their financial assistants had prepared the plan with little involvement of subordinate line and staff personnel.

In 1971, Mr. Rockwell put increased emphasis on the generation of new projects utilizing the "project priority reporting system." To emphasize the importance of the Major New Venture, the format for the Planned Growth Conference held that year in March, was changed to include presentations of the best two ventures and the best long-range plan. Time was also devoted to a discussion of the Management by Objective Program introduced by Mr. Rockwell. The long-range financial plan was then assembled during the next five months by the divisions and consolidated by the Controller's Department. While an improvement, the second planning cycle continued to fall short of the long-range strategic view intended by the planning manual.

One benefit, however, was the generation of a considerable number of investment proposals. Those projects which appeared to Mr. Rockwell to warrant serious attention were frequently assigned to a task force, usually composed of younger managers in the bank, for further study. The results of these investigations, which followed a general format, spelled out in the project priority reporting system manual, figured heavily in the eventual decision to proceed or hold off on the venture.

In the fall of 1971, Mr. Rockwell selected Mr. Gallant to be Vice President of Corporate Planning. He also appointed a Planning Committee to look after the planning function and insure that it extended its concerns beyond financial forecasting. It was composed of Mr. Rockwell (as chairman) and Mr. Nichols as permanent members, three members-at-large to serve for one-year terms (Messrs. Benson, Merrill and Miller[4] for 1972) and ex officio, Mr. W. B. Walker[5] and Mr. Gallant. The Corporate Planning Office was vested with the privilege of convening the committee to recommend courses of action and policy changes to the chief executive.

The Planning Manual defined the planner's job in these terms:

> The ultimate responsibility for all the planning activities of the bank lies with the chief executive who is to be assisted in this task by the corporate

---

[4] Division Head of Automated Customer Services, Subsidiary Manager of SSB Investments, Inc., and Division Head of Credit and Loan respectively.

[5] First Vice President and Corporate Staff Coordinator.

planner. The primary responsibility of the corporate planner is to act as the communicating and coordinating link between all parties involved in the planning process. It is his function to see to it that the planning gets done, and done effectively.

Mr. Rockwell commented on three additional tasks he had come to feel were important:

First, I would like him to evaluate and analyze the marketplace for opportunities and trends and advise management of his findings. However, that doesn't mean he should consider himself a specialist in any area. Second, he should motivate planning from the bottom of the organization. And third, he should provide me and the division managers with advice and counsel but without putting himself in a position—actual or perceived—of power. His job is not to direct action.

MR. GALLANT VIEWS HIS JOB

Several weeks after Mr. Gallant assumed his new position and moved into Mr. Rockwell's old office in the executive suite, complete with adjoining conference room, he outlined for the researcher the tasks he felt he should undertake:

Coordinate the formal process.

As coordinator of planning, in effect, all strategic plans are sent here directly. Financial plans initially go to the Comptroller, but finally end up here also. My job is to evaluate and assess these plans and advise management of my conclusions.

Act as a catalyst to encourage creative planning.

My job is to identify opportunities as opposed to problems. It is here that I think the corporation is beginning to lose sight of the fact that the primary objective of the planning process is to maximize ideas in order to generate opportunities.

In fact, what I see happening is that managers spend their time studying problems, meeting after meeting, rather than studying opportunities. I have to attempt to steer them away from the problem orientation to more innovative thinking that will result in changes which will in turn satisfy the business goals of the bank.

I am beginning to see that the education job is going to be a real time-consumer. At the last planning committee meeting I asked each committee member to provide me with a memo listing what he thinks the bank's priorities should be. At first reading I was astounded. All of the items were problems, none of them were opportunities. I think they are missing the point of strategic planning, even though they have all sat in on the training and education sessions.

Advise the Chief Executive Officer.

When a specific division submits his plan, strategies, and goals, I see myself advising the Chief as to whether they are in line with his philosophy of management by objectives; are they innovative goals? Will the strategies proposed actually achieve those goals?

Ideally, divisions should present their plans to me. I will then counsel the Chief as to my judgment of the plan. I will also informally advise the division manager of how he may best satisfy his audiences—the Chief and the Board of Directors. It is the Chief's prerogative then to determine what is reasonable, and whether or not he wants me to provide my evaluation to the manager.

Evaluate the organization.

It is part of my job with other members of management to evaluate product lines, determine strategies through "what if, ivory tower" planning, but within the realm of reality, and come up with best possible mix of products and strategies.

The next thing to do is determine if the organization is set up to implement those strategies. Are we properly and effectively aligned?

I would not see my job as being concerned about the quality of management. I do not think I could make a judgment about a manager. But, if I did see that there was an advantage, long-run, to centralizing a function, I would recommend it—but not who should fill the position.

Monitor the various management systems.

There is a constant danger that management by objectives and incentive compensation programs will be misinterpreted. The basic problem with incentive compensation, for example, is that a short-term financial orientation may arise when some of the long-range goals are intangible. I must work closely with the Personnel Division and the Chief Executive in reviewing division goals to insure that strategic factors are not slighted or overlooked.

Evaluate major new ventures and act as an advocate of new ideas.

Feedback on ideas has been a problem. One purpose of having this office which can spend almost full time on strategic planning, is that we could study ventures in detail, list them by priority in our best judgment and then sit down with Rockwell and request his opinion. Rockwell can then ask me to discuss his opinion with the division managers. I can do this on a more timely basis and am able to give the divisions faster feedback on how he feels.

Organize and systematize the diversification process.

This is the one office which is formally responsible for having knowledge about who is researching what areas, and what the status of this research is. By preparing a periodic status report, I can coordinate these activities while permitting a free flow of ideas. The President then doesn't have to go to a division head. He comes to me to request research of a specific area, to assign the area to a specific division, and to assess the status of the research.

There was one further task that Mr. Gallant was anxious to undertake, although he felt it might be controversial. Based on his knowledge of various segments of the bank, he wanted to provide advice on various tactical matters to the divisions. To play this role he thought it would be necessary to talk directly with managers down in the organization without the presence of their superiors.

In theory it is wrong, a violation of organizational principles, of the line manager's prerogative to manage his own people. But I think if I can do it with his awareness and permission, but without his presence—and I would only do it on a selective basis where I know the managers reasonably well—I would still like to do so.

It depends on the degree of confidence he has in me as an individual. Most would want to be there and then I don't know if I would want to do it. Their subordinates might not be able to open up to me. They must believe in my integrity and believe that I can give them some ideas to help them in their particular area.

In addition to these planning activities, Mr. Gallant also attended the Salary and Budget Committee meetings. He saw one aspect of his function there as that of reviewing the goals proposed by the various managers under the incentive compensation system and making recommendations regarding feasibility and orientation in an attempt to avoid targets which were too short-term oriented and neglected long-term strategic goals.

REACTION TO PLANNING

The need for planning appeared to have gained wide acceptance in the bank. For instance, Mr. Woodworth, formerly in charge of the Credit and Loan Division and currently chairman of the Executive Committee, commented:

Long-term planning is needed to determine how you want to expand your business; to determine the manpower required for the expansion; and to establish contingency plans in the event problems arise.

Mr. John Benson, recently appointed head of the Automated Customer Services Division, noted some additional benefits:

Historically, banking had some pretty solid trends that were relatively easy to follow, for example, deposit and loan growth. We are now in a period when historical projections have become less reliable and thereby less valuable. The planning exercise has helped us in every division to start thinking about how our business is changing.

Another manager reflected on the stress placed on the plans by Mr. Rockwell:

I don't know how men could exert more pressure. I don't have experience with what a manufacturing firm would do, but here it involves calling in a man from an ineffective area and saying, "This was your plan, you're off target. I want a new plan and you'll live by it. If that plan doesn't meet corporate goals, you will go back and do your homework; tell me whether to sell the business, merge with another division, set up a special subsidiary, or bring in a new manager."

He is no dictator. He will ask if he is being reasonable, "Is it fair to ask you to give me a plan you can live with?"

Although the need for long-range planning was recognized in the corporation, there was less agreement on the role of the corporate planner. Mr. Woodworth stated one extreme:

> There is no real need for a separate corporate planner. He should be the Chief Executive Officer, since only he can make the decisions and he must hang with them. However, if a planner does exist, he should be an accountant who just adds up and consolidates the division's numbers. How can he evaluate a line manager's decisions without any background or experience in the business? It is the line manager's responsibility to identify market needs and plan to fulfill them.

Mr. Benson had a different view and stated that the corporate planner should coordinate the planning process and act as a stimulant to the decision process by presenting new ideas for discussion:

> I think the best thing the planner can do is to pull stuff together so that people can explain it and make some decisions, clarify the options, and come up with some analysis of what other banks are doing, and how and why they are performing in the way they are.
>
> He should also be concerned with working with division managers on the strategy things for the long run. However, he should not be concerned with how we [division managers] are going to get it done. I report the results and tell Rockwell why I did or why I did not do it. He [the planner] certainly should never get into the position of judging people on their performance. There is this temptation because of his close involvement with top management. For him to be successful as a planner, he must have the confidence of the guys who are actually responsible for generating the plan.
>
> Consequently, he has to figure out how he can work closely with top management without alienating the division managers. A planning process does not occur by edict. It is worked out with line management. No staff guy can call me up and tell me what to do. His strength will come from maintaining a low profile by presenting things for discussion and withholding opinions as much as possible.

PLANS FOR PLANNING IN 1972

In the final weeks of 1971 Mr. Gallant worked out with Mr. Rockwell the strategic and financial planning activities reproduced in Exhibits 7 and 8.

One major change from previous years was the function of the Planned Growth Conference. Scheduled for May 21–23, the three-day meeting was to be devoted to the study of nine topics considered to be of critical importance to State Street. During the second day, seven-member teams were to analyze the bank's position in each area, guided by suggested issues for study, and make whatever recommendations they felt were appropriate. Each team was also to identify at least one new product/service line during the presentation scheduled for the third day.

Exhibit 7   THE STATE STREET BOSTON FINANCIAL CORPORATION

Strategic Planning Timetable

Activity	Target Dates 1972
Strategic planning period—Divisions and subsidiary corporations solicit ideas from their staffs relative to possible new business opportunities and methods for solving current problems	Jan. 4– May 1
Prepare and circulate environmental assumptions for the planning period 1972—1976	Feb. 23
Divisions and subsidiary corporations submit major new ventures and other programs and projects	Mar. 1
Top Management to provide feedback to the divisions and subsidiary corporations relative to project priorities	Mar. 31
All divisions and subsidiary corporations submit Division Position Reports for Planned Growth Conference	May 1
Planned Growth Conference	May 21– May 23

Source: State Street Planning Manual, 1973.

Exhibit 8   THE STATE STREET BOSTON FINANCIAL CORPORATION

Financial Planning Timetable

Activity	Target Dates 1972
Line divisions and subsidiary corporations submit selected statistical data for use by staff and operating divisions	June 14
Line divisions and subsidiary corporations submit long-range plans to director of long-range financial planning*	June 30
Staff and operating divisions submit long-range plans to director of long-range financial planning	July 17
Comptroller's to prepare consolidated financial statements	Aug. 1
Comptroller's to prepare profit center statements and make distribution to profit center managers as applicable	Aug. 1–15
Profit center managers to review 5 year profit and loss statements and bring any questions or proposed changes to the attention of Comptroller's management no later than August 30	Aug. 30
Comptroller's to submit final long range plans to Corporate Planning Office	Sept. 15
Support divisions review and sign off on line division/subsidiary plans and vice versa	Sept. 29

* The Director of Long-Range Financial Planning reports to the Comptroller of the bank.

Source: State Street Planning Manual, 1973.

The first team, comprised of Messrs. Rockwell, Nichols, Walker, Miller, Benson, Merrill, Lewis and Gallant, were to examine "where should SSB Financial Corporation be headed?" Captains chosen for the remaining teams were asked to select three managers from the list of invited participants and submit their names to Mr. Gallant. Should a manager be requested more than once, he was to select the topic he preferred. The remaining three slots were then to be filled by a special task force of the Corporate Planning Committee. This procedure was adopted to encourage a feeling of participation in the planning process as well as to increase the quality of the workshop sessions.

By March 1, the divisions and subsidiaries were to submit Major New Ventures and other programs to the planning office. Top management feedback was to be given by the end of the month. "Position papers," summarizing division strategy and providing preliminary financial forecasts were then to be submitted by May 1.

Final division plans were to be submitted to the Director of Long-Range Financial Planning by June 30. During this period and later, while the Comptroller's Department consolidated the plans and broke them down into profit center statements, Mr. Gallant anticipated that informally he should provide the divisions with guidance in establishing profit targets and relating financial forecasts to supporting strategies.

In September after line division plans had been formally delivered to the Corporate Planning Office, support division heads (Personnel, Accounting, etc.) were to review and "sign off" on them. Similarly, line division heads were to sign off on support division plans. The purpose of these joint reviews was to insure that the interdivisional implications of forecasted activity levels were anticipated throughout the bank.

In October, Mr. Gallant anticipated that Mr. Rockwell would meet with each division manager to review the plan in the light of corporate goals. The meeting would also serve as a preliminary goal-setting session prior to the development of the budget for 1973.

These procedural steps in the upcoming planning cycle described some of the formal tasks Mr. Gallant realized he would be involved in during the coming months. He was aware, at the same time, that the planning system did not constitute a full description of his role at State Street. It was to this larger issue that he turned his attention in January 1972.

Case 3

The Quaker Oats Company*

Harry T. Ambrose had recently been appointed The Quaker Oats Company's Director—Long-Range Planning. An MBA with nine years of managerial experience (but no previous exposure to the management of formal planning systems), in early 1971 Mr. Ambrose had the task of guiding the company through what was essentially the initiation of formal, long-range planning.

THE COMPANY

During the five-year period ended June 1970, Quaker Oats' per-share earnings grew at an average annual rate of 11%. That performance was in striking contrast to the company's record in the five previous years, when earnings were almost on a plateau, and represented one of the best records achieved in the packaged-food industry in the second half of the 1960s. Exhibit 1 presents a five-year review of Quaker Oats' financial performance.

A highly successful product-development program was the principal contributor to the improved earnings record of the company. Out of fiscal 1970's revenues of $598 million, the company spent $7.4 million on research and development, 21% higher than in fiscal 1969 and almost twice the amount spent five years earlier. Management felt that those expenditures were fully justified by the success achieved in the introduction of such new products as Aunt Jemima Complete Pancake Mix, Aunt Jemima Frozen French Toast, Quaker Instant Oats, King Vitamin (a nutritional cereal for children), and Ken-L Ration Burgers.

Also contributing to the company's improved earnings record was management's decision to minimize commodity operations and emphasize consumer-product areas in order to take greater advantage of the company's marketing capabilities. The decision to reduce commodity operations resulted in the divestiture of a line of country elevators in 1967 and a sizable feed operation early in 1969 and the acquistion of Fisher-

* This case was prepared by Ronald M. Hall, Research Assistant, under the supervision of Professor Richard F. Vancil.

Exhibit 1 THE QUAKER OATS COMPANY AND SUBSIDIARIES

Statement of Consolidated Income and Reinvested Earnings

Year Ended June 30	1970	1969	1968	1967	1966
			(thousands of dollars)		
Revenues:					
Net sales	$597,652	$553,879	$547,194	$555,133	$498,358
Other income—net	2,745	2,738	956	881	432
	$600,397	$556,617	$548,150	$556,014	$498,790
Cost and Expenses:					
Cost of goods sold	399,426	375,661	382,419	403,010	358,178
Selling, general and administrative expenses	142,572	129,675	122,693	115,132	103,750
Interest expense	4,433	2,083	2,315	2,417	1,950
	546,431	507,419	507,427	520,559	463,878
Income before federal and foreign income taxes	53,966	49,198	40,723	35,455	34,912
Federal and foreign income taxes	25,823	23,492	19,400	16,673	17,340
Income before extraordinary items	28,143	25,706	21,323	18,782	17,572
Extraordinary (charges) credits (net of income taxes)	—	(1,092)	—	898	—
Net Income	28,143	24,614	21,323	19,680	17,572
Reinvested Earnings					
Dividends: Preferred stock	490	495	507	528	568
Common stock	11,737	10,704	9,710	8,868	8,864
Earnings reinvested during the year	15,916	13,415	11,106	10,284	8,140
Balance at beginning of year	139,567	129,996	118,890	108,606	100,466
Transfer to common stock re stock split	(3,731)				
Excess of cost over par value of treasury preferred stock retired (95,489 shares)		(3,844)			
Balance at end of year	$151,752	$139,567	$129,996	$118,890	$108,606
Per Common Share: (A)					
Income before extraordinary items	$ 2.21	$ 2.04	$ 1.72	$ 1.51	$ 1.41
Extraordinary (charges) credits		(.09)		(.07)	
Net income	2.21	1.95	1.72	1.58	1.41
Dividends declared	$ .94	$ .87	$ .80	$ .73	$ .73
(A) Adjusted for stock splits.					

Price Toys, a manufacturer of toys for preschool children, later that year. In addition, Quaker made several acquisitions outside the United States, including pet food companies in England and Canada and a leading manufacturer of chocolate in Mexico.

In recognition of the change in the company's product line and the broadening scope of its operations, Robert D. Stuart, Jr., the President and chief architect of Quaker Oats' growth since 1962, announced in September 1970 a reorganization of the company's management structure. The reorganization decentralized all operations into four major profit centers called groups: grocery products (United States and Canada), international grocery products, industrial and institutional products, and toys and recreational products. Mr. Stuart stated that the toy and recreational group would be expanded considerably by means of internal growth and acquisitions. The decentralized corporate structure was expected to facilitate the implementation of top management's plans to continue to expand and diversify the enterprise. Exhibit 2 presents Quaker Oats' management structure prior to, and after the 1970 reorganization.

PLANNING HISTORY

Quaker began long-range planning in fiscal 1965. The plans created that year, and annually thereafter, were primarily numbers-oriented estimates of income and requirements of capital. Emphasis was placed on the first year of the annual, three-year plans; the last two years were more or less extrapolations of the first year. Concentration was on existing businesses, which were treated in great financial detail.

Initially, responsibility for supervision of both long and short-range plans reposed with a director of corporate planning. However, the corporate planner's heavy involvement in acquisition studies and negotiations coupled with his limited staff capability forced him to rely upon the controller's office for staff support in supervising, reviewing and consolidating the company's plans. By mid-1968 responsibility for short-range planning (annual two-year plans) had been shifted to the corporate controller's office, which created a department entitled Profit Planning & Analysis (PP&A) to handle the task. Responsibilities for long-range planning and acquisitions were split. When the director of long-range planning left the company in early 1969, the long-range planning position was left vacant.

Robert A. Bowen, Vice President and Controller since the mid-1960s, stated that while he had been in a position to directly influence the company's planning he had endeavored to gain a more explicit grasp of what made the business tick. He had collected, through the planning

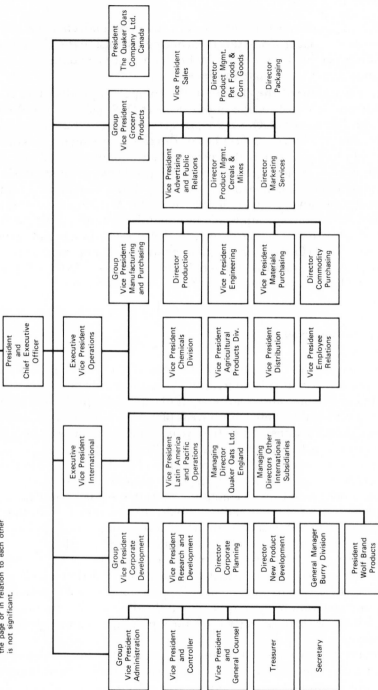

This organization chart shows official lines of authority and responsibility, but does not limit channels of contact in any way. Location of positions on the page or in relation to each other is not significant.

BOARD OF DIRECTORS Chairman and Vice Chairman

President and Chief Executive Officer

Executive Vice President International

Executive Vice President Operations

Group Vice President Administration
- Vice President and Controller
- Vice President and General Counsel
- Treasurer
- Secretary

Group Vice President Corporate Development
- Vice President Research and Development
- Director Corporate Planning
- Director New Product Development
- General Manager Burry Division
- President Wolf Brand Products

Executive Vice President International
- Vice President Latin America and Pacific Operations
- Managing Director Quaker Oats Ltd. England
- Managing Directors Other International Subsidiaries

Executive Vice President Operations
- Vice President Chemicals Division
- Vice President Agricultural Products Div.
- Vice President Distribution
- Vice President Employee Relations

Group Vice President Manufacturing and Purchasing
- Director Production
- Vice President Engineering
- Vice President Materials Purchasing
- Director Commodity Purchasing

Group Vice President Grocery Products
- Vice President Advertising and Public Relations
- Director Product Mgmt. Cereals & Mixes
- Director Marketing Services
- Vice President Sales
- Director Product Mgmt. Pet Foods & Corn Goods
- Director Packaging

President The Quaker Oats Company Ltd. Canada

Exhibit 2A The Quaker Oats Company Executive Reporting Relationships April 1, 1968

232

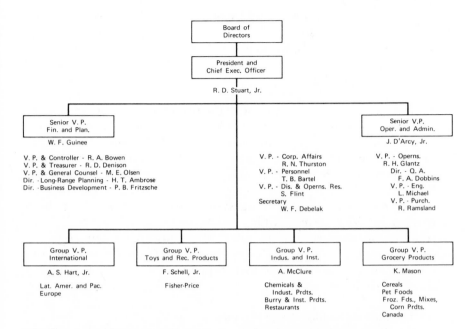

Exhibit 2B   The Quaker Oats Company Executive Reporting Relationships

process, detailed quantitative indicators of product group performance over the previous 3–4 years. The "back data," as he termed this information, included historical comparisons of product expenses and asset utilization. In addition, Mr. Bowen had accumulated comparative information on ten of Quaker Oats' chief competitors. He had distributed relevant portions of the back data to Quaker's managers annually as a part of the planning process. Mr. Bowen intended to continue this practice which he believed aided operating managers in formulating realistic operating plans.

However, in 1969 overall responsibility for Quaker's long-range planning processes was assumed by W. Fenton Guinee. Previously, the Vice President—Marketing Services, Mr. Guinee had recently been appointed to the position Group Vice President—Corporate Development. (In September 1970 his title was again changed to Senior V.P. Finance & Planning.) After, in his words,"'taking awhile to figure out what long-range planning was . . . through reading and discussion with the president and business school contacts," Mr. Guinee decided that Quaker needed more strategic thinking and fewer numbers in its plans. He characterized the company as evolving from a rather homogeneous business to a montage of partial profit centers and functional organizations in substantially different businesses and having different needs. Mr. Guinee thought that the information flows represented by plans should be altered to fit the changing management structure. In particular, plans should reflect the rationale behind operating management's decisions and performance.

HARRY AMBROSE'S JOB

Following extensive discussions with the president, in September 1970 Mr. Guinee appointed Harry T. Ambrose to the position of Director —Long-Range Planning. Mr. Ambrose was to aid Mr. Guinee in designing and overseeing a formal planning system which recognized the changing management needs of the company. Mr. Ambrose was instructed to work closely with the head of the Profit Planning & Analysis Department in coordinating a formal planning system which accounted for both short-term and long-term planning needs.

To guide Mr. Ambrose in his work, Mr. Guinee gave him copies of memorandums exchanged by Messrs. Stuart and Guinee which laid out their expectations regarding the formal planning system. Following is a summary of their position:

1. The purpose of long-range planning was to be:
   a. Develop agreement among divisional, group and corporate management on written goals and strategies based on projections of long-term needs.
   b. Identify future resource needs of skills, personnel, organization, finances, and new businesses to allow for their development in an orderly manner.
2. No substantive changes in the concept, content, and administration of the two-year planning effort were to be contemplated.
3. The long-range plan was to cover five fiscal years beginning after the current fiscal year. (Quaker's fiscal year ran from July 1 to June 30.) The content of the long-range plan was to include:
   a. Description of current state of the business and of each of its major functional areas.
   b. Assumptions about future economy, social, and political environment, technological developments, and competition.
   c. Recommended objectives.
   d. Recommended strategies.
   e. Identification of risks.
   The plans were to include statements describing a selected strategy supported by numbers defining the magnitude of growth, investments and risks. The alternative strategies considered were to be described along with the reason for the one recommended. Compared to the two-year plan, in the five-year plan relatively greater emphasis was to be placed on the written statements and recommendations with numbers being used to provide reasonably quantified approximations of the direction chosen

rather than as an instrument for controlling or for measuring managerial performance.

4. Responsibility for development of divisional plans was to rest with divisional vice presidents and/or general managers; for group plans, with group vice presidents; and for corporate plans with the planning committee (identified as the president plus the two senior vice presidents).

5. Divisional management was to be responsible for securing approval of their plans from group management, who in turn was to be responsible for securing approval of group plans from the planning committee. The latter was to review group plans in detail, direct appropriate modifications and the development of a consolidated corporate plan for presentation to the executive committee of the board of directors.

6. Responsibility for the format and administration of both two-year and long-range plans was to be that of the senior vice president—Finance and Planning. Responsibilities of individual departments in Finance and Planning were to be as indicated in Exhibit 3.

7. For the first annual planning process, both the two-year and long-range planning efforts were to proceed concurrently, commencing in January 1971 and concluding in June of that year. Timing of future planning was to be reviewed after the completion of 1971's planning.

8. Review of the five-year plans was to be focused upon the quality of current and previous analyses and conclusions rather than the accuracy of numerical projections. Whereas responsibility for achievement of two-year plan goals was to rest primarily with the person responsible for operating a

Exhibit 3 THE QUAKER OATS COMPANY

Delineation of Responsibilities in Planning

	Two-Year		Five-Year	
	PP&A (1)	L-R P (2)	PP&A	L-R P
Develop manual	Primary	Collaborative	Collaborative	Primary
Develop financial format	Primary	None	Primary	Collaborative
Develop format for statement & recommendations	Primary	None	Collaborative	Primary
Provide financial back data	Primary	None	Primary	None
Coordinate planning	Primary	None	None	Primary
Consolidate into corporate figures	Primary	None	Primary	None
Critique plans	Primary	Collaborative	Collaborative	Primary
Identify deviations from plan	Primary	None	None	Primary

(1) PP&A—Profit Planning and Analysis under direction of Vice President-Controller.

(2) L-R P—Long-Range Planning.

particular area, responsibility for the strategies selected in the five-year plan was to be shared between the person recommending the plan and the person approving it.

REMARKS BY FENTON GUINEE

What we are trying to accomplish with our planning system must be considered in light of the corporate situation. Our determination to achieve profitable diversification as a basis for future growth has spurred some notable changes in the way the company is managed.

Operational responsibilities were restructured last September so that many of our managers now have overall responsibility for all four functions (marketing, finance, production, and personnel) instead of only one. We have found that this is a very difficult reorientation for some managers to make.

Even if we had not reorganized in 1970, we probably would reintroduce long-range planning now. Quaker needs to be looking beyond its immediate future and next year's profits to the issues which will determine its long-term viability.

But, also, we expect the introduction of a planning system at a time when the managers' tasks are changing to help them to define their new tasks. Sure the work load is going to be enormous, but we are forcing them to look beyond their own previous functional expertises immediately. Therefore they are going to develop as general managers much quicker.

Harry's task is to work out a working balance between the amount and quality of effort managers put into short-term versus long-term planning. Right now we don't know what this balance should be. We do know, however, that each type of planning is important in its own right.

Short-term planning is well established at Quaker. We have fine budgeting and control systems. The managers use them and seem to believe in them. But the quality of the decisions made through these systems may begin to deteriorate if the decision-makers lose pace with corporate objectives and strategies. Long-range planning should function to maintain this pace through the introduction of new information, analysis, and properly disseminated decisions.

HARRY AMBROSE'S COMMENTS

I suppose that I was selected for this job because my background was in line management (not staff) and because I am on good terms with most of the division managers. I was formerly director of materials purchasing under the old functional corporate set-up and I got to know most of the present division managers pretty well because my job took me all over the company.

Mr. Stuart and Mr. Guinee have pretty well thought out what they want planning to do and how Quaker ought to go about doing it. Nevertheless, there always remain a number of practical problems to be ironed out. This much I know from my own experience as a manager and from my investigations into how other companies plan.

I don't expect that we are going to leap into an ideal planning system immediately. With the uncertainty arising from the new corporate structure and the two-year planning going on at the same time as long-range planning, I expect that long-range planning is not going to get as much attention as I would like.

Therefore, I think that I should try to achieve some limited objectives in planning this year. First, I would like to establish in the managers' minds that long-range planning is here to stay and is an important part of their jobs. Second, I would like to educate them in the rationale of long-range planning. In particular, I need to break them away from thinking that long-range planning is the extrapolation of short-term quantitative relationships. Quaker's managers must come to realize that different kinds of factors are at work in the long term and that because many of these factors are very intangible their handling requires the use of a disciplined, logical, technique.

There are a lot of factors which will determine the ultimate success or failure of the planning program. Certainly one of these factors will be the kind and quality of cooperation that I get from PP&A. It appears to me that the delineation of responsibilities in planning between PP&A and the long-range planning department was based primarily upon existing staff capabilities. In essence, any of the planning which dealt with financial statements was assigned to PP&A. Financial analysis is their specialty and they have a staff of about 12 skilled people. The long-range planning department consists of myself plus an assistant and a secretary.

Fortunately I have a good working relationship with the head of PP&A. We have managed to resolve amicably differences of opinion relating to the format and content of the long-range plans. In general, he tends to see more of a need in the plans for detailed, precise information than I do. For example, one of our arguments revolved around whether to round all financial data in the plans off to the nearest thousand dollars or the nearest million dollars. I finally managed to persuade him that the larger figure was adequate to indicate the direction and magnitude of financial results —which was all that was necessary for the long-range plans.

The head of PP&A also would like to see (as would I) the long-range plans precede the short-range plans so that the former could be used to provide direction for the latter. However, we differ on the question of how tight the linkage between long-range plans and short-range plans should be. His opinion (which is shared by Mr. Guinee) is that the forecast performance in the first two years of the five-year plan should be required to match precisely the forecast performance in the short-range plan. I believe that he feels that this requirement is necessary to gain commitment to, and inject reality in, the long-range plans. I feel that it would be more useful at this time to concentrate more upon developing the managers' ability to create alternative strategies than to tie them to a rigid planning program.

Case 4

The Galvor Company—R-3

CONTROL SYSTEM

When M. Barsac replaced M. Chambertin as Galvor's Controller in April of 1964, at the age of 31, he became the first of a new group of senior managers resulting from the acquisition by Universal Electric. It was an accepted fact that in the large and sprawling Universal organization, the Controller's Department represented a key function. M. Barsac was a skilled accountant and had ten years' experience in a large French subsidiary of Universal.

He recalled his early days with Galvor vividly and admitted they were, to say the least, hectic:

> I arrived at Galvor in early April 1964, a few days after M. Chambertin had left.[1] I was the first Universal man here in Bordeaux and I became quickly immersed in all the problems surrounding the change of ownership. For example, there were no really workable financial statements for the previous two years. This made preparation of the Business Plan, which Mr. Hennessy and I began in June, extremely difficult. This plan covers every aspect of the business, but the great secrecy which had always been maintained at Galvor about the company's financial affairs made it almost impossible for anyone to help us.

Mr. Barsac's duties could be roughly divided into two major areas: first, the preparation of numerous reports required by Universal, and, second, supervision of Galvor's internal accounting function. While these two areas were closely related, it is useful to separate them in describing the accounting and control function as it developed after Universal's acquisition of Galvor.

To control its operating units, Universal relied primarily on an extensive system of financial reporting. Universal attributed much of its success in recent years to this system. The system was viewed by Universal's European Controller, M. Boundry, as much more than a device to "check up" on the operating units:

[1] M. Chambertin remained on the payroll as a part-time consultant for legal problems.

In addition to measuring our progress in the conventional sense of sales, earnings and return on investment, we believe the reporting system causes our operating people to focus their attention on critical areas which might not otherwise receive their major attention. An example would be the level of investment in inventory. The system also forces people to think about the future and to commit themselves to specific future goals. Most operating people are understandably involved in today's problems. We believe some device is required to force them to look beyond the problems at hand and to consider longer range objectives and strategy. You could say we view the reporting system as an effective training and educational device.

Background[2]

The Galvor Company had been founded in 1936 by M. Georges Latour, who continued as its owner and president until 1964. Throughout its history, the company had acted as a fabricator, buying parts and assembling them into high-quality, moderate-cost electric and electronic measuring and test equipment. In its own sector of the electronics industry—measuring instruments—Galvor was one of the major French firms; however, there were many electronics firms in the more sophisticated sectors of the industry which were vastly larger than Galvor.

Galvor's period of greatest growth began around 1950. Between 1950 and 1961 sales grew from 2.2 million 1961-new francs to 12 million, and after-tax profits from 120,000 1961-new francs to 1,062,000. Assets as of December 31, 1961 totalled 8.8 million new francs. (One 1961-new franc=$.20.) The firm's prosperity resulted in a number of offers to purchase equity in the firm, but M. Latour had remained steadfast in his belief that only if he had complete ownership of Galvor could he direct its affairs with a free hand. As owner/president, Latour had continued over the years to be personally involved in every detail of the firm's operations.

In 1962, M. Latour explained to a casewriter how he controlled Galvor:

> At the month's end, M. Chambertin sends me the following figures for the month: net sales, total purchases, direct and indirect labor, R&D expenses, manufacturing overhead, inventory levels, gross profits, commissions, sales taxes, my personal account, and net profit. I check these figures against previous levels in order to determine whether we are up to standard or should take some corrective measures. Finally, I check our balance sheet, total overhead as a per cent of sales, and our sales to each country. Of all these figures, I am most interested in the net profit figure. Since I sign all our important checks, this gives me another way of keeping an eye on our purchasing.

As of early 1962, M. Latour was concerned about the development of adequate successor management for Galvor. In January 1962 Latour

[2] This section has been summarized from earlier cases in the Galvor series.

hired a "technical director" as his special assistant, but this person re-
signed in November 1963. Following the 1963 unionization of Galvor's
workforce, which Latour had opposed, Latour (then 54 years old) began
to entertain seriously the idea of selling the firm and devoting himself "to
family, philanthropic, and general social interests." On April 1, 1964
Galvor was sold to Universal Electric Company for $4.5 million worth of
UE's stock. M. Latour became Chairman of the Board of Galvor, and
David Hennessy was appointed as Galvor's Managing Director. Hennessy
at that time was 38 years old and had been with UE for nine years.

The Business Plan

The heart of Universal's reporting and control system was an extremely
comprehensive document—the Business Plan—which was prepared annually by each of the operating units. The Business Plan was the primary
standard for evaluating the performance of unit managers and everything possible was done by Universal's top management to give authority
to the plan.

Each January, the Geneva headquarters of Universal set tentative
objectives for the following two years for each of its European operating
units. This was a "first look"—an attempt to provide a broad statement of
objectives which would permit the operating units to develop their detailed Business Plans. For operating units which produced more than a
single product line, objectives were established for both the unit as a whole
and for each product line. Primary responsibility for establishing these
tentative objectives rested with eight product-line managers located in
Geneva, each of whom was responsible for a group of product lines. On
the basis of his knowledge of the product lines and his best judgment of
their market potential, each product-line manager set the tentative objectives for his lines.

For reporting purposes, Universal considered that Galvor represented
a single product line, even though Galvor's own executives viewed the
company's products as falling into three distinct lines—multimeters,
panel-meters and electronic instruments.

For each of over 300 Universal product lines in Europe, objectives were
established for five key measures:

Sales
Net income
Total assets
Total employees
Capital expenditures

From January to April, these tentative objectives were "negotiated" between Geneva headquarters and the operating managements. Formal meetings were held in Geneva to resolve differences between the operating unit managers and product-line managers or other headquarters personnel.

Negotiations also took place at the same time on products to be discontinued. Mr. Hennessy described this process as a "sophisticated exercise which includes a careful analysis of the effect on overhead costs of discontinuing a product and also recognizes the cost of holding an item in stock. It is a good analysis and one method Universal uses to keep the squeeze on us."

During May, the negotiated objectives were reviewed and approved by Universal's European headquarters in Geneva and by corporate headquarters in the United States. These final reviews focused primarily on the five key measures noted above. In 1966 the objectives for total capital expenditures and for the total number of employees received particularly close surveillance. The approved objectives provided the foundation for preparation of Business Plans.

In June and July, Galvor prepared its Business Plan. The plan, containing up to 100 pages, described in detail how Galvor intended to achieve its objectives for the following two years. The plan also contained a forecast, in less detail, for the fifth year hence—e.g., for 1971 in the case of the plan prepared in 1966.

Summary Reports

The broad scope of the Business Plan can best be understood by a description of the type of information it contained. It began with a brief one-page financial and operating summary containing comparative data for:

Preceding year (actual data)
Current year (budget)
Next year (forecast)
Two years hence (forecast)
Five years hence (forecast)

This one-page summary contained condensed data dealing with the following measures for each of the five years:

Net income
Sales

Total assets
Total capital employed (sum of long-term debt and net worth)
Receivables
Inventories
Plant, property and equipment
Capital expenditures
Provision for depreciation
% return on sales
% return on total assets
% return on total capital employed
% total assets to sales
% receivables to sales
% inventories to sales

Orders received
Orders on hand
Average number of full-time employees
Total cost of employee compensation
Sales per employee
Net income per employee
Sales per $1,000 of employee compensation
Net income per $1,000 of employee compensation
Sales per thousand square feet of floor space
Net income per thousand square feet of floor space

Anticipated changes in net income for the current year and for each of the next two years were summarized according to their cause, as follows:

Volume of sales
Product mix
Sales prices
Raw material purchase prices
Cost reduction programmes
Accounting changes and all other causes

This analysis of the causes of changes in net income forced operating managements to appraise carefully the profit implications of all management actions affecting prices, costs, volume or product mix.

Financial Statements

These condensed summary reports were followed by a complete set of projected financial statements—income statement, balance sheet, and a statement of cash flow—for the current year and for each of the next two years. Each major item on these financial statements was then analyzed in detail in separate reports which covered such matters as transactions with headquarters, proposed outside financing, investment in receivables and inventory, number of employees and employee compensation, capital expenditures, and nonrecurring write-offs of assest.

Management Actions

The Business Plan contained a description of the major management actions planned for the next two years with an estimate of the favorable or unfavorable effect each action would have on total sales, net income and total assets. Among some of the major management actions described in Galvor's 1966 Business Plan (prepared in mid-1965) were the following:

Implement standard cost system

Revise prices

Cut oldest low-margin items from line

Standardize and simplify product design

Create forward research and development plan

Install punch-card inventory system

Implement product planning

Separate plans were presented for each of the functional areas— marketing, manufacturing, research and development, financial control, and personnel and employee relations. These functional plans began with a statement of the function's mission, an analysis of its present problems and opportunities, and a statement of the specific actions it intended to take in the next two years.

Among the objectives set for the control area in the 1966 Business Plan, M. Barsac stated that he hoped to:

Better distribute tasks.

Make more intensive use of IBM equipment.

Replace nonqualified employees with better trained and more dynamic people.

The Business Plan closed with a series of comparative financial statements which depicted the estimated item-by-item effect if sales fell to 60% or to 80% of forecast or increased to 120% of forecast. For each of these levels of possible sales, costs were divided into three categories: fixed costs, unavoidable variable costs, and management discretionary costs. Management described the specific actions it would take to control employment, total assets and capital expenditures in case of a reduction in sales and when these actions would be put into effect. In its 1966 Business Plan, Galvor indicated that its programme for contraction would be put into effect if incoming orders dropped below 60% of budget for two weeks, 75% for four weeks or 85% for eight weeks. It noted that assets would be cut only to 80% in a 60% year and to 90% in an 80% year "because remodernization of our business is too essential for survival to slow down much more."

Approval of Plan

By mid-summer the completed Business Plan was submitted to Universal headquarters, and, beginning in the early fall, meetings were held in Geneva to review each company's Business Plan. Each plan had to be justified and defended at these meetings, which were attended by senior executives from both Universal's European and American headquarters and by the general managers and functional managers of many of the operating units. Universal viewed these meetings as an important element in its constant effort to encourage operating managements to share their experiences in resolving common problems.

Before final approval of a company's Business Plan at the Geneva review meeting, changes were often proposed by Universal's top management. For example, in September 1966, the 1967 forecasts of sales and net income in Galvor's Business Plan were accepted, but the year-end forecasts of total employees and total assets were reduced about 9% and 1% respectively. Galvor's proposed capital expenditures for the year were cut 34%, a reduction primarily attributable to limitations imposed by Universal on all operating units throughtout the corporation.

The approved Business Plan became the foundation of the budget for the following year, which was due in Geneva by mid-November. The general design of the budget resembled that of the Business Plan except that the various dollar amounts, which were presented in the Business plan on an annual basis, were broken down by months. Minor changes between the overall key results forecast in the Business Plan and those reflected in greater detail in the budget were not permitted. Requests for major changes had to be submitted to Geneva no later than mid-October.

Reporting to Universal

Every Universal unit in Europe had to submit periodic reports to Geneva according to a fixed schedule of dates. All units in Universal, whether based in the United States or elsewhere, adhered to essentially the same reporting system. Identical forms and account numbers were used throughout the Universal organization. Since the reporting system made no distinction between units of different size, Galvor submitted the same reports as a unit with many times its sales. Computer processing of these reports facilitated combining the results of Universal's European operations for prompt review in Geneva and transmission to corporate headquarters in the United States.

The main focus in most of the reports submitted to Universal was on the variance between actual results and budgeted results. Sales and expense data were presented for both the latest month and for the year to date. Differences between the current year and the prior year were also reported because these were the figures submitted quarterly to Universal's shareholders and to newspapers and other financial reporting services.

Description of Reports

Thirteen different reports were submitted by the Controller on a monthly basis, ranging from a statement of preliminary net income which was due during the first week following the close of each month, to a report on the status of capital projects due on the last day of each month. The monthly reports included:

Statement of preliminary net income
Statement of income
Balance sheet
Statement of changes in retained earnings
Statement of cash flow
Employment statistics
Status of orders received, cancelled and outstanding
Statement of intercompany transactions
Statement of transactions with headquarters
Analysis of inventories
Analysis of receivables

Status of capital projects
Controller's monthly operating and financial review

The final item, the controller's monthly operating and financial review, often ran to 20 pages or more. It contained an explanation of the significant variances from budget as well as a general commentary on the financial affairs of the unit.

In addition to the reports submitted on a monthly basis, approximately 12 other reports were required less often, either quarterly, semi-annually, or annually.

Cost of the System

The control and reporting system, including preparation of the annual Business Plan, imposed a heavy burden in both time and money on the management of an operating unit. M. Barsac commented on this aspect of the system in the section of Galvor's 1966 Business Plan dealing with the control functional area.

Galvor's previous Administrative Manager (Controller), who was a tax specialist above all, had to prepare a balance sheet and statement of income once a year. Cost accounting, perpetual inventory valuation, inventory control, production control, customer accounts receivable control, budgeting, etc. did not exist. No information was given to other department heads concerning sales results, costs and expenses. The change to a formal monthly reporting system has been very difficult to realize. Due to the low level of employee training, many tasks such as consolidation, monthly and quarterly reports, budgets, the Business Plan, implementation of the new cost system, various analyses, restatement of prior year's accounts, etc. must be fully performed by the Controller and Chief Accountant, thus spending 80% of their full time in spite of working 55-60 hours per week. The number of employees in the Controller's Department in subsequent years will not depend on Galvor's volume of activity, but rather on Universal's requirements.

Implementation of the complete Universal Cost and Production Control System in a company where nothing existed before is an enormous task, which involves establishing 8,000 machining and 3,000 assembly standard times and codifying 15,000 piece parts.

When interviewed early in 1967, M. Barsac stated:

Getting the data to Universal on time continues to be a problem. We simply don't have the necessary people who understand the reporting system and its purpose. The reports are all in English and few of my people are conversant in English. Also, American accounting methods are different from procedures used in France. Another less serious problem concerns the need to convert all of our internal records, which are kept in francs, to dollars when reporting to Universal.

I am especially concerned that few of the reports we prepare for Universal are useful to our operating people here in Bordeaux. Mr. Hennessy, of course, uses the reports as do one or two others. I am doing all that I can to encourage greater use of these reports. My job is not only to provide facts, but to help the managers understand and utilize the figures available. We have recently started issuing monthly cost and expense reports for each department showing the variances from budget. These have been well received.

Mr. Hennessy also commented on meeting the demands imposed by Universal's reporting system:

Without the need to report to Universal, we would do some things in a less formal way or at different times. Universal decides that the entire organization must move to a certain basis by a specified date. There are extra costs involved in meeting these deadlines. An example was applying the punch-card cost system to our piece-parts manufacturing operation before we were really ready to tackle the job. It should be noted, also, that demands made on the Controller's Department are passed on to other areas such as marketing, engineering and production.

M. Boudry, Universal's European Controller, acknowledged that the cost of the planning and reporting system was high, especially for smaller units:

The system is designed for a large business. We think that the absolute minimum sales volume for an individual unit to support the system is about $5 million; however, we would prefer at least $10 million. By this standard, Galvor is barely acceptable. We really don't know if the cost of the system is unnecessarily burdensome in the sense that it requires information which is not worth its cost. A reasonable estimate might be that about 50% of the information would be required in any smartly managed independent business of comparable size, another 25% is required for Universal's particular needs, and 25% is probably "dead underbrush" which should be cleaned out. Ideally, every five years we should throw the system out the window and start again with the essentials.

As an indication of some of his department's routine activity, M. Barsac noted that at the end of 1966 Galvor was preparing each working day about 10,000 punch cards and 200 invoices. At that time the company had approximately 12,000 active customers.

Early in 1967, 42 people were employed in the Controller's Department, about 6% of Galvor's total employees. The organization of the department is described in Exhibit 1.

Headquarters Performance Review

Galvor's periodic financial reports were forwarded to M. Boudry in Geneva. The reports were first reviewed by an assistant to M. Boudry, one of four financial analysts who together reviewed all reports received from Universal's operating units in Europe.

In early 1967, M. Boudry described the purpose of these reviews:

The reviews focus on a comparison of performance against budget for the key measures—sales, net income, total assets, total employees, and capital expenditures. These are stated as unambiguous numbers. We try to detect any trouble spots or trends which seem to be developing. Of course, the written portions of the reports are also carefully reviewed, particularly the explanations of variances from budget. If everything is moving as planned, we do nothing.

The reports may contain a month-by-month revision of forecasts to year-end, but if the planned objectives for the year are not to be met we consider the situation as serious.

If a unit manager has a problem and calls for help, then it becomes a matter of common concern. He can probably expect a bad day in explaining how it happened, but he can expect help too. Depending on the nature of the problem, either Mr. Forrester, Galvor's product-line manager, or one of our staff specialists would go down to Bordeaux. In addition to the financial analysts, one of whom closely follows Galvor's reports, we have specialists on cost systems and analysis, inventory control, credit and industrial engineering.

We have not given Galvor the help it needs and deserves in data processing, but we have a limited staff here in Geneva and we cannot meet all needs. We hope to increase this staff during 1967.

With reference to Galvor's recent performance, M. Boudry stated:

Galvor is small and we don't give it much time or help unless its variances appear to be off. This happened in the second half of 1966 when we became increasingly concerned about the level of Galvor's inventories. A series of telexes on this matter between Mr. Hennessy and M. Poulet, our Director of Manufacturing here in Geneva, illustrate how the reports are used. (See Exhibits 2 through 5.)

We feel the situation is under control and the outlook for Galvor is okay despite the flat performance between 1963–65 and the downturn in 1966. The Company has been turned about and 1967 looks promising.

Although the comprehensive reporting and control system made it appear that Universal was a highly centralized organization, the managements of the various operating units had considerable autonomy. For example, Mr. Hennessy, who was judged only on Galvor's performance, was free to purchase components from other Universal units or from outside sources. There were no preferred "in-house" prices. A slight incentive was offered by Universal to encourage such transactions by not levying certain headquarters fees, amounting to about 2% of sales, against the selling unit.

Similarly, Universal made no attempt to shift its taxable income to low-tax countries. Each unit was viewed as though it were an independent company subject to local taxation and regulation. Universal believed that this goal of maximizing profits for the individual units would in turn maximize Universal's profits. Forcing every unit to maximize its profits precluded the use of arbitrary transfer prices for "in-house" transactions.

Recent Developments at Galvor

A standard cost system, which included development and tooling costs as well as manufacturing and assembly, had been in effect since March 1966.

According to Mr. Hennessy:

> We had hoped to start in January, but we were delayed. On the basis of our experience in 1966, all standards were reviewed and, where necessary, they were revised in December. We now have a history of development and tooling experience which we have been accumulating since 1965. This has proved extremely useful in setting cost standards. Simultaneously we have integrated market and sales forecasts more effectively into our pricing decisions.
>
> Before Universal acquired Galvor, a single companywide rate was used to allocate factory overhead to the costs of products. For many years this rate was 310% of direct labour. In a discussion of his pricing policies in 1962, M. Latour said, "I have been using this 310% for many years and it seems to work out pretty well, so I see no reason to change it."

M. Chambertin had long argued that the less complex products were being unfairly burdened by the use of a single overhead rate, while electronic products should bear more.

M. Latour's response to this argument was:

> I have suspected that our electric products are too high-priced, and our electronic products are too low-priced. So what does this mean? Why should we lower our prices for multimeters and galvanos? At our current prices we can easily sell our entire production of electric products.

M. Chambertin remained convinced that eventually Galvor would be forced by competitive pressures to allocate its costs more realistically.

In 1966, as part of the new standard cost system, Galvor did indeed refine the procedure for allocating overhead costs to products. Fifteen different cost centers were established, each with a separate burden rate. These rates, which combined direct labour cost and overhead, ranged from 13.19 francs to 38.62 francs per direct labour hour.

Concluding his comments about recent developments, Mr. Hennessy said:

> A formal inventory control system went into effect in January 1967. This, together with the standard cost system, allows us for the first time to really determine the relative profitability of various products, and to place a proper valuation on our inventory.
>
> We are installing a new IBM 6400 in February which we will use initially for customer billing and for marketing analysis. We hope this will reduce the number of people required in our customer billing and accounts receivable operations from six, or seven.

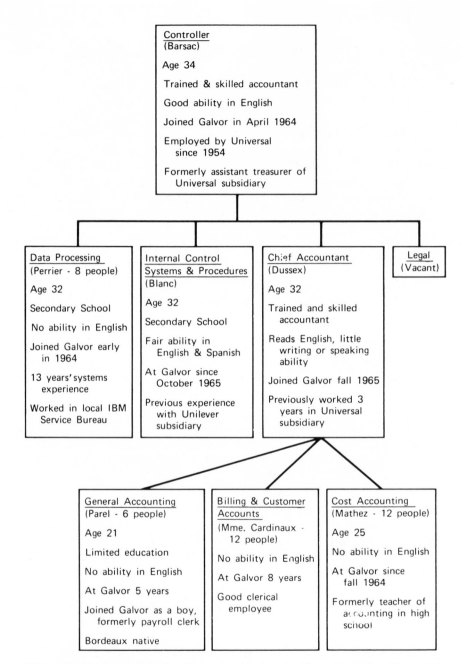

Controller
(Barsac)

Age 34

Trained & skilled accountant

Good ability in English

Joined Galvor in April 1964

Employed by Universal
since 1954

Formerly assistant treasurer of
Universal subsidiary

Data Processing
(Perrier - 8 people)

Age 32

Secondary School

No ability in English

Joined Galvor early
in 1964

13 years' systems
experience

Worked in local IBM
Service Bureau

Internal Control
Systems & Procedures
(Blanc)

Age 32

Secondary School

Fair ability in
English & Spanish

At Galvor since
October 1965

Previous experience
with Unilever
subsidiary

Chief Accountant
(Dussex)

Age 32

Trained and skilled
accountant

Reads English, little
writing or speaking
ability

Joined Galvor fall 1965

Previously worked 3
years in Universal
subsidiary

Legal
(Vacant)

General Accounting
(Parel - 6 people)

Age 21

Limited education

No ability in English

At Galvor 5 years

Joined Galvor as a boy,
formerly payroll clerk

Bordeaux native

Billing & Customer
Accounts
(Mme. Cardinaux -
12 people)

No ability in English

At Galvor 8 years

Good clerical
employee

Cost Accounting
(Mathez - 12 people)

Age 25

No ability in English

At Galvor since
fall 1964

Formerly teacher of
accounting in high
school

---

* Immediately prior to Galvor's takeover by UE, there had been fewer than 20 people in the Controller's Department.

Exhibit 1 Galvor Company Organization of Controller's Department* (January 1967)

Exhibit 2 THE GALVOR COMPANY

Telex from Poulet to Hennessy Concerning Level of Inventory

TO: HENNESSY - GALVOR
FROM: POULET - UE
DATE: SEPT. 26, 1966

FOLLOWING ARE THE JULY AND AUGUST INVENTORY AND SALES FIGURES WITH THEIR
RESPECTIVE VARIANCES FROM BUDGET.

THOUSANDS OF DOLLARS

	ACTUAL	JULY BUDGET	VARIANCE	ACTUAL	AUGUST BUDGET	VARIANCE
INVENTORY	2,010	1,580	(430)	2,060	1,600	(460)
SALES TO DATE	3,850	3,900	(50)	4,090	4,150	(60)

LATEST AUGUST SALES FORECAST REFLECTS DECREASE IN YEAR-END SALES OF 227 VS
INCREASE OF 168 IN YEAR-END INVENTORIES OVER BUDGET.

Exhibit 2 (continued)

REQUEST TELEX LATEST MONTH-BY-MONTH INVENTORY AND SALES FORECAST FROM
SEPTEMBER TO DECEMBER, EXPLANATION OF VARIANCE IN INVENTORY FROM BUDGET
AND CORRECTIVE ACTION YOU PLAN IN ORDER TO ACHIEVE YEAR-END GOAL. INCLUDE
PERSONNEL REDUCTIONS, PURCHASE MATERIAL CANCELLATIONS, ETC.

POULET

Exhibit 3 THE GALVOR COMPANY

Telex from Hennessy to Poulet Concerning Level of Inventory

TO: POULET - UE
FROM: HENNESSY - GALVOR
DATE: SEPT. 27, 1966

YOUR 26.9.66
MONTHLY INVENTORY FORECAST SEPTEMBER TO DECEMBER BY CATEGORY FOLLOWS:

THOUSANDS OF DOLLARS	SEPT. 30	OCT. 31	NOV. 30	DEC. 31
RAW MATERIALS	53	51	50	50
PURCHASED PARTS	180	185	190	195
MANUFACTURED PARTS	95	93	93	91
WORK IN PROCESS	838	725	709	599
FINISHED GOODS	632	694	683	705
OTHER INVENTORIES	84	84	82	80
ENGINEERING IN PROCESS	55	58	48	44
RESERVE	(14)	(14)	(14)	(20)
INDICA[1]	50	52	55	55
TOTAL	1,973	1,928	1,896	1,799

[1]Indica S.A. was a wholly owned Parisian subsidiary of Galvor, which made dials and faces for measuring instruments. Only 10% of Indica's sales were to its parent.

Exhibit 3 (continued)

THE MAIN EXPLANATIONS OF PRESENT VARIANCE ARE THREE POLICIES ADOPTED END 1965 AND DISCUSSED IN MONTHLY LETTERS BUT WHICH LEFT DECEMBER 1966 BUDGET OPTIMISTICALLY LOW. FIRST WAS TO HAVE REASONABLE AMOUNTS OF SELLING MODELS IN STOCK WITHOUT WHICH WE COULD NOT HAVE ACHIEVED 19% INCREASE IN SALES WE ARE MAKING WITH OUTMODED PRODUCT.

SECOND POLICY WAS TO MANUFACTURE LONGER SERIES OF EACH MODEL BY DOUBLE WHEREVER SALES WOULD ABSORB IT, OTHERWISE MANY OF OUR COST REDUCTIONS WERE NEARLY ZERO. THIS MEANS OUR MANUFACTURING PROGRAM ANY MONTH MAY CONTAIN FIVE MONTHS WORTH OF 15 MODELS INSTEAD OF 10 WEEKS WORTH OF 30 MODELS (OUT OF SEVENTY).

THIRD WAS NEW POLICY OF REDUCING NUMBER OF PURCHASE ORDERS BY MAINTAINING A MINIMUM STOCK OF MANY THOUSANDS OF LOW VALUE ITEMS WHICH YOU AGREED WOULD AND DID INCREASE STOCK UPON FIRST PROCUREMENT BUT WE ARE ALREADY GETTING SLIGHT REDUCTION.

CORRECTIVE ACTIONS NUMEROUS INCLUDING RUNNING 55 PEOPLE UNDER BUDGET AND ABOUT 63 BY YEAR END PLUS REVIEWING ALL PURCHASE ORDERS MYSELF PLUS SLIDING A FEW SERIES OF MODELS WHICH WOULD HAVE GIVEN SMALL BILLING IN 1966 INTO 1967 PLUS THOSE POSTPONED BY CUSTOMERS. THIS WILL NOT HAVE DRAMATIC EFFECT AS NEARLY ALL THESE SERIES ARE PROCURED AND HAVE TO BE MADE FOR RELATIVELY SURE MARKETS BUT SOME CAN BE HELD IN PIECEPARTS UNTIL JANUARY. WE ARE WATCHING CAREFULLY STOCK OF SLOW MOVING MODELS AND HAVE MUCH CLEANER FINISHED STOCK THAN END 1965.

Exhibit 3 (continued)

FINAL AND GRAVE CONCERN IS ACCURACY OF PARTS, WORK IN PROCESS, AND FINISHED
GOODS VALUATION SINCE WE BEGAN STANDARD COST SYSTEM. INTERIM INVENTORY
COUNT PLUS VARIANCES VALUED ON PUNCH CARDS STILL DOESNT CHECK WITH MONTHLY
BALANCE USING CONSERVATIVE GROSS MARGINS BUT NEARLY ALL GAPS OCCURRED FIRST
FOUR MONTHS OF SYSTEM WHEN ERRORS NUMEROUS AND LAST 4 MONTHS NEARLY CHECK
AS WE CONTINUE REFINING. EXTENSIVE RECHECKS UNDERWAY IN PARTS, WORK IN
PROCESS, AND FINISHED GOODS AND CORRECTIONS BEING FOUND DAILY.

YOUR INVENTORY STAFF SPECIALISTS ARE AWARE OF PROBLEM AND PROMISED HELP
WHEN OTHER PRIORITIES PERMIT. WILL KEEP THEM INFORMED OF EXPOSURE WHICH
STARTED WITH RECODING ALL PARTS AND BEGINNING NEW BALANCES WITH NEW
STANDARDS AND APPEARS CLOSELY RELATED TO ERRORS IN THESE OPERATIONS. WE
CAN ONLY PURGE PROGRESSIVELY WITHOUT HIRING SUBSTANTIAL INDIRECT WORKERS.

HENNESSY

255

Exhibit 4

THE GALVOR COMPANY

Telex from Poulet to Hennessy concerning level of inventory

TO: HENNESSY - GALVOR
FROM: POULET - UE
DATE: NOV. 10, 1966

SEPTEMBER INVENTORY INCREASED AGAIN BY 64,000 COMPARED TO AUGUST WHILE
SEPTEMBER SALES WERE 145,000 UNDER BUDGET REFERRING TO YOUR LATEST TELEX
OF SEPTEMBER 27 IN WHICH YOU GAVE A BREAKDOWN OF THE SEPTEMBER FORECAST.
REQUEST DETAILED EXPLANATION FOR NOT MEETING THIS FORECAST IN SPITE OF YOUR
CURRENT CORRECTIVE ACTIONS.

SEPTEMBER	YOUR FORECAST	ACTUAL	VARIANCE
RAW MATERIALS	53	96	(43)
PURCHASED PARTS	180	155	25
MANUFACTURED PARTS	95	108	(13)
WORK IN PROCESS	838	917	(79)
FINISHED GOODS	632	723	(91)
OTHER INVENTORIES	84	87	(3)
ENGINEERING IN PROCESS	55	52	3
RESERVE	(14)	(14)	
INDICA	50	51	(14)
TOTAL NET	1,973	2,175	(1)
			(202)

256

Exhibit 4 (continued)

IN ORDER TO MEET YOUR DECEMBER FORECAST OF 1,799 YOUR WORK IN PROCESS HAS TO BE REDUCED BY 318. THIS MEANS A REDUCTION OF ABOUT 100 PER MONTH FROM SEPTEMBER 30 TO DECEMBER 31. THEREFORE, I ALSO WOULD LIKE ACTUAL ACHIEVEMENTS AND FURTHER REDUCTION PLANS DURING OCTOBER, NOVEMBER, AND DECEMBER CONCERNING THE POINTS MENTIONED IN YOUR SAME TELEX OF SEPTEMBER 27. CONSIDER AGGRESSIVE ACTIONS IN THE FOLLOWING SPECIFIC AREAS:

1. REALISTIC MASTER PRODUCTION SCHEDULES.
2. SHORT TERM PHYSICAL SHORTAGE CONTROL, TO INSURE SHIPMENTS.
3. WORK-IN-PROCESS ANALYSIS OF ALL ORDERS TO ACHIEVE MAXIMUM SALEABLE OUTPUT.
4. MANPOWER REDUCTION.
5. ELIMINATION OF ALL UNSCHEDULED VENDOR RECEIPTS. HAVE YOU ADVISED OTHER UNIVERSAL HOUSES NOT TO SHIP IN ADVANCE OF YOUR SCHEDULE UNLESS AUTHORIZED?
6. ADVISE FULL DETAILS ON ALL CURRENT SHORTAGES FROM OTHER UNIVERSAL HOUSES WHICH ARE RESPONSIBLE FOR INVENTORY BUILD-UP.

POULET

Exhibit 5 THE GALVOR COMPANY

Telex from Hennessy to Poulet concerning level of inventory

TO: POULET - UE
FROM: HENNESSY - GALVOR
DATE: NOV. 15, 1966

YOUR 10. 11. 66

WE NOW HAVE OCTOBER 31 FIGURES. OUR ACTUAL
ACHIEVEMENTS FOLLOW: RAW MATERIALS 54
VARIANCE PLUS 3, PURCHASED PARTS 173 VARIANCE
MINUS 12, MANUFACTURED PARTS 110 VARIANCE PLUS
17, WORK IN PROCESS 949 VARIANCE PLUS 224,
FINISHED GOODS 712 VARIANCE PLUS 18, OTHER 82
VARIANCE MINUS 2, ENGINEERING 54 VARIANCE MINUS
4, RESERVE MINUS 14 VARIANCE NIL, INDICA 55 VARI-
ANCE PLUS 3, TOTAL 2, 175 VARIANCE PLUS 247.
EACH ITEM BEING CONTROLLED AND THE ONLY SIG-
NIFICANT VARIANCES 224 WORK IN PROCESS AND 18
FINISHED GOODS ARE MY DECISION UPON SALES DE-
CLINE OF SEPTEMBER AND OCTOBER OF 311 TO
DELAY COMPLETION OF SEVERAL SERIES IN MANU-
FACTURE IN FAVOR OF ANOTHER GROUP OF SERIES,
MOSTLY GOVERNMENT, WHICH ARE LARGELY BILL-
ABLE IN 1966 IN ORDER TO PARTLY REGAIN SALES.
LAST EIGHT DAYS ORDERS AND THEREFORE SALES
ARE SHARPLY UP AND NONE OF THIS WORK IN PRO-
CESS WILL BE ON HAND MORE THAN 3 TO 6 WEEKS
LONGER THAN WE PLANNED.

NEVERTHELESS YOU SHOULD BE AWARE WE MANU-
FACTURE 4 TO 8 MONTHS WORTH OF MANY LOW
VOLUME MODELS AND EXAMPLE OF HOW WE DETER-
MINE ECONOMIC SERIES WAS FURNISHED YOUR STAFF
SPECIALIST THIS WEEK. WE CANNOT OTHERWISE
MAKE SIGNIFICANT COST REDUCTIONS IN A BUSINESS
WHERE AT LEAST 70 OF 200 MODELS HAVE TO BE ON
SHELF TO SELL AND TYPICAL MODEL SELLS 15 UNITS
MONTHLY. REGARDING YOUR 5 SUGGESTIONS AND TWO
QUESTIONS WE ARE CARRYING OUT ALL 5 POINTS
AGGRESSIVELY AND HAVE NO INTERHOUSE SHORTAGES
OR OVERSHIPMENTS.
                                                    HENNESSY

PART THREE

Developments in Management Technology

The final part of this book examines the implications of recent developments in management technology on the design and implementation of strategic planning systems. Three topics are studied: (1) the role of computer-based models, (2) planning in matrix organizations, and (3) resource allocation of strategic expenses.

In "A Framework for the Application of Computer-Based Models in the Long-Range Planning Process," we argue that although much progress has been made in the design and implementation of computer-based planning models, there are three major constraints that are crucial for good planning modeling approaches. The first factor requires that there be a specific recognition of the nature of the variables at each stage and level of the planning to be modeled. This in turn will influence the kind of quantitative modeling technique that might be appropriate. The second constraint relates to present and expected state-of-the-art of our computer technology. The third constraint relates to the capabilities of line management to undertake successful implementation of planning models. It is necessary to address these constraints, and to sense which of these might be expected to remain more or less permanently over the years and which will be expected to diminish as the technology evolves. Failure to observe these constraints is almost certain to lead to opportunity losses in modeling cost-effectiveness.

In the second reading, "A Framework for Strategic Planning in Multinational Corporations," we show that many multinational corporations (and many complex domestic organizations as well) will need to be managed along more than one organizational dimension, that is, adopt a so-called matrix structure that combines functional, product (business), and geographical dimensions. In practice it turns out that most matrix organizations can disregard one dimension; of the two remaining dimensions, one will typically be more dominant. To achieve both effective *adaptation* to environmental opportunities and threats and effective *integration* of the long-term ongoing pattern of corporate activities, we propose that the stronger, traditionally better developed dimension should assume primary responsibility for the integration task, and the less powerful, newer dimension should be more heavily involved with adaptation. Thus, the integration planning tasks will closely follow the formal organization pattern, but the adaptation planning tasks generally will not. Furthermore, adaptation will probably be relatively more important in the earlier planning stages, particularly during objectives setting. Integration, on the other hand, will probably be relatively more important during the latter stages of the planning and budgeting cycles. Thus, there is a natural "division of labor" between the two matrix dimensions, a feature that should increase the effectiveness of planning in complex, matrix settings. Considering that planning cost patterns are substantial for a matrix organization, however, planners do not develop a matrix organization structure unless they have to.

The third article, "Better Management of Corporate Development," describes a way to approach the process of managing internally generated growth, including a new type of planning and control system. The key to this is to plan the use and control of the corporation's development expenses, that is, items charged against income in current year, but not giving rise to profit until some subsequent year. Typical examples of development expenses are R & D expenses, marketing expenses, manufacturing overhead, and general administration overhead. In the decision process regarding development expenses, top management must focus on determining the scope of its resources, and how to mobilize and properly allocate them. The five proposed analytical steps to be followed are: identification of the resources, chief among which will be skilled people; classifying projects according to their expected effects on *new* business through research, product development, or marketing introduction versus their effects on *existing* businesses through product modification, marketing extensions, or cost engineering; deciding on the division of funds among projects; integrating by *first* developing plans for the projects and *then* consolidating the effects of the plans for each functional department; and, finally, measuring and reviewing the progress and effectiveness of the projects.

The three cases presented give practical illustrations of how to apply the various developments in management technology that have been discussed. In the first case, American Airlines, Inc., a large domestic airline carrier with centralized strategic decision making and planning, describes the design and implementation of a computer-based planning model. The model is a large simulation of the route pattern of the company, showing which routes to fly with the various types of aircraft, nonstop versus stopover routes, seat/mile configurations, and so on. The model is used by the corporate planning department as an efficient substitute for the old "pit-of-the-stomach" approach in its route scheduling planning—an operating planning task rather than a strategic one. However, the model also indicates the need for new aircraft to be acquired and the effects on the existing network of new route acquisitions, indeed strategic planning decisions. Thus, the model is serving a dual strategic and operating planning purpose.

The second case study, A. B. Astra, deals with strategic planning in a multinational corporate setting. The company is divisionalized; its huge pharmaceutical division is organized along the product dimension for its Swedish (home country) operation, along geographical areas for the rest of Scandinavia, and along a product/area matrix structure for the rest of the world. The four smaller divisions are organized along the product dimension. The challenge of the planning process is how to achieve both effective environmental adaptation and integration within such a complex setting. In addition to tailoring the planning system to this organizational structure, there is a problem of achieving realism in the plans, given the diverse set of inputs to and participants in the process, and of finding a proper role for top management in the planning process.

The final case, Texas Instruments Incorporated, exemplifies a company that has developed a sophisticated planning system for internal growth. The company has a rather unique organizational setup, in which many of the upper level management wear "two hats"—one for strategic management responsibilities and one for operating management responsibilities. The strategic mode of operations is structured through a hierarchy of objectives, strategies, and tactical action programs. The operating mode is structured around another hierarchy—groups, divisions, and product-customer centers. Through this dual structure, Texas Instruments has laid the foundation for achieving both effective adaptation and integration. The method of achieving this balance is further strengthened by a resource allocation process with two pools of resources—an operating pool and a strategic pool. The planning system is built around the two modes of operations and their separate resource allocation pools. Reinforcement of the strategic management task comes from other administrative systems within Texas Instruments, examples of which are the incentive compensation system, the information system, and the reporting system. In fact, the case gives an excellent example of what we might call an integrated *administrative* system. A strategic planning system, to be effective, must fit in as *one* of a family of systems; in isolation it probably will not work.

1

A FRAMEWORK FOR THE USE OF COMPUTER-BASED MODELS IN THE PLANNING PROCESS

PETER LORANGE AND JOHN F. ROCKART

INTRODUCTION

The use of computer-based models in the planning process has attracted much attention over the past decade. Heightened understanding of the mathematical tools and skill required for model building together with ever-better computer technology have increased activity in designing and implementing models for planning purposes. Although several successful planning model applications have emerged, we feel that the rate of success is not proportional to the level of resource commitments to these efforts. Many attempts fail to recognize that the models must comply with a number of constraints that affect the freedom of choice of modeling approaches. Such limiting factors are consistency with (and therefore recognition of) the overall planning process, the capabilities and limitation of the mathematical tools available, computer hardware and software constraints, and capabilities of line managers for successful implementation of planning models.

Perhaps most important is the first of the above constraints. In the past, too many modeling attempts have either assumed a simplistic attitude about the planning process or have not acknowledged the nature of the planning process at all. Unrealistic assumptions about the conceptual elements of the planning process have lead to unrealistic designs of computer-based models to support planning activities. Even where model builders have had a rather good perception of the nature of this factor, they have, unfortunately, often coupled this with an overly simplistic view, or "underperception," of some of the other constraints. For instance, ignorance of the computer hardware and software technology has often led to an unrealistic modeling approach.

In this chapter we will discuss some major factors constraining the development of computer-based planning models, arriving at a "constraint-based" conceptual scheme for planning models. We will discuss the following limiting factors in turn: consistency with the overall planning process and the consequences this has for the choice of modeling techniques; computer hardware and software technology developments; and implementation considerations.

PLANNING FRAMEWORK

To define whether models are integrated well into the planning process, one needs to have a scheme for that process, which provides a breakdown of the planning process into its relevant parts. We work with the Vancil-Lorange model, which defines three *cycles* in the planning process and three different *levels* in the organization of which planning takes place (see Exhibit 1). Vancil and Lorange identify three distinctly different strategic planning activities that take place respectively at the corporate, divisional, and functional levels.[1] The designations for these planning activities are portfolio planning, business planning, and functional planning. A brief discussion of each of these forms of planning will reveal clear differences in the tasks that must be handled by computer-based models to support each type of planning.

Portfolio planning at the corporate level involves balancing the corporation's portfolio of business activities. Are the business activities of some divisions to be emphasized relatively more or less than others? Should some businesses be eliminated? Are there venture opportunities in entirely new areas? A major concern in this form of planning is the balancing of the financial flows that result from the activities of the various businesses. Among factors that must be considered are funds generation/consumption patterns, absolute funds return from investments, and the quality of the funds flows in terms of risk, volatility, and such. A second concern in portfolio planning is the need to consider the probable effects on these funds flows caused by the company's economic outlook. General environmental scanning is, therefore, also part of the portfolio planning activity, with emphasis on such factors as monitoring the outlook for wages, inflation, interest rates, currency fluctuations, availability of credits, and so on.

Business planning at the divisional level is different. The emphasis here is on planning for the long-term success of the division through successful launching of new products and maintenance of established ones, maintenance of adequate R & D, production, sales, and distribution forces. The emphasis is on competitive moves, advances as well as responses, and is nonfinancial in flavor. A secondary emphasis, however, in business planning is to evaluate the balance between funds generation and funds consumption from established products and new products, in order to estimate the funds contribution or need of a division.

[1] See Reading 2, Part 1.

At the functional level within a division there are two major types of *functional planning* activities. "Programming" comes first, with the departments cooperating in strategic programs intended to strengthen the business position of the division; for example, the development and launching of a new product, a new marketing campaign, or a cost-cutting effort. After the programming stage comes the "functional budgeting" stage, which emphasizes bringing departmental budgets into accord with the programmed activities of each department. While the programs may be largely nondollar-dominated in terms of critical variables, the functional budgeting stage is heavily dollar-dominated.[2]

As Exhibit 1 shows, Vancil and Lorange also identify a second dimension in the planning process. Believing that the purpose of planning is to undertake a systematic "narrowing down" of strategic options in as intelligent a manner as possible, they suggest that this can best be done by going through a series of three increasingly more detailed planning cycle steps. In the first cycle, there is decision on objectives—corporate and divisional. The second cycle is the period in which multiple-year plans are developed in some detail at each organizational level to accomplish one's objectives. The third cycle is the budgeting stage, in which options are narrowed down even further and a coordinated set of action plans is determined for the company. It should be noted that the degree of specificity and sharpness of focus increases as one moves from the first objectives—setting cycle through cycle two and finally to the third cycle, the budgeting cycle. The differing types of data processed in each stage has obvious implications for the computer-modeling approach that should be employed.

A further aspect of the Vancil and Lorange model is that the planning process taking place within the "three by three" scheme just described is one dominated by the interaction of people. Communication flows have to be defined, the "negotiation" process is based on certain rules for interaction and is an iterative one. We shall return to this later. This breakdown of "the planning process" into parts results in a matrix with a number of cells, each one representing a different planning task and involving unique planning variables. Exhibit 1 portrays this matrix of planning variables.

The pattern of planning tasks portrayed in Exhibit 1 gives us guidelines for the modeling tasks that might be performed in each part of the planning process, if we are to utilize computer-based models at any stage/level of the planning process.[3] To emphasize this point, we shall discuss several of these cells briefly.

The different nature of the planning tasks, as exemplified by the

[2] See Reading 4, Part 2.
[3] See also Reading 1, Part 1.

Exhibit 1. Matrix of Variables for Planning Models

Step in Planning Organi-zation Level	Cycle 1 *Objectives Setting*	Cycle 2 *Specific Multiyear Planning*	Cycle 3 *Budgeting*
Corporate—Portfolio Plans	1) Set overall corporate performance targets given the environment.	3) Evaluate divisions' business plans. Modify balance of portfolio, if necessary.	6) Set quantitative targets. Modify balance of portfolio, if necessary.
Divisional—Business Plans	2) Identify key strategic success factors in business. Develop general strategy for business-major resource allocations.	4) Develop multiple-year action plan for business. Develop funds flow consequences of multiple-year action plan.	7) Develop budget for business in terms of strategic variables *and* dollar variables.
Functional—Programs/Budgets		5) Develop programs across functions.	8) Develop functional budgets in accordance with existing programs.

variable differences just discussed, will have a profound impact on the choice of modeling techniques in each cell. Differences in the nature of the various cycles in the planning process requires relatively different emphasis on the tasks of *adaptation* to environmental opportinities and/or threats versus *integration* of the diverse, ongoing activities of the company from cycle to cycle. For instance, during the objectives-setting cycle, the problem of selecting effective approaches to ensure adaptation to environmental opportunities and threats is typically a rather "messy," unstructured process. At the more constrained budgeting stage, on the other hand, the problem of efficient allocation and coordination of internal resources is much better defined. Thus, the degree of specificity of the model requirements is relatively more structured in the budgeting cycle than in the objectives-setting cycle. The degree of specificity of the modeling task in the second cycle—multi-year planning—falls somewhere in-between.

A similar argument can be made for the expected difference in complexity of the modeling task at the corporate, divisional, and functional levels of the corporation. At the functional level the degree of data specificity is relatively high when it comes to modeling production planning, marketing planning, or R & D planning. When attempting to model a combination of these functional tasks as one integrated business activity at the divisional level, the degree of data specificity is considerably less. At the corporate level, finally, the degree of data specificity is even less. Thus, we go from relatively high data specificity to relatively less data specificity as we move up the organizational hierarchy.

Just as the *data* used gets more specific as we move from the top left of the three-by-three matrix to the bottom right, so does the degree of *structure* of the decision process. In the functional budgeting area, many exact algorithms exist to make decisions. In the corporate objectives setting cell, however, most decisions are uncertain, unstructured, and opportunistic. We would expect that more exact models would be used in the lower right. We might summarize our discussion of where to find relatively more versus relatively less specific structure and data in planning modeling settings in Exhibit 2.

Models for objectives-setting assistance. Let us now consider what specific modeling tools we should find at various stages of the planning process, given the general nature of the planning variables (as summarized in Exhibit 1) and the degree of data structure to be the basis for our planning models (as summarized in Exhibit 2). During the objectives-setting stage of planning (cycle 1), we expect relatively less reliance on formal computer-based planning models than for the other planning stages, given the qualitative, creative nature of planning at this stage. This, however, does not imply that computer-based planning models might not be of some use. Particularly, econometric models of the economy or of

Exhibit 2. Planning Structure Differences In Relative Degree of Specificity as a Function of Stage in the Planning Process and Organization Level

Stage in Planning Process / Organizational Level	Cycle 1 Objectives Setting	Cycle 2 Specific Multiyear Planning	Cycle 3 Budgeting
Corporate	LITTLE	SOME	MORE
Divisional (Business)	DATA AND STRUCTURE	DATA AND MODELING	DATA AND MODELING
Functional		STRUCTURE	STRUCTURE

specific industries might provide a useful "feel" for macro trends in the environment in which the organization (corporation or division) exists. At the corporate level this will be used for getting a better feel for the sections of the economy that are potentially more versus less attractive. Thus, the output of such models will facilitate the corporate strategy formulation in terms of which business to emphasize and which to de-emphasize. At the division level an industry model might similarly give a better feel for where a business is going and what major business strategies to consider.[4]

Cycle 2 models. During the second planning cycle there are several different model-approaches that potentially might be useful. At the divisional level, industry-based econometric models can provide insight as to what might be the attractiveness of one's business, say, in terms of expected growth rate. Other models might provide forecasts for own and major competitors' market shares. The division will be further in need of models to assist in the consolidation of funds flows. Capital budgeting models are useful as well. Models to assist the selection of new business lines, such as PIMS, are clearly of use.[5]

At the corporate level pro forma models for evaluating funds-flow combinations from the divisions will be needed.[6] Capital investment models will also be needed.

At the functional level within each division, on the other hand, there will be a need for an even wider variety of models. We have functional planning models such as advertising planning models and R & D selection models. Warehouse and plant location models might be used. PERT/ production planning might also be useful.

Budgeting Cycle Models. While the modeling applications at the second planning cycle primarily took the form of industry and firm simulations and *multiple-year* pro forma financial statements, the modeling in cycle three will typically focus on one-year pro forma budgeting applications as

---

[4] Data Resources Institute (DRI) provides a well-known service of industry-specific as well as larger econometric models. Another well-known large model is the Wharton econometric model. See M. D. McCarthy, "The Wharton Quarterly Econometric Forecasting Model, Mark III," Wharton School of Finance and Commerce, University of Pennsylvania, and V. D. Duggal, L. R. Klein, and M. D. McCarthy, "The Wharton Model Mark III: A modern IS-LM Construct," *International Economic Review*, October 1974. See also Robert S. Pindyck, and Daniel L. Rubinfield, *Econometric Models and Economic Forecasts*, (New York: McGraw-Hill, 1976), Ch. 12.

[5] See Bruce D. Henderson, "Perspectives on Experience," Boston Consulting Group 1968, and "The Experience Curve Revisited," Boston Consulting Group 1970; and Reading 4. Part 2. The so-called PIMS project also addresses this; see S. Schoeffler, R. D. Buzzell, and D. F. Heany, "Impact of Strategic Planning on Profit Performance," *Harvard Business Review*, March-April 1974, and R. D. Buzzell, B. T. Gale, and R. G. M. Sultan, "Market Share—A Key to Profitability," *Harvard Business Review*, January-February 1975. See also *The PIMS Program*, Strategic Planning Institute, 1033 Massachusetts Avenue, Cambridge, MA 1976.

[6] See E. Eugene Carter, *Portfolio Aspects of Corporate Capital Budgeting*, (Lexington, Mass.: D. C. Heath Publishing, 1974).

well as one-year physical budgets.[7] The latter typically will be found within the functions of each division, in the form of operations management and scheduling models. At the divisional and corporate levels we find budgeting models, primarily emphasizing financial variables at the corporate level but also containing some nonfinancial data (such as market share and price and volume data) at the division level.

Exhibit 3 provides a summary of the major modeling applications that fit each of the cells. (The blank cell for functional objective setting exists since we have seen no models that assist this area.)

TECHNOLOGICAL FACTORS

To the best of our knowledge, there is no good compendium on the "history of models to assist the planning process."[8] To write such a history would be an heroic undertaking, for the number of attempts at developing models for one phase or another of the planning process has undoubtedly been in the thousands—with too few successes. Companies are notoriously unwilling to talk about failures, and even less willing to talk about planning models that are of significant use to them.

The flavor of the history, however, is rather well documented in an article by Hayes and Nolan.[9] The article is concerned with the "successful" development of "fairly detailed corporate models that have been used for at least a couple of years to help senior managers make strategic decisions." They could find no such model in existence, but they do shed some light on the process of computer-based corporate modeling. In particular, they contribute an interesting categorization of the three major periods or phases of corporate modeling. It is worth reviewing these periods, which, although not scientifically separable, do tend to fit our intuition and experience and provide some perspective on the processes of development of planning models.

Hayes and Nolan summarize the three major periods, characterized as "bottom-up" from 1956 to 1963, "top-down" from 1964 to 1969, and "inside-out" from 1970 to the present. The first two periods can be summarized—and lumped together—in the following way: In general

---

[7] Although in-house developments of these systems are common, programs to process this data are also available from many service bureaus. Some of the major organizations providing these services are Accounting Corporation of America, Automatic Data Processing, and the Service Bureau Corporation. Other examples are Haskins and Sells' Falcon/Forecast system; IBM's Budplan and PGS II system. Literature on these systems is available from these organizations.

[8] There are, however, several survey studies of planning model practices. See George W. Gershefski, "Corporate Models—The State of the Art," *Management Science*, No. 16, 1970; Peter H. Grinyer, "Corporate Financial Simulation Models for Top Management," *Omega*, Vol. 1, No. 4, 1973; and Peter H. Grinyer, and Christopher D. Batt, "Some Tentative Findings on Corporate Financial Simulation Models," *Operations Research Quarterly*, Vol. 25, 1974.

[9] Robert H. Hayes, and R. L. Nolan, "What Kind of Corporate Modeling Functions Best?" *Harvard Business Review*, May-June 1974.

Exhibit 3. Modeling Tools to be Used at Various Stages/Levels of the Planning Process

Stage in Planning Process / Organizational Level	Cycle 1 *Objectives Setting*	Cycle 2 *Specific Multiyear Planning*	Cycle 3 *Budgeting*
Corporate	national econometric models (DRI, Wharton)	pro forma port-folio funds flows (multiple years), capital invest-ment models (multiple years).	budgeting models ▲
Divisional (Business)	industry econometric models (DRI, Wharton)	(DRI, PIMS) pro forma busi-ness funds flows (multiple years), capital invest-ments (businesses).	│
Functional	/////	mktg models, R&D models, warehouse/plant location, capital invest-ment (function).	operations management, models scheduling ▼

the prevailing computer technology of these first two periods was good enough to tempt designers into developing ambitious models to assist the planning process. But in neither period was the technology—either hardware or software—*really* adequate. In the "bottom-up" period, second generation computer hardware did not have a cost/benefit ratio adequate enough to allow much significant competitive use of models for day-to-day management. More significantly, the software that was available at that time required a computer technician to interact with the computer—and, then, only slowly and painstakingly. On-line interaction with the model was unavailable.

The hardware and software for the "top-down" generation was somewhat better. Availability of larger data storage capacity, time-sharing techniques, and better interactive languages expanded mathematical modeling horizons. But data, stored in separate files, was still hard to get to. And interactive languages still required many days of study before they could be used.

Even more significant than the hardware constraints during the "bottom-up" and "top-down" periods was the inability on the part of those designing planning models to understand the conditions under which managers used models. In both periods, the model development process was essentially turned over to "technicians"—to "operations researchers" in the first period, and to approximately the same people, renamed in the second period as "management scientists," and aided by "systems analysts." In both periods, line managers were seldom found in the planning model development loop. When they were involved, the models developed were simpler and more useful.

There are many examples of well-publicized "corporate planning models" during both of these periods. In the latter era the Sun Oil model[10] and the Boise Cascade Linear Programming model[11] were typical. Developed by staff groups of management scientists and systems analysts, both were eventually found too static, too complex, too removed from the real world, and too "sophisticated" to be useful to operating managers.

In the past five years, seven major factors in the area of computer technology (hardware and software) have contributed to the more successful development and use of models to assist the planning process. These seven factors and expectation about their direction over the next five years are:

1. *Central processing unit cost reduction.* Initial cost reductions with the System 370 introduced early in this period were on the order of a threefold increase in computing power for approximately the same money. During the last few years, this initial increase has been enhanced even more. Thus, the hardware cost of running a model has been reduced by a factor of 4 to 5 over the last five years. Hardware costs are expected to continue their downward trend. According to our interpretation of forecasts provided from organizations such as Arthur D. Little, Quantum Sciences, and Internation Data Corporation, hardware costs will decrease over the next five years so that the cost of equivalent processing power to a user will be approximately 15% to 20% of what it is today.

2. *Decreased cost of data storage.* In the past few years costs of on-line, direct-access storage have dropped precipitously, as indicated by Table 1.

MONTHLY ON-LINE STORAGE COST PER 1,000,000 CHARACTERS[12]

Year Introduced	IBM Storage Device	Storage Type	Storage Cost
1965	2314	Disk Storage	$25.00
1969	2319	Disk Storage	13.00
1970	3330	Disk Storage	6.80
1975	2850	On-Line Tape Storage	20¢-50¢

[10] See George Gershefski, "Building a Corporate Financial Model," *Harvard Business Review,* July-August 1969.

[11] See Albert N. Schrieber, ed., *Corporate Simulation Models* (Seattle: University of Washington, 1970).

[12] According to IBM sources.

Since planning models are run intermittently, very fast access to data is unnecessary; direct access, however, is necessary. All of the above mechanisms provide direct access to data, the most recent 2850 file at a vastly reduced cost per character of data storage, although access time to this data is relatively slow. These storage costs will continue to decline precipitously.

3. *The coming of age of time sharing.* Although time sharing was available in the late 1960s, it was not until the early 1970s that the industry really began to shake out. Today, time-sharing networks are available world-wide. This leaves a "planner" with access to alternate sources of computation as well as to specialized data bases and models. Thus, planning departments, if frustrated by a lack of activity on their behalf by the data processing department, can turn to outside sources of supply. The on-line service bureau industry and in-house time sharing is currently growing at about 25% a year, as opposed to half that growth rate in hardware generally. This supports the trend to more on-line, interactive availability of equipment for planning personnel desiring to use computers.

4. *Access to specialized data bases.* Also during this period, many time-sharing vendors built up data bases which, formerly unavailable, can now be accessed by the corporate planner. This data is available at costs much lower than those that would exist if each planner had developed the same data base by himself for use in the planning process.

5. *The availability of planning models.* During the past few years, there has been an explosion of "packaged models" for use by planners. These models are available either from time-sharing vendors for use on their time-sharing systems, or as "packages" that can be installed on the planner's own computer hardware. They range from very simple regression and moving average packages to slightly more complex, pro forma, profit and loss extrapolation models to econometric models. Depending upon the planner's sophistication in the world of modeling, and his place in the three by three framework described earlier, he can today choose models fitted to his needs (and understanding) from a very extensive cafeteria of offerings. The package software field is currently growing at approximately 35% a year with an equivalent growth expected over the next several years. This should mean that additional planning model "packages" of varying types will be available to planners who desire to use them.

6. *Data base languages.* Until recently, much corporate data has been buried in various corporate files accessible only by particular programs and particular languages. Gathering the data for a corporate planning effort—even for a corporation's own data base—has been a tiresome and very expensive process. The advent of data base languages, typified by IBM's IMS and CinCom's TOTAL,[13] provides data in a common, well-defined, accessible corporate pool. All data under a common data base system can be accessed by any program. The "data base revolution" is proceeding slowly,

---

[13] See R. G. Canning, "Trends in Data Management, Part 1 and Part 2," *EDP Analyzer,* Vol. 9, Nos. 5-6, May-June 1971. See also James Martin, *Computer Data-Base Organization,* (Englewood Cliffs, N.J.: Prentice-Hall, Inc., 1975).

however. Most data base languages are expensive to use in terms of computer time, difficult to implement, and only partially implemented in most companies. They provide little help with planning models at this time, but they augur well for the future.

7. *Better interactive languages.* Although on-line interaction with computers has been going on for more than a decade, it is only recently that simple, easy-to-use languages have been available. In a very real sense, BASIC was the first of these languages developed with the user in mind rather than the computer. The APL language and other user-oriented languages are just now beginning to make a favorable impact on the ability of nontechnicians (and technicians) to interact effectively and quickly with a computer system.

Perhaps most significant is the increasing availability of user-oriented languages such as APL. The user-oriented features are very significant. Sun Life of Canada estimates that they got a planning model up in approximately three and a half months, which would have taken about that number of years to program under some of the older languages. As one report notes, "The feature of the APL environment that cannot be reproduced in any other environment is the capability that provides the chains of specifications many times each day during the development period. Sun Life believes that their ability to perform hundreds of trial and error runs was essential in getting their model working.[14]

The design of APL encourages the manager/user to modify directly and expand his planning model without reliance on programmer substitutes. Many other companies, including Xerox, are now using APL for interactive modeling in the planning area. At the present time, APL-based systems aimed at planners are being offered by several firms. Included among these are the IP Sharp Associates of Toronto (with their AIDS package), Scientific Time Sharing of Bethesda, Maryland (with its FPS System), and IBM.[15] These systems have appeared in the last three or four years. One can only expect that more planning-oriented, user-oriented software interactive languages will be forthcoming within the next several years.

All of the above extrapolations into the future suggest that the hardware and software available today to assist the planner in modeling in the various parts of the planning process will be vastly more seductive in the future. Models will be easier to develop and much less costly to run. Crucial for planning purposes is the ability to run and rerun a model to test sensitivity in several directions; the cost of each run will be vastly diminished. And, as noted above, both major costs of running planning

[14] "Applying EDP Techniques to Corporate Planning," *EDP In-Depth Reports,* Vol. 3, No. 7, March 1974.
[15] Ibid.

models—programming the model and relevant changes into the computer, and actually running the model—will be reduced.

IMPLEMENTATION OF MODELS

We noted at the start of this chapter that there were three necessary steps for the development of effective computer planning models. Two of these—understanding of the planning process with its implications for model applicabilities and improved computer technology—have been discussed. This section turns to what is an equally crucial step—the development of an understanding of the necessary factors in the *implementation* of useful and usable planning models.

We noted earlier that prior to 1970 the development of planning models was turned over to technicians—and this did not work very well. During the last several years, an increasing amount of knowledge has been built up around the factors in model development that facilitate the absolutely critical process of the development and use of planning models. What has been discovered is what we probably should have known all along. Among their "lessons learned," Nolan and Hayes suggest that:[16]

1. Large models overwhelm the manager's ability to understand the assumptions of the model and to integrate its output into the decision-making process.
2. The manager must be intimately involved in the model-building process.
3. Simple models are usually the way to start.
4. The models should evolve in complexity or size as required by the decision maker and at *his* pace.

In a discussion of why "strategic planning models" have failed, Hall notes some of the same factors.[17] He underlines the need for quick interaction with planning models since change occurs very quickly in the corporate planning environment. And he underlines the differences between the technician and the manager in the way they see the world and see the process of model development.

One can only agree with these observations. We *have* learned over the last several years that models, planning or otherwise, are only abstractions of reality. No line manager is going to work with an abstraction or compaction of reality that is different from his own. As a result, he must understand the model he is using. This gives him only one of four choices. These are:

---

[16] Hayes and Nolan, "Corporate Modeling."
[17] William K. Hall, "Strategic Planning Models: Are Top Managers Really Finding Them Useful?" *Journal of Business Policy,* Vol. 3, No. 2, 1973.

1. Accept a "packaged" model to be used as part of the planning where the model fits a small enough part that the manager can verify the input and the output and observe that the model is performing as he believes it should. An outside model to be accepted therefore, must treat a very simple part of the planning process—such as the extension of pro forma profit and loss statements and balance sheets.

2. Develop the model himself. This means there must be interaction between the manager and the technician, and the initial model must be simple.

3. Have a technician program a simple aid to the planning process where the constraints are similar to those in 1.

4. Utilize a model such as an econometric model on a time-sharing basis, which is being used by enough other people and constantly checked by an "expert" to give it validity.

It is clear that the conditions which allow any of the four choices above to take place are increasing. The keystones for having a useful model then are: (1) credibility (either from an outside "expert"—an internal technician will *not* suffice—or from the manager himself having been involved in the development process of a simple, understandable model); (2) the ability to get the model "up" quickly; (3) cost effectiveness; (4) the development of the "right" model for the right part of the planning process; and (5) evolutionary capability so that the model can keep pace with both environmental changes and the manager's continuing gain in understanding of his environment.[18]

Given the above factors, most successful, newly developed planning models are likely to be relatively small and address only one or a few aspects of the planning process. A model is likely to be most effective when it can assist a manager at a given point in the planning process to analyze and understand better his alternative options, to provide a better basis for the manager's interaction with other relevant managers in the negotiation process leading to a "narrowing down" of strategic options, and, finally, to be of help to the manager during the revision and iteration stages that typically characterize the planning process.

The planning models that we see emerging primarily then, will typically be "special purpose" rather than large and all-encompassing. Assisting the manager in his planning thought process, they will more often be one shot rather than intended to be used year in and year out—reflecting the manager's planning focus at a given point in time —and they will typically be interactive, allowing for "what if" questioning and supporting the interactive, iterative nature of planning.

[18] See also Harvey M. Wagner, "A Managerial Focus on Systems Implementation," in *Proceedings of a Conference on the Implementation of Computer-Based Decision Aids,* Peter G. W. Keen, ed., MIT, 1975; Steven L. Alter, *A Study of Computer Aided Decision Making in Organizations,* MIT, Ph.D. thesis, 1975; and John S. Hammond, "The Roles of the Manager and Management Scientist in Successful Implementation," *Sloan Management Review,* Winter 1974.

We feel that the recognition of these aspects of the types of planning models that will be emerging in many ways will facilitate the implementation of these models. Given that the models satisfy the considerations outlined, they will be perceived easily by the manager as useful and cost beneficial to him. This, together with the relatively small size of the models, will make implementation manageable. The major concern of implementation, then, is that the model satisfies the requirements for providing meaningful, specific support to a manager who is involved in the planning process, positioned at a given organizational level, and functioning during a particular stage of the planning process.

CONCLUSIONS

While there has been a strong interest in the development and application of computer-based planning models, both among practitioners and academicians, we feel that progress has been marred by failure to observe three classes of factors that should impact the modeling approaches. First, there should be a specific recognition of the nature of the variables that must be taken into account. These are somewhat different in each cell of the planning process. These differences also constrain our use of modeling techniques in different parts of the planning process. Second, there should be acknowledgment about the types of constraints that realistically will be imposed due to the state of current computer technology. Further, we should have a sense of those constraints that will be lifted given the evolution of the development of computer technology. Third, the successful implementation of computer-based planning models depends on the recognition that models must be developed in such a way as to provide realistic support to the manager who is facing a given planning task. To have this occur, the manager must have faith in the model. There certainly are other factors that will influence a successful application of computer-based models in the planning process, but these three classes of constraint provide a useful framework for the task of developing more appropriate models.

2

A FRAMEWORK FOR STRATEGIC PLANNING IN MULTINATIONAL CORPORATIONS*

PETER LORANGE

INTRODUCTION

Strategic planning in a multinational corporation has a twofold task: to identify the strategic options most relevant to the corporation and to "narrow down" these options into the one best plan. Stated this way there is, of course, nothing fundamentally different between the strategic planning task of a multinational corporation and that of any other large corporation. However, since multinationals offer several complex and distinctively different approaches to organizational design and planning, it is useful to examine some of the problems of strategic planning in the context of the multinationals.

The broad definition of the strategic planning tasks given above has several implications. To be able to identify the most relevant strategic options, the corporation needs to *adapt* continuously to the environment. Also, to narrow down the strategic options into the one best plan, the corporation must be able to *integrate* its many diverse activities. In this chapter we shall attempt to clarify the major purposes of planning in the multinationals in terms of adaptation and integration needs.

Given the diversity of settings in which multinationals operate, the adaptation and integration tasks will not be the same for all multinationals. Indeed, the opposite is true; each multinational will be faced with unique adaptation and integration tasks. However, for us to develop some generalizations about the adaptation and integration tasks of planning in multinationals, we shall start out by identifying a few multinational corporate archetypes, followed by a discussion of their planning purposes in terms of adaptation and integration. We shall then present some normative propositions about adaptation/integration and the costs of striking a reasonable balance between the two in planning systems.

Empirical findings on long-range planning in multinationals reported by others indicate that (1) it is hard to find actual examples of multina-

*Reprinted from Journal of Long Range Planning, June 1976.

tionals that in all respects fit into any of the archetypes to be suggested[1] and (2) the formal planning systems of multinationals seem to be much less developed than those we recommend here.[2] However, we do not see this as limiting the value of the arguments to be presented. We intend to propose some fundamental dimensions of planning for multinationals that might be useful to improve the understanding of the planning phenomenon. Obviously the proposed normative framework is not intended for uncritical adaptation in specific cases.

A TAXONOMY OF MULTINATIONAL CORPORATIONS

We shall distinguish between types of multinational corporations according to the dimension along which the organization has been structured.[3] There seem to be two dimensions that might dominate the organizational structure: the product dimension, which occurs in companies that have adopted a so-called divisional structure, with each division responsible for one class of products; and the geographical area dimension, wherein each division is responsible for carrying out all the corporation's business within a given geographical area.

Complete domination of corporate structure by one dimension can prove to be inefficient. For instance, there might be considerable duplication of effort by having the product divisions operate their own separate organizations in one country. When evolving from such a product structure, the matrix structure might be described as consisting of a *leading* product dimension and a *grown* area dimension.[4] Alternatively, when evolving out of an area-dominated structure the matrix structure would have a leading area dimension and a grown product dimension.[5]

So we perceive four types of multinationals, depending on the degree of emphasis they put on the product dimension and/or the area dimension. This continuum of multinationals is shown in Exhibit 1.

---

[1] See Derek F. Channon, "Prediction and Practice in Multinational Strategic Planning," paper presented at the 2nd Annual European Seminar on International Business, European Institute for Advanced Studies in Management, 1974.

[2] See John S. Schwendiman, "International Strategic Planning: Still in Its Infancy," *Worldwide P&I Planning*, Sept.-Oct. 1971.

[3] This section is based heavily on Peter Lorange, "Formal Planning in Multinational Corporations," *Columbia Journal of World Business*, Summer 1973. See also Peter Lorange, "La Procedure de Plantification dans les Entreprises Multinationales," *Revue Economique et Sociale*, March 1973. Other classifications have been proposed in David P. Rutenberg, "Organizational Archetypes of a Multinational Company," *Management Science*, Vol. 16, No. 6, Feb. 1970; Howard V. Perlmutter, "L'Entreprise Internationale-Trois Conceptions," *Revue Economique et Sociale*, May 1965; and Richard D. Robinson, *International Business Management*, (New York: Holt, Rinehart and Winston, Inc., 1973).

[4] Davis has developed the concepts of "leading" and "grown" dimensions of matrix structures. See Stanley M. Davis, "Two Models of Organization: Unity of Command versus Balance of Power," *Sloan Management Review*, Fall 1974.

[5] We shall, however, not imply that the evolution of matrix structures will have to be toward an ultimate equal balance between the two dimensions.

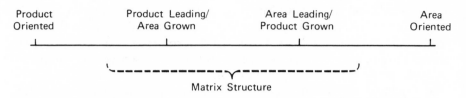

Matrix Structure

Exhibit 1. The Taxonomy of Multinational Corporations According to Relative Emphasis on Product Orientation vs. Area Orientation.

It should be stressed that typologizing into four categories is an over-simplification, since we are really dealing with a continuum. Further, dimensions other than product versus area orientation are likely to be considered in a realistic taxonomy of multinational corporations. Also, the taxonomy adopted does not apply to the early evolutionary stages of corporate internationalization. Thus, much richer and probably also more realistic classifications may conceivably be developed.[6] However, keeping the purpose of this chapter in mind, little seems to be gained by adopting a more detailed taxonomy of multinationals.

PLANNING PURPOSES: ADAPTATION AND INTEGRATION NEEDS

Let us analyze the nature of the requirements for adaptation and integration in each of the four multinational archetypes we are considering.

The product-organized corporation

This corporation will conduct its worldwide activities by means of several divisions, each responsible for carrying out the business strategy for one class of products on a worldwide basis. In terms of *adaptation,* then, each *division* will be responsible for scanning its own business environment. This implies a heavy pressure on each division to adapt to changes in each national market. How should the marketing promotion campaign be laid out for the promotion of a division's products in a particular country? Which models seem particularly worthwhile emphasizing in a given country? The pressures for scanning and adaptation within each worldwide product division will be on monitoring changes in area trends and taking advantage of the resulting opportunities. The major responsibility for carrying out this scanning rests on functional managers within each

[6] See Robinson, *International Business.*

division. Among the advantages of this form of adaptation will be a basis for the development of strong international plans for each business, which may enjoy the benefits of economies of scales in worldwide product strategies. Among the disadvantages may be the lack of adaptation to diverse geographical area inputs. Potential duplication of efforts by several divisions in interpreting the need for adaptation to the same geographical area may also be a problem.

At the *corporate* level of the product-division type of corporation *adaptation* tasks will center on the "mix" of the portfolio of divisions. Multinational strategy questions will not be addressed at headquarters, except when reviewing division plans to probe their soundness. Important issues for corporate management are how to adapt to changing patterns of inflation/deflation and/or devaluation/revaluation, and which divisions should receive added/diminished emphasis, given differences in the nature of products, capital intensity, and relative strength in an area that is becoming more/less attractive. At the extreme, these resulting corporate adaptation needs may lead to the triggering of acquisitions, that is, involvement in new business lines on a worldwide basis, or divestitures, that is, pull-out of a business on a worldwide basis.

The *integrating* task of the worldwide product *division* will be primarily to make sure that the overall activities of the division are consistent. There will be a need to integrate the strategic programs within each product division as well as the various functional activities. On the other hand there will probably be relatively less need for area integration, since each program and/or function is slated to work independently within the worldwide area. Thus, the main coordination focus will be on each worldwide business line activity.

At the *corporate* level there will be a need to integrate and coordinate the portfolio of worldwide business divisions, emphasizing financial funds flow interrelations among the divisions. Again, any portfolio adjustments resulting from a need for stronger integration eill be in modification of the plans of one or more of the product divisions, and not in area coordination directly.

It can be deduced that the formal organization structure itself plays a major role in facilitating the integration task. A major reason for the particular choice of the worldwide product division structure is in fact the need to integrate this type of company's worldwide activities along the product dimension. Thus, the formal organizational chart will typically be a reflection of the integration needs of an organization.[7]

---

[7] See Alfred D. Chandler, "Strategy and Structure," M.I.T. Press, 1962, and Jay Galbraith, *Designing Complex Organizations* (Reading, Mass.: Addison-Wesley, 1973).

The geographically area-organized corporation

To dichotomize the adaptation needs among the various multinational archetypes as clearly as possible, we shall consider the opposite of the product-organized multinational. This is the multinational corporation that is organized in a number of geographical divisions, each undertaking a relatively broad spectrum of businesses within its own area of the world. We shall first discuss the adaptation needs within each area division, and then consider adaptation challenges at the corporate level.

A primary task for each area *division* will be adapting its product portfolio to the area conditions and determining which products or businesses to emphasize. This will be the main responsibility of the general manager of the division, who will rely to a large extent on his business managers within the area. Thus, each area division will have considerable autonomy in providing environmental scanning data from its part of the world. Headquarters for the area divisions will probably be staffed with executives mostly from the host country and have broader local expertise than the product-oriented divisions. The latter divisions will probably have general worldwide rather than local geographical expertise and will most likely be staffed with executives from several nations. Divisions of the area-dominated multinational will have the potential for strong geographical area strategies and plans. The biggest disadvantage is probably the lack of adaptation of product strategies to several geographical areas. The adaptive efforts might lead to too much duplication of efforts in production, new product development, and so on among the areas and the risk of too much fragmentation, particularly if the geographical areas are small.

At the *corporate* level the *adaptation* requirements will be related to balancing the portfolio of area divisions. The task will be to assess the long-term health of each area given the composition of products of each division. Given devaluation/revaluation and/or inflation/deflation opportunities and/or threats, corporate will evaluate which products seem to have the best future in various areas and which should be de-emphasized; this may lead to changes in the portfolio. The central question will be whether the firm is emphasizing a set of products that result in the best worldwide geographical balance. We shall expect to find a much higher need for international staffing and broad worldwide expertise at the corporate level in the area-dominated multinational than in that which is product-oriented.

There seem to be diametrical differences between the two multinational archetypes in their needs for international competence and staff skills to carry out the adaptation tasks of planning at corporate as well as at divisional levels.[8] This is not surprising, since the adaptation needs for the geographical area-organized multinational generally are so different from the adaptation needs of the worldwide product-oriented multinational. The product division will focus on adapting to changing geographical area patterns, the geographical area division to changing business or product opportunities. At the corporate level, too, the adaptation challenges will be fundamentally different, although in both instances the task will be to monitor the balance of the portfolio of divisions according to devaluation/revaluation and/or inflation/deflation patterns. Thus, the adaptation needs for the divisional and corporate levels of the two types of multinationals will be structured along the *opposite* dimension to the one on which the corporation is organized.

The *divisional* level needs for *integration* will focus on pulling together the diverse business activities within the given area. This implies that product policies within the area should be integrated, and that the program and/or functional activities within the area will be coordinated. There will probably be less pressure to integrate the business worldwide, however, since each division is responsible for adapting a business or product exclusively to its given area. The *corporate* level will coordinate the several area divisions so that the portfolio may become integrated; portfolio adjustments will probably be in terms of areas, not products. Again, the choice of organizational structure, which in this case is primarily along the area dimension, directly reflects the integrative needs of the corporation.

Let us now leave the two extreme positions and consider the matrix structures, which will be faced with adaptation and integration tasks along *both* the product *and* area dimension. Before discussing the adaptation and integration tasks of our two matrix-based archetypes, however, let us review some relevant facts about coordination between the dimensions of a matrix structure. Effective coordination between the matrix dimensions must involve people; managers representing each dimension must get together to share information and work out decisions that take into account the considerations of each dimension. To facilitate coordination, then, it seems reasonable to form committees.[9] Staffing of these committees should reflect the matrix dimensions involved and should be done with executives from appropriate organizational levels. A major implication of the decentralized organizational structures considered here is that the responsibility for business strategy formulation and implementation

---

[8] Some of the differences in staffing patterns for nationals vs. nonnationals of four large European-based multinationals found by Davis, Edstrom, and Galbraith support this. See Harry Davis, Anders Edstrom, and Jay Galbraith, "Transfer of Managers in Multinational Organizations," European Institute for Advanced Studies in Management, Working Paper 74-19, Brussels 1974.

[9] See William Goggin, "How the Multi-Dimensional Structure Works at Dow-Corning," *Harvard Business Review*, Jan.-Feb. 1974. See also Davis, Edstrom, and Galbraith, "Transfer of Managers."

as well as the bulk of the action program decisions will be made at the division level. Consequently, it will be at this level that integration of the inputs from the various dimensions will have to take place, as each dimension should influence the way that business strategy decisions are made and carried out. It should be noted that a matrix structure does not imply that representatives from each dimension will have to cooperate in detail to reach decisions at each level of the organization. Rather, the multidimensional cooperation will take place at *one* level, namely through the business coordination committees at the division level. Below this, there will generally be unidimensional reporting to cope with the functional strategy tasks. At the corporate level only the leading dimension will be represented to formulate and implement a portfolio strategy.

Product leading/area grown matrix structure

This type of multinational will have a product-dominated organizational structure. However, going all the way along the product dimension with parallel business divisions operating worldwide would mean forfeiture of many of the benefits of being a large multinational and not merely a collection of business divisions. Thus, the rationale for the matrix structure is the acknowledgment that more than one dimension might be beneficial and a willingness to capitalize on potential economies of scales.

What requirements for *adaptation* face the product leading/area grown matrix structure? The answer is a combination of the adaptation requirements facing the worldwide product division organizations and the geographical area division organizations, but with relatively more emphasis of the factors discussed for the product division organization. Thus, at the divisional level the adaptation requirement will be dominated by changes in the area conditions. However, some emphasis will also be put on assessing changes in the business product dimension within each area. At the corporate level, similarly, adaptation of the portfolio should be primarily a response to area reconsiderations but also for business line reconsiderations.

In this type of corporation, which typically has evolved from a very strong dominance of the product dimension to the present balance, the *integrating* needs will probably not be too different from those of the worldwide product-organized corporation. At the division level the primary integrative concern will be to get the product lines together. However, a secondary concern will be to insure the product integration in such a way that the areas also are integrated to the largest possible extent. At the corporate level the product dimension will again be the one receiving the most attention for integration, so that the portfolio of worldwide product activities will be coordinated. However, this portfolio will need to be modified to take into account area coordination.

Area leading/product line grown matrix structures

For this last type of matrix structure the opposite of what was the case in the previous section will be the pattern. The *adaptation* requirements of the product dimension will be the most important, both at divisional and corporate levels. However, the area adaptation dimension will also play a role.

The *integrative* needs are likely to be similar to those of the corporation that is geographical area divisionalized. At the divisional as well as the corporate level, the area dimension will probably be the one requiring the most integrative attention. This should be modified by the need to integrate the product dimension as well.

SUMMARY PATTERN OF ADAPTATION AND INTEGRATION REQUIREMENTS

A summary of the adaptation and integration requirements of each of our four multinational archetypes is presented in Exhibit 2. As we see, there is a continuing shift in adaptation and integration requirements as we go from one organizational extreme to the other. It is important to recognize that the adaptation needs fall into a pattern along a continuum that goes *contrary* to the product/area organizational structure continuum of multinationals, while the integration needs fall along a continuum that goes in the *same* direction as the organization structure. This leads us to our first normative statement, namely that while the *integration task* of planning should be undertaken in such a way that it *follows the organizational structure*, the *adaptation task* should be carried out in a direction *contrary to organizational structure*.

Exhibit 2. SUMMARY OF THE INTEGRATION AND ADAPTATION PLANNING TASKS OF THE MULTINATIONAL CORPORATIONS IN OUR TAXONOMY

Taxonomy of Corporations	Adaptation	Integration
Worldwide Product Divisions	Along Area dimension	Along Product dimension
Product Leading/ Area Grown Matrix	Primarily along Area dimension; some along Product dimension	Primarily along Product dimension; some along Area dimension
Area Leading/ Product Grown Matrix	Primarily along Product dimension; some along Area dimension	Primarily along Area dimension; some along Product dimension
Geographical Area Divisions	Along Product dimension	Along Area dimension

COSTS OF PLANNING IN MULTINATIONALS

In this section we shall consider some of the costs of undertaking planning in each multinational archetype. One might ask whether it would not have been more natural to discuss first the issues of design and implementation of planning systems so that they might fulfill the requirements outlined in the previous section, then to consider the costs associated with the systems design alternatives. It will turn out, however, that cost considerations may have a major influence on the choice of the planning systems design approach. Thus, by discussing costs of planning at this point, we shall be able to advance a more cost-effective planning systems design approach.

The relative proportion of overall planning costs attributed to the area dimension versus the business dimension of course changes as one moves from the one extreme to the other, as illustrated in Exhibit 3.

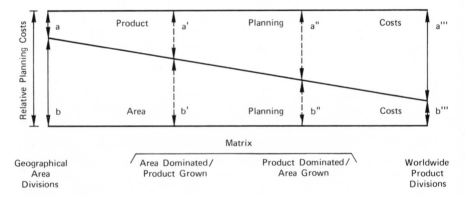

Exhibit 3.   The Relative Proportion of Planning Costs Attributable to the Product Dimension vs. the Area Dimension. The a's Indicate Product Dimension Cost Functions. The b's Indicate Area Dimension Cost Functions.[10]

We see that the relative importance of each dimension's planning cost segment will be dependent on the multinational archetype at hand. This, however does not imply that the *absolute* costs of planning remain the same for each archetype. For instance, evolving from a structure with geographic area divisions to a matrix with the area dimension dominated and product dimensions grown, the purpose will be to maintain a planning strength along *both* dimensions. The planning costs of the area

---

[10] Galbraith has suggested this exhibit. See Jay R. Galbraith, "Matrix Organization Design; How to Combine Functional and Project Forms," *Business Horizons,* Summer 1964 (Exhibit 3), p. 70.

dimension will remain more or less the same, and the planning costs of the product dimension will be added. Thus, the nature of the absolute costs of planning implies that Exhibit 3 will have to be modified, as illustrated in Exhibit 4.

From Exhibit 4 one will see that the choice of organized structure is not a free one, since the planning costs associated with a matrix structure may be substantially higher than for "extreme" structures dominated by one dimension. Thus, one may conclude that only in instances in which the added benefits accrued by carrying two dimensions outweigh the added costs will the adoption of a matrix structure be justified. Also, the instances in which a matrix planning structure will be justified cost benefit-wise will probably be fewer than commonly anticipated, given the significantly higher than expected planning costs associated with such systems.

Diminishing the costs of planning in matrix archetypes

Given the obvious potential payoffs of adapting and integrating along more than one dimension, and disregarding the added planning costs, we should discuss the two ways of changing the cost benefit tradeoff point: increasing the benefits from planning in the matrix archetypes and decreasing the planning costs of these archetypes. We shall propose a way of

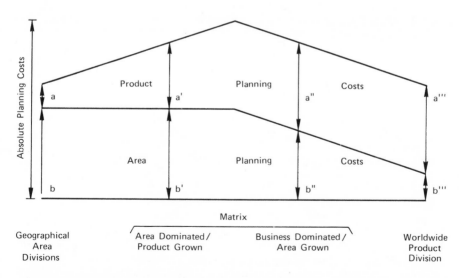

Exhibit 4. The Absolute Proportion of Planning Costs Attributable to the Product Dimension vs. the Area Dimension. The a's Indicate Product Dimension Cost Functions. The b's Indicate Area Dimension Cost Functions.

decreasing the planning costs that turns out also to increase the benefits of planning.

Keeping in mind that the planning process implies a narrowing down of strategic options, which may come about through a series of stages, say objectives-setting, planning, and budgeting, we may ask the following question: Are the adaptation and integration requirements equally important at each stage of progressive narrowing down?

First, we should consider which is the more important purpose of the objectives-setting stage, to ensure adaptation or integration. At this stage the major planning task should be to reexamine the fundamental assumptions for being in business, evaluate opportunities and threats, and consider whether the rationale for the firm's policies is still valid; in other words, where the firm stands relative to the environment. A realistic and effective adaptation to the current environmental conditions is the major concern. Integration, on the other hand, plays a lesser role at the objectives-setting stage.

At the next narrowing down stage, the planning stage, we still have to cater to the need for adaptation. More detailed plans will be developed in order to follow up on the major issues for adaptation to the environment identified in the objectives-setting stage. Typically, there will be the calculation and evaluation of a number of "what ifs" to assess the effects of various environmental changes. There will, however, be an increasing need for integration at this stage to ensure that the various parts of the plans are consistent, that they are exhaustive when taken together, based on common assumptions, and that all relevant people have had a chance to contribute to the plans.

At the third and final stage of narrowing down, the task will be to prepare more detailed budgets within the framework set out in the plans. Here the major thrust will be on integration, with little concern for adaptation at this stage.[11]

We have shown that in each of the matrix archetypes there will be different roles for the business and the area dimensions with respect to performing the adaptive and integrative tasks, and that the relative importance of these tasks shifts over the stages of narrowing down. We can now suggest a division of labor between the dimensions, as indicated in Exhibit 5.

We see that the adaptation task, to be performed primarily by the grown dimension (in accordance with the argument summarized in Exhibit 2), will play a *relatively* more important role in the early part of the narrowing down process than the integration task to be performed by the leading dimension. Later in the narrowing down process, however,

---

[11] See Reading 2, Part 1 for an approach to a three-step narrowing down of strategic options.

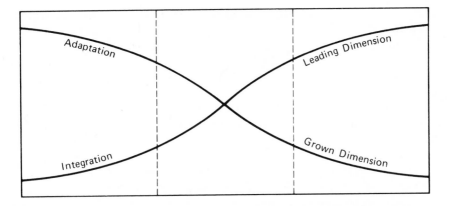

Exhibit 5. The relative importance of the adaptation function of the grown dimension vs. the integration function of the leading dimension at each of the "narrowing down" stages.

the roles will be reversed and the leading dimension will be relatively more dominating.

Before discussing the specific implications of this opportunity for division of labor in the planning function of the matrix archetypes, let us emphasize that we are talking about *relative* importance of the tasks of the two dimensions. For instance, in a matrix structure with a mature and strong worldwide product dimension and a recent and weak area dimension, the *absolute* importance of the leading dimension may prevail at all stages, although the relative emphasis will nevertheless follow the pattern indicated in Exhibit 5.

Let us also consider how the planning tasks of our two extreme organizational structures, the worldwide product organization and the area organization, can be interpreted in terms of Exhibit 5. If neither of these organizational forms has a grown dimension, will the adaptation task be taken care of? Yes, to some extent, since the leading dimension will adapt to environmental changes within relatively narrow limits. However, a lesser need for environmental adaptation will be perceived in a structure organized along one of the two extreme archetype forms. Also, the capacity for environmental adaptation will be much greater in a matrix organization. In fact the environmental adaptation need is probably the major reason for organizing along a matrix structure.

What are some of the implications that the pattern outlined in Exhibit 5 will have on the division of labor in the execution of the planning function? We see that extensive interaction among executives of the two dimensions of the matrix structure does not have to take place all through the narrowing down process, but only during the middle stage, that is, the planning stage. An added sense of direction can probably be achieved in that it will be clearer which group of people will be primarily responsible at each stage of the narrowing down. The communication flows of the planning system can be simplified and be more explicit in terms of indicating who is responsible for what.

In addition to improving planning by instilling an added sense of task direction there will probably also be considerable cost savings. The cost of planning in a matrix should be considerably less through division of labor than if the conventional approach were followed, namely full-blown interaction between the dimensions at each stage of the narrowing down process.

This brings us to our second general normative statement, that *costs of planning* should be a major consideration in establishing an *appropriate balance* between adaptation and integration. The relative balance will be skewed toward more integration emphasis and less adaptation emphasis because of the costs associated with planning. However, emphasizing adaptation during the early stages of planning and integration during the later stages will tend to counteract this relative imbalance and will allow for a strengthening of the system's adaptation ability.

Conclusion

We have analyzed the adaptation and integration requirements of several corporations within a taxonomy of multinationals and have come up with a pattern of planning tasks for the multinationals. It turned out that to carry out this planning would be exceedingly expensive for several of the corporations. However, we were able to suggest a way to simplify planning and utilize task specialization. We suggest that this approach might lead to an operational, simplified, more effective, and less expensive planning activity in multinational corporations.

3

BETTER MANAGEMENT
OF CORPORATE DEVELOPMENT*

*Planning and control systems should focus more
on internally generated growth*

RICHARD F. VANCIL

The development of successful new products is a critical element in the strategy of most large business corporations. Acquisitions as a panacea for corporate growth objectives have been largely discredited—they are marvelous when they work, but the odds are long. The odds on new products are long, too, but the individual risks are smaller; the payoffs from a winner are greater; and, perhaps most important, the process of introducing a continuing stream of new products is manageable. How should top executives try to plan and control that process?

DEVELOPMENT COSTS

To begin, let us consider the kind of corporation commonly referred to as a "growth company." It is likely to be publicly held, to have a good performance record, and to enjoy a high price/earnings multiple. Its primary financial objective is growth in earnings per share, and let us suppose management recognizes that most such growth must be internally generated—i.e., acquisitions will not be the prime growth element. The company is organized along divisional lines, reflecting the increasing diversification of its businesses, and the divisions have a fair amount of managerial autonomy.

What permits a company like this to generate continual growth? Or, to state the question in more operational terms, what is the constraint that inhibits even faster growth? In order to manage such growth, management must have a clear fix on the critical controllable resources that produce increases in future sales and profits. The economist's concept of a "scarce resource" is highly relevant here. Identifying and allocating the utilization of that resource is management's primary task.

In many companies, the traditional scarce resource is considered, appropriately, to be capital—whether obtained from internal cash flow,

*(Reprinted from *Harvard Business Review* Sept.-Oct., 1972)

or through borrowing, or from the sale of stock. However, for a growing company with an above-average performance record, capital is not scarce; such a company has expanding debt capacity, and the sale of common stock may cause only a temporary, negligible dilution in earnings per share. In such growth companies, there is a dollar resource far larger and much less well-identified and controlled than capital.

I call this scarce resource "development expenses." I define them as expenditures that are charged against income in the current year but that do not give rise to profits until some subsequent year.

It should be borne in mind that profits are a managed figure in many growth companies. This does not mean that profits are "manipulated" in an accounting sense, but rather that they are the first figures to emerge from the budget-making process, not the last.

Given an objective of steady earnings growth, the profit requirement for next year is a simple extrapolation from the past. To fall short of this requirement is bad and is likely to have an adverse effect on the company's price/earnings multiple. To exceed this requirement is unnecessary and may be almost as bad as falling short, for it both increases the level of profits that must be reported in the following year and raises shareholder expectations (thus making management's task more arduous and the risk of failure higher in the future). As a result, if profits look as though they will be higher than needed, management finds ways to plough pretax dollars back into the development of the business, attempting to insure that future growth can more easily be sustained.

New accounting concept

Exhibit I illustrates the concept of development expenses. Here we see two versions of the annual profit and loss statements for a growth company that is relying on internally generated funds for capital.

Conventional statement. The left-hand column in this exhibit is simply a more detailed version of the income statement that is condensed in the annual stockholder's report. It shows that this company spends 5% of sales on research and development and that it has a good technological edge in its field so that its marketing costs are reasonably low at 10% of sales. Its after-tax profit margin is 7.5%, which gives it a respectable return on investment. Retained earnings are large enough both to permit capital expenditures that are 50% larger than current depreciation and to cover the working capital needs arising from growth. In short, the conventional income statement shows a stable, steady growth situation.

New statement. However, this company is not really so placid as these figures might imply. Management is able to generate growth consistently

Exhibit I. STATEMENT OF ANNUAL CORPORATE
DEVELOPMENT EXPENSES

(In millions of dollars)

	Conventional statement	New statement	
		Base business	Development expenses*
Sales	$1,000	$1,000	
Less cost of goods sold			
Labor and material	400	400	
Manufacturing overhead	175	150	$ 25
Depreciation	50	50	
Total	$ 625	$ 600	
Manufacturing profit	375	400	
Less other expenses			
Research and development	50		50
Marketing	100	50	50
General administration	75	50	25
Total	$ 225	$ 100	
Profits before tax	150	$150	
Profits after tax	75		
Dividends	25		
Capital expenditures (including reinvested depreciation)	75		
Increase in working capital	25		

*Column I minus Column 2.

because there are many projects in progress designed to increase sales and profits in future years. These projects all cost money. Where does this money come from?

The middle column in *Exhibit I* shows the same company's income statement presented in an unconventional manner. The only expenses, sales, and profits figures shown are those relating to the "base business"—that is, the established, profitable product lines. Expenditures which are not recovered in the current year through higher sales or lower costs are excluded in the middle column. The effect of this procedure is to change every expense item except prime costs and depreciation —reflecting the fact that this corporation, like so many others, charges some items to current expenses that are really an investment for the future.

I am not arguing here for a change in the way accountants calculate net income, but current accounting conventions do obscure, even for management, what is going on in the company.

The difference between the two income statements is, of course, the development expenses. These are shown in the right-hand column of *Exhibit I*.

Component expenses

As can be seen, development expenses break down into *four* broad categories which, in total, amount to $150 million:

1. *R&D expenses* are fairly obvious. Managers traditionally think of this type of cost as an investment in the future, even though it is charged against current income in most large companies. The mission of R&D is clear: to produce the ideas and technology that permit the company to introduce new or improved products. The activity is critical, but it is only the beginning of the total effort required to provide growth in sales and profits.

2. *Marketing expenses* contain another major segment of corporate development funds. The nature of these outlays varies greatly from one company to another, but every growing corporation incurs substantial current expenses in marketing that have a delayed profit payoff. The two most common examples are the costs of launching a new product and the start-up costs of getting established in new market segments or new geographical areas. Advertising, too, has long-run payoffs.

3. *Manufacturing overhead* has development costs hidden in it. As a percentage of the total overhead, this cost may not be large but the total dollars are still significant. The two main types of development activities at the plant level are (1) the pilot plant operations and debugging costs associated with manufacturing a new product, and (2) the engineering efforts aimed at reducing manufacturing costs for current product lines. Both of these activities trade current expenses for future profits.

4. *General administrative overhead* is traceable in part to the fact that this corporation is trying to grow. The company is intentionally overstaffed; it is doing more than what is required simply to run the base business. The extra people are scattered across a variety of functions, including new-products departments, venture teams, market research groups, and others. These people are not employed to produce today's business; their job is to improve profitability in the future and to provide growth.

The numbers in *Exhibit I* are not significant; what is important is looking at the operations of the business in the way described. The size of this pool of funds and the projects for which it is used vary greatly from one company to another, but usually growth companies have a substantial amount of such funds. In terms of order of magnitude, it is probably safe to make two generalizations.

First, if the corporation has a formal R&D effort and costs it out in the conventional manner, this expense is likely to be only a fraction of total development expenditures (one third in our example).

Second, capital expenditures, which deservedly get a lot of management attention, are also only a fraction of the corporation's total future-oriented expenditures (expense dollars are twice as large in this example.

REALISTIC PERSPECTIVE

How do most managements look at capital expenditures and development expenses? Although the purpose of both types of outlay is the same—to lay out money today in the hope of getting it back with a profit in the future—the two categories tend to be managed quite differently.

Most companies have elaborate systems and procedures to guide the decision process for capital investments; they specify careful gradations of spending authority at each hierarchical level, create complex manuals on capital budgeting procedures, and work up elaborate analytical formulas to calculate the probabilistic present values of projects. Development expenses, on the other hand, usually get buried in the conventional operating budgets. While the highly visible R&D budget may get management attention (and indeed some companies capitalize these costs), the bulk of the expenses identified in *Exhibit I* are never identified separately, let alone managed as the scarce resource of the company. Why is this so?

One reason is mainly historical and shows the power of accounting conventions to influence thinking. Accountants capitalize the amount of investment in fixed assets while writing off other investment-type expenses primarily because the former are intangible, have some salvage value, and can be recorded easily.

A second reason, as accountants and financial executives point out, is that capital expenditures are irreversible; money put in bricks and mortar is "sunk." Ironically, this is even more true for development expenses. A plant or a machine may be the wrong size or in the wrong place, but it may still have a value to someone else and part of the investment may be recouped. However, development expenses that go awry are not just sunk—they are gone.

And a third reason is that capital investments frequently represent large, separable decisions that deserve the best possible assessment of the risks and rewards. There is some validity to this viewpoint but, in terms of the dollars involved, the expense side of a new product—from research to market acceptance—is frequently much larger than the equipment required to manufacture it. The real difference is in the timing. The development program for a new product may take five years or more and require a series of sequential decisions to proceed from one stage to the next. The final decision, to build a new plant after a successful market introduction, is not risky; it is practically a foregone conclusion after the earlier, high-risk money has paid off. Also it is an explicit decision, whereas the series of unrecorded earlier investments are forgotten.

This is not to say that, given their obligations, the accountants' careful distinction between capitalized and written-off expenditures is not defensible or rational. It is to say that the distinction has been given too much importance by managers. Dollars are dollars, and any corporation has too few of them with which to buy growth in future profits.

Economics of growth

The validity of development expenses as the scarce resource in a growth company is illustrated in *Exhibit II*. It shows the profit projection if all development expenses were discontinued. Profits would decline because no new businesses would be added and the franchises of the old businesses would eventually wither. Fortunately, the company can meet its growth objectives for the coming year with substantially less profit than that available from the base businesses. Therefore, $150 million can be spent to perpetuate old businesses and develop new ones. If the money is spent wisely, management hopes that the reported profits will continue to grow at a steady rate. Achieving that goal requires the management of many development projects, simultaneously and continuously.

Exhibit III shows the profit and cash-flow profiles of a typical development project. For most such projects the curves fall into this well-known

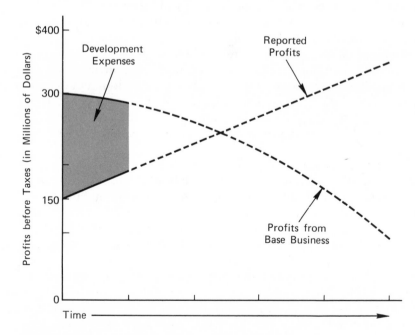

Exhibit II. Effect of development expenses on profit profile.

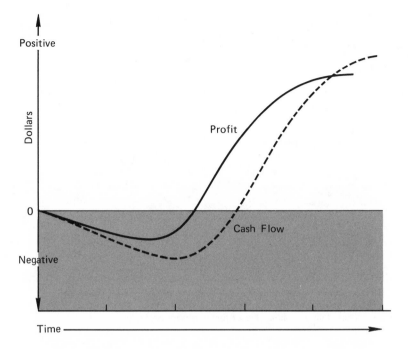

Exhibit III.   Profit and cash-flow effects of a typical development project.

pattern, the difference between cash flow and profits being accounted for by expenditures that are capitalized and depreciated (over the life of the project the total amount of profit and cash flow will, of course, be the same). The actual shape of the curve naturally varies substantially from one project to another, particularly with regard to the length of time before profits come in and with regard to the amount of the accumulated deficit up to that time. However, the expected pattern for any successful development project will always have this basic shape.

Exhibit IV shows the collective effect on the company of a continuing stream of development projects. Each year, if the prior year's development funds have been spent successfully, the residual profit potential in the base businesses is higher than the year before. The result is that the pool of development funds also grows a little, even after allowing for an increase in reported profits.

The fact that the economics of internal development are complex, as illustrated in *Exhibits II-IV,* is well known. Less well appreciated, perhaps, is (1) the complexity of the development process, and (2) the challenges that it poses for management. I shall devote the balance of this article to these two topics.

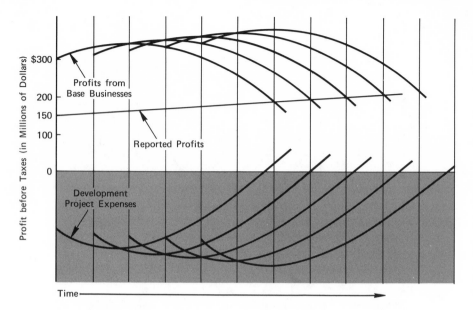

Exhibit IV.　Cumulative profit profile of development projects.

COMPLEXITIES OF ANALYSIS

There are not many parts of the business which do not incur development expenses of some kind. In order to understand the management task, let us break down the development process into four parts.

1. Identifying resources

Development resources are essentially people, and development expenses are almost entirely made up of payroll costs. Simply identifying the personnel working on future-profit activities in a large corporation is a difficult task since these individuals are scattered throughout the organization. The more complex the company is, the greater the variety of talents that are deployed in development tasks.

In the situation on which *Exhibit I* is based, determining that the company was spending $150 million per year required a careful analysis of the activities of each department. The company found that personnel in more than 100 departments were engaged either full or part time in development projects. These people were scientists, market researchers, product-development specialists, members of new-product teams, designers, engineers, planners, and others. Moreover, it was not merely a question of pure development departments as such, for throughout the organization there were individuals whose tasks were largely future-oriented—even when their departments were primarily involved with current business. In fact, there were not many organizational units that did not look past the current base businesses in some way.

Management also found that the people engaged in development work tended to be some of the best employees in the organization. A company seeking to grow internally must, as a general rule, employ higher caliber personnel than a similar company must that is content to maintain the status quo. And these people almost inevitably are assigned to development tasks. This makes the management of the development process more difficult because direction and tight control are difficult to combine successfully with the creativity, imagination, and dedication of innovative people.

2. Classifying activities

The diversity of development activities in a growth company is enormous. In the company used for *Exhibit I*, each person engaged in developmental tasks was asked to describe the project or projects he was working on. Two main findings emerged. First, many projects involved the efforts of personnel in more than one department. The bigger the project, the more likely that a half-dozen or more departments, at both the corporate and division levels, were involved. Typically, each individual was aware of some of the related activities of other groups, but no one manager was well informed about the magnitude or rate of progress of the combined efforts. Second, many projects were proceeding simultaneously—nearly 500 in all—so that the management of the entire process was almost impossible without the benefit of specialized planning and control systems.

One helpful way to deal with such complexity is to categorize activities so that they can be dealt with at a summary level by top management as well as at a detailed level by operating people. In the company in question, management classified *new-business* projects as follows:

Research. In the pure exploratory sense, research comprised only about 5% of the total development expenses. These projects were designed to expand the frontiers of technological knowledge in the hope of developing new materials and processes for commercial exploitation.

Product development. Projects in this category were in the early phases of the development cycle shown in *Exhibit III*. A project entered this category when the first, crude specifications for the new product were delineated. The project was reclassified into the next category as soon as it began yielding any sales revenue from market tests, even though product development activities continued concurrently with the initial marketing efforts.

Market introduction. This category included all the expenditures concerned with launching a new product. The projects were at the loss-reversal stage in the cycle shown in *Exhibit III;* losses tended to increase in the early stages of market introduction, but if successful the product subsequently became profitable. (At the point where a new-product line crossed the profitability threshold, it was reclassified as an existing business—although various kinds of developmental activities would continue over the life of the product, as will be described later.)

Projects for *existing* businesses involved a more diverse and diffuse range of activities, but again some broad subcategories were designated:

Product-modification projects designed to extend the life cycle of existing products by improving and expanding the line (e.g., changes in product design, packaging, or flavors).

Marketing-extension projects aimed at opening new market segments or new geographical areas to existing and modified products (e.g., special promotional campaigns).

Cost-engineering projects designed to improve processes, programs, and other activities.

3. Allocating

A useful analogy for thinking about the allocation process is as an investment portfolio. After deciding on the amount of development funds available, the management of a diversified corporation had to divide the funds among competing projects. A wide range of risks is involved, from very safe cost-reduction projects to high-risk, new-product programs with high payoff. This situation closely parallels the choice facing the manager of an investment portfolio, who has to choose among investments ranging from triple-A bonds to highly speculative common stocks.

The corporate task is more complex than the portfolio manager's. For one thing, the funds to be allocated are less flexible; people resources are mobile only to the extent that they can be reassigned, making major rapid shifts impractical. For another, choices made in one year both constrain and increase opportunities for choices next year.

4. Integrating the system

In order to pull together the identification, organization, and allocation of development resources, management needs to modify the planning and budgeting systems of the corporation. The integrated system that I recommend is illustrated conceptually in Part A of *Exhibit V*. This matrix shows a two-step management process involving first planning and then budgeting. Planning, on the horizontal axis, is the process of *deciding*

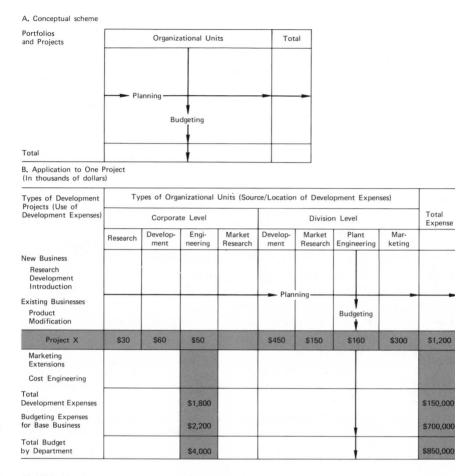

A. Conceptual scheme

B. Application to One Project
(In thousands of dollars)

Exhibit V. Integrated planning and budgeting.

which projects should be funded and what resources (what talents and how much of each) are needed for each project in each organizational unit. Budgeting, on the vertical axis, may be thought of as the process of *obtaining* the necessary resources or ensuring their availability. This means that the budgeting system must identify and separate development personnel and expenses from base-business personnel and expenses.

As Part B of *Exhibit V* indicates, Project X is a proposal to spend $1.2 million to develop an improved product for one of the existing lines of business. The effort required is primarily at the division level, but $140,000 must also be spent by personnel in three different corporate staff groups (research, development, and engineering). The data suggest that the engineering department, which is budgeting $50,000 for Project

X, is heavily engaged in current operations; $2,200,000, or slightly more than half, of its total budget is devoted to the base business of the company.

Because the nature of each project changes over time and is never precisely predictable, the integration of needs and resources in this way is no easy task. Moreover, the resources are people whose talents are not interchangeable and who cannot be turned on and off like a tap. Nor can such people—least of all, the dedicated, creative, high-caliber personnel in development work—be moved at random around the organization.

CRITICAL ISSUES

We have seen that development expenses, broadly defined, are the critical resources to be managed in a growth company and that the development process is complex. Many of the managerial implications of this discussion are already apparent: major changes in executives' thinking may be required to reconceive the management task along the lines described; and concomitant changes in the corporation's planning, budgeting, and reporting systems will also be required. More specifically, these issues are of pervasive importance to top management.

Strategy and objectives

The conventional wisdom of corporate planning is that the strategic process begins with a clear and explicit statement by the chief executive officer of his objectives for the corporation and the broad strategy that he proposes to pursue. Such an approach is no doubt appropriate in some situations, but it is not at all clear that it is the right approach for a diversifying growth company like the one discussed earlier. Should a statement of strategy and objectives be issued at the beginning *or the end* of the annual planning effort?

Turning back to *Exhibit II,* I suggest that this simple chart is a concise illustration of the objectives and strategy of a company which seeks to grow by internal development. The objective—at least the financially quantifiable one—is expressed by the slope of the growth line. That, in turn, is a function of both the availability of expense dollars for development (the shaded area), and the time-phased payoff of the opportunities available. For a diversified corporation, strategy is best expressed as the choice of which and how many developmental activities to pursue. Viewed in this way, the decisions about *how much* to spend on development and *how* to spend it are the very essence of what most businessmen mean by strategy.

There are advantages in delaying the preparation of a statement of corporate strategy and objectives. A delayed statement can be much more explicit and thus can provide a much better sense of direction and purpose than the typical "motherhood" statements obviously drafted by staff planners. Moreover, the very fact of a delay is, in itself, a statement that the corporate strategy is somewhat opportunistic, as it has to be for a growth corporation. In a statement that is issued as a *wrap-up* of the process of allocating developmental resources instead of as a preamble to that process, the corporate objective can be clear and the available resources can be explicit; yet there can also be an acknowledgment that the biggest elements of change in the equation are the opportunities.

Division autonomy

Who is responsible for growth in a divisionalized company, corporate management or divisional management? Answers to this question vary greatly in U.S. business today.

At one extreme, the president tells his division managers to run their businesses as if they were independent companies—each responsible for its continuing growth. The attractiveness of this approach is that it creates many centers of initiative, which are each highly motivated to be innovative and to grow. One disadvantage is the problem of communicating corporate objectives to a diverse group of managers. A greater danger is suboptimization; since some divisions have more and better development opportunities than others, they may end up rejecting some projects that are better than the ones accepted by another division.

For a diversified, growing company the answer to this problem does not lie at the other extreme, where the division managers are mere functionaries overseeing today's business while all new-product development is handled at the corporate level. The most promising answer is to institute the same careful sharing of authority for committing development resources as is common in the authorization of capital expenditures. Rather than put dollar limitations on a division manager's authority, however, management can draw a line between development projects for new and for existing businesses. It might proceed as follows:

The primary initiative for development projects in an *existing* business must lie with the divisional personnel; they are the ones who know the most about that business.

But the amount to be spent in each such business should be approved at the corporate level, determined in the context of the opportunities available in other existing or new businesses. (Specific projects connected with the business can then be approved and monitored by the division manager in a way analogous to conventional capital budgeting procedures.)

The divisional personnel, along with their counterparts in the various corporate staff departments, are a major source of ideas for new business developments. Funding such projects, however, is strictly a corporate-level decision because: (1) new businesses tend to be much riskier, if only because they are harder to appraise; (2) in the early stages, a new business or major new-product line may deserve investigation even if it lacks divisional sponsorship or support; (3) while selecting the set of new-business projects—with their complex patterns of risk and reward—can scarcely be an analytically rational process, it can and should reflect the strategic choices of top management.

Implementing this approach, particularly in companies where the divisions have been highly autonomous, is likely to be viewed as a diminution of division managers' responsibility. In fact, in some companies this may be exactly what is needed. If divisional operating budgets include a substantial amount of development expenses, corporate management may have delegated away too much authority over activities that are vital to future corporate growth. For instance, in the company used as an example earlier, roughly two thirds of the total corporate development expenditures were included in divisional budgets until procedures like those described were established.

Measurement and review

Every project, no matter how small, must have a manager who is responsible for achieving the results that were expected when the project was approved. For most small projects, project management is not a full-time job; it is an addition to the individual's responsibilities in the base business. Most small projects are also related to the existing businesses, thus simplifying the cost-measurement problem to some extent.

In the case of new business development, the management and measurement tasks are complicated by the fact that such projects may stretch out over several years, requiring different kinds of management skills at different points in time. Also, in their latter stages, these projects may be very large, drawing on development resources from many departments.

In order to handle the long development period and the episodic nature of progress, new-business developments should be funded from event to event. Each proposal for an allocation of development funds should specify one or more milestones at which progress will be reviewed and new funds authorized for the next steps. At these review points, official responsibility may be transferred. For example, it might rest first with an engineer in the corporate development lab, then with a senior analyst in the corporate market research department, and finally with a new venture manager or a marketing manager in the division that expects to add the new business to its existing businesses.

To deal with the large, cross-departmental nature of new-business developments, a project accounting system analogous to work-order accounting for capital expenditures may be needed. This approach has the virtue of removing development expenses from the regular departmental operating budgets, thus permitting easier accountability for the manager of each project. (Such a system could also be used for smaller projects but is probably not worth the effort.)

CONCLUSION

What is the most effective approach to the management of internally generated corporate growth? While no simple set of rules is possible, executives should consider these guidelines:

They should identify and mobilize the developmental resources of the corporation. Most corporate managements do not know, at least not in terms of the broad definition of development expense dollars used in the article, how much they are spending for the future or where it is spent within the organization. But it is possible to find out, and the result may be a surprise. Many growth companies are engaged in an unbelievable range of developmental projects carried out by people scattered all across the organization chart and representing a vast array of risks, rewards, and time patterns of payoff. Quantifying these activities is a critically important first step.

Top management must focus attention on the use of developmental resources. This set of decisions is *the* critical resource allocation problem and the most tangible expression of corporate strategy. Some sort of formal system to aid in the management of development resources is a necessity, even though it will take a while to work it out.

Top management must reexamine the distribution of authority for committing resources to developmental projects. One thing is certain: the expenses should not be buried in divisional or departmental operating budgets; the amounts involved are too important. Division managers need some discretion, but top management overview is probably more critical here than it is in the case of capital expenditures.

Systems must be devised to monitor the effectiveness of utilization of development funds. This step, too, takes time and may never be done in a completely satisfactory manner, but without some such effort top management will never achieve a sense of control over the destiny of the company.

This approach is not a one-shot analysis of a critical resource; it is a whole new way of thinking about the management of a growth company. Managing change is not a problem that managers solve; it is a problem that they live with. If they decide to devote their efforts to that problem, then they should design the planning, budgeting, and reporting systems to bring the problem into focus. This is a major task, but the potential payoff is enormous.

Case 1

American Airlines, Inc.*

In 1969 American Airlines, Inc. was awarded the right to fly several new routes in the Pacific. The Corporate Planning Department, headed by American's Vice President, Mr. Harry A. Kimbriel, was responsible for revising aircraft acquisition plans, adjusting previously developed transcontinental flight schedules and scheduling the new routes.

Strict time constraints, the immense scope of the problems to be solved, and American's history of advanced systems development were important factors in the Planning Department's decision to make its Corporate Planning Model the focal point of the Pacific planning process.

Mr. Kimbriel explained, "We at American were naturally pleased to have won the Pacific routes. However, for those of us in Corporate Planning, the award posed urgent problems. Since the Pacific routes were to be opened for traffic in June 1970, we had approximately one month's time to develop our overall plans. The Operations and Marketing Departments needed our planning outputs so they could make necessary preparations before American inaugurated regular service."

BACKGROUND

Since 1934 the U.S. airline industry had been subject to strict supervision and legal regulation by the Civil Aeronautics Board (CAB). Three governmental powers—the power to certify all air carriers to operate; the power to assign air routes to specific carriers; and the power to adjust fares—had a pronounced effect upon strategies pursued by the domestic air carriers. Against a background of industry-government negotiation on routes and fares, the individual carriers competed on the basis of

---

* This case was prepared by Peter Lorange, Research Assistant, under the supervision of Professor Richard F. Vancil.

scheduled frequencies and standards of service, while struggling to keep their operating costs as low as possible.

Through 1968 the airline industry had generally experienced a high and continuous annual rate of growth, measured both in terms of dollar volume of revenue and magnitude of capital investment. For American, a major U.S. trunkline, this was reflected in the following annual revenues and profits:

	1961	1965	1966	1967	1968
Operating Revenue	$421.3	$612.2	$724.6	$841.5	$957.2
Net Profit	7.2	39.7	52.2	58.8	35.5

American Airlines' management believed that first and foremost the company was a service industry involving just one product—the transportation of people and goods by air. American did engage in some peripheral activities such as contract maintenance, catering, and hotel service; however, each of these ventures existed to support the primary business of air transportation.

As of January 1970, American served 43 cities in the U.S., Canada, and Mexico with a fleet of 247 jet aircraft. The fleet in operation or on order is listed below. Current purchase prices for the various aircraft still in production are also recorded in millions of dollars:

Type	In Operation or On Order or Option	1970 Purchase Price Per Plane
"First Generation Jets"		
Boeing 707	53	$6.7
Boeing 707-Intercontinental	10	8.1
Boeing 707-Convertible	20	8.3
Boeing 707-Airfreighter	17	8.0
Boeing 720	22	6.0
Boeing 727	57	4.8
Boeing 727-Stretch Version	41	5.6
BAC 400	27	3.3
Total	247	
"Second Generation Jets"		
McDonnell-Douglas		
DC-10-"Air Bus"	50	16.0
Boeing 747-"Jumbo"	16	24.0
Total	66	

ORGANIZATIONAL STRUCTURE

The organizational structure of American Airlines in January 1970 is shown below:

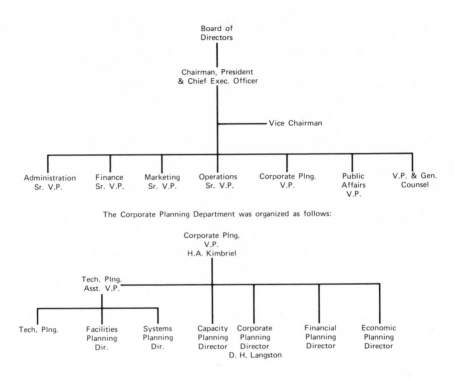

The Corporate Planning Department was organized as follows:

ROLE OF THE PLANNING DEPARTMENT

The formal planning process at American Airlines began with the Corporate Planning Department in January each year and involved the simultaneous development of macro and micro forecasts. From five-year economic and environmental projections total industry traffic and required aircraft capacity were determined. Then an American Airlines share of total market was formulated. As a check to this industry or macro approach, micro forecasts were also developed and cumulated for each individual route segment. Once the macro-micro approach yielded acceptable traffic volume forecasts, revenues and operating costs contributing to an initial profit and loss projection were developed.

After the preparation of this "rough cut," extensive efforts were made throughout the company to improve the plan. The Marketing and Operations departments were particularly active in this revision process. By late August a proposed five-year plan was submitted to the Chief Executive Officer. Normally some refinements were necessary, and the completed plan was approved in the early fall.

Talking about planning activities at American, Mr. Douglas Langston, Director—Corporate Planning, said, "In broad terms, the role of the

Planning Department is to focus corporate attention on basic policy questions and decision points, and to provide the ground rules, the stimulation and the coordination of the various departmental planning efforts. We monitor current results of operations in order to update our planning assumptions and try to identify problems and their profit impact to give appropriate guidance to the operating departments.

"There are many factors that place limitations on the strategic choices of an airline. Some of these are institutional, such as the federal requirements concerning fares, routes, and safety, and some result simply from the competitive situation of the industry. The challenge of planning is to help management figure out how to make a satisfactory profit while still living within these various constraints. Today, this challenge has taken on some new dimensions, three of which are particularly critical.

"Growth forecasting has always been one of the biggest and most difficult problems we have," Mr. Langston continued. "Although the basic route structure is relatively stable and a vast amount of high quality historical data is available from regulatory agencies and corporate files, it has never been easy to forecast traffic growth with accuracy. Today the accuracy of long-range forecasting has become essential. Because of the increasing technical and financial requirements inherent in developing new aircraft for service in the 1970s, the lead time for "second generation" planes may be four to five years instead of the twelve- to eighteen-month lead time characteristic of the '50s and '60s.

"A second new dimension in airline planning problems is financing. Most major airlines have now completed their first jet equipment cycle and are looking immediately ahead to two new equipment cycles that will follow each other in rapid succession, the "Jumbo" jet and the "Air Bus," and then the supersonic transports. Although the airlines have for years been one of the nation's major capital consuming industries, spending for these new aircraft will accelerate the capital requirements tremendously.

"The third area where planning problems and penalties have increased in dimension," Mr. Langston went on, "is in the timely acquisition of the ground equipment and facilities necessary to support the operation of the existing and prospective fleets. Thorough planning can help to minimize maintenance and other nonoperating time of increasingly expensive aircraft. Also, careful planning has been mandatory in the redesign of passenger terminals with respect to gate requirements, corridor widths, baggage handling areas, curb space, and so forth.

"All of these new pressures have just exaggerated the importance of planning for the acquisition and utilization of aircraft, the two main, continuing tasks of my department. The two most critical factors in our success are the acquisition of new routes and the acquisition of new aircraft. I'm not too involved in the first, but when we do win a route such as the Pacific award, I'm in the thick of the second issue.

"The reason why aircraft acquisition is so important is straightforward. The capacity that we have available at any point in time, both the quantity in terms of seat-miles and the quality in terms of the types of planes, frequencies and desired departure times, affects our ability to win a share of the market on our routes. The more successful we are, the larger our revenues. The problem is one of profits and the major consideration is capacity. If we have excess capacity, our revenues may go up but our profits down because we're flying too many empty seats. If we're short of capacity, or our competitors are offering better equipment, we've lost a profit opportunity. Either way, we stand to lose. The trick is to find the right balance.

"Another major consideration of fleet management is aircraft utilization. It might be considered a tactical problem, because it is constrained by previous decisions, but it's a very important problem. Since we can't really add new capacity on short notice, we've got to do the best we can with what we have. The type of aircraft is an important factor in the passenger's appraisal of the quality of our service, but departure times, nonstop service, and convenient connections are also important. On competitive routes particularly, we know that our market share is directly affected by how good our flight schedule is.

"Just as with the acquisition decision, you can't really win the scheduling game, the tradeoffs are too complex. Utilizing a given fleet, you can gain on one route by offering more frequent service, but then that plane isn't available to offer an extra flight on another route."

NEW MANAGEMENT TOOLS

During the decade prior to the Pacific route award the management of American Airlines was actively developing new approaches for dealing with the problems of the airline industry. The most important of these techniques was the application of computer technology to airline planning and operating problems.

The joint development of the SABRE ticket reservation system by American Airlines and IBM Corporation was the first milestone in American's history as an aviation industry "systems" pioneer. In 1961 when SABRE was inaugurated it was limited to handling reservations functions for ticket offices and airport reservation counters. By 1969 the system also stored each passenger's name, phone number, and address. Additional data was collected for each flight and went into historical files to become basic source material.

THE CORPORATE PLANNING MODEL

In 1967 American began the development of a corporate planning model, setting as its first goal the creation of a better and more efficient method for sizing and scheduling its fleet and for evaluating the economic implications of alternative schedules.

No theoretical solution to the aircraft utilization problem, described earlier by Mr. Langston, was considered practical. Instead, the typical scheduling practice was one of progressive refinement. By this method a trial schedule, generally patterned on the itineraries previously flown by the fleet, was introduced, and the flows and load factors of each route segment were reviewed. Adjustments were then made in successive revisions of the schedule in order to even out load factors, provide more direct routing for traffic flows, and strengthen or terminate uneconomic segments. American's approach to the problem was to program a computer to stimulate this iterative procedure of schedule adjustments as closely as possible.

Since 1967 the structure of the model had been continuously revised. As of early 1970 the model handled itinerary generation, traffic routing, balancing aircraft movements, equipment, and revenue calculations. The output provided a list of feasible and legal aircraft routings, load factors (percentage of revenue-generating seat-miles to total seat-miles of capacity offered), and traffic flow information. Rerunning the model permitted an evaluation of the consequences of any further specifications or revisions that the planner wished to introduce. The flow chart of the Corporate Planning Model as of early 1970 is shown in Exhibit 1.

Several constant inputs were built into the model, but six variable data groups had to be supplied for each computer "run."

A description of the six categories of variable inputs follows:

1. Fleet Composition and Characteristics—A specified number of aircraft of each type were assumed to be available. Data inputs for each type included range, seat capacity, speed, ground time at through stops, direct operating costs and take-off and landing capabilities.

2. Cities served—Characteristics such as time zone, longitude, latitude, and runway information were provided for each individual city.

3. City-pair information—The distance, origin and destination traffic available and the competitive status of the market were necessary.

4. Route Restrictions—Governmental regulations or bilateral agreements with other airlines established legal limitations.

5. Run Parameters—Program branch instructions determined the amount of detail in the printout and the search procedure of the itinerary-generator. A predetermined load factor was entered to terminate the generation of new itineraries.

6. Inputted Itineraries—The computer assigned traffic to the inputted itineraries, and, if so instructed, generated new itineraries which supplied better service. Whether or not new itineraries were sought, the computer reported passenger routings, load factor, traffic flows, and other information useful to the planner.

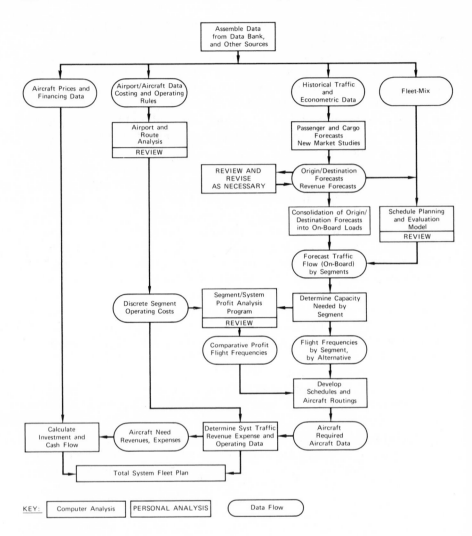

Exhibit 1

Output from the model enabled the planners at American to determine revenue and return on investment for the most practical and competitive utilization of a specified fleet. Additional applications included the ability to study an airline system market by market, and to do a detailed airport traffic and gate requirement study for each city within the system. The same outputs labeled Exhibit 2 and Exhibit 3 illustrated the depth of airline system simulation. The output tables discussed below are summaries of more detailed reports.

The Daily Passenger Allocation Report (Exhibit 2) summarized results

PC 303

Exhibit 2

SEGMENT	NO. OF STOPS	DAILY PASSENGER ALLOCATION AND FLOW, BY SEGMENT NO-CHANGE ROUTES					ONE-CHANGE ROUTES VIA			
		0	1	2	3	4&	A			
NYC - SDF	NO. OF ROUTES	2	1	0	0	0				
	PASSENGERS	134	4	0	0	0				
NYC - MEM	NO. OF ROUTES	1	4	0	0	0				
	PASSENGERS	87	34	0	0	0				
NYC - MEX	NO. OF ROUTES	0	1	0	0	0				
	PASSENGERS	0	9	0	0	0				
NYC - BNA	NO. OF ROUTES	2	2	0	0	0				
	PASSENGERS	170	7	0	0	0				
NYC - OKC	NO. OF ROUTES	0	1	2	0	0				
	PASSENGERS	0	28	16	0	0				
NYC - PHL	NO. OF ROUTES	3	0	0	0	0				
	PASSENGERS	32	0	0	0	0				
NYC - PHX	NO. OF ROUTES	2	0	0	0	0				
	PASSENGERS	134	0	0	0	0				
NYC - PIT	NO. OF ROUTES	3	0	0	0	0				
	PASSENGERS	78	0	0	0	0				
NYC - PVD	NO. OF ROUTES	7	0	0	0	0				
	PASSENGERS	269	0	0	0	0				
NYC - ROC	NO. OF ROUTES	9	1	0	0	0				
	PASSENGERS	539	2	0	0	0				
NYC - STL	NO. OF ROUTES	5	5	0	0	0				
	PASSENGERS	268	23	0	0	0				
NYC - SAT	NO. OF ROUTES	0	0	1	0	0	DAL			
	PASSENGERS	0	0	7	0	0	2			
NYC - SAN	NO. OF ROUTES	2	2	0	0	0				
	PASSENGERS	153	24	0	0	0				
NYC - SFO	NO. OF ROUTES	6	1	0	0	0				
	PASSENGERS	743	12	0	0	0				
NYC - SYR	NO. OF ROUTES	9	0	0	0	0				
	PASSENGERS	436	0	0	0	0				
NYC - TUS	NO. OF ROUTES	0	3	0	0	0				
	PASSENGERS	0	69	0	0	0				
NYC - TUL	NO. OF ROUTES	0	3	0	0	0				
	PASSENGERS	0	67	0	0	0				
NYC - YYZ	NO. OF ROUTES	8	0	0	0	0				
	PASSENGERS	575	0	0	0	0				
NYC - WAS	NO. OF ROUTES	16	1	0	0	0				
	PASSENGERS	792	0	0	0	0				
OKC - ACA	NO. OF ROUTES	0	1	0	0	0				
	PASSENGERS	0	0	0	0	0				
OKC - ALB	NO. OF ROUTES	0	0	0	0	0	ORD	NYC	STL	WAS
	PASSENGERS	0	0	0	0	0	1	1	0	0
OKC - BAL	NO. OF ROUTES	0	0	0	0	0	BNA			
	PASSENGERS	0	0	0	0	0	0			

Exhibit 2

of the simulation of flight selection decisions passengers make, reflecting the possible and most probable origin to destination (O-D) passenger routing. The computer determined every no change (single plane) and one-change (connecting) routing that a passenger could consider for his flight. The number of routes listed in the no-change columns by number of O-D stops equaled the total number of daily flights available to the passenger. The number of passengers assigned to each column indicated the daily number that fly the segment and their routing distribution by number of stops.

The program excluded itineraries which exceeded four stops printing a message which explained that passengers had not been routed and were receiving poor or no service.

The Flight Summary Report in Exhibit 3 recorded the results of the passengers' simulated evaluation of the flight schedule, listing each segment of every flight and indicating passenger movements. The following

Exhibit 3

FLIGHT NO.	A/C TYPE	START TIME	FROM	TO	ENPL	CONT	CONN	COMP	CONT	CONN	LOCAL	SUM	CITY FLOWS	LOAD FACTOR	BLOCK	LOCAL	GRND	TOTAL	REVENUE $/DAY
2	747	8.45	LAX	JFK	251	0	0	246	0	5	246	251	2	0.661	4.48	7.48	0.0	7.48	28811.50
15	747	18.15	JFK	SFO	238	0	1	239	0	0	238	239	2	0.629	5.38	2.38	0.0	2.38	28698.06
254	747	12.00	SFO	ORD	169	0	0	139	0	30	139	169	5	0.445	3.39	5.39	0.0	5.39	14693.80
183	747	18.45	ORD	LAX	156	0	24	180	0	0	156	180	3	0.474	3.54	1.54	0.0	1.54	14829.27
196	747	0.40	LAX	ORD	98	0	0	52	0	46	52	98	3	0.258	3.29	5.29	0.0	5.29	8092.61
181	747	9.50	ORD	LAX	156	0	6	162	0	0	156	162	3	0.426	3.54	1.54	0.0	1.54	13433.94
30	747	13.00	LAX	JFK	185	0	0	185	0	0	185	185	1	0.487	4.48	7.48	0.0	7.48	21163.41
59	747	9.30	JFK	SFO	179	0	1	180	0	0	179	180	2	0.474	5.38	2.38	0.0	2.38	21461.93
16	747	13.30	SFO	JFK	198	0	0	197	0	1	197	198	2	0.521	4.59	7.59	0.0	7.59	23666.41
1	747	9.00	JFK	LAX	170	0	2	172	0	0	170	172	2	0.453	5.24	2.24	0.0	2.24	19701.19
182	747	12.50	LAX	ORD	200	0	0	196	0	4	196	200	3	0.526	3.29	5.29	0.0	5.29	16640.43
219	747	19.30	ORD	SFO	110	0	28	138	0	0	110	138	6	0.363	4.07	2.07	0.0	2.07	12003.05
14	747	8.30	SFO	JFK	271	0	0	263	0	8	263	271	4	0.713	4.59	7.59	0.0	7.59	32209.1?
21	747	18.00	JFK	LAX	227	0	2	229	0	0	227	229	2	0.603	5.24	2.24	0.0	2.24	26177.00
60	949	9.00	LAX	PHL	130	0	0	130	0	0	130	130	1	0.922	4.41	7.41	0.0	7.41	14442.60
61	949	17.45	PHL	LAX	164	0	0	156	0	8	156	164	2	1.163	5.00	2.00	0.0	2.00	18256.83
88	949	0.25	LAX	DTW	88	0	0	81	0	7	81	88	2	0.624	4.05	6.05	0.0	6.05	8214.77
99	949	11.35	DTW	LAX	66	0	1	67	0	0	66	67	2	0.475	4.33	2.33	0.0	2.33	6266.35
176	949	15.00	LAX	DTW	61	0	0	61	0	0	61	61	1	0.433	4.05	6.05	0.0	6.05	5687.49
580	949	8.25	DTW	JFK	97	0	0	97	0	0	97	97	1	0.688	1.17	2.17	0.0	2.17	2912.79
3	949	12.00	JFK	LAX	67	0	1	68	0	0	67	68	2	0.482	5.36	2.36	0.0	2.36	7772.??
4	949	16.30	LAX	JFK	61	0	0	61	0	0	61	61	1	0.433	5.00	8.00	0.0	8.00	7002.65
265	949	6.30	JFK	BDL	44	0	0	41	3	0	41	44	2	0.312	0.32	0.32	0.0	0.12	537.82
		7.32	BDL	ORD	73	3	0	53	14	9	50	76	8	0.539	2.00	1.00	0.30	2.02	3022.85
		9.02	ORD	SFO	77	14	5	96	0	0	77	96	4	0.681	4.17	2.17	1.00	4.49	8436.41
214	949	13.30	SFO	ORD	102	0	0	70	23	9	70	102	6	0.723	3.49	5.49	0.0	5.49	8998.21
		19.49	ORD	YYZ	46	23	15	84	0	0	46	84	8	0.596	1.09	2.09	0.30	8.28	2031.41
455	949	8.55	YYZ	ORD	64	0	0	49	2	13	49	64	9	0.454	1.20	0.20	0.0	0.20	1631.2?
		9.55	ORD	TUS	57	2	19	78	0	0	57	78	10	0.553	3.18	1.18	0.40	2.18	5360.65
144	949	13.00	TUS	PHX	37	0	0	24	13	0	24	37	2	0.282	0.30	0.30	0.0	0.30	312.95
		14.10	PHX	JFK	47	13	0	54	0	6	41	60	3	0.426	4.32	7.32	0.40	8.42	5967.48

Exhibit 3

heading definitions helped clarify the types of passenger movements analyzed:

ENPL = Number of enplaned passengers, i.e., originating passengers at this location.

CONT = Number of continuing passengers from previous leg on multistop flight.

CONN = Number of connecting passengers travelling this leg based upon time of day and circuity.

COMP = Passengers completing their trip on this leg.

LOCAL = The number of people that flew only on a specific segment.

SUM = Total number of passenger movements over this segment.

CITY FLOWS = Number of cities that supplied passengers for the given city pair.

LOAD
FACTOR = Average daily load factor for each segment.

BLOCK
TIME = Hours and minutes of actual flight time.

LOCAL
TIME = Block times corrected for time zones.

GROUND
TIME = Time spent on the ground at a terminal.

REVENUE = Yield reflecting the passenger movements, calculated from an equation which considered costs to board and costs per mile. The fare was computed on O-D rather than actual itinerary.

Exhibit 4, the system summary, provided a daily breakdown of aircraft activity for the system.

Another report, the Systems Distribution Analysis, related the network of flights to the passenger O-D figures. The average stage length, great circle distance from passenger origin to destination, was computed and compared to haul or distance the plane actually flew. This ratio monitored the efficiency of flight itineraries in serving passenger demand. A high ratio revealed that O-D passengers were flown excess miles due to multistops, indirect flight routings, or flight irregularities.

An important application of the Corporate Planning Model was the generation of five-year forecasts for all American Airlines city pairs. Planners supplied the following inputs:

American's market share by city-pair.

1. Domestic industry traffic base.

2. American market share by city-pair.

3. Segment growth rates.

SYSTEM DAILY SUMMARY							
AIRCRAFT TYPE	NO. OF DEPARTURES	PLANE MILES	BLOCK HOURS	PASSENGERS BOARDED	PASSENGER MILES	YIELD %CENTS/MI.<	LOAD FACTOR
747	14	30855.	64.2	2672	6039447.	4.661	0.515
949	77	98537.	223.2	5884	9473244.	4.778	0.682
939	235	245022.	570.5	17578	22596192.	4.893	0.715
989	104	84054.	203.3	6803	7315492.	5.011	0.798
929	236	130219.	353.9	13798	8821196.	5.524	0.555
959	365	209916.	566.3	20922	14044654.	5.454	0.727
119	203	42607.	170.4	6588	1687464.	7.258	0.609
TOTAL	1234	841210.	2151.8	74245	69977648.	5.119	0.671

233 PASSENGERS NOT ROUTED.

Exhibit 4

Then a current forecast schedule was entered into the computer. The model was designed to flow previously computed passenger volumes over the route segments and divide passenger loads among available flights. As a final step, the model pinpointed poorly accommodated passenger flows and developed alternative aircraft schedules to improve service. In this process equipment types were assigned to each flight on the basis of equipment characteristics and passenger preference criteria.

After each successive manipulation the model could provide computer printouts itemizing the total flight schedule by fleet mix, including plane miles, flight hours, ramp hours and load factors. Arrivals and departures by station might be arranged by time of day to identify gate activity levels for all airports served by American.

Given a traffic forecast the model calculated in individual "runs" the economic consequences of alternative fleet assumptions. Although the Corporate Planning Model was not able to "make the decision" on optimum fleet size and composition, by trial and error it assisted the planner in determining the most profitable and competitive fleet size and mix. From that determination an aircraft acquisition plan could be developed.

THE PACIFIC ROUTE AWARD

The extensive planning procedure resulting from the Pacific Route Award was an actual example of American's corporate planners at work. It was also illustrative of the interplay between mechanical planning aids and purely human inputs.

Mr. Kimbriel, Vice President of Corporate Planning, described the decision making process, "The Pacific route award allows us to extend our transcontinental route network to Hawaii, and to the international routes; Honolulu—Sydney, Australia, Honolulu—Auckland, New Zealand, and Honolulu-American Samoa. For each of these so-called city-pairs, we have to project the future traffic activity of American. For example, for the city-pair Honolulu—Sydney, involving a flying distance of 5,078 miles, we expect the number of passengers that will fly American will be something like this:

	1970	1971	1972	1973	1974	1975	1976
Passengers per year	11,900	12,320	12,740	13,160	13,570	14,000	14,400

"To carry this stream of passengers," Mr. Kimbriel continued, "several types of aircraft might be used. Of course, we have our Boeing 707—Intercontinentals. These planes, costing approximately 8.1 million dollars, have a capacity of 131 passengers and a speed of 518 m.p.h. Soon we will also be able to use our new second generation planes. We could put the Boeing 747 into service on the Pacific routes in 1971, if we choose to do so. The "Jumbo" will carry 380 passengers at 530 m.p.h. The price tag, however, is uncomfortably high, 24 million dollars. From 1973 we'll also be able to fly the routes with the long distance version of the McDonnell-Douglas DC-10. The "Air Bus" has a capacity of 254 passengers, speed 530 m.p.h., and costs 19.1 million dollars.

"I see several possible flight combinations over the coming years for a route like Honolulu-Sydney. For instance, we might plan to use the Boeing 707 for the entire period 1970-1976. Another alternative is to fly the 707 for three years and then switch to the DC-10 from 1973. On the other hand, instead of switching to the DC-10 in 1973, we might plan to fly our 747's. With these passenger flows," Mr. Kimbriel said, pointing to the figures below, "our load factors would clearly be highest if we used the 707 all the way.

	1970	1971	1972	1973	1974	1975	1976
Passengers per flight (One flight per day, each way)	32	33	34	36	37	38	39

"If we disregard the effects of competition on the route, the choice of aircraft is quite obvious. We will be best off flying our smallest plane, the 707, which has more than enough capacity. Also, our load factor will improve if we cut our frequency of service from one flight a day to, say, three flights per week, losing some passengers but probably carrying more on each flight.

"The nature of competition, however, is such that we are forced to compete in terms of capacity offered, frequency of service, technological advantage of equipment, et cetera. Because of competition from the Australian national line, Qantas, we know that it is essential that the route should be flown daily at least once each direction and our traffic estimates are based on that frequency. With lower frequency, or older equipment, we wouldn't get as large a market share. Therefore, as soon as Qantas introduces the 747 or the DC-10, American will have to consider following:

"Using our computer model, we've been able to find the most profitable flight schedule pattern for the Pacific as a whole. By modifying our over-all domestic flight schedule, reflecting the repercussions from the new flights between several U.S. continental cities and Honolulu, we know how many new planes of what type we ought to buy to serve the

Pacific. The model tells us to fly 707's to Sydney. However, the competition may leave us with little choice as to aircraft type and route service frequencies. As a practical matter, we may have to disregard the solution that our model has given us and order several more large aircraft."

Case 2

A. B. Astra*

Astra was a Swedish-based industrial company, working mainly in the fields of pharmaceuticals and chemical products. Group sales in 1972 were 848 million Swedish Kronor (*S.Kr.*),[1] up 19 percent from the previous year, and almost quadrupled during the ten-year period since 1962. Most of the sales growth was in foreign markets, whose share of group sales increased from 35 to around 50 percent between 1967 and 1972. The group had 5,900 employees, of whom slightly more than 2,800 worked outside Sweden.

Astra, headquartered in Södertalje, south of Stockholm, was founded in 1913. The company had grown to be the leading pharmaceutical company in Scandinavia, and had approximately one fourth of the Swedish market. However, it was small in relation to the world-wide industry leaders. Compared to Astra's 1972 sales of 589 million S.Kr. in the pharmaceutical sector, the world leader, Swiss-based Hoffman-La Roche, had pharmaceutical sales equivalent to 4,590 million S.Kr. (see Exhibit 1 for financial data on Astra).

Astra had actively attempted to diversify into other areas, and was presently engaged in several non-pharmaceutical sectors. The organizational setup, in effect since 1968, consisted of five autonomous divisions: pharmaceuticals, industrial anticorrosion chemical specialties, chemical-based consumer products, agricultural feed products, and fish protein products (see Exhibit 2 for the formal corporate organization chart). The company was in the middle of a transitional period with increased emphasis on planning and management in its international operations. The

---

* This case was written by Peter Lorange, Assistant Professor Management, Massachusetts Institute of Technology. Copyright 1976 by L'Institut pour l'etude des Methodes de Direction de l'Entreprise (IMEDE), Lausanne, Switzerland.

[1] The exchange rate between Swedish Kronor and U.S. dollars was S.Kr. 4.85 to U.S. $1.00.

Exhibit 1. FINANCIAL STATEMENTS

Consolidated Profit and Loss Statement (in thousand S.Kr.)

	1972	1971
Operating income	849.231	715.903
Operating expenses	761.434	643.289
Operating earnings before depreciation	87.797	72.614
Calculated depreciation	26.500	23.400
Operating earnings after depreciation	61.297	49.214
Interests and dividends received	3.236	3.369
Interests paid	8.170	7.590
Earnings after nonoperating income and expenses	56.363	44.993
Minority interests in subsidiary earnings	− .191	+ 1.972
Earnings before appropriations and taxes	56.172	46.965
Fiscal depreciation in excess of calculated	− 6.996	− 6.309
To inventory and investment reserve	− 9.202	− 3.412
Earnings before taxes	39.974	37.244
Taxes	18.003	14.731
Minority interests in subsidiary appropriations and taxes	+ 1.072	− 8
Net earning for year	23.043	22.505

Consolidated Balance Sheet

Assets	1972	1971
Current assets	352.521	305.942
Blocked account in Bank of Sweden	1.734	4.434
Fixed assets	304.208	283.882
	658.463	594.258
Liabilities and Stockholders' Equity		
Current Liabilities	166.791	142.037
Long-Term Liabilities	157.509	135.851
Untaxed reserves	134.166	120.622
Minority interests	5.389	4.545
Stockholders' equity		
Capital stock	100.000	100.000
Restricted statutory reserves	35.937	32.637
Free reserves	35.628	36.061
Net earnings for year	23.043	22.505
	658.463	594.258
Assets pledged (incl. mortgages)	92.946	87.398
Contingent liabilities	24.417	27.319

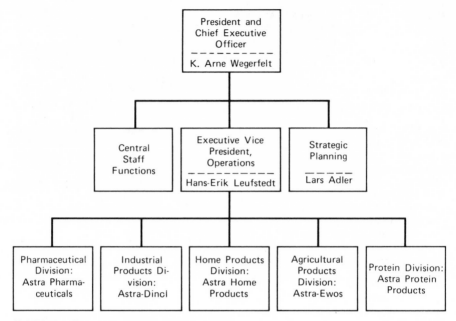

Exhibit 2. Corporate Organization Structure

following table indicates the magnitude of Astra's *sales* in each of its businesses.

1972 SALES IN MILLION S.Kr.

Division	Total	International	Sales increase Over 1971 %
Pharmaceutical Products	589	282	14%
Industrial products	38	21	26%
Home Products[2]	114	37	28%
Agricultural Products	60	18	15%
Protein Products	47	47	45%

The chairman of the board of Astra was Mr. Jacob Wallenberg, a leading figure in Swedish industry and finance. The president and chief executive officer was Mr. K. Arne Wegerfelt, 53, and the executive vice president and chief operating officer was Mr. Hans-Erik Leufstedt, 49.

BUSINESS INVOLVEMENTS

Pharmaceutical Division—Astra Pharmaceuticals

Organization. Astra Pharmaceuticals, headquartered in Södertalje, Sweden, was responsible for the group activity in the pharmaceutical

[2] Chemical-based consumer products.

field. Research and development and marketing were carried out at five subsidiaries—denoted product companies: Astra Läkemedel, located in Södertalje; Hässle, in Gothenburg; Draco, in Lund; Astra Pharmaceutical Products, Inc. (Astra-U.S.A.) in Worcester, Massachusetts; and Lematte et Boinot in Paris, France. Marketing was further handled by subsidiaries—denoted marketing companies—in sixteen countries and by agents and licensees in an additional 100 markets. Manufacturing of pharmaceutical products in Sweden was centralized, with one major plant at Södertalje. Minor pharmaceutical manufacturing units existed at a number of the foreign subsidiaries. (Exhibit 3 gives the formal organization chart for the pharmaceutical division.)

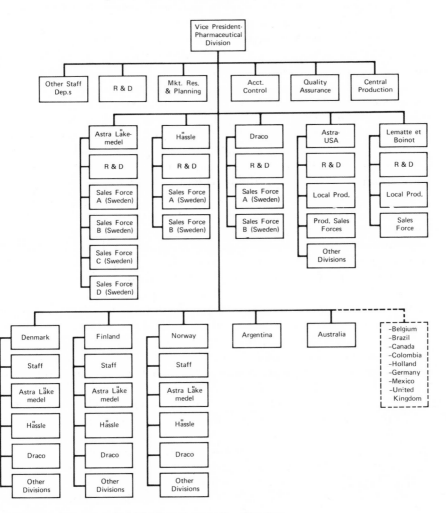

Exhibit 3. Pharmaceutical Division: Organization Structure

Each of the three Swedish product companies had its own marketing organization for Sweden and several sales forces; thus, a total of eight different sales forces were actively selling drugs in the home market. Marketing responsibility was with the product companies for their own product lines.

In each of the other Scandinavian countries (Denmark, Finland, Norway), there was a national Astra company president in charge of a service staff and physical properties. Each of the pharmaceutical division's product companies had its own sales organization operating within this common services setup, with independent profit and loss responsibilities at each product company headquarters.

Outside Scandinavia there were a number of marketing companies, each tied to a particular geographical region. For instance, there were marketing companies for England and Germany, headquartered locally. The marketing companies were responsible for handling all Astra drug sales within their particular areas. They would thus deal with the products of all five product companies. The marketing companies, not the product companies, would by tradition have profit and loss responsibility for the performance of Astra drug sales in their own regions. Thus, although the product companies were responsible for R&D and product-oriented marketing know-how on a global basis, they got credit only for profits from domestic and Scandinavian sales. Profits on international selling were credited directly from the marketing companies to the division.

Astra-U.S.A. had started out as a marketing company, producing and marketing the Astra local anesthetic product line for the U.S. market. Due largely to the superior characteristics of Astra's local anesthetic, Xylocain, the company had managed to get a market share of more than 50% of the U.S. local anesthetic market. Over the years the Worcester organization accumulated a lot of knowledge about local anesthetics and this led to the initiation of research at Worcester. Research leading to cardiovascular applications of Xylocain was one of the successful undertakings pioneered at the new laboratory. In 1972 Astra-U.S.A. became an independent product company, with worldwide responsibility for the development of cardiovascular antiarrhythmic products. The present organizational structure of Astra-U.S.A. had been in effect since the spring of 1972, when marketing efforts were organized around four product groups. (See Exhibit 4 for organization chart.) The intent was to delineate between the company's function as a marketing company for the U.S.A. and the worldwide product company function. Its four product managers would coordinate the activities of their own groups with members of the R&D, manufacturing and marketing forces.

The Paris-based product company Lematte et Boinot was much smaller than the four other product companies. Although in principle it too functioned as both a product company and a marketing company for France, the modest magnitude of its research and product development activities made its operations comparable to the ordinary marketing companies.

Much of the interaction and communication between the product companies and the marketing companies was carried out via product managers. The idea was that each product company would have product managers for the different groups of lines it handled. Similarly, each of the marketing companies would have product managers handling one

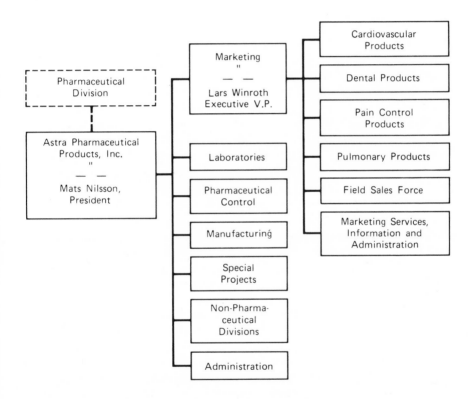

Exhibit 4. Organization Chart, Astra Pharmaceutical Products, Inc.

or a few lines each. There would be a close communication between pairs of product managers responsible for the same product. It was felt, however, that with the lack of size of most of the marketing companies it would simply be uneconomical and close to impossible with a similar matching of products in both product and marketing companies. Consequently, a typical product manager in most marketing companies handled a substantial number of lines.

Product company activities. The product companies were somewhat specialized in their products reflecting their comparative areas of strength in research and development. For instance, Astra Läkemedel had a strong competence in local anesthetics and antibiotics. Draco concentrated on pulmonary diseases and Hässle on cardiovascular related drugs. Each product company was thus active within a number of fairly specific areas of activities. This specialization was made in order to minimize interdependencies in R&D, marketing, and other functions. There was some overlap between the product companies' areas of activities, however, partly because of the nature of research and development in the drug industry. One company might start a research project on a new drug for one specific use and find a different use for it. Although a project from one company thus might edge into other companies' areas of interest, such a project would usually stay with the originating product company. Another reason for overlapping areas of interest was that a drug originally used for one purpose might turn out to have applicability in other areas, with or without small product modifications. One example was Xylocain of the Astra Läkemedel product company, which originated as a local anesthetic but lately had found wide uses in intensive care treatments after heart attacks. Xylocain for cardiac arrhythmia was not transferred to Hässle, although this application of the drug was within Hässle's area of interest. In 1972, however, Xylocain was transferred to Astra-U.S.A.; this unusual move coincided with the elevation of Astra-U.S.A. to a product company. Both Astra Läkemedel and Astra-U.S.A. were thus active as product companies in Xylocain-based applications, and both Hässle and Astra-U.S.A. were in the cardiovascular area, due to a set of circumstances analogous to those just described.

The product companies were thus responsible for their own R&D. Their success, as well as the sucess of the pharmaceutical division as a whole, depended on their ability to launch good new products at regular intervals. Astra's overall R&D costs in 1971 were 8.4% of sales and this expenditure had risen steadily over recent years, both in absolute and relative terms. The growing importance of R&D was a phenomenon in the pharmaceutical industry worldwide, yet the rate of drug innovations was decreasing. Most of the large pharmaceutical companies found it necessary to increase research because they were highly dependent on a steady outflow of product innovations to utilize fully their worldwide, expensive marketing organizations.

Given the difficulty and importance of the R&D task, the assumptions underlying Astra's P&D strategy became crucial. Astra had decentralized its R&D efforts to each of the product companies. The three Swedish companies were located close to the three major Swedish universities, permitting intimate cooperation in basic research tasks and use of faculty expertise. The research was centered as closely as possible around ten to twelve new drug developments, and an attempt was made to establish clear goals for each research effort. Thus efforts were concentrated within a few specialty sectors.

There were a number of distinctive steps that a new drug project went through from the time when research was initiated until full-scale marketing was carried out. A project would typically have an "investment life cycle." For each of the stages in the drug's development cycle a number of funds outflows would be incurred. Funds inflows would start occurring only after the marketing stage was under way.

Much of the Astra organization's skill lay in the fact that it had highly competent specialists to carry out the tasks at each development stage. These tasks were generally quite different, and could be undertaken only by the specialist unit in question. For the manager of a product company, it became important to utilize these specialized human resources at a fairly steady rate. In line with this, a high-priority, long-term task for management was balancing R&D and marketing. On the other hand it would be suboptimal to allocate so many resources and efforts to R&D that product innovations would result faster than they could effectively be marketed. Nor should the marketing apparatus be so extensive that R&D would be unable to develop enough new innovations to utilize it fully. Mr. Leufstedt, the executive vice president, felt that Astra's strengths and weaknesses worldwide in the pharmaceutical field might be broadly illustrated by means of the following diagram:

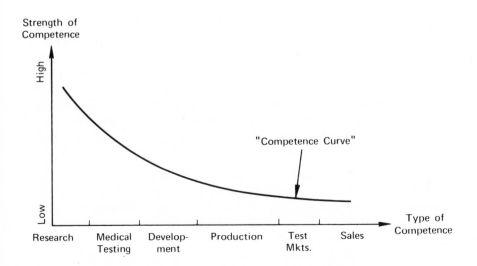

The Nonpharmaceutical Divisions

Over the years Astra had diversified into a number of nonpharmaceutical areas, a spread of activities that in 1968 prompted the reorganization of the company along divisional lines. The reasons behind the action were to strengthen a diversification move into areas related to pharmaceuticals so as to enable capitalization on the technical and marketing know-how, and to attempt to lower overall risk by engaging in businesses not exposed to the same type of risks. Each division was given a formal organizational status similar to that of the pharmaceutical division.

Industrial Products Division–Astra-Dinol. Headquartered in Hässleholm, this division specialized in producing and marketing products through its two companies Tikamin, which concentrated on rust preventives, and Alkalion/Nordiens, which specialized in institutional dishwashing detergents and cleansers. In addition to those in the Nordic countries, the division had its own marketing organizations in France, Holland, Germany, Austria, and the United States, where it had formed a joint venture with Tuff-Cote, Inc., a U.S.-based rust preventive company, which in turn franchised out the rust-preventive process. It was represented by agents in several other countries. The division's sales were greatly influenced by the sales of automobiles, since car owners were one of the largest groups of customers. It was anticipated that the division's sales would increase 20 to 25 percent per year over the coming two to three years, and that earnings would increase as well.

Home Products Division–Astra Home Products. The division, headquartered in Stockholm, developed, marketed and, in some cases, manufactured consumer household goods and articles for use in sports and leisure activities. Operations were divided among four product companies: Wallco, which was in the business of personal hygiene products and cleansers; Sunco, which concentrated on food products and chemical specialties; Wallco Sport/Arjon, which produced sporting goods and leisure articles; and Gema, which was in the low price range of toiletries and cosmetics. The division was active in Sweden, Denmark, Finland and Norway. Much of its expansion had resulted from takeovers of smaller companies engaged in production, wholesaling, and distribution within the division's broad area of activity.

Agricultural Products Division–Astra-Ewos. The division headquartered in Södertalje (but separately from the corporate and the pharmaceutical division headquarters) developed, manufactured and marketed special preparations for animal breeding through the Ewos corporation, and plant culture through the Plantex corporation. The division was now firmly established with its own marketing setup in all the Scandinavian countries. In addition it also had minor marketing arrangements in England, France, Germany, Canada, the United States, and Australia. Research and development was an integral part of the division's activities. Over the last few years new or improved products had been developed which accounted for 70 percent of the division's present sales. The division also attempted to apply the group's know-how in fish proteins.

Protein Division–Astra Protein Products. Headquartered in Gothenburg, this division had its operations concentrated in three fields: food protein, proteins for animal feeds, and fish meal, the last being produced aboard the factory ship M/S Astra, operated by Astra Overseas Fishing, and jointly owned by Astra and a Norwegian shipping group. The commercial break-through in food proteins that was expected had not yet materialized, and this line of operations suffered a loss. International interest in the products was however, substantial. The division planned to extend its efforts by enlisting the cooperation of international relief organizations on various nutritional programs. Astra had held the leading position in the world for many years in the area of fish protein technology and production but thus far had not had much success in the potential market for utilizing fish protein as a food additive. Fish protein was an entirely new food additive and the biggest problem was to overcome tradition, prejudices, and costs. As anticipated, regional shortages of skim milk had begun to open some markets for fish protein as an animal food. The company was convinced that interest in new protein sources for human use would also be increased.

ASTRA'S LONG-RANGE PLANNING SYSTEM

Start-up planning

The president, Mr. Wegerfelt, had stated that planning would be a way of life at Astra and that his office was ultimately responsible for the overall strategic planning activities of the corporation. However, the heads of divisions and subsidiaries were to be responsible for developing their own plans. The intention was that the corporate strategic planning would to a considerable extent set guidelines and limitations for the planning activities of the divisions, and the division's planning, in turn, would direct the subsidiaries' activities. The director of corporate planning, Mr. Lars Adler, was hired from outside the company in late 1968, and was to assist the president and the heads of divisions and subsidiaries on matters of strategic planning. In 1971 the president's special responsibility for strategic planning was further underscored by the establishment of the office of executive vice president (Mr. Leufstedt), responsible primarily for operations, to allow the president more time for strategic and long-range activities.

The first formal strategic plans were developed on a systematic basis in 1969 by those units of the corporation which previously had undertaken planning on their own and thus had some experience in the field. By 1971, all the divisions and most of the subsidiaries had offered their strategic plans, and the first consolidated strategic plan for the entire corporation, culminating in the identification of a number of planning issues requiring immediate attention, was presented. The first stage in introducing a formalized strategic planning in the Astra Company had emphasized a "bottom-up" approach. The guidelines and constraints set by the corporate level were mainly key target figures concerning expansion, profit margin, return on investment, and investment in R&D and plants as a percentage of sales.

During the start-up phase Mr. Adler had put heavy emphasis on trying to develop an enthusiasm for and understanding of planning among the operating units. He was heavily involved in field visits to "sell" planning and introduce tailor-made systems for almost three years, from the time he joined Astra in 1968 until the first full-scale planning effort in 1971. The first round of planning was intended as a perception process, with the emphasis on listing major planning issues based on environmental conditions, available competence, and general target figures. For later rounds a more "systematic" input of economic evaluations and sales figures was scheduled.

The corporate policy statement

To give further direction to the planning effort, corporate issued a written policy statement defining Astra's basic values and objectives. Its purpose was to provide general and long-term guidelines, not to define operating procedures in detail. Corporate emphasized that the company's policies—excluding its very basic goals—would have to be continuously reviewed and revised, as markets and other external and internal conditions changed.

The operating objectives were an effort to utilize Astra's research capabilities for the development, production and marketing of medical, health and nutritional products and systems for the Scandinavian and international markets, with an increased emphasis on the international markets (80% of the growth were seen to come from the international markets). In addition, the company should be active in other fields where its specialized research and marketing skills might be applied productively. Targets and minimum requirements for profitability and sales expansion were also proposed. Finally it was stated that the necessary product development for these targets should be assured primarily through comprehensive "in-house" research. However, although not the usual means to growth, acquisitions were not ruled out when they might be more advantageous than internal growth.

The planning process

The planning process was characterized by a predominantly bottom-up approach, with the conscious attempt to utilize management tools already existing in Astra's divisionalized corporate structure, such as autonomous budgets and economic targets and evaluation systems, and to tailor plans to fit the situation and problems of a particular division or subsidiary. To avoid formalizing the contents of the plans while allowing some degree of consolidation of the decentralized plans, a number of questions were specified:

"What sort of business are you in?" (You" = you as head of your division or subsidiary company.)
"How do you want to operate within this business?"
"What will be the results you expect to achieve?"
"What will be the consequences of your results for the rest of the group (cash flow, materials flows, organization, personnel, know-how, synergy, etc.)?"

Three initial questions were also to be answered:

"What have been the key events in your business up to now?"
"What are your distinctive skills or competences?"
"What core process or key decisions will make or break your business?"

The corporate planning department had also developed a manual, in the format of a detailed checklist, for the development of divisional and subsidiary plans. The main headlines were as follows:

Company policy and objectives—
    company philosophy and business concepts
    goals and targets

Analyses and forecasts—
  forecasts and analysis of the environment such as the industry and
    the national economic patterns
  analysis of the particular company or division
  Summary (strengths and weaknesses, threats and opportunities)
Planning issues—
  perception and identification of major problems, key factors for
    success and possible future actions
  priority-setting of planning issues
Plans and new policies including structural changes—
  development of existing fields of business
  penetrating new areas of activities
  discontinuation of present activities
Economic evaluations—
  cash flow, resource requirements and resource generation
  results and contribution to group profits

The developing strategic planning system needed to be coordinated
with the many other planning systems that would recur at various
intervals in the company, such as the annual budgeting, and functional
planning for R&D, personnel, production, marketing, and finance;
accordingly, during 1972 the corporate planning department had introduced a system by which strategic plans should be revised sufficiently early in the year to provide one of the bases for marketing
planning and budgeting. Exhibit 5 reflects the critical sequence of dates
for these planning activities at corporate, divisional and subsidiary
levels.

The R&D function was given specific recognition as an important
part of the planning activity. A scientific committee met once a year to
establish research priorities. This committee consisted of the heads of
the company's pharmaceutical research laboratories as well as three
outside scientists who had been retained by the chairman, Mr. Wallenberg, and the president, Mr. Wegerfelt, as their personal advisors on
scientific matters, reflecting the chairman's desire to strengthen this
important part of corporate decision-making. The R&D planning was a
separate system in Astra, running from the product companies via the
pharmaceutical division to the board. In the strategic planning of the
pharmaceutical division the total resources allocated to R&D was
stated, usually as a percentage of sales. Within this frame the R&D
planning system allocated the resources to different projects. The
balancing of the research project portfolio had been done very informally, with no review procedure of all the projects in the portfolio,
either at the level of each of the product companies or at the divisional
or corporate levels. This procedure had operated well because at the

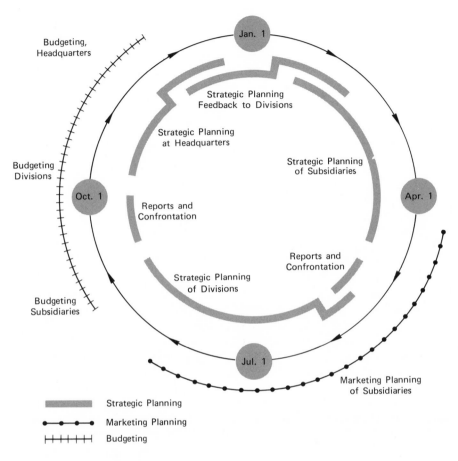

Budgeting,
Headquarters

Jan. 1

Strategic Planning
Feedback to Divisions

Strategic Planning
at Headquarters

Strategic Planning
of Subsidiaries

Budgeting
Divisions

Oct. 1

Apr. 1

Reports and
Confrontation

Reports and
Confrontation

Strategic Planning
of Divisions

Budgeting
Subsidiaries

Jul. 1

Marketing Planning
of Subsidiaries

▬▬▬ Strategic Planning

●—●—● Marketing Planning

┼┼┼┼┼┼ Budgeting

Exhibit 5.   The annual planning cycle

product company level the R&D people had very close contact with marketing people and the medical market. However, there was no formal long-range balancing of resources between R&D, marketing and manufacturing. The R&D planning system ran parallel with the general long-range planning system, the two being informally coordinated through close personal and operational contacts.

The control system

By tradition Astra had strong central control, except for R&D, with emphasis on short-term budget performance. With the attempt to decentralize, culminating in the adoption of the divisional organizational form in 1968 and the introduction of strategic planning, the unique position of the tight budget system as a steering instrument had diminished, but even today the budget played a central role in the president's control of the group.

Budgeting took place during the period of September to December, starting with the subsidiaries, continuing with the divisions, and ending up with the whole group. Thus, although budgeting coincided with the final stages of strategic planning for the group as a whole, it was in fact based on all the separate strategic and marketing plans made earlier. Comparing performance to budget was done on a regular basis, with results reported for both products and markets. Top management generally paid great attention to the follow-up of the budgets, since the process indirectly gave an indication of managerial competence.

PLANNING ISSUES OF MANAGERIAL CONCERN

Top management's involvement in strategic planning

By 1973 each of the divisions had a strategic planning system. There was, however, no formalized system to consolidate the divisional plans and to plan for relative changes over the years in allocation of funds among the divisions. Mr. Leufstedt attributed this lack primarily to size-difference among the divisions, the pharmaceutical division plan itself being close to the entire company plan. Each division plan was therefore reviewed and the sum of the approved plans became the corporate plan. At the budget stage, however, Mr. Leufstedt claimed some overall balancing took place among the divisions regarding their budgeted capital needs.

There was a growing pressure from several of the organizational line units to receive more formal corporate feedback to their plans, although many saw the pattern of resource allocation allotments as indirect corporate feedback. Agreeing that something more systematic was needed, Mr. Adler stated that the next step was to sell the need for and to secure additional commitment by top management in strategic planning, and to assure the top-down half of a two-way communication of strategic thinking. One staff analyst at the pharmaceutical division suggested building some sort of model to bring in "what if" thinking and sensitivity analysis in the evaluation of major strategic issues of the plans.

"I feel that it would have been useful if the major proposed investments in Astra had been discussed at the same time," Mr. Mats Nilsson, president of Astra-U.S.A., related. "At least the plans of the five or six biggest organizational units should be reviewed together. Now, I fear that we may be taking a partial view. In fact, a problem with the concept of divisionalized structure as we practice it seems to be that there is not enough overall portfolio planning. A coordinated point of view with regard to planning should take place at two levels, for the resource allocation within the pharmaceuticals division and for the resource allocation among the divisions."

Mr. Nilsson felt that the smaller divisions might be occupying too much of top management's time, and that the pharmaceuticals division had not gotten as much top management attention as possible. He suggested that the smaller divisions might operate more effectively in independent settings if put under "rule of thumb" capital restrictions. Until now the smaller divisions had generally been given most of the capital they asked for. A tighter policy would force the divisions to reallocate resources that were tied up in less than absolutely necessary uses. He claimed that such a trimming process would encourage more prudent independent financial behavior in the smaller divisions.

Mr. Nilsson commented on the planning review process as follows: "Obtaining corporate commitment to my plan depended very much on my own initiative. I gave a 45-minute presentation of my 1972 plan to the top executive group of the pharmaceutical division, explaining my key assumptions, planned action programs and expected financial development, and got only three questions back, all relating to relatively minor issues. I then took my plan directly to the president, then to our chairman of the board and finally to the board. A number of good questions came up and a penetrating discussion developed. I felt that a mutual understanding of the consequences of the plan developed and that, in fact, I had gotten a reasonable commitment from top management. Subsequently, I spent time with the executive vice president, Mr. Leufstedt, to discuss the operational implications of my plan."

Degree of realism in plans

One senior line executive felt that there was often too little realism in the plans, and gave as an example some of the minor divisions' optimistic planning activity in the spring versus their realistic budget preparation in the fall. He also noted that when the incoming plans were consolidated into the corporate plan this would not necessarily represent a fair expression of the corporation's direction for the future, partly because a simple aggregation of overoptimistic subplans would lead to a too optimistic corporate plan. However, corporate level also had realized that some units were understretched. Even if faster growth were possible some divisions "played safe" and stayed at established target figures. It was also felt that the long-range plans were getting so rigid in terms of financial figures that there was a danger of extrapolating numbers instead of addressing the inventory of opportunities at hand. There would be a temptation to stress the economic evaluations so much that the plan would become a five-year rolling budget. The senior line executive felt that one way of achieving more realism and strategy-orientation in the plans would be for corporate headquarters to provide more initial steering in the planning process by specifying operational objectives for each of the organizational units. The planning job for each unit would then be to codify these objectives by suggesting strategic actions to reach the desired objectives.

Mr. Leufstedt realized that some of the incoming divisional plans (as well as budgets) would be more optimistic than others, reflecting the division management's attitude towards risk and its understanding of the business. To some extent overoptimism as well as pessimism might be detected from comparisons with past performance. However, this would be of little help when dealing with newly acquired, rapidly growing or rapidly changing operations, such as several of the smaller divisions and foreign subsidiaries. In order to cope with this problem Mr. Leufstedt felt that a more effective analytical support unit was needed at central headquarters to back up central management with analyses, detect unreasonable aspects of the plans, and facilitate interdivisional comparisons as well.

According to Mr. Adler, there were many examples, especially in the smaller divisions, of unforeseen additional resource requirements. He believed this was due mainly to failure in realizing the limitations of competence and capability of the units in question. This failure would, of course, turn up later as unexpected scarcity of financial resources, inability to generate the expected cash, build-up of stocks of unsold goods, or various forms of managerial "crises."

Regarding the separation of R&D planning from the rest of the planning efforts, Mr. Nilsson noted that the pharmaceutical division's investment allocations into R&D projects tended to be decided almost solely on the basis of scientific knowledge, and he was concerned that this important class of strategic decisions was not encompassed in the formal planning process. He felt that the evaluation of an R&D project should include an additional production and marketing plan, to get a better feel for the additional investment requirements as well as the approximate payback for the project. Further, no project should be decided in isolation, but in the context of an evaluation of the portfolio of projects to ensure that the quality of each project would be judged relative to others. A staff assistant to Mr. Adler saw no way of including in the plans the financial consequences of R&D projects in their early stages, and he felt that it would be difficult to get the research organizations to cooperate because of the inherent uncertainty of research and lack of financial aptitude among the researchers. Also, in inclusion of R&D decisions in planning would open another potential conflict area between the product companies and the marketing companies because of the need to agree on which research projects to undertake while allowing for future product portfolio needs. Time-horizon problems would probably also enter into such a discussion. "Our independent resource allocation to R&D is a company philosophy and you have to remember that the R&D people really are the most important and significant professional group in Astra. We have not yet formed a better working system," Mr. Adler stated.

The planning system and organizational structure

One senior line officer felt that the organizational dilemma regarding the tasks of the product companies relative to the marketing companies was not satisfactorily settled, and that there was too much short-term decision-making to improve the immediate profit and loss performance. The marketing company managers should instead be encouraged to think "in balance sheet terms," i.e., to increase their feeling for the importance of an effective utilization of the capital employed. The officer did not feel that the present system with use of return on investment (ROI) calculations was of much help, partly because of the marketing managers' basic sales attitudes and partly because of lack of appreciation of the importance of the ROI-figures. Even if the present system were modified to cope with disfunctions due to the marketing companies' short-range profit and loss behavior, this would not be sufficient to ensure a reasonable balance between products and markets. Thus, he felt that considerable benefits might be achieved by reorganizing the pharmaceutical division into four or five product group areas with global profit and loss responsibility. These should then be responsible for product development as well as for marketing on a global basis.

Mr. Adler felt that the present system of delineation of responsibility had worked fairly well as long as the Swedish market was the major profit-generating source, but with rapidly expanding international sales, confusion was setting in. He indicated, however, that Astra need not abandon its present organization of product companies in order to get global profit and loss responsibility. A matrix organization system might achieve this.

Mr. Nilsson felt that the nonpharmaceutical divisions would not get the right sorts of information and support from the pharmaceutical division when attempting to utilize this division's international organization for their own internationalization. A smaller division going into a new geographical area should be required to pay its own expenses. This would, of course, not prevent the smaller division from buying certain services from the pharmaceutical division's organization in the given area. Mr. Nilsson believed that it was important that the smaller divisions should be separately capitalized all the way and have to work with their own realistic profit and loss statements and balance sheets. This would give the proper motivation to these divisions' international arms.

In this respect, one senior executive felt that it was important that Astra-U.S.A. had achieved the status of a product company, because this might enforce a realization of the duality of the U.S. subsidiary's present task, being both a product company on a worldwide basis and a geographical marketing company. Anticipating potential conflict between these two tasks, the officer indicated that the U.S. executives were trying to develop informal contacts with executives at each of the other product companies to effect joint approaches to future R&D and marketing. The discussion on organizational structure had been going on for five years, ever since the decision to expand internationally had been taken. He felt that the most suitable way for the company's organizational structure to adapt to an international strategy would be to abandon present product companies as key decision-making units and instead organize and plan through worldwide product groups.

In terms of Astra's future organizational development, Mr. Leufstedt saw the need to preserve the strong competence apparent in some areas while strengthening competence in weaker areas—the worldwide marketing company structure, for one. Given Astra's new strength in the pharmaceutical area with the increased need for rapid and full-scale worldwide marketing efforts to capitalize on a new product's advantages and uniqueness, Mr. Leufstedt was concerned that the strengthening would take too long. Also, since the economic magnitude of developing new pharmaceutical products from initial research to commercial launching had increased dramatically, the cost of *not* doing a top job in marketing was considerable. Merging with another company with complementary strengths and weaknesses was ruled out, as written in the group policy statement, mainly for reasons of political infeasibility. Instead experts were sent out from Sweden to build up the foreign marketing company organizations. Mr. Leufstedt felt, however, that this approach would only represent a temporary and short-term solution and only in relatively untapped markets. To ensure the long-term success of Astra in a given geographical area it seemed essential to draw heavily on nationals for key management positions. This was also felt to be necessary to facilitate the implementation of Astra's stated policy of becoming a full-fledged international company.

Benefits and disappointments from the planning experience

To the question of whether it was possible to point out specific positive as well as negative consequences of planning so soon after full-scale planning had been introduced at Astra, Mr. Leufstedt replied: "The most important positive benefit had been the perception of new alternatives, policies and growth paths. Another benefit has been in the discussion of why certain targets do not get achieved. Today, we are much better equipped to judge the relative importance of the various reasons for setbacks, and to keep a "clean" discussion focusing on this. Through planning we have gotten early warning about a number of problems that we previously were unaware of, and we have been able to take corrective actions. For instance, we were not aware of the degree of overlap that turned out to exist in the activities of a number of our units, particularly between our product companies in the pharmaceutical division, between our home products and agricultural products divisions, and between our protein division and agricultural products division. We have already been able to tackle this, or have the problem under close monitoring. Another problem that became apparent was that some of the smaller divisions diversified rapidly, taking over new companies, their major objective seeming to be more to boost growth and performance figures in plans, budgets and internal accounting than to add new businesses that logically fitted in with and could complement existing activities. Maybe the biggest problem with having the divisions undertaking their own diversification policy turned out to be that they got involved with a relatively large number of smaller acquisitions. Given all the extra administrative problem-solving created by this, it would in retrospect probably have been better if Astra spent its money and administrative talents on consummating one or a few large mergers instead. What turned out to be appropriate size in a merger candidate differed from the divisional and corporate points of view.

"Planning might also have created a feeling of unrealism and overoptimism, together with a tendency to overlook less comfortable problems. More probing and questioning would be necessary in order to reinforce realism in planning, Mr. Leufstedt felt. He also felt that central management maybe had had a tendency to say "yes" to the division managers, in order not to dampen a division's initiative, and also because it was difficult for corporate headquarters to argue against the special knowledge of the divisions. "A major challenge for us at corporate management is to have enough competence and knowledge to be a skillful partner in the strategic discussions with units that cover many separate areas and business ideas," he stated.

Mr. Leufstedt also saw a need to push some of the marketing companies to develop more useful plans. Mr. Leufstedt was particularly concerned that lack of emphasis on planning might lead to overlooking environmental scanning and markets monitoring needs for product modifications or discontinuance, or new product opportunities. Given the lead-times required to develop a new drug he felt that a strong worldwide marketing scanning function was necessary. Mr. Leufstedt thus saw as essential giving frequent support to the marketing companies for their planning efforts, particularly in terms of planning assumptions and information enabling the marketing companies to make relatively reasonable priority decisions in their plans. In rare cases of conflicts between the plans of a marketing company and those of the product companies the divisional management would have to step in as a problem solver or decision maker.

Mr. Adler felt that the call for the set of highly quantified economic evaluations had turned out to be a rather awkward hurdle in the implementation of planning. Economic computations of this kind might discourage the "visionary" and perceptive element of the planning process, provoke a mechanical extrapolation of earlier developments, or create a deceptive feeling of precision. Thus, it might lead to a degree of stated accuracy, or the taking up of a definite position, that might not always be possible or even desirable. Finally, the role of plans might get to be confused with that of budgets, even to the extent that they might be compared a number of years later with actual results.

The quantification of the plans was, however, also felt to yield a number of positive benefits. Above all, it might facilitate the perception and identification of structural changes. Also, it might add pressure to give substance to the plans, serve as a way to check the realism of the plan, and signal possible obstacles. Finally, economic data would be necessary for certain parts of corporate planning, such as the allocation of economic resources, financial planning, and planning for risk, Mr. Adler stated.

When asked about the usefulness of the plan for the management of their operation, senior executives answered variously. One noted an increased sense of a coordinated pattern, permitting a better judgment of the consequences of changing assumptions. Another spoke of a general increase in the level of conscience. It was felt that the plan would be useful for the divisional headquarters too. U.S. subsidiary executives already credited the plan for a revised and in their opinion more meaningful pattern of resource allocations to the subsidiary, recently decided on at the divisional and corporate headquarters.

Planning Issues Ahead

In a recent statement the president, Mr. Wegerfeldt, had given a standing order on cutting down resources and time spent by corporate staff on corporate planning. This had led a number of managers to question if the long-range planning process should be changed or not, and, if to be changed, in what ways? How might one arrive at a proper balance of commitment by top management to corporate planning? Would it be necessary to attempt to arrive at a different match between organization structure, top management style, and the design of the planning system?

Case 3

Texas Instruments Incorporated*

Management Systems

Since the end of World War II, sales of Texas Instruments Incorporated (TI) had grown at an average compound rate of 25% per year, reaching $764 million in 1971. Over the same period, profits had grown at a rate of 24%. This growth had been internally generated, with the exception of one acquisition in 1959 which amounted to about 25% of TI sales in that year. Exhibit 1 presents a 10-year review of the company's growth which indicates that it was accompanied by conservative financial policies. Publicly traded shares of TI stock had historically sold at a higher-than-average multiple of earnings.

This case describes the management systems that were developed within TI to assist its executives in achieving a sustained rate of internally generated growth. The particular focus of this case is on the company's formal system for strategic long-range planning, a system which TI called its Objectives, Strategies, and Tactics system (OST). The case also discusses TI's organization systems and reporting systems.

Corporate Structure

In 1972 TI was a technologically oriented company with diversified interests in industrial, government/military (about one-third of sales) and consumer markets. Operations were organized into four groups. These groups were not based on such typical organizing categories as product lines or types of customers served. Instead, each of the four groups reflected a different perspective as to how TI products and

* This case was prepared by R. F. Vancil with the assistance of Texas Instruments Incorporated, as a basis for class discussion rather than to illustrate either effective or ineffective handling of an administrative situation.

services could be related to a customer's processes and systems. The *Materials Group* dealt with products that would be raw materials for a customer's production process. The *Components Group* was concerned with products that would be subassemblies in the customer's process or replaceable parts in his equipment. The *Equipment Group* produced machines that would perform sensing or processing operations in the customer's system. The *Services Group* provided systems support and services for a customer's operations.

Given this operational structure depicted in Exhibit 2, the various groups within TI were all natural customers for each other. Moreover, the development of any new product or service to be marketed by TI was likely to require the coordinated, cooperative effort of most, if not all, of the four groups.

The four operating groups were broken down further into divisions and then again into 77 Product Customer Centers (PCCs) which operated like complete small business organizations with their own short-term profit responsibility. Texas Instruments credited the PCC with contributing much toward developing a spirit of customer responsiveness and innovation in management and also toward developing entrepreneurial managers.

OBJECTIVES, STRATEGIES, AND TACTICS

The primary reason that TI had developed its OST system was to facilitate the management of innovation. The need for such a system was expressed by Mr. S. T. Harris, Officer of the Board, as follows:[1]

"As the organization grows, it gets more complex. Hundreds and then thousands of customers are involved, often in multiple locations. The number of customers grows. Operations extend into many states and often into many countries. Governments all over add complexities of reporting and of regulation—some of them necessary, some of them not. To exploit an invention or innovation fully and to get broad distribution, the price must come down. The margin between price and costs gets narrower. At a relatively early stage in the development, so far as this invention or innovation is concerned, it becomes far more important that the principal managers be good administrators than good innovators. The administration in a technologically based business may often require good, or even deep technical skill, but at this stage what counts is the aid that kind of knowledge brings to administration, not to innovation.

"To handle the growth and increasing complexity, the organization

---

[1] These remarks by Mr. Harris are excerpted from a speech he delivered at the London Graduate School of Business Studies on May 22, 1970.

Exhibit 1 TEN-YEAR REVIEW TEXAS INSTRUMENTS
INCORPORATED AND SUBSIDIARIES *IN*
THOUSANDS OF DOLLARS

Years Ended December 31	1971	1970	1969	1968
Operations				
Net sales	**$764,258**	$827,641	$831,822	$671,2
Income before provision for income				
taxes	**59,478**	52,043	60,301	50,3
Provision for income taxes	**25,755**	22,182	26,790	24,0
Net income	**33,723**	29,861	33,511	26,3
Earned per common share (average				
outstanding during year)†	**3.05**	2.71	3.06	2
Cash dividends paid per common				
share†	**.80**	.80	.80	
Financial Condition				
Total current assets	**$414,706**	$349,642	$336,924	$277,3
Total current liabilities	**153,308**	138,685	147,653	120,2
Working capital	**261,398**	210,957	189,271	157,1
Property, plant, and equipment (net)	**154,954**	171,436	182,377	145,8
Long-term debt, less current portion	**94,778**	86,801	94,595	52,9
Shareowners' equity	**328,702**	303,236	281,548	253,4
Common shares (average				
outstanding during year)†	**11,042,736**	11,036,115	10,959,489	10,909,6
Employees at year-end	**47,259**	44,752	58,974	46,7
Shareowners at year-end	**16,210**	17,738	17,808	18,6

† Adjusted for stock split in 1966 and for stock distribution in 1963. Except for 1966, there
would have been no significant difference if earnings per share had been computed on basis of
shares outstanding at year-end. In 1966, earnings per common share outstanding at year-end
were $3.14.

decentralizes into groups, divisions, departments, and branches. The
total job is divided up and cut into the size pieces that a good administrative manager can get his arms around. This is logical and good management practice. But unless the general managers understand their jobs
thoroughly, the company is in danger of becoming no more than the sum
total of the decentralized parts loosely governed at the corporate level,
primarily from a financial point of view.

"Consequently, though the organization as a whole may have far more
of the tools, the opportunity, and the skilled people needed for innovation, the exposure of any one manager is restricted. He simply fails to see
the larger opportunities to solve problems of the right scale for the whole
corporation.

"Another undesirable pattern which too often develops is the gravita-
tion of resources toward short-term problems with a consequent neglect
of long-term, major impact programs. As a result, the organization can be

1967	1966	1965	1964	1963	1962
$568,507	$580,314	$436,369	$327,579	$276,477	$240,693
41,098	63,722	46,273	34,857	25,087	16,381
18,243	29,768	21,434	16,816	12,948	7,824
22,855	33,954	24,839	18,041	12,139	8,557
2.11	3.30†	2.46	1.80	1.22	.85
.75	.55	.50	.40	.32	.24
$242,915	$253,705	$186,721	$123,500	$105,967	$ 90,263
97,520	112,142	89,072	65,627	50,985	37,216
145,395	141,563	97,649	57,873	54,982	53,047
138,883	123,752	81,215	56,354	47,852	42,634
54,265	51,935	48,708	3,937	5,700	7,463
234,134	217,320	132,618	111,293	97,761	88,651
10,845,663	10,291,973	10,091,248	10,011,217	9,894,919	9,866,837
38,736	38,686	34,519	24,551	21,616	18,166
20,065	19,903	16,566	15,867	15,827	17,031

misled into believing that it is making sound investments for the future, when, in truth, the resources may be largely consumed in responding to current crises."

The system which TI developed to improve its management of innovation was based on a formal structure of hierarchial goals. This structure was described by Mr. Grant A. Dove, Vice President for Corporate Development, in the following terms:[2]

"The OST system amounts to a statement of goals and the plans for achieving these goals at the appropriate level in the organization. The goals expressed in OST form a structure, of hierarchy, beginning with the Corporate Objective and extending downward to Business Objectives and Strategies, and finally, Tactics [Figure 1.].

"Our Corporate Objective states the economic purposes, the reasons for existence of the organization. It also states in broad terms our product, market, and technical goals. It defines our responsibilities to our employees, our shareowners, our community, and society as a whole. And, it

[2]These remarks, and other quotations attributed to Mr. Dove in this case, are excerpted from his speech at the London School of Business Studies on May 22, 1970.

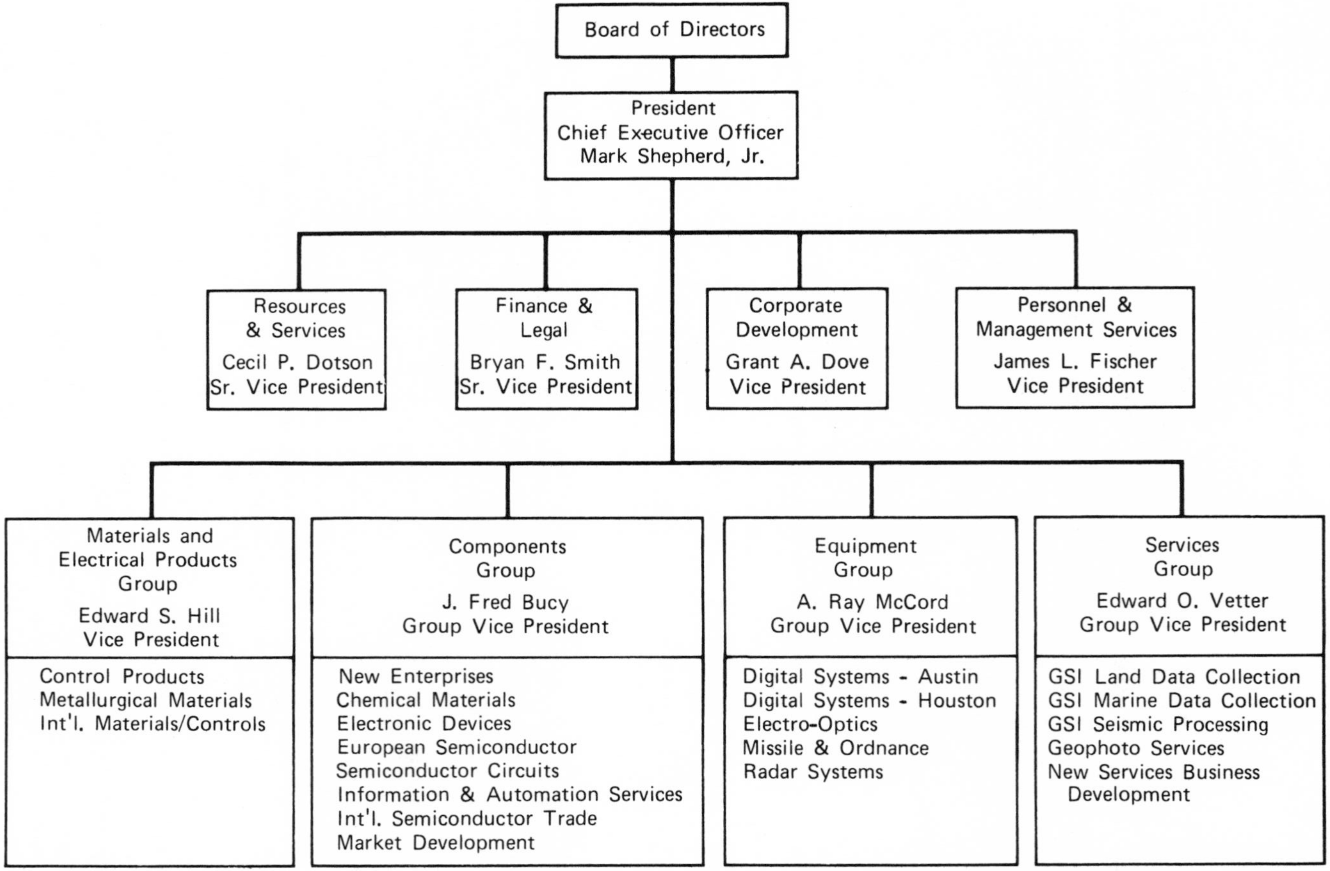

Board of Directors

President
Chief Executive Officer
Mark Shepherd, Jr.

Resources & Services
Cecil P. Dotson
Sr. Vice President

Finance & Legal
Bryan F. Smith
Sr. Vice President

Corporate Development
Grant A. Dove
Vice President

Personnel & Management Services
James L. Fischer
Vice President

Materials and Electrical Products Group
Edward S. Hill
Vice President

Control Products
Metallurgical Materials
Int'l. Materials/Controls

Components Group
J. Fred Bucy
Group Vice President

New Enterprises
Chemical Materials
Electronic Devices
European Semiconductor
Semiconductor Circuits
Information & Automation Services
Int'l. Semiconductor Trade
Market Development

Equipment Group
A. Ray McCord
Group Vice President

Digital Systems - Austin
Digital Systems - Houston
Electro-Optics
Missile & Ordnance
Radar Systems

Services Group
Edward O. Vetter
Group Vice President

GSI Land Data Collection
GSI Marine Data Collection
GSI Seismic Processing
Geophoto Services
New Services Business
Development

Exhibit 2 Texas Instruments Incorporated

342

A HIERARCHY OF GOALS

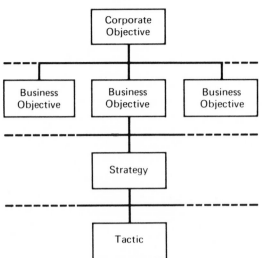

Figure 1

establishes the financial goals by which we measure our contribution to the economic development of society.

"The Corporate Objective is supported by a set of Business Objectives. Each of these is expressed in terms of (1) a business charter which establishes the boundaries of the business, (2) an appraisal of the potential opportunities we perceive in this business, (3) a study of the technical and market trends, and (4) the overall competitive structure of industry serving this business.

"Performance measures are established which include specific goals for financial factors, such as sales, profit, return on assets, and served available market penetration for five and ten years ahead.

"In addition, we attempt to project the market and the product mix, to establish technical goals, and to identify obstacles or boundaries limiting the business.

"Finally, we attempt to look at ourselves in a mirror and critique the overall Objective. We carefully evaluate the competition, the threats and contingencies we might have to meet, market shifts we might anticipate, and attempt to evaluate what we must make happen in order to achieve success of the Objective. The ranking of these key factors, then provides a priority list for future management attention.

"We expect the Objective to be challenging enough, even shocking enough, to force a radical rethinking of the Strategies and Tactics. For example, any time we have enough well-defined Strategies to give us a

EXHIBIT 3

TEXAS INSTRUMENTS INCORPORATED

Examples of Tactical Action Programs

TI's management selected three examples to illustrate three
different types of TAPs: (1) a technology - product development program with long-time horizon and relatively large
investment, (2) a marketing-oriented program with rather
specific short-term goals and relatively small-scale investment, and (3) an internal capability development program
of moderate scale and time horizon, oriented neither to
products nor markets but to the generalized manufacturing
process.

1. Under our overall strategy in the Radar Systems
    Business, we have a TAP to accomplish certain
    specific business objectives in air traffic control,
    which has a well-developed milestone structure out
    for three years, and less frequent milestones on out
    to six or seven years. Funding of the TAP is ac-
    complished on an annual basis using the OST decision
    packages. This TAP is technologically oriented, and
    aimed at developing the next generation radar, dis-
    play, and information management systems required
    for future air traffic control problems.

2. Another TAP is designed to impact our long-estab-
    lished line of products for thermal overlead protec-
    tion of electric motors. Basically this is a market-
    ing-oriented program, with only secondary impact
    on product design activities. It contains specific
    actions relating to certain markets and certain ac-
    counts, with goals of specified increases in market
    penetration during the planned year. This program
    has a much shorter time horizon than (1) above, and
    tends to be a one-year program typically, subject to
    revaluation of its continuing need at year end.

EXHIBIT 3 (continued)

3. Another example is selected from a non-product type
   strategy. We have an overall strategy for development and implementation of advanced manufacturing
   techniques containing a TAP to integrate directly the
   mechanical design process into the manufacturing
   process. This involves using automation and software skills to put the designer into the manufacturing
   loop.

high confidence level in exceeding the goals stated in a business Objective, then that business Objective probably is not ambitious enough, and the probability of truly innovative strategic thinking is likely to be slow.

"At the next level in the goal structure is the Strategy statement. The Strategy describes in detail the environment of the business opportunity to be pursued in support of the Objective. Normally, there will be several Strategies supporting each Objective. Altogether, we had more than 50 Strategies operating in 1969. For example, if we had an Objective to achieve certain goals in the automobile market, we might have one Strategy involving automobile electronics, one involving material applications, and perhaps another for safety systems. The Strategy looks ahead over a number of years, normally from five to ten, and intermediate check points are defined along the way providing milestones against which to judge progress. Progress measurement is an element of a Strategy not included at the Objective level. Finally, the contribution of the Strategy to the overall Objective is defined in quantitative measures and a critique is formulated which assigns a success probability to the Strategy.

"Next in the goal hierarchy is the Tactical Action Program, or TAP. [Examples are given in Exhibit 3.] A TAP is a detailed action plan of the steps necessary to reach the major long-range check points defined by the Strategies. It normally is short term, covering 6 to 18 months of effort. For each planned Tactic, a responsible individual is designated, a start and finish schedule is established, and the required resources are defined.

"As we progress downward through the OST system, plans are formulated at an increasing level in detail. We have major goals at the Objective level, major milestones at the Strategy level, and individual responsibility with resource allocation at the Tactic level. Below the Tactic level, each TAP is broken down into individual work packages which we manage by means of standard program management techniques. The detailed planning at this level provides the basis for planning and control of resources through the OST structure."

ORGANIZATION SYSTEMS

Mr. Dove described how the OST system operated within the context of the corporation's formal organization structure, as follows:

"What we have with OST is a system that gives us a method of planning, review and control which cuts across the operating structure of groups, divisions and PCCs. It provides a mechanism for assembling capabilities and challenging efforts to achieve results that could not be achieved by any one organizational element."

ORGANIZATION MATRIX
OST/OPERATING

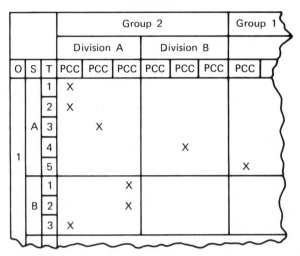

O	S	T	PCC	PCC	PCC	PCC	PCC	PCC	PCC
			Group 2						Group 1
			Division A			Division B			
1	A	1	X						
		2	X						
		3		X					
		4					X		
		5							X
	B	1			X				
		2			X				
		3	X						

Figure 2

The Two-Hat Concept

"One way to visualize this overlay is to use a matrix with the traditional organizational units across the top and the OST structure at the left margin [Figure 2]. Typically, the matrix organization concept has been used to illustrate the overlapping of a project organization with a functional technology organization. Here, the matrix is showing something entirely different. It is showing the relation between a strategic mode and an operating mode within the same organization.

"One of the roles of a Strategy Manager, as indicated here, is to identify the TAPs required, represented by Xs in the matrix, and to pull them together from across the company into a coordinated strategic plan. Many times the Strategy Manager also is the manager of a Product-Customer Center, especially if there is one PCC able to take a dominant role in the Strategy. Nearly always, the Strategy or Tactic Manager also will have an operating role to play. Only in rare cases does the Strategy Manager or Tactic Manager have that job as his full-time assignment.

"Frequently, an Objective Manager also will be a Division Manager, though this is not always the case. When it is the case, we simply have a single manager wearing two hats with clearly designated goals for both growth and profitability. This now gives us a way to tie our long-range strategic plans to our short-term operational planning and control activities.

"Through the OST overlay, we have a goal structure for strategic activities as well as operating activities. Not only can we measure profit and loss performance operationally, but we also can allocate resources through the OST structure and measure our progress toward these strategic goals. Now, your new idea has a home. It can be given resources for further development and, if the progress warrants, heavier support later. A number of outcomes are possible. Your idea might develop as a Tactic. Or, it might even be the catalyst which would lead to a new major corporate goal at the Objective level. Whatever the case, your idea would be clearly a part of the OST structure and would be recognized and supported by deliberate choice. It won't have to be bootlegged, or dropped completely through the crack.

"Thus, at Texas Instruments, our managers are given a dual responsibility for both Strategies and Operations. In recent years, we have deliberately tried to create an environment in which it becomes natural for managers to distinguish between their operating and Strategic modes. Lest I mislead you, let me re-emphasize that we are talking about two modes within the same organization, and not about two distinct organizational structures. In fact, in the majority of cases—say about 75%—the execution of both modes is through a single manager.

"There are a number of reasons why we have chosen to develop the second, or strategic, mode, within the organization. First, the strategic mode gives us a mechanism for large-scale opportunities, or those requiring combinations of resources not found in a single unit. Second, it gives us a mechanism for planning and controlling our investments for the future, and for making sure that we do achieve the desired balance of priorities between short-term and long-term activities.

"To achieve this balance, it was necessary to structure the system so that each manager, in his strategic role, would have roughly the same influence and stature as in his operating role. [This structuring involved two distinct steps.] The first involved the simple decision to allocate strategic resources through the Strategy Managers. In the case of a single manager serving both the operating and strategic role, this amounted to a separation of strategic investments from operating activities in a manager's profit and loss statement. In other words, he and his managers were given visibility to plan and control both the strategic and operating components of his business. In the exceptional case where we would have full-time Strategy Managers, this created a mechanism for the allocation of a strategic budget apart from the operating profit and loss statement. In either case, the strategic budget represents funds that the Strategy Manager can choose to spend anywhere in the organization to get the skills and resources which he needs.

Incentive Compensation Systems

"The second step was the development of a compensation structure, which measured strategic performance as well as operating performance. An important part of this structure is what we refer to as Key Personnel Analysis (KPA). KPA is a system of annual comparative assessment of individual TIers. The procedure involves classification of TIers into five comparative rating groups, and eventually a paired comparison based upon contributions during the current year, for individuals in the top group.

"Starting with the immediate supervisor, individuals are rank-ordered on the basis of their relative performance and contribution, and an adjustment to base salary is recommended. The ranks are combined at successive levels of the organization until the department level is reached. The department manager identifies 'bench mark' people among those in his department. Bench marks are those people judged as having made equal contributions, even though they are in different functions and job grades. This procedure permits merging of the rankings reaching the department level into a single department ranking. Each person then is placed in one of five comparative rating groups of 20% each. The top 20% group is paired-compared—that is, each person is paired with every other person, and one of each pair is selected against the contribution criterion. From this, a new rank ordering is achieved. The process is repeated at Division and Group levels, bench-marking each time to produce merged rankings. Several cross-cuts are made on job grade and job function, including a separate ranking by the President of all Strategy and Objective managers. Incentive bonus award recommendations based on the rankings are made for up to 20% of the salaried population. The KPA approach has provided an effective way to award strategic performance.

"During a series of interviews in the spring of 1972, several TI executives acknowledged that one effect of the KPA system was to create a competitive environment within the company. These executives thought the system was constructive, nevertheless, because peer rivalry encouraged better performance. 'As a practical matter,' one manager said, 'KPA is not as much of a zero-sum game as it sounds like. The system does force us to examine performance at the very lowest levels in the organization and attempt to identify people who have done a superlative job. As the ranking process moves up the hierarchy, however, only a very few people from the lower levels manage to survive the screening. The informal test that each of us uses in identifying our key personnel is, who is contributing most to the success of the business? The net effect of the process is that almost all of the managers in the higher ranks participate in the bonus pool. It would be a rare event, for example, for a PCC manager not to receive a bonus.'

"Another aspect of TI's incentive compensation systems was a stock-option plan. One participant in this program commented, "It's really a very unusual plan. Most stock-option plans involve an award of so many shares to an individual, and the only restriction on his right to exercise the options is that he must stay with the company for several years; the options vest at, say, 20% of the shares each year. In our plan, an award is made for a certain number of shares, but vesting is conditional upon the company meeting a specified earnings per share target each year. The fact that all executive options are tied to the same EPS target thus establishes a common goal for the management team. To some extent, this group goal tends to mitigate the individual competition that is inherent in our KPA system."

Committee Structure

TI's top management had formed two important operating committees, the OST Committee and the Management Committee. Commenting on the composition and role of these committees, Mr. Gene Helms, TI's manager of Advanced Corporate Planning, spoke as follows:

"In 1969, TI created an OST Committee to make strategic resource allocations, and review strategic activities. The OST Committee has 13 permanent members including the president, the four group vice presidents, and other officers including the vice president of corporate development (to whom I report). The committee meets about 18 times a year for a full day. The agenda for each meeting normally is settled beforehand and includes a rigorous re-examination of at least one business objective or consideration of a major new business opportunity. Topics discussed are: (1) the appropriateness of the objective in light of current information; (2) progress in the strategic development of the objective; (3) any actions which should be taken at the corporate level to accelerate or otherwise modify the strategic programs for that objective. Besides this, managers of key strategies and tactics frequently meet with the OST Committee for progress reviews, or when initiation of new programs is under consideration.

"Since each of the eight business objectives is reviewed at least once a year, and because most TI managers have some tasks to perform for at least one and often several objectives, there is now more of a tendency on the part of our managers to look upon OST as a living and important system. Also, the OST meetings provide a forum for the consideration of new objectives in light of our changing corporate situation.

"Another important feature of the OST Committee's function is the impact that it has had upon strategic conflict resolutions. All of our objective managers now report (in the strategic mode) to the OST Committee. In the operational mode they report to their group vice presidents who sit on both the OST and Management Committees. (The latter committee has nearly the same composition as the OST Committee, but at separate meetings it treats operational issues and the overall allocation of resources between the operating and strategic modes.) In the OST Committee meetings, members are expected to adopt a corporate perspective. The fact that no member is associated exclusively with any single objective, but that all members are responsible for the management of the objectives, facilitates unbiased consideration of the objectives."

THE RESOURCE ALLOCATION PROCESS

Continuous Review

Mr. Dove described the review process of the OST Committee in the following terms:

"The Objectives and Strategies contain all the essential elements of our long-range plan. In fact, the OST documentation is our long-range plan. In the operational mode, we budget and control to an annual plan, which is just a snapshot of one year of the long-range plan.

"Figure 3 is a schematic representation of our planning cycle.

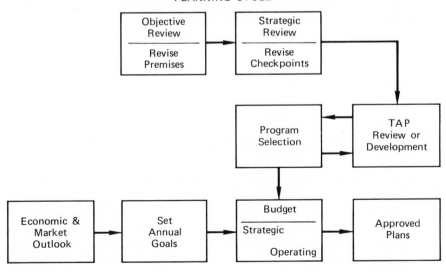

PLANNING CYCLE

Figure 3

Throughout the year we are concentrating on our Objectives and Strategies, revising the basic premises and checkpoints. This gives us the environment and guidelines we need for the more detailed annual planning to follow. Then, in the fall and winter, with the economic and market outlook in mind, we set our annual goals and the split of funds between the strategic and operating modes. Tactics are revised and new ones generated. We normally have many more defined Tactics than we can afford to undertake at any one time.

"The Tactics are then grouped into logical, stand-alone decision packages which are rank-ordered by the Strategy managers. Based upon the guidelines for strategic funding of business objectives and individual strategies a cut-off line is drawn, and packages above the line are given a tentative approval. Those falling below the line are not discarded, but remain in what we call our 'creative backlog' and have an opportunity to move up for approval at a latter time when resources become available. This process is repeated at the Objective level, where adjustments in the allocation between Strategies may be made, and decision packages falling below the cut-off line at the strategy level have another opportunity for approval. Finally, we allocate a segment of the strategic funding directly from the corporate level to certain decision packages. This provides an opportunity to fine-tune the resource allocation below the cut-off line at the Strategy and Objective level. But mostly, this gives us a mechanism for starting new ventures which for the various reasons could not normally be undertaken by one of the operating units.

"What I want to emphasize here is that the Objectives and Strategies give us a living and dynamic long-range plan, tying the activities together from top to bottom. We are attempting to space our Objective reviews throughout the year so that top management can devote time for an in-depth study of each Objective, and yet never be more than 12 months away from the most recent Objective review."

Elaborating on Mr. Dove's comments, Mr. Helms said, "One of the reasons that this continuous updating process works as well as it does is because of our computer-assisted planning model. We call it modplan, for 'model planning,' but it's really nothing more than a very simple computer program which takes much of the arithmetic out of revising any long-range plan, or shorter-term forecast. An Objective Manager can specify ten key variables for his business over the next 10 years and have these converted by the computer into condensed conventional financial statements and related statistics. Having such a tool thus permits the OST Committee to focus on the specific actions that the manager must take in order to make his assumptions come true."

"The net effect of this planning flexibility," Mr. Helms continued, "is that at any particular point in time we *do* have a long-range plan, represented by the sum of the modplans that have currently been approved for each of our Objective Managers. On the other hand, changes in these plans are so frequent that we really don't take the trouble to prepare a nice thick volume called 'The Plan' the way many companies do. The only real plan, therefore, is the set of TAPs that will be undertaken during the next year or two, and the specific funding of those takes place as a part of the annual budgeting process.''

Budgeting and Forecasting

"We really have two budgets for the year," Mr. Helms continued, "one for OST funds and the other for operating expenses. The key point is that expenditures associated with each category appear as separate and distinct line items on the P/L statement for each unit. We begin with P/L models for the coming year consolidated from each unit to give a first approximation to our scale of operations and expected profitability. At this point, all OST funds are considered discretionary, and in effect, are accrued in one big pot for allocation purposes. Zero-based budgeting is applied to the operating segment of expenses. The OST package is allocated among Objectives, and then to strategies and TAPs using the OST decision package approach."

"The balance between the OST expenses package and the operating expense package is a top-level, long-term/short-term type tradeoff. The key principle is that operating profit (as measured before OST expenditures) must meet certain standards for each business, and the zero-based budgeting approach gives visibility to help at the operating profit level. The size of the OST pot, of course, is influenced strongly by the total operating profit, and the pressure naturally is to beat down operating expenses so that we can invest more in OST programs.

"The preceding remarks primarily apply to the setting of targets for key P/L indices (operating expense, operating profit, OST expense, etc.) at the corporate level. In succeeding phases of the planning cycle, new information appears as both operating and OST decision packages which are matched to the available budgets. The iterative loop is closed by providing for appeals upward which can result in adjusting the original targets.

"We simply are dividing a total expense package into two segments so that we can look at each segment from a different viewpoint. The operating segment is examined from the viewpoint of operating efficiency and maximizing year-ahead profits. The strategic segment is considered on a companywide basis as though it were completely discretionary and is the element in our resource allocation process which permits decisions to change the business mix, product emphasis, or overall direction of the company.

"The entire OST pool is not necessarily allocated to the Objective

Managers at the beginning of the year. We retain approximately ten percent of it as a contingency for subsequent use by the OST Committee for new opportunities that may arise. The use of OST funds can be modified during the year by managers at any of the three levels. A TAP Manager is permitted to change the nature of his activity on his own discretion, as long as it doesn't change the Tactical goal which he is committed to achieve. Similarly, changes and reallocation of funds may be made at the Strategy Manager or Objective Manager level as long as there is no change in the goal which has been approved by higher authority.

"We had a recession in 1970, as you will recall, and that spring, as it became apparent that we were going to have trouble meeting our earnings' commitment, we did begin to cut back on OST funding. By early summer, however, it was apparent that the downturn was hitting us rather severely. The choice that top managemet had to make was whether or not to continue to reduce the spending on OST projects. Mark Shepherd finally drew a line, saying that he would not cut OST funds below a certain level. There is no way of knowing what the right answer is in such a situation, of course, but he believed strongly that we should not mortgage our future simply for the sake of current year profitability. Subsequently, we held OST funding at about the same level in 1971 until we were sure we were out of the woods. Our funding for 1972 now exceeds the amount we were spending in 1969.

"Once our OST and operating expense budgets are set for the coming year, our detailed budgeting then proceeds. We only budget future performance by quarter. Actually, we prepare our quarterly budget as much as 10 quarters in advance. Right now, each of our PCCs has a quarterly budget running through the balance of this year and for all of 1973. This summer they'll extend that budget, again by quarters, through 1974. This is not as much work as it sounds like, because the level of detail is still not very great; the quarterly budget is also prepared with computer assistance and uses somewhat more input assumptions than the objective models. In effect, preparing a quarterly budget is simply the task of providing more detailed assumptions for the modplan that has been approved by the OST Committee.

"As the year progresses, each manager prepares a rolling forecast four to six months in advance. In December, for example, the manager will submit a revised monthly forecast for the next three months and will, for the first time, provide a monthly forecast for the three months of the second quarter of the coming year. In January, the forecast for the five months February through June is revised. The forecast is revised again in February for the remaining four months, and in March the cycle starts over again with a revision of the forecast for April through

June and a presentation of the first monthly forecast for July through September. These forecasts are at the level of detail sufficient for analysis of actual performance. We think it's the right way to do planning and budgeting; we start with annual gross data 10 years out in modplan, convert that to quarterly budget data for up to 10 quarters out, and then convert that to monthly forecasts for up to six months. Another advantage of this approach is that it eliminates any problem of interface between the long-range planning activity and budgeting. All budgeting and forecasting are coordinated by the corporate operation's controller; he starts to track expected corporate performance more than two years ahead of the event. Starting at that point, it's easy to get consistency between the first quarterly budget and the then current modplan. Any subsequent revisions in the budget that may be necessary are then coordinated through the Controller's Department."

Planning Methodology

"As you've gathered by now," Mr. Helms continued, "we're not very enthusiastic around here for elaborate methodological approaches to planning. Speaking philosophically, it seems to me there's a major problem of injecting methodology into a human organization. The literature abounds with elegant solutions to well-formulated problems. However, very well-formulated problems appear in strategic business management. Even fewer businessmen are prepared to accept someone else's strategic model as a guide to their own behavior. Too often, we've tried to extend into the strategic planning area the same points of view which have proved successful operating planning approaches. Because they have been applied to more routine tasks, these approaches have not been required to interact strongly with variations in management style. In strategy, style is everything, and planning approaches must deal with style variations effectively, or fail."

"At TI, we have proceeded on the premise that long-range planning can be imbedded successfully within the primary operating organization. Our commitment to accomplish this has placed first priority on matters of organization development and culture, rather than on matters of pure planning methodology. This had been implemented by creating the OST structure of goals, and superimposing it upon our traditional organization structure. By doing so, we are building in a consciousness of the future. We are creating a distinct orientation toward two different time frames. When successful, this creates two management modes within the same organization: a strategic mode and an operating mode.

"Consistent with this philosophy," Mr. Helms continued, "we do formalize the results of our planning activities with an annual planning conference. It's held in early December each year, lasts for three days, and about 500 of our managers attend some part of that conference. Each operating group is allocated a part of the agenda, and in the course of three days each division manager, each PCC manager, each Objective Manager, and each Strategy Manager will speak briefly to the group; that's about 90 men in all. About 150 of the highest ranking managers attend the entire three-day conference, and other managers come in to listen to the part that is relevant to their sphere of activities. The purpose of such a conference, of course, is primarily communication; it helps to keep the corporation knit together. Another advantage, however, is that each manager makes a public commitment of what he proposes to achieve during the coming year, and we think that helps to ensure that he really will try to deliver on his commitment."

REPORTING SYSTEMS

"Our reporting systems are not all that unique," Mr. Helms explained, "but obviously they're very important in allowing us to ensure that our plans are being executed as intended. Because of our dual-mode approach to management, our reporting systems focus on both the PCC Manager and the TAP Manager."

Mr. Dove described the effects of dual responsibilities on a profit-center on a PCC manager in the following terms:

"Suppose we have a common situation where you happen to be a Strategy Manager and a PCC Manager, both at the same time. You are responsible both for current operating results and for a long-range Strategy. How will you reconcile the two roles, and how will you avoid the temptation to delay and cut back strategic efforts every time an operating crisis comes along?

"Let's look at a simplified profit and loss statement for the PCC [Figure 4]. As a typical PCC Manager, you will be expected to wear two hats, the first as an Operating Manager concerned with today's operating results, and the second as a Manager of Strategic activity for longer range results. For today's operations, you will be measured relative to your planned operating profit. Within limits, you are free to make adjustments in the operating expense budget in order to bring about a maximum operating profit. But remember that you also have a strategic hat to wear. This means that you also are going to be measured by how effectively you utilize the strategic expense. In other words, how well are you achieving the milestones and checkpoints established at the time the strategic expenditures were approved?

"Once the plans are made and resources allocated, Objective, Strategy

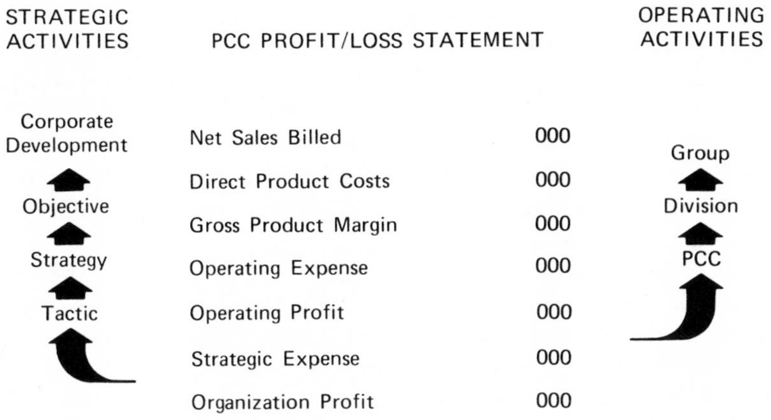

STRATEGIC ACTIVITIES	PCC PROFIT/LOSS STATEMENT		OPERATING ACTIVITIES

Corporate Development

Net Sales Billed 000

Group

Objective

Direct Product Costs 000

Division

Gross Product Margin 000

Strategy

Operating Expense 000

PCC

Tactic

Operating Profit 000

Strategic Expense 000

Organization Profit 000

Figure 4

LONG RANGE OBJECTIVE MODEL

Dollars ($000,000's) ☐   ☐ Indices ($K/$MNSB)

Objective _____   Manager _____

		1971	1972	1973	1974	1975	1976		1981
	Served Available Market								
	Net Sales Billed								
	GPM								
	Operating D + A								
	Operating Profit								
	OST D + A								
	Total D + A								
	Div. Oth Inc/(Exp)								
	Organization Profit								
	Total People (000's)								
	Net Space Avail (ft^{2}000's)								
	Current Assets								
	Net Fixed Assets								
	Total Assets								
	Capital Expenditures								
	Depreciation								
	Organization Pft ROA %								

Exhibit 4

and TAP Managers are given decentralized authority to obligate the expense, capital, and people resources, make adjustments as necessary to meet the goals, and resolve conflict as it occurs. The results and progress on strategic activities will be reviewed first by the TAP Manager, and then successively at the Strategy Manager level, the Objective Manager level, and by the Corporate Development function. Through this path, the strategic resources are allocated and controlled. Accountability for operating profit, on the other hand, is through the Product-Customer Center to the Division and Group levels. As we shall see, the responsibilities for strategic and operating activities tend to converge closer and closer to single individuals as we move up higher in the organization. As a result, Group and Division Managers are wearing both hats and have responsibilities for both operating profit and strategic expense. This, in turn, means that they are accountable for the bottom line on the P/L statement—the organization profit."

"In fact, of course," Mr. Helms said, "our reporting system is much more detailed than the simplified example Mr. Dove displayed. Here (Exhibit 5) is a copy of one page from the actual report for one PCC Manager for one month. As you can see, we make the usual comparisons of actual against budget and forecast. In addition, on other pages in the report, we get an opportunity to see how good a forecaster the manager is because we can track actual against several previous months' forecasts."

"One of the problems in getting a system like OST started is in framing the definitions of just what expenses fall into the OST pool. We started out by asking each group manager to present his own proposal for the expenses which he viewed as "discretionary." We then tried to resolve the differences in perspective among the group managers, but even today we have slightly different definitions of what types of expenses constitute OST activities. More important than a rigid definition that is applicable to all groups is the consistency of the definition within any given operating unit. Here it's very important for top management to take a hard-nosed approach in order to make sure that OST activities are not being funded sub rosa out of operating expenses.

"When each TAP is funded, it's given a project order number, and all costs on that TAP are charged against that account number. About 80 percent of the total OST expenditure is for personnel costs—primarily engineering. Fortunately, because of our early history in government contracting, our engineers were used to keeping records of their time. Accumulating TAP costs by project greatly facilitates separating out OST expenses from the operating expenses in any given PCC.

MONTHLY COMPARISON
MARCH

OPERATING UNIT   RESPONSIBILITY

	YEAR TO DATE			PCT OF PLAN	DESCRIPTION	CURRENT MONTH COMPARISON				
	ACTUAL	PLAN	LAST YEAR			MONTH ACTUAL	MONTH FORECAST	QTR ACT/FCST	QTR PLAN	QTR VARIANCE
1	10473	6960	6069	150	NSE $	4085	2600	10473	6960	3513
2	12003	10546	11339	114	BACKLOG TOTAL	12003	11908	12003	10546	1457
3	1747		1071		BACKLOG DELINQ	1747	1600	1747		-1747
4	62908	54200	49439	116	NUB	22418	19200	62908	54200	8708
5	7744	6680	7268	116	NSB - TOTAL	2798	2400	7744	6680	1064
6	563	550	372	102	DIRECT LABOR	215	195	563	550	-13
7	3124	3125	3534	100	DIRECT MATL	1218	1038	3124	3125	1
8	881	880	755	100	MFG OVERHEAD	307	310	881	880	-1
9	356	365	276	98	OTHER OVERHEAD	126	124	356	365	9
10	136	130	120	105	COST ADJ - NET	48	48	136	130	-6
11					OTHER MFG COST					
12	638	-160	189	-999	INV REDUCTION	125		638	-160	-798
13	2046	1790	2022	114	GPM	759	685	2046	1790	256
14	26.4	26.8	27.8	99	GPM % NSB	27.1	28.5	26.4	26.8	-.4
15	175		187		OPER D+D EXP	61	59	175		-175
16	56		55		OST D+D EXP	18	18	56		-56
17	1815	1790	1780	101	DIV PROFIT	680	608	1815	1790	25
18	23.4	26.8	24.5	87	DIV PF % NSB	24.3	25.3	23.4	26.8	-3.4
19	917	915	993	100	OPERATING D+A	310	308	917	915	-2
20	11.8	13.7	13.7	86	OPER D+A % NSB	11.1	12.8	11.8	13.7	1.9
21	44.8	51.1	49.1	88	OPER D+A % GPM	40.8	45.0	44.8	51.1	6.3
22	-292	-278	-209	105	DIV OTH INC/EXP	-103	-100	-292	-278	-14
23	837	597	820	140	OPER PROFIT	346	277	837	597	240
24	10.8	8.9	11.3	121	OPER PF % NSB	12.4	11.5	10.8	8.9	1.9
25	75	75	55	100	OST D+A EXP	25	25	75	75	
26	992	990	1048	100	TOTAL D+A EXP	335	333	992	990	-2
27	12.8	14.8	14.4	86	TOT D+A % NSB	12.0	13.9	12.8	14.8	2.0
28	48.5	55.3	51.8	88	TOT D+A % GPM	44.1	48.6	48.5	55.3	6.8
29	762	522	765	146	ORGAN PROFIT	321	252	762	522	240
30	9.8	7.8	10.5	126	ORGAN PF % NSB	11.5	10.5	9.8	7.8	2.0
31	19.5	13.6	20.6	143	ORGAN PRF ROA	25.0	19.1	19.5	13.6	5.9
32	870	668	1080	130	TOTAL OTH ASSET	870	810	870	668	-202
33	4524	4612	4121	98	RECEIVABLES	4524	4750	4524	4612	88
34	146	173	142	84	REC/MIL NSB	146	162	146	173	27
35	3196	3395	2905	94	INV - NET	3196	3425	3196	3395	199
36	103	127	100		INV/MIL NSB	103	117	103	127	24
37					UNLIQ PROG PAY					
38					UPP/MIL NSB					
39	2022	2485	2415	81	NFA-MFG EQ OWN	2022	2362	2022	2485	463
40	6167	6632	7038	93	NFA - TOTAL	6167	6512	6167	6632	465
41	199	240	242	80	NFA/MIL NSB	199	222	199	248	49
42	14757	15307	15144	96	EOM ASSETS	14757	15497	14757	15307	550
43	476	573	521	83	ASSETS/MIL NSB	476	527	476	573	97
44	1168	486	265	240	ORGAN CASH FLO	1507	729	1168	486	682
45	205	400	73	51	TOTAL CAP EXP	-114	80	205	400	195
46	325	335	320	97	TOTAL DEP EXP	112	21	325	335	10
47	219	308	113	71	TOTAL CAP AUTH	81	78	219	308	89
48	737	700	655	105	DIRECT PEOPLE	737	740	737	700	-37
49	161	162	183	99	INDIR EX PEO	161	162	161	162	1
50	1165	1116	1124	104	TOTAL PEOPLE	1165	1164	1165	1116	-49
51	26.6	23.9	25.9	111	NSB/PERSON	26.6	25.2	26.6	23.9	2.7
52	2.6	1.9	2.7	137	ORGAN PRF/PER	2.6	2.4	2.6	1.9	.7
53	1316		1105		TOTAL PAYROLL	468		1316		-1316
54	91	95	96	96	NET SQ FT AVAL	91	101	91	95	4
55	2938	3555	3302	83	SQ AVL/MIL NSB	2938	3437	2938	3555	617

Exhibit 5

"Then, of course, we track the performance on each TAP with a monthly status report such as that shown in Figure 5.

"For management review, the status of each TAP is reported monthly in a simplified format which enables us to tell at a glance how the TAP stands on a number of critical factors. Yellow and red bars indicate that higher level management action is needed to solve a problem. Monthly reports covering detailed financial data and manpower resources also are distributed to TAP, Strategy, and Objective Managers."

EFFECTIVENESS OF MANAGEMENT SYSTEMS

At lunch, midway through the interviews in the spring of 1972, several TI executives chatted with the casewriter about the effectiveness of TI's planning system. One of the executives described the operation of the system in the following terms: "The sum total of our efforts to change the future of TI can probably be divided into three pieces: (1) efforts which should be managed as a part of the system but which escape the system and occur as sub rosa activities, (2) efforts which are managed as a part of the system but are not affected by it—that is, activities that would be undertaken whether we had such a system or not, and (3) efforts which are affected because of the system by which proposals are reviewed and approved."

In the ensuing discussion, there was general agreement among the TI

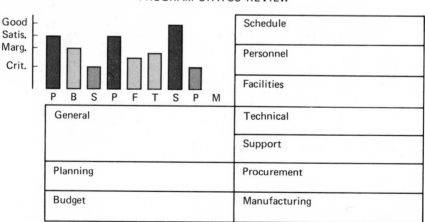

Figure 5

executives at that lunch that perhaps 15 percent of the total discretionary efforts of the corporation were in Category 1, perhaps 30 percent in Category 2, but that more than 50 percent of the company's innovative, future-oriented activities were being better managed because of the OST system.

SELECTED BIBLIOGRAPHY

ACKOFF, RUSSELL L., *A Concept of Corporate Planning*, Wiley Interscience, 1970.
Contains a number of fundamental ideas for the experienced planner. It stresses how to impose "common sense" on planning.

AGUILAR, FRANCIS, *Scanning, The Business Environment*, Macmillan, 1967.
Discusses a useful first approach to environmental scanning for systematic data collection for the planning process.

ALLISON, GRAHAM T., *Essence of Decision*, Little, Brown, 1971.
Although concerned primarily with strategic decision-making processes in government, there are easy analogues to be drawn to large corporations. The strategic planning process is seen to have rational, behavioral and political elements.

ANDREWS, KENNETH, *The Concept of Corporate Strategy*, Dow Jones, Irwin, 1971.
An excellent book on how to develop and revise corporate strategy, based on the Harvard Business School business policy tradition.

ANSOFF, H. IGOR, *Corporate Strategy*, McGraw-Hill, 1965.
A classic book on how to develop long-range corporate strategies. Discusses how to attain "synergy," i.e. engage in activities that make "2 + 2 = 5."

——— (editor), *Business Strategy*, Penguin Books, 1969.
A number of useful articles on strategy and top management decision-making.

ANTHONY, ROBERT N., *Planning and Control Systems: A Framework for Analysis*, Harvard Business School, 1965.
A classic; the first book to develop the distinction between strategic planning, management control and operational control.

ANTHONY, ROBERT N. and JOHN DEARDEN, *Management Control Systems*, 3rd Edition, Irwin, 1976.
A classic textbook on management control containing several cases.

ARGENTI, JOHN, *Systematic Corporate Planning*, Wiley, 1974.
The book provides a framework for top-down, centralized corporate planning.

ARROW, KENNETH J., *The Limits of Organization*, Norton, 1974.
This small book by a famous economist and Nobel Prize winner discusses the role of information as a limiting factor for organizations' growth.

EMERY, JAMES, *Organizational Planning and Control Systems*, Macmillan, 1969.
Quite theoretical, and with a number of thought-provoking ideas, particularly on the cost of information dissemination and handling.

GALBRAITH, JAY, *Designing Complex Organizations*, Addison-Wesley, 1973.
Discusses how to modify the organization's structure in order to make the information processing as effective as possible. Major emphasis is on matrix organizations.

GERSHEFSKI, GEORGE W., *The Development and Application of a Corporate Financial Model,* Planning Executives Institute, Oxford, Ohio, 1968.
Describes the development of the Sun Oil corporate model, a large scale integrated planning model effort.

HELLRIEGEL, DON and JOHN W. SLOCHUM JR., editors, *Management: A Contingency Approach,* Addison-Wesley, 1974.
This collection of articles give many interesting examples of contingency design of systems to particular situational corporate settings, in planning as well as in other areas.

JANTSCH, ERICH, *Technological Planning and Social Futures,* Cassel (London), 1972.
An up-to-date but fairly technical book by one of the leading authors on technological forecasting.

LORANGE, PETER, *Behavioral Factors in Capital Budgeting,* Norwegian University Press, Universitetsforlaget, Bergen, Norway, 1973.
Based on the Harvard Business School long-range planning data bank of 87 large U.S. corporations. Explores particularly how the planning system should be tailored to different managerial styles.

LORSCH, JAY and STEPHEN ALLEN III, *Managing Diversity and Interdependence,* Division of Research, Harvard Business School, 1974.
A research report on how to better handle the integration task between divisions in decentralized, divisionalized corporations.

MALM, ALLAN, *A Framework for Design of Planning Systems,* Lund, Sweden, 1975.
An elaborate conceptual model for strategic planning based on an extensive literature study and in-depth field studies with several corporations. Reflects the state-of-the-art of research within the field.

MORRIS, WILLIAM T., *Decentralization in Management Systems,* Ohio State University Press, 1968.
This book gives a good treatment of mathematical models for decentralization, transfer pricing procedures, etc. The book assumes some familiarity with calculus.

NEWMAN, WILLIAM H., *Constructive Control,* Prentice-Hall, 1975.
A very readable (and short) book about control as a forward-oriented process, closely related to strategic planning.

RHENMAN, ERIK, *Organizational Theory For Long-Range Planning,* Wiley, 1973.
Based on action-research in several organizations this book provides a theory for how to plan the corporation's adaptation to various environmental settings and challenges.

ROTHBERG, ROBERT R., editor, *Corporate Strategy and Product Innovation,* The Free Press, 1976.
This book deals with the process of new product development as part of strategic business planning, and consists of a collection of managerially oriented articles.

STEERS, RICHARD M., and LYMAN W. PORTER, editors, *Motivation and Work Behavior,* McGraw-Hill, 1975.

An up-to-date collection of papers discussing the more recent theories of individuals' motivation.

STEINER, GEORGE A., *Top Management Planning,* Macmillan, 1969.
This is a comprehensive book on long-range planning. A must for planners as an encyclopedia.

WARREN, E. KIRBY, *Long-Range Planning: The Executive Viewpoint,* Prentice-Hall, 1966.
A survey of long-range planning practices in 15 major companies. Although old, it still contains a number of basic points about "how to do it."